THE ADDICTION PROCESS
EFFECTIVE SOCIAL WORK APPROACHES

Edited by

Edith M. Freeman

School of Social Welfare
University of Kansas

The Addiction Process: Effective Social Work Approaches

Longman, 95 Church Street, White Plains, N.Y. 10601

Associated companies:
Longman Group Ltd., London
Longman Cheshire Pty., Melbourne
Longman Paul Pty., Auckland
Copp Clark Pitman, Toronto

Senior editor: David J. Estrin
Production editor: Ann P. Kearns
Cover design: Paul Agule Design
Text art: Pompeo Designs
Production supervisor: Anne P. Armeny

Library of Congress Cataloging-in-Publication Data

The addiction process : effective social work approaches / [edited by]
 Edith M. Freeman.
         p.   cm.
   Includes indexes.
   ISBN 0-8013-0377-X
   1. Compulsive behavior—Treatment.   2.   Substance abuse—Treatment.
 3.   Social work.   I. Freeman, Edith M.
RC533.A32   1991
616.86'0651—dc20

91-13839
CIP

1 2 3 4 5 6 7 8 9 10-DO-9594939291

To the individuals and families
who struggle daily
with the recovery process

Contents

Contributors

Robert J. Battjes, DSW
Associate Director for Planning, Division of
Clinical Research, National Institute on Drug
Abuse
Rockville, Maryland

William E. Berg, PhD
Associate Professor, School of Social Work,
University of Wisconsin-Milwaukee
Milwaukee, Wisconsin

Sara Boomhower-Kresser, MSW, ACSW
Alcoholism-Drug Dependence Program of
Lutheran Social Services of Illinois
Chicago, Illinois

Betty A. Burrows, PhD
Staff Psychologist, DePaul University
Community Mental Health Center
Chicago, Illinois

Mary E. Connors, PhD
Community Coordinator-ABtec Unit
Chicago, Illinois

Peter Delany, MSW, LCSW
National Catholic School of Social Services,
Catholic University of America
Washington, D. C.

Nancy Ellis-Ordway, MSW, ACSW
Community Coordinator-ABtec Unit, St. John's
Mercy Medical Center
St. Louis, Missouri

Jerry P. Flanzer, DSW, LCSW
Metropolitan Psychiatric Group, Psychiatric
Institute of Washington, D. C.
Washington, D. C.

Edith M. Freeman, PhD, ACSW
Professor, School of Social Welfare, University
of Kansas
Lawrence, Kansas

Ronald Gaudia, MSW
Deputy Executive Director, Westchester Jewish
Community Services
Hartsdale, New York

Gary W. Holden, M.S.
Research Associate, School of Social Work,
Columbia University
New York, New York

Barbara Lynn Kail, DSW
Associate Professor, Graduate School of Social
Work, University of Texas at Arlington
Arlington, Texas

Linda Farris Kurtz, DPA, ACSW
Professor, Department of Social Work, Eastern
Michigan University
Ypsilanti, Michigan

Toby Landesman, ACSW, CAAC, CEAP
Private Practice, Landesman, Inc.
Chicago, Illinois

Carl G. Leukefeld, DSW
Deputy Director, Division of Clinical Research,
National Institute on Drug Abuse
Rockville, Maryland

Sadye M. L. Logan, DSW
Associate Professor, School of Social Welfare, University of Kansas
Lawrence, Kansas

Michael S. Moncher, JD, MS
Senior Research Associate, School of Social Work, Columbia University
New York, New York

Patricia A. Pape, LCSW, SCAC
President, Pape & Associates
Wheaton, Illinois

Steven Perlow, PhD
Director, On Track Program for Child and Adolescent Obesity, St. Joseph Hospital and Health Care Center
Chicago, Illinois

Joanne Pilat, MSW
American Telephone & Telegraph
Chicago, Illinois

Steven P. Schinke, PhD
Professor, School of Social Work, Columbia University
New York, New York

Sanford Schwartz, PhD
Assistant Professor, School of Social Work, Virginia Commonwealth University
Richmond, Virginia

Susan Shrifter, MSW, ACSW
Clinical Coordinator, On Track Program for Child and Adolescent Obesity, St. Joseph Hospital and Health Care Center
Chicago, Illinois

Roosevelt Wright, Jr., PhD
Professor and Dean, Graduate School of Social Work, University of Texas at Arlington
Arlington, Texas

Foreword

Concern for the victims of addiction has grown immeasurably during the past twenty years. In that time, theorists, researchers, clinicians, and practitioners from a host of academic disciplines and professional backgrounds have all joined ranks in the study of addictions and addictive phenomena (e.g., drugs, other behavioral problems, and compulsions). This incipient trend, however, is hardly cause for celebration since for the most part it is difficult, if not impossible, to specify exactly the nature and magnitude of the progress that has resulted from all this work and effort.

As there is about most constructs in the social and behavioral sciences, there is continuing debate about what in the real world addiction (and by extension the addictive process) refers to. Even when such controversy is ignored, however, the term *addiction* is, indeed, singularly difficult to define or conceptualize since it means so many things to different people. In the main, one conceptualization of addiction does not satisfy all cases. For the most part, the word addiction has been used to describe and characterize a wide array of behaviors ranging from a strong habit to an intense and overwhelming compulsion. In this connection, the enormity of the task of conceptualizing addiction in a way that is theoretically sophisticated, intuitively satisfying, and operationally rigorous is fraught with difficulty, particularly in view of constantly changing scientific and ideological perspectives about addiction. The conceptualization of addiction that is so masterfully articulated in the introductory chapter of this book is in many ways a very useful one. One virtue of such a conceptualization is that it allows us to employ the intensity of behavior and compulsion as criteria for addiction and it allows us to classify addictive phenomena on the basis of the kinds of psychological, biochemical, and physiological changes they produce. A further virtue is that strongly reinforced behaviors such as anorexia, bulimia, compulsive overeating, excessive sexual activity, and compulsive gambling are not necessarily seen as separate classes of dependencies (addictions) or qualitatively different entities. Each of these behaviors is carried out in a highly compulsive and addictive manner and, to a large extent, each can persist despite the possibility of deleterious personal, familial, and social consequences.

This book, *The Addiction Process: Effective Social Work Approaches*, edited by Edith M. Freeman, is a ground-breaking effort to present, implicitly or explicitly, a universalistic model on the nature and source of a variety of addictions. Each characterization of addiction and dependency examined in the various chapters does this by harmoniously examining the triple themes of addiction etiology, assessment and intervention methodologies (including self-treatment processes), and analytical approaches to prevention. Professor Freeman has, without a doubt, amassed an outstanding group of social work educators and practitioners (and leading scholars on the subject), who have produced a thorough, thoughtful, scholarly, challenging, and remarkably insightful collection of essays on the problem of addiction in our society.

With the varied content presented in the book, readers will come to appreciate that it is a volume that covers, for the most part, every important aspect of addiction and the addictive process. Each contributor presents a broad range of theoretical ideas, empirical research, and clinical data that are absolutely essential for a better understanding of the addiction field today. As a result, readers of this book need to carefully consider the different perspectives and points of view that are presented, while at the same time they should make personal efforts to develop a systemic and functional framework concerning addiction for themselves.

As a collection of essays, this book does justice to the identification of similarities and differences (some of which are unique) in the process(es) through which individuals develop addictive manifestations. With its overarching emphasis on an ecological "strength and wellness" approach—an approach that encourages human service practitioners to help clients build on appropriate individual, familial, and environmental strengths—this book offers an innovative perspective to the analysis, treatment, and prevention of addictions. The book's firm theoretical framework is a useful metaphoric alternative for understanding the problem of addiction and for formulating differential approaches to individual, group, and societal change. Therefore, it will be relevant and useful to professionals (from a host of disciplines), addiction theorists, addiction researchers, and, most importantly, addicted individuals, their families, and society.

Professor Freeman has compiled a well-organized collection that addresses the multifaceted and multidimensional nature of addictive behaviors. In editing this book, which in my professional judgment provides a scientific and unbiased exploration of addiction, she has performed a distinct service to the human service field in particular and to the social and behavioral sciences in general. The astute and open-minded reader of this book cannot help becoming more knowledgeable and sensitive (and possibly alarmed) about the destructive impact of many addictions on individuals, families, communities, and society. Hopefully, this book will be widely read, discussed, and critiqued and, as a result, will stimulate the systemic and rational development of additional effective approaches to research and analysis, treatment, and prevention of addiction in our society.

Roosevelt Wright, Jr.

University of Texas at Arlington

Preface

There are many concerns being voiced about changes in the addictions field. Larger numbers of individuals are becoming addicted now than in the past to new and existing substances, while smaller numbers are entering and completing treatment programs. Treatments that were effective with drugs such as heroin are being questioned in terms of their effectiveness with other drugs—with cocaine, for instance, and especially crack. Cross addictions are not uncommon, making it difficult for practitioners to reach clinical judgments about how treatment should proceed. With substance abuse and other addictions becoming more pervasive, possibly the risk of relapse has become greater for those who do complete treatment.

Research has shown how recovery can be enhanced through specific treatment designed to help the abuser as well as the environment change. Despite the advances made in understanding and treating the different addictions, important knowledge gaps exist, particularly about the common aspects of addictions across substances, activities, and relationships. The purpose of this book is to summarize the common process through which individuals develop addictions such as chronic alcohol abuse, abuse of other drugs, eating disorders, addictive relationships, and compulsive gambling.

In the course of summarizing common aspects of addictions, it has become apparent that researchers do not agree on how the term should be defined. Some experts assume that, in spite of some important commonalities, differences between the various dependences, compulsions, and addictions have made it impossible to develop a common definition. Although the editor does not agree with this assumption, it is important to acknowledge such state-of-the-art limitations at the outset. Thus, the editor's definition is subject to the same limitations. Nevertheless, the term is being defined as follows in this book: a psychological and/or physical dependence on a substance, activity, or relationship as manifested by an inability to abstain in the face of serious physical, emotional, social, and legal consequences. Examples of addictions that are consistent with this definition include those identified above. It is important to note that alcohol and other drugs differ from these other addictions because the former contain psychoactive components that distort the user's affect, cognitions, and perceptions.

It is not clear to what extent the definition of addictions in this book and others in the literature should include or exclude certain ritualistic and repetitive behaviors such as handwashing or water intoxication. Nor is it clear at this point how the general category of obsessive-compulsive disorders is related to a common definition of addictive behaviors, although some examples of addictions included in this book are obviously characterized by compulsive-type behaviors. Other attempts to define the concept of addictions and important state-of-the-art issues are addressed more fully in Chapter 1. Even with these acknowledged limitations in the field, this book makes an earnest attempt to grapple with significant issues involved in defining the term *addiction* and in preventing and treating the consequences of addictions.

The book builds on the part of the professional literature that is beginning to explore similarities between particular addictive behaviors and the common effects on family life and society. It underscores some effective social work approaches to prevention, treatment, and social changes at community and societal levels. Intervention strategies are conceptualized on a continuum. They range from those used in situations in which there is mild use (pregnant women and minor children) to those used in situations involving an addiction (abuse by several members of one family, or IV drug use among members of a drug network). This indicates that social work intervention in this book is based not only on the severity of the use or abuse, but also on the seriousness of the consequences. The book also helps readers understand more clearly the unique role of social workers in this field, while also pointing out specific benefits of interdisciplinary practice.

The book's purpose is grounded in a philosophical stance that emphasizes a strengths or wellness perspective; this is compatible with a social work frame of reference. Such a perspective assumes that all persons strive toward wholeness and functional behavior and that environments can enhance or inhibit this innate tendency. It also discourages a focus on pathology. Addictive behaviors are viewed as efforts to cope with complex stressors that block the movement toward wholeness, while treatment is useful for facilitating the person's struggle to reach that inherent tendency and develop more functional ways of coping. Generalization of adaptive coping is emphasized during discussions about recovery as a way of preventing relapse. This perspective necessitates using a range of practice theories and approaches that are discussed fully in the book.

The book is organized into four major sections, following an introductory chapter describing state-of-the-art issues within the addictions field. Part I is focused on alcohol abuse and addiction, Part II covers other drugs, Part III includes chapters on eating disorders, and Part IV contains material on other addictions that are not easily categorized within the previous sections.

Case, program, or community-level examples are used in each chapter to illustrate the varied approaches to treating addictions that are included in the book. This should make the book's material more useful to the reader at a practical level. Another unique feature of the book is its focus on the needs of special populations integrated throughout the chapters—women, children and youth, minorities, the poor, and the elderly. Each chapter is followed by a brief list of supplemental and annotated readings. For the reader's convenience, a glossary containing key concepts and definitions from the various chapters is included at the end of the book. Finally, each of the book's first three sections has a lead-in chapter focused on a particular aspect of research and addictions that lays a foundation for the practice chapters in the same section.

This book is intended for use as a primary text in alcohol and drug courses; in addictions courses; and for health, mental health, and family, children, and youth specializations/courses in graduate schools of social work. It is designed as a supplementary text for methods or direct practice courses given the widespread incidence and consequences of addictive behaviors for a cross section of the general population. It also may be useful as a backup text for specialized electives such as crisis intervention and criminal justice courses. This means that the content will be relevant to the situations of most clients encountered by graduate students in social work programs as well as by students in graduate programs for other helping professions. Included are alcohol and drug counselors, psychologists, nurses, psychiatrists and other physicians, physical and occupational therapists, and administrators in treatment programs that serve addicted clients and their families. Such programs are provided in alcohol and drug treatment or prevention facilities, inpatient and outpatient psychiatric units, residential treatment centers for children, probation and parole agencies, hospitals, mental health centers, schools, public and private child welfare services, and family service agencies.

The book will be a useful reference for professional libraries in schools of social work and in graduate programs of the other helping professions. It may be useful for inservice education programs. Finally, experienced practitioners will find it helpful even in an informal reading.

The writing of this book has truly been uplifting. It has confirmed my belief that ''writing is learning.'' Moreover, it has allowed time for rethinking and expanding some ideas, for challenging others. May the reader have a similar journey.

ACKNOWLEDGMENTS

I wish to thank each of the contributing authors, not only for the chapters they have furnished for the book, but also for the opportunity to share ideas about the field in the process of writing and editing the book. My special thanks go to Kim Ray for typing the manuscript with such thoroughness and skill. Sadye Logan was very supportive in reviewing and providing feedback on portions of the manuscript.

Finally, I am most grateful to my family for their continuing belief in the value of my work in general, and specifically the value of this book on addictions in the current troubling times.

Edith M. Freeman

It was the best of times; it was the worst of times.

–Charles Dickens

CHAPTER 1

Addictive Behaviors: State-of-the-Art Issues in Social Work Treatment

Edith M. Freeman
University of Kansas

All change is revolutionary.

Anonymous

Shaffer and Gambino (1984) indicate that the field of addictions is in a "pre-paradigm" stage of development. Those authors believe that clinicians have, as a consequence, been left to develop their own "working" models of addiction. This state-of-the-art phenomenon is puzzling when one considers that the diagnosis of drug addiction became officially recognized in 1934 when it was included as a mental illness for the first time by the American Psychiatric Association (Szasz, 1974). Bratter and Forrest (1985) assume that this shift occurred for social control rather than clinical reasons, implying that clinical concerns about addictions may have arisen at a later period. This may be one factor that accounts for the current stage of development in the field of addictions.

A focus on addictions encourages attention to an intricate behavioral pattern or process (Bratter & Forrest, 1985), not to isolated behaviors. The value of such a broad focus is that all the multifaceted, biopsychosocial aspects in each person's situation are more likely to become apparent. Another benefit is that the focus can be extended beyond substances; nonconsummatory, but equally compulsive, processes such as gambling and sex can also be included.

Moreover, knowledge building related to how addictions develop can help to pinpoint common etiological issues and, therefore, common factors that can hinder or support effective treatment. For instance, the process of addiction development seems to involve the common use of substances, behaviors, or relationships to suppress and mask feelings (Miller, 1980; Wegscheider, 1981; Agras, 1987; Gaudia, 1987; Peele, 1976). And support groups based on the Alcoholics Anonymous model have been found to be useful when combined with other treatments (Freeman, 1985) for a wide variety of addictions (Miller, 1980).

There are problems involved in this approach as well as the benefits noted above. There is little consensus among scholars and service providers about how addictions should be defined; further, some of the addictions do not fit neatly within even the broad areas of agreement. Chaudron and Wilkinson (1988) indicate that anorexia involves limiting and restricting behaviors rather than the problems of excess that have been noted in other addictions. Another limitation is the tendency of scholars to specialize in the study of a specific addiction and not in the range of addictions. Thus, until recently much of the literature has been compartmentalized with few opportunities for generalizing what is known across the various addictions. One additional issue has been the problem of confusing the notion of addictions with the disease concept of alcoholism. This practice has caused some authors who challenge the disease concept to reject the framework of common addictions.

Given the potential benefits and limitations of focusing on the addiction process, the purpose of this chapter is to summarize major conclusions about this way of conceptualizing the problem. More specifically, the concept of addictions is defined, and alternative frameworks for describing the process such as the disease and adaptive models are included. Theories about the etiology of addictions are discussed also as well as their fit with descriptive models. The unique interaction of race, gender, and social class with addictions is reviewed, and a discussion about state-of-the-art social work treatment and roles concludes the chapter.

DEFINITION OF ADDICTION

Bratter and Forrest (1985) define an addiction as "a behavior pattern of compulsive drug use characterized by overwhelming involvement . . . with the use of a drug and the securing of the supply, as well as a tendency to relapse after completion of withdrawal" (p. 250). These authors state that the difference between use and addiction is quantitative rather than qualitative. They note that addiction is not determined by quantity alone, but, moreover, is additionally determined in terms of the effect on the individual in his or her social context. Table 1.1 illustrates Bratter and Forrest's definition of addiction and "a continuum of involvement," based on the extent to which the behavioral pattern pervades the total life of the user.

TABLE 1.1. Continuum of Involvement with a Substance or Behavior: Extent to Which the Substance, Activity, or Behavior Pervades the Person's Total Life

	Use	Abuse or Problem Use	Addiction
Context of the life situation	The person "wants to use," for recreation, celebration, or medication, and can control amount, manner of use, appropriate context of use.	The person "must use," increasing involvement in a compulsive manner; uncontrollable consequences occur but abuse continues nevertheless.	The person "must not stop using"; overwhelming involvement with a substance or behavior is carried compulsively into the person's daily life. Day to day patterns or routines of living are disrupted —with use —with securing a supply —with a strong tendency to relapse after completion of withdrawal.
Social parameters	Use is socially condoned for adults, and often encouraged. Mixed messages to youth, the elderly, and women in some instances.	Use in a manner that deviates from approved religious, medical, or social patterns within a given culture so social disapproval results.	Same as Abuse or Problem Use.
Tolerance	Increased tolerance can occur.	Increased tolerance has occurred.	Same as Abuse or Problem Use.
Dependence	Psychological and physiological dependence is not present.	Psychological and physiological dependence is indicative of abuse (the person feels it is necessary to have the substance or behavior to tolerate a social situation or feeling; the person must have the substance or behavior to prevent shakiness, anxiety, nausea, sweating, weakness).	Same as Abuse or Problem Use.

The Relationship of the Concept of Addiction to Other Concepts

The continuum in Table 1.1 illustrates a number of other important points about how addiction is defined and about its parameters. It implies that the concept of addiction is descriptive, rather than explanatory, in nature. The concept of addiction is not expected to provide an explanation of why the process occurs, but simply what occurs. The concept's usefulness is not dependent on any particular theory about the etiology of substance abuse or other addictions. Nor is it to be confused with descriptive *models* such as the disease concept of alcoholism that will be discussed in the next section of this chapter.

There is an important relationship between addictions and dependence (see Table 1.1); Bratter and Forrest's (1985) analysis of this relationship is enlightening:

Anyone currently addicted would be considered drug-dependent; but those who are psychologically dependent may not necessarily be addicted. (p. 250)

Tolerance, on the other hand, is possible even when involvement is at the "use" level in terms of the continuum. Tolerance is said to occur when a given substance or behavior, after repeated administration, produces decreased effect. Increased tolerance is certain when the level of involvement is indicative of abuse or addiction.

Common Aspects of Addictions

In defining addictions, some authors have questioned whether there are common elements involved in the process across substances, relationships, and behaviors. Baker (1988) notes that there is an implicit assumption that the types of addictions are more similar than dissimilar. In this same vein,

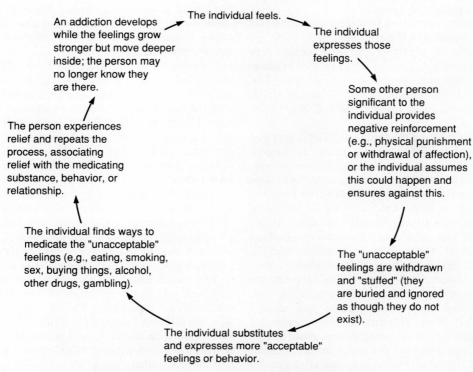

Figure 1.1. Common Elements in Addiction Development

Drew (1986) has pointed out that there is a "giving oneself to" aspect in all addictions, while others have wondered whether distinctions *should* be made among the addictions (Peele, 1985; Saleebey, 1985).

Burden's (1989) description of Dr. Linda Moore's concept of coping in children who are raised by addicted parents offers some interesting possibilities in this area. The concept developed out of practice experiences and fits with Shaffer and Gambino's (1984) assumption mentioned earlier about "working" models of addiction. The question is whether this concept, as shown in Figure 1.1, can be generalized to a wide range of addictions including alcohol, other drugs, eating disorders, compulsive gambling, and sexual addictions.

Similarly, many researchers have grappled with this question. Some common signs of addiction have been identified including

1. a preoccupation with a substance, relationship, or behavior;
2. a loss of control over the use of a substance or a pattern of behavior;
3. concerns expressed by others about the loss of control and the effects;
4. continued, persistent use of a substance or involvement in a behavior in spite of negative consequences (Bratter & Forrest, 1985; Sinnett, Judd, & Olson, 1983; Filstead, Parrella, & Ebbit, 1988; Murray, 1984; Cohn, 1987).

Scott (1983) and Filstead et al. (1988) note that eating disorders and substance abuse are similar conditions that share a common addictive process. Other researchers indicate that several addictions can often coexist in study populations. For instance, researchers have found that from 14 to 33 percent of the women with eating disorders in their studies were heavy users of alcohol and other drugs (Hatsukami, Eckert, Mitchell, & Pyle, 1984; Mitchell, Hatsukami, Eckert, & Pyle, 1985; Garfinkel, Moldofsky, & Garner, 1980). Still others have found a similar pattern in those who abuse cocaine and cannabis (Murray, 1984) and cocaine and alcohol (Cohn, 1987). Even with these findings, additional research is needed to answer questions about a common addiction process. The need includes epidemiological, outcome evaluation, and ethnographic

research. Such research can further clarify salient models of addiction as well.

MODELS FOR DESCRIBING ADDICTIONS

Models, frameworks, or concepts of addiction were developed to describe what typically happens and how it happens during this process. These three terms are often used interchangeably throughout the literature. Regardless of how they are labeled, they are not the same as theories that offer an explanation of why addiction occurs (Chaudron & Wilkinson, 1988). The "what" that the models describe varies greatly. For instance, the disease model focuses on addiction as an illness, the adaptive model looks at it as a way of coping, and the way-of-life model emphasizes life-styles or roles.

The Disease Model

The disease model provided "threshold" information about addictions when not much was known about the subject from research and practice experiences. It was introduced as an overt reaction to the moral condemnation and indifference that were being directed toward the addicted (Watts, 1981). This view of addiction authenticated drug use as a medical problem (Drew, 1986), tying it inexorably to the medical model and its focus on pathology and disease (Fingarette, 1989). In so doing, it provided a much needed alternative to the pattern of blaming the victim, but it also assumed that addiction involves a linear cause-and-effect relationship, similar to the development of diseases like diabetes.

Both the model's lack of emphasis on clients' strengths and the more narrow, nonsystemic view of addictions make it incompatible with social work (Weick, 1985; Freeman & Palmer, 1989). Challenging the disease model, however, is not only a professional judgment but also a political one. Acceptance of this model has given the medical profession a dominant role in the treatment of substance abuse that it will not yield easily. The field of addictions is now in a different time and place in terms of conceptualization. The disease model should be viewed in terms of its relationship to other emerging descriptive models, rather than as *the* model of addiction.

The Adaptive Model

The adaptive model assumes that certain problems and conditions (faulty upbringing, environmental inadequacies, and inborn physical or psychological disability) can cause a person not to grow up or to maintain adult integration. This can be seen in a lack "of self-reliance, competence, social acceptance, and self-confidence which are the basic expectations of society" (Alexander, 1987, p. 48). Various substitute adaptations may be drawn upon; they are labeled as substitutes because they do not provide the satisfaction that comes from adult integration. However, they fill a void even when they are harmful, as in the use of substances or other addictions. Proponents of this model cite that its benefits include the following:

1. A view of actions as purposive (involving search and choice)
2. A belief that addicted people are responding adaptively within their limitations at the time (Drew, 1986; Alexander, 1987)

The Way-of-Life Model

While the adaptive model views substance abuse and other addictions as a way of coping with an inability to achieve adult integration, the way of life model assumes that addictions develop when individuals are unable to achieve balance between their various life-styles or roles.

Essential to this model is the assumption that each person has a number of life-styles or roles that more or less hold together; this involves a behavior pattern that is repeated and valued. One or more ways of life can relate to work, home, recreation, community involvement, relationships, or the way persons make meaning out of life. Life-styles can conflict, coexist, or reinforce one another as well as change over time (Edwards, Arif, & Hodgson, 1981). The objective in life is to achieve some balance and integrity among the different life-styles.

According to Drew (1986), drug use as a way of life can assume a position of dominance; it can also become a persistent and destructive life-style (Taylor, 1985). In this model, self-destructive behavior occurs when people have "trouble organizing their lives" (Drew, 1986, p. 270). Self-destructive

behaviors differ primarily in terms of the object of the behaviors (drugs instead of work or sex). Drug abusers are said to eventually find themselves in a predicament; they may need help to get their ways of life in balance again. Of benefit is the model's way of taking into account the drug, the person, and the environment, although there seems to be less emphasis on the latter than on the first two. These models of addiction are examples of traditional frameworks, and some new ones that are being proposed currently. They serve as a foundation for a discussion on explanatory theories of addiction.

THEORIES OF ADDICTION

Explanatory theories build on descriptive models by incorporating their focus on what happens and how in the process of addiction, but they then extend the focus to the reasons addictions occur. Moreover, unlike descriptive models, they are capable of being tested empirically and they are generalizable. Some are more compatible with a particular descriptive model. Psychoanalytic theory and the disease concept are both based on the medical model, for example, while systems theory and the adaptive model emphasize the positive, adaptive capacities of individuals and their environments (Alexander, 1987; Chaudron & Wilkinson, 1988).

These theories on the etiology of addictions have been summarized in detail by a number of authors (Chaudron & Wilkinson, 1988; Blane & Leonard, 1986; Lettieri, Sayers, & Pearson, 1980). (See also Chapter 8 of this book.) For this reason, they will not be described here. Typically, the following theories have been included:

1. Biological or genetic theories.
2. Social learning and behavioral theories.
3. Theory of classical conditioning.
4. Stage theory.
5. Theories of access and availability.
6. Personality theory.
7. Psychoanalytic theory.
8. Systems theory.
9. Anthropological theories.
10. Economic theory. (Chaudron & Wilkinson, 1988, p. xix)

Connecting Theories of Etiology and Treatment

A recent trend has been to conceptualize the development of addictions as a biopsychosocial process, encouraging the integration of a number of interconnecting theories of etiology (Chaudron & Wilkinson, 1988). Using a combination of theories rather than one narrowly focused theory to explain addiction emphasizes all the interacting factors that may influence both its development and treatment outcomes.

When the focus for understanding the reasons for addictions is broad, this facilitates the use of treatment theories that are equally broad and comprehensive (connecting systems theory and family therapy, for example). Such theories of treatment point out who within the client's situation should be involved in treatment and suggest the types of changes in the person and environment that are considered necessary to initiate and maintain recovery (Bowen, 1974; Steinglass, 1989; Pearlman, 1988). This broad focus is even more important in understanding addiction development and treatment in special populations.

Theories and Special Populations

It is useful to question to what extent etiological theories consider the social context of special populations in addiction development. Special populations include, but are not limited to, women, minorities, and the poor. The roles of gender socialization, institutional racism, and socioeconomic barriers in the addiction process are just beginning to be examined in research and practice. Those aspects of the social context determine risk factors for special populations in terms of addictions, and their responses to those factors as well as societal responses. Heath (1988) acknowledges that the increasing attention being paid to special populations indicates a growing acceptance of the importance of the following sociocultural perspectives:

1. It has been found from epidemiological research that different populations have different rates of addictions, different responses to substances in particular, and different beliefs and behavior about them.
2. Such ethnographic data on cultural differences provide insights about practical applications, such as a search for effective measures for prevention.
3. Without a good understanding of the norms of a population, it is difficult to make early identification of individuals who are at high risk for (or are showing early signs of) addiction.
4. Similarly, a great many of the addiction problems in any population defy diagnosis unless one is familiar with the cultural norms and expectations of the population.
5. Among the several approaches to treatment that are available, some are appropriate to members of one culture but not to members of another. (pp. 398–399)

While it appears that some progress is being made by the addictions field in the area of special populations, there is much more that needs to be done. For instance, sociocultural theoretical perspectives focus primarily on the culture of the individual and the person, but they do not examine the role of the larger environment (e.g., gender bias and racism) within that social context (Schuckit & Duby, 1983; Wright, Kail, & Creecy, 1989; Schwartz, Thompson, & Johnson, 1983). Moreover, few culture-specific treatment approaches exist except for a few examples (Bell & Evans, 1983; Covington, 1984). These current deficits and other issues discussed throughout this chapter have special implications for social workers and other helping professionals in the addictions field.

IMPLICATIONS FOR PRACTICE

If the addictions field is on the threshold of change, so are its practitioners and those who suffer from addictions. And while "all change is revolutionary," change nevertheless represents both opportunities and risks.

Special Opportunities

An important task is for social workers to integrate their clinical roles and skills with a full knowledge of addictions. Those roles and skills that have been found to be effective in other fields of practice can be generalized, modifying them as needed in terms of the dynamics of addictions. An example of a role that can be generalized is that of case manager. That role has proven to be effective with other client groups such as the chronically mentally ill and pregnant teenagers. The emphasis on a continuum of services and intensive problem solving around daily tasks appears to be critical for improved adaptation and coping in those populations (Benjamin & Ben-Dashan, 1983; Freeman, 1983). This is likely to be true in work with addicted clients if the role of case manager is indeed generalized as recommended.

Examples of generalizable skills include social network interventions, crisis management, and advocacy. Drinking and drugging networks as well as high-risk communities present real-life opportunities for social workers to influence the social context of addicted clients. Advocacy skills are often needed to help clients negotiate for resources in the form of employment, housing, or addictions treatment. Crisis management skills are extremely useful for preventing and helping a client to learn from relapse experiences.

A second opportunity involves work with interdisciplinary teams in the addictions field and related areas of practice such as mental health. The team is a useful mechanism for helping practitioners to stay focused on all the biopsychosocial variables in each situation. It is also useful for preventing burnout in this high-stress field and for obtaining support from colleagues. Further, since value conflicts are inevitable in this area of practice, the team provides an opportunity to reality test and maintain objectivity. It may assist practitioners in working on their own unfinished business or personal experiences with addictions.

Third, assessment of the current state of the art helps to identify gaps in addictions treatment to which social workers can recommit themselves. Two areas identified in this chapter are the need for descriptive models that emphasize a strengths perspective, and the need to identify risk factors in the social context of special populations and to participate in relevant theory building. Such a commitment is consistent with professional values and priorities about serving vulnerable populations in general. While these opportunities are available to practitioners in the area of addictions, the current state of the art also involves some noteworthy risks.

Current Risks

Social work, after years of struggle to increase its status by embracing the medical model, is currently moving away from that model (Weick, 1985) and from its offspring: the disease concept. As more and more social workers are drawn into the addictions field due to the drug epidemic and other social conditions, there may be a tendency to move back toward the dominant force in the field. This could result in a loss of focus on client strengths and on a belief in the adaptive potential of individuals. This is a significant risk for the profession *and* for the addictions field.

Social workers who are already in the addictions field have and will continue to struggle with the dilemma of how to "begin where the client is" when the client denies the problem due to an addiction. As the pressures mount to increase treatment effectiveness with the growing numbers of addicted clients, this struggle will no doubt intensify. Therefore, there is a potential for losing the focus on mutuality between client and practitioner in treatment *and* the professional value of beginning where the client is.

Finally, a number of social policy, prevention, and environmental impact issues are emerging as the field is shifting. Some of these are "new twists" on old issues and others are completely new issues due to changes in prevalence rates and the development of new, illicit substances. A sample of some of these issues includes the following:

1. Mandatory drug testing policies and laws
2. Drug-exposed fetuses and how child abuse reporting laws apply to them
3. Clean needle campaigns for IV drug users
4. Tobacco brands and ad campaigns targeted specifically for high-consuming and high-risk special populations (women, young males, and minorities)
5. Labeling issues in terms of dual diagnosis conditions
6. Personal values among practitioners that support casual drug use
7. Media ad campaigns that equate femininity and social acceptance with ideal body weight
8. Campaigns to raise the drinking age laws
9. A socialization process that encourages individuals to seek immediate gratification or relief from stressful situations.
10. State lotteries and the role they play in social and compulsive gambling

11. Competition for funding resources and separation of research from prevention and treatment programs in addictions
12. The controversy over whether primary prevention works and whether it can be effectively evaluated
13. Conflicts about how to allocate national resources between law enforcement, treatment, and research in the addictions field

The risk is that social workers and other helping professionals will mistakingly view these issues as too complex to resolve and somewhat distant from their daily practice. This could mean that some very basic and significant issues would not be addressed by the professionals whose input is critical and that policymakers would address some of those issues inadequately or not at all.

CONCLUSION

The addictions field may be in the process of overturning some of its traditions; this could have both positive and negative consequences. Some common aspects of addictions could be clarified, old models could be challenged, new explanatory theories might be developed or existing ones combined differently, and the needs of special populations could be addressed more effectively with improved treatments. The potential negative consequences for social workers relate primarily to a loss of professional values and frame of reference. Social workers can choose to be in the forefront of this change process or they can be merely swept along in the backlash. This is a time for reflection and, then, for action.

REFERENCES

Agras, W. S. (1987). *Eating disorders: Management of obesity, bulimia, and anorexia nervosa.* New York: Pergamon Press.

Alexander, B. K. (1987). The disease and adaptive models of addiction: A framework evaluation. *Journal of Drug Issues, 17,* 47–66.

Baker, T. B. (1988). Models of addiction: Introduction to the special issue. *Journal of Abnormal Psychology, 97,* 115–117.

Bell, P., & Evans, J. (1983). Counseling the black alcoholic client. In T. D. Watts and R. Wright (Eds.), *Black alcoholism: Toward a comprehensive understanding* (pp. 100–121). Springfield, IL: Thomas.

Benjamin, M. L., & Ben-Dashan, T. (1983). Case management: Implications and issues. In C. J. Sanborn (Ed.), *Case management in mental health services* (pp. 43–50). New York: Haworth Press.

Blane, H. T., & Leonard, K. E. (1986). *Psychological theories of drinking and alcoholism.* New York: Guilford Press.

Bowen, M. (1974). Alcoholism as viewed through family systems theory and family psychotherapy. *Annals of the New York Academy of Science, 233,* 115–122.

Bratter, T. E., & Forrest, G. G. (1985). *Alcoholism and substance abuse: Strategies for clinical intervention.* New York: Free Press.

Burden, S. (1989). *Adult children of alcoholics.* Paper presented at Cedar Ridge Treatment Center, Grand Rounds Series. Shawnee Mission, KS.

Chaudron, C. D., & Wilkinson, D. A. (1988). *Theories on alcoholism.* Toronto: Addiction Research Foundation.

Cohn, V. H. (1987, Summer). New studies on the interaction of alcohol and cocaine. *Alcohol Health and Research World, 10,* 26–27.

Covington, S. S. (1984). *Treatment for women: What do we do with what we know?* Paper presented at the 30th International Institute on the Prevention and Treatment of Alcoholism. Athens, Greece.

Drew, L. R. H. (1986). Beyond the disease concept of addiction: Drug use as a way of life leading to predicaments. *Journal of Drug Issues, 16,* 263–274.

Edwards, G., Arif, A., & Hodgson, R. (1981). Nomenclature and classification of drug- and alcohol-related problems: A WHO memorandum. *Bulletin of the World Health Organization, 59,* 225–242.

Filstead, W. J., Parrella, D. P., & Ebbitt, J. (1988). High-risk situations for engaging in substance abuse and binge-eating behaviors. *Journal of Studies on Alcohol, 49,* 136–141.

Fingarette, H. (1989). *Heavy drinking: The myth of alcoholism as a disease.* Berkeley: University of California Press.

Freeman, E. M. (1983). *Training manual for case managers in programs for teenage parents.* Lawrence, KS: University of Kansas.

Freeman, E. M. (1985). Toward improving treatment effectiveness with alcohol problems. In E. M. Freeman (Ed.), *Social work practice with clients who have alcohol problems* (pp. 83–105). Springfield, IL: Thomas.

Freeman, E. M., & Palmer, N. (1989). *Reconceptualizing dynamics in the alcoholic family: A preliminary study.* Research Report. Lawrence: University of Kansas.

Garfinkel, P. E., Moldofsky, H., & Garner, D. M. (1980). The heterogeneity of anorexia nervosa. *Archives of General Psychiatry, 37,* 1036–1040.

Gaudia, R. (1987, May/June). Effects of compulsive gambling on the family. *Social Work, 32,* 254–256.

Hatsukami, D., Eckert, E., Mitchell, J. E., & Pyle, R. (1984). Affective disorder and substance abuse in women with bulimia. *Psychological Medicine, 14,* 701–704.

Heath, D. B. (1988). Emerging anthropological theory and models of alcohol use and alcoholism. In C. D. Chaudron and D. A. Wilkinson (Eds.), *Theories on alcoholism* (pp. 353–410). Toronto: Addiction Research Foundation.

Lettieri, D. J., Sayers, M., & Pearson, H. W. (1980). *Theories on drug abuse: Selected contemporary perspectives.* Rockville, MD: National Institute on Drug Abuse, U.S. Department of Health and Human Services.

Miller, W. (1980). *The addictive behaviors: Treatment of alcohol, drug abuse, smoking, and obesity.* New York: Pergamon Press.

Mitchell, J., Hatsukami, D., Eckert, E. D., & Pyle, H. (1985). Characteristics of 175 patients with bulimia. *American Journal of Psychiatry, 142,* 482–485.

Murray, G. F. (1984). The cannabis-cocaine connection: A comparative study of use and users. *Journal of Drug Issues, 14,* 664–676.

Pearlman, S. (1988). Systems theory and alcoholism: In C. D. Chaudron and D. A. Wilkinson (Eds.), *Theories on alcoholism* (pp. 289–384). Toronto: Addiction Research Foundation.

Peele, S. (1976). *Love and addiction.* New York: Signet.

Peele, S. (1985). How can addiction occur with other than drug involvement? *British Journal of Addictions, 80,* 23–25.

Saleebey, D. (1985). A social psychological perspective on addictions: Themes and disharmonies. *Journal of Drug Issues, 15,* 17–28.

Schuckit, M. A., & Duby, J. (1983). Alcoholism in women. In B. Kissin and H. Begleiter (Eds.), *The pathogenesis of alcoholism: Psychosocial factors* (pp. 215–241). New York: Plenum.

Schwartz, D. M., Thompson, M. G., & Johnson, C. (1983). Anorexia and bulimia: The sociocultural context. *International Journal of Eating Disorders, 1,* 23–25.

Scott, D. W. (1983). Alcohol and food abuse: Some comparisons. *British Journal of Addictions, 78,* 339–349.

Shaffer, H., & Gambino, B. (1984). Addiction paradigms III: From theory-research to practice and back. *Advances in Alcohol and Substance Abuse, 3,* 135–154.

Sinnett, E. R., Judd, B., & Olson, M. A. (1983). Food, drugs, and alcohol—A common pattern of use. *Perceptual Motor Skills, 57,* 375–379.

Steinglass, P. (1989). *The alcoholic family.* New York: Basic Books.

Szasz, T. (1974). *Ceremonial chemistry: The ritual persecution of drugs, addicts and pushers.* Garden City, NY: Doubleday.

Taylor, D. (1985). The sick child's predicament. *Australian and New Zealand Journal of Psychiatry, 19,* 130–137.

Watts, T. (1981). The uneasy triumph of a concept: The "disease" conception of alcoholism. *Journal of Drug Issues, 11,* 451–460.

Wegscheider, S. (1981). *Another chance: Hope and help for the alcoholic family.* Palo Alto, CA: Science & Behavior Books.

Weick, A. (1985). Overturning the medical model. *Social Work, 30,* 310–315.

Wright, R., Kail, B. L., & Creecy, R. F. (1989). Culturally sensitive social work practice with black alcoholics and their families. In S. M. L. Logan, E. M. Freeman, & R. G. McRoy (Eds.), *Social work practice with Black families: A culturally specific perspective* (pp. 203–222). White Plains, NY: Longman.

SUPPLEMENTAL READING LIST

Antonovsky, A. (1985). *Health, stress, and coping.* San Francisco: Jossey-Bass.
This book proposes a health continuum model that provides new insights about a wellness perspective and ways of coping; the discussion has implications for how addictions are viewed.

Crawford, J. R., Thomson, N. A., Guillion, F. E., & Garthwaite, P. (1989). Does endorsement of the disease concept of alcoholism predict humanitarian attitudes to alcoholics? *International Journal of the Addictions, 24,* 71–77.
The study results in this article raise interesting questions about the efficacy of promoting the disease concept to influence humanitarian attitudes toward alcoholics.

Fingarette, H. (1988, November/December). Alcoholism: The mythical disease. *The Utne Reader, 35,* 64–69.
This article provides an analysis of factors that challenge the validity of the disease concept, including those related to economic interests, scientific requirements, and social policy implications.

Thorpe, G. L., Parker, J. D., Bush, M. J., & Magill, S. J. (1987, Summer). Alcohol and cocaine abuse treatment in Maine: An integrated approach. *Alcohol Health and Research World, 11,* 28–31.
Treatment guidelines are provided in this article for situations where clients have alcohol and cocaine addictions; the differences and common aspects of the two addictions are included.

PART I

Alcohol Abuse and Addiction

Treatment for alcohol abuse and addiction is complex, not only because of effects from the substance itself, but also because of the many biopsychosocial variables that influence the situation. Further, social workers who provide services to these clients struggle to integrate their professional skills and values into addictions counseling. They must manage the strains involved in meeting differing, and sometimes conflicting, expectations. Part I attempts to place alcohol treatment within the context of these issues while identifying what strategies of intervention are effective with what types of clients in what circumstances. Each chapter in this and the three other sections of the book identifies roles and skills for social workers and other helping professionals in relation to the unique crosscutting issues being addressed.

Chapter 2 reviews research on alcohol recovery in terms of natural healing, mutual and self-help groups, and formal treatment. Little is known about the ''spontaneous'' recovery process that occurs for some individuals without the assistance of the two other approaches to treatment. The chapter discusses how the three ways individuals recover work best for particular types of clients and how they can be combined. A section on new research paradigms points to possibilities of involving recovering clients in developing research with natural, ethnographic methods.

That chapter lays a useful foundation for the other chapters in Part I. Chapter 3 examines the importance of differential diagnosis in assessment and discusses variables, such as race and gender, that determine the least restrictive treatment for a client. Some examples are provided to clarify how differential diagnoses can be developed while the practitioner is utilizing a strengths perspective, especially when nonvoluntary court-ordered clients are referred for treatment.

In Chapter 4, a unique type of codependent relationship is discussed: adult children of alcoholics (ACOAs) and their parents. The focus is on how that relationship influences all others until ACOAs become involved in treatment of a long-term nature, with group work being the treatment of choice. Common issues among ACOAs are identified and work on those issues is described clearly through a focus on the group process. The focus in Chapter 5, however, is on a more complex addictive system in which several members of a family are alcohol dependent. Guidelines are discussed for monitoring the elimination of alcohol from the system, along with predictable responses of the system to reintroduce alcohol. Also discussed is treatment that includes family systems and paradoxical interventions. Again, issues related to coerced treatment, along with the social worker's concerns about ethical standards, are explored in this chapter.

Similarly, the thrust of treatment in Chapter 6 on alcohol and child sexual abuse is directed toward all members of the unit rather than toward the perpetrator only. The common and unique factors that are present when alcoholism and child sexual abuse coexist are identified, with emphasis on the risk of ignoring either problem in favor of designating one as the primary focus for the work. Because of the stressful nature of the work, the social worker's role with the interdisciplinary team is highlighted.

CHAPTER 2

Research on Alcohol Abuse and Recovery: From Natural Helping to Formal Treatment to Mutual Aid

Linda Farris Kurtz

Eastern Michigan University

We will comprehend the word serenity and we will know peace.

Alcoholics Anonymous, *The Big Book*

Many people stop alcohol abuse without help, but we do not know how many. Many people who do get help do not stop alcohol abuse, but again we are not sure how many. Our research on the abuse of alcohol and efforts to stop it, both in individuals and in society as a whole, is limited. We as social workers and as members of society also must face our limitations and do the best we can with what we know. This chapter reviews some of the theory and research on treatment and recovery from alcohol abuse. It first furnishes an overview of natural healing and supports in order to show how friends, family, and helpers outside the formal alcoholism treatment field can either help or hinder the alcohol abuser's path of dysfunctional use. It also reviews research and theory on formal treatment and mutual help, and ends with a discussion of future directions for social work practice and research.

NATURAL HEALING AND NATURAL HELPERS

Family, friends, and co-workers are the basis for a well-functioning social support system. Evidence

shows that adequate social support reinforces positive physical and mental health (Garbarino, 1983; Lin, Ensel, Simeone, & Kuo, 1979). On the other hand, friends can harm the health of others when drinking buddies and social groups support heavy use rather than moderation or abstinence (Denzin, 1987; Selnow & Crano, 1986). In contrast to theories of social control that assume that the substance abuser is violating societal norms, theories of social deviance suggest that misuse occurs because social groups reinforce abuse of alcohol (Hawkins & Fraser, 1983). Alcohol use is an accepted norm in modern American society and, for certain social or peer subgroups, abuse of alcohol is the norm as well (Fine, Akabas, & Bellinger, 1982). These norms may have equal relevance to how individuals recover and whether this process can occur spontaneously or naturally (Ludwig, 1985).

Dynamics of Natural Healing

Researchers have attempted to discover the extent to which alcohol-abusing members of society recover spontaneously without formal treatment. Factors such as family, friends, family doctors, jobs, and individual cognitions appear to play a very important role in moderating excessive use of alcohol. For example, when one sample of problem drinkers who had received formal treatment was interviewed, instead of citing aspects of the treating agency as factors in recovery, 88 percent cited internal psychological or social factors as reasons. Vaillant's 20-year longitudinal study (1983) found that nontreatment factors, such as substitute dependencies, medical consequences, religious involvement, and personal relationships, were most instrumental in the recovery of alcoholics. Vaillant's study, as well as others cited by him, suggest that 2 to 3 percent of alcoholics become abstinent and another 1 percent return to asymptomatic drinking without treatment (Vaillant, 1983, p. 123). Additionally, natural social supports contribute importantly to recovery following formal treatment.

Tuchfeld's (1981) sample of spontaneous remitters gave not wanting to hurt the family as one reason for quitting or controlling alcohol use and designated the family as a means of social control once changes in use occurred. A prospective study found that alcohol abusers who quit consumption of alcohol were more likely to be married than were those who only reduced intake or who continued abuse (Hermos, Locastro, Glynn, Gouchard, & DeLabry, 1988).

Having a family life can also be a negative factor in recovery, if the actions of family members reinforce drinking or produce a hostile climate that triggers a drinking response (Steinglass, 1981). Moos, Finney, and Chan (1981) compared recovering and relapsed alcoholics on measures of family environment. They found that recovering subjects assessed their family as more cohesive, more expressive, more organized, and less conflicted than relapsed subjects. Recovering families were also more involved in recreation and social events than relapsed families.

The same patterns were found in a study of teenagers who belonged to Alateen, a mutual-aid group sponsored by Al-Anon Family Groups (Peterson-Kelley, 1985). Spouses of alcoholics traditionally have been seen as meeting neurotic needs in their marriage to a drinking, dependent spouse. This theory has given way to research that shows dysfunctions in spouses to be the result of the alcoholism rather than the cause of it (Paolino, Mc-

Crady, Diamond, & Longabaugh, 1976). Although wives of some alcoholics do not see that having a drinking spouse meets their needs, they do see that spousal behavior can encourage further use (Ablon, 1974; Gorman & Rooney, 1979). They "enable" the drinking when they cover up the drinker's behavior, accept unacceptable behavior, and engage in threats and futile efforts to control the drinker.

Friends, too, can either be supportive of recovery or become obstacles to moderation and good judgment in the use of alcohol. Tuchfeld's (1981) study found that friends, like family, were an important factor in the maintenance of recovery and served as informal social controls. On the other hand, friendships developed prior to the onset of a stigmatizing illness, such as alcoholism, may depart; the resulting alienation and loss can become another stressor (Borkman, 1984). Additionally, alcohol abusers frequently, if not usually, break ties to those who do not share their preoccupation with the substance; thus the existing social network is often one that promotes continued misuse (Denzin, 1987).

Health problems caused by alcohol are the most frequently mentioned reason given for spontaneous recovery (Tuchfeld, 1981; Ludwig, 1985; Hermos et al., 1988). Therefore, the family doctor and other medical personnel become a crucial part of the natural helping network; they can promote abandonment of alcohol abuse and continue to remind the recovering abuser that personal health depends on abstinence or reduction of use.

Religion and religious groups are another support that can assist the drinker to recover. Vaillant (1983) contends that Marx's slogan "religion is the opiate of the masses" contains an important therapeutic principle (p. 193). Religion provides new sources of self-esteem, hope, and forgiveness. It also gives support for converting what is cherished (alcohol) into that which is hated and rejected, while providing a more socially accepted replacement for the alcohol.

The work environment can be a powerful force for recovery by being another natural reinforcer of moderation. However, the workplace may be a subculture that encourages heavy drinking (Trice & Roman, 1979). Work site drinking cultures, according to Fine et al. (1982), result in three sets of consequences: socialization of new workers to drinking, normalization of drinking on the job, and obstruction of treatment for problem drinkers. The Alaskan oil spill of 1989 represents a spectacular example of what can happen when work site norms encourage drinking instead of sobriety. This broadened definition of drinking cultures has special implications for diverse population groups and their natural support networks.

Natural Helping: Special Populations

Natural helping factors can present both positive and negative factors for special populations. The elderly, for example, rarely fit the stereotype of the alcoholic and usually do not have the workplace as a control against alcohol abuse. Furthermore, the elderly are prescribed, more than other age cohorts, psychoactive medications that interact dangerously with alcohol; the results are often ascribed to senility or seen as merely enjoyment of one's final years, rather than correctly identified and treated (Blackmon, 1985).

For some African Americans, drinking is more social than in most white groups and also has reinforcing status implications. According to at least one authority on substance abuse in the African American community, one's social class is denoted by the brand and price one pays for liquor (Harper, 1976). In addition, African American communities often contain more liquor stores than other communities, which serve as places to congregate and socialize (Harper, 1976). In contrast, the church is often a positive force against alcohol abuse in African American communities (Brisbane & Womble, 1985).

Women also have unique characteristics that reduce the influence of natural helping resources. Women are more likely to have alcoholic spouses, or, if the woman is the alcohol abuser, her husband is more likely to leave her as a result of the abuse (Fewell, 1985; Kimball, 1978). Physicians, who are major contributors toward recognition of alcohol abuse in men, unwittingly exacerbate the problem for women by failing more often to diagnose their addictions and by prescribing cross-addicting tranquilizers (Kimball, 1978).

In conclusion, the research on spontaneous abstinence establishes that recovery from alcohol misuse can occur without formal treatment or self-help groups and that members of the abuser's support network have a profound impact on that recovery.

Furthermore, natural helpers also serve as adjuncts to formal treatment and self-help groups. The significance of family, friends, work, and leisure underscores the salience of natural healing and of ecological approaches to social work practice with alcoholics (Tuchfield, 1981).

FORMAL TREATMENT FOR ALCOHOLISM

There are several models of formal, professional intervention for alcoholism that are based loosely on theoretical explanations of the nature and the cause of alcohol dependence. Research on outcome has given support for some of the approaches, but has not yet been reported for others. Effectiveness studies must account for multiple factors that influence outcomes, such as the competence of the helper, bias in the evaluation process, presence or lack of methodological rigor, the presence of aftercare and follow-up services, and the general availability of supports and other resources to the discharged client. The available research is not always well connected to a theoretical approach, nor does it "prove" the effectiveness of one treatment over another or of any treatment at all. It may be that any theoretical approach works well when applied in a coherent manner, by competent caregivers, to persons motivated to improve, who have a good support system and a lot to lose if they fail to control their drinking.

Does professional treatment help according to available research? George Vaillant (1983) summed up the dilemma posed to the professional when he wrote, "Follow-up studies suggest that elaborate treatment may be no better than brief sensible advice . . . but to ignore a chronic malady as painful . . . as alcoholism . . . is unconscionable" (p. 281). He resolves the dilemma by pointing out that, while treatment may not cure the illness, it does prevent death, contribute to the overall set of curative factors available, and gives hope. Although many, if not most, alcoholics relapse, the relapse itself is simply one step in the ongoing recovery process, not the end of it. The range of formal treatment models currently in use varies in terms of how this recovery process is conceptualized and implemented.

The Minnesota Model

The Minnesota Model, sometimes called the Hazelden Model, has become the standard for inpatient alcoholism programs in the United States (Anderson, 1981). The Minnesota approach rests on the disease theory of alcoholism. Although the Hazelden approach has been referred to as using primarily ''ex-alcoholics'' as care providers (Pattison, 1985), this description misleads. Although recovering counselors are an important component, the Minnesota Model also depends upon professionals who complement the recovering counselor.

A key aspect of the Minnesota Model is the concept of the continuum of care that includes diagnosis and detoxification as the first step in treatment, residential treatment during which the philosophy of Alcoholics Anonymous (AA) is introduced along with professional counseling, and discharge planning, which may include time in a halfway house (Anderson, 1981). Aftercare services typically include educational services, continued participation in AA, and returns to the treatment center as part of an alumni organization. During and after treatment this model emphasizes the importance of education about the illness for the alcoholic and his or her family. The Hazelden program in Minnesota has been routinely evaluated. Discharged patients have maintained sobriety in 55 percent of cases followed for a period of *one year*. The percentage increases to 80 percent for those with steady jobs, an intact family, and a home to return to (Anderson, 1981).

The Minnesota Model has been more comprehensive than some historical and current approaches: the medical detox model, traditional psychiatric approaches, the developmental model, the biopsychosocial model, behavior modification approaches, and controlled drinking approaches (Anderson, 1981). Some of these models continue to be used alone or in combination with other approaches in order to enhance their effectiveness and scope.

The Medical Detox Model

Detoxification remains an essential element in any treatment program for those who need it but is rarely used alone. Psychotherapy has proven unsuccessful with alcoholics who were still drinking but may be more effective with motivated persons after recovery has begun (Vaillant, 1981). While alcohol remains in the system, even though the individual has stopped drinking, the dysfunctional behavior that can threaten recovery will continue. This includes inadequate communication, guilt and shame reactions, blaming others, hiding feelings, and inadequate problem solving. Detoxification eliminates alcohol from the system *and* makes it possible for other treatment approaches to be useful in changing these dysfunctional behaviors. According to the literature (Saunders, 1985; Vaillant, 1983), medical detox can be provided effectively in freestanding clinics that then refer clients for alcohol treatment or in treatment programs in which detox is an essential component of a continuum of services.

Traditional Psychiatric Approaches

In many respects, psychodynamic theories of alcoholism infuse the AA approach, which is a fundamental aspect of the Minnesota Model, as noted previously. AA's founders made use of Thibout's understanding of the alcoholic's basic narcissism and the importance of surrendering control or letting go of the illusion of omnipotence (Mack, 1981; E. Kurtz, 1979). Recent contributions from the ranks of psychiatry (Bean & Zinberg, 1981) propose a self-psychology approach to understanding alcohol abuse and its effects on the abuser. These insightful and thoughtful contributions give understanding of how and why AA works for some recovering people and how professional therapy can become compatible with involvement in AA. For example, Khantzian (1981) believes that AA works because it helps the alcoholic regulate emotions and maintain self-esteem and related dependency needs, which he posits are ego functions deficient in many alcoholics.

The Developmental Model

The Developmental Model proposed by Brown (1985) rests on Piaget's theory and incorporates AA principles as part of the treatment. Brown considers the act of alcohol abuse as both a behavior and a thinking disorder in which the loss of control seems instead to *be* control; the drinker maintains a false ''nonalcoholic'' identity through cognitive denial. In treatment, the drinker moves through three developmental stages. In the first phase, the patient's identity changes from ''nonalcoholic'' to an alcoholic identity. In the second stage, many alcoholic behaviors continue, but dependency on others replaces dependency on alcohol. In the final stage, treatment encourages reflection on anxiety and discomfort, ways of coping with distress by means other than alcohol, and a new interpretation of self in interaction with others. The latter change reflects a shift in beliefs and cognitions and, thus, is similar to cognitive approaches (Rollnick, 1985). Brown (1985) bases the Developmental Model on his empirical study with 80 abstinent AA members, but does not present outcome data from application to treatment.

The Biopsychosocial Model

The Biopsychosocial Model is a systems framework that considers the interaction of biological, psychological, and social factors in assessing a person for clinical intervention and stresses matching treatment to individual needs (Donovan, 1988). This model, though eclectic in name, incorporates a social learning or behavioral approach to treatment. It relies on carefully kept records of drinking stimuli and measures of functioning before and after treatment. It advocates behavioral, cognitive, and social support approaches. Unlike other models, the biopsychosocial model is not dependent upon AA principles nor is it insistent upon total abstinence as a goal of treatment. This model also spans the various addictive behaviors, including smoking, drinking, drug taking, and overeating (Donovan & Marlatt, 1988). The authors cited here base some of their eclectic conclusions on a substantial body of behavioral research literature but do not report outcome data on the full use of the Biopsychosocial Model.

Behavioral Approaches

The behavioral school is much more grounded in empirical research than is the Biopsychosocial Model. It contains numerous theoretical subschools, such as social learning theory, expectancy theory, stress response dampening, and others (Blane & Leonard, 1987). Social learning theory also furnishes a theoretical base for Marlatt and Gordon's (1985) relapse prevention approach. This approach teaches the recovering person methods of coping with future situations (immediate determinants) that have previously triggered use of alcohol (Marlatt & Gordon, 1985). It combines behavioral skill train-

ing, cognitive interventions, and life-style change. Although the authors do not present outcome data from application to problem drinkers, social learning approaches to other problems have been studied under controlled experimental conditions as well as in the field (Rollnick, 1985).

Controlled Drinking Approaches

Finally, there is the controversial controlled drinking approach and interventions designed to teach moderated drinking. The debate over teaching alcoholics to drink "normally" is probably the most controversial issue in the alcoholism field. One side contends that controlled drinking is unsafe for anyone with a correctly diagnosed problem of alcoholism, that one drink will lead to others, if not now, then at some time, and that the ability to drink socially is not worth the risk (Pendry, Maltzman, & West, 1982). On the other side, controlled drinking proponents argue that, for some heavy drinkers, controlled or comfortable drinking is theoretically attainable and should be studied further in an open-minded fashion (Heather & Robertson, 1981). And further, because total abstinence has not been proven necessary for all persons, heavy drinkers in treatment should be told honestly of the possible option of learning to drink moderately.

Methodological Problems across All Treatment Models

Research on outcomes after treatment reveals a jumble of conflicting findings and persistent uncertainty regarding treatment effectiveness, regardless of the treatment model applied. Saunders (1985) argues that treatment does not work, as evidenced both by the failure to reduce the number of alcoholics in the population and by the fact that most reliable follow-up studies show little success that can be ascribed to treatment alone. Other factors such as motivation to stop abuse, employment, and other environmental supports might also be involved. On the other hand, one of the studies Saunders cites to support his contention (Vaillant, 1983) differs regarding the significance, if not the effectiveness, of treatment. According to Vaillant, early treatment can interfere with the natural history of alcoholism by shortening the period of suffering. Moreover, treatment does save lives until natural healing processes can take over.

Also on the other side of the treatment effectiveness argument, Cartwright (1985) states that controlled experimental studies are inappropriate for evaluating treatment efficacy. He points out that treatment effectiveness must distinguish between therapists, citing research that shows skilled therapists can be 100 percent effective when they relate empathically with clients, whereas less empathic therapists have very low success.

Those programs that follow up with clients after the initial treatment period also show positive results in outcome. Marlatt (1988) reports that relapse is the most common outcome of alcoholism treatment. Others have found that long-term outcome is more dependent on events that occur after treatment is completed than on what happens during treatment (Moos, Finney, & Chan, 1981). In one experimental study, for example, the authors contrasted aggressive aftercare, consisting of home visits by therapists, with traditional aftercare appointments and case management (Gilbert, 1988). The results after one year showed that the aggressive method improved treatment compliance, decreased dropout rates, and, for those who completed treatment, improved outcome.

Variations on the treatment package, such as provision of treatment for the family, marital counseling, or special programs for the elderly, women, and minorities, further complicate research on treatment effectiveness. Research reviewed in the previous section highlights the significance of supportive environments, stable marriages, and other functional relationships to the recovery of the alcoholic. The existence of family dysfunctions or mental illness in alcoholic families is not a new concept (Jackson, 1954); however, inclusion of family treatment in formal alcohol treatment centers has not been widespread (Regan, Conners, O'Farrell, & Jones, 1983). Evaluations of outcomes of family treatment are few, but those that have been done support its usefulness (Wright & Scott, 1978; Kaufman, 1985).

Issues of Diversity, Formal Treatment, and Research

A small number of specialized treatment programs for women, minorities, and the elderly are being developed, especially in larger population centers where demand for treatment beds and competition in

the marketplace lead to segmentation and targeting of special groups. Special programs for women need to be offered because of the unique character of women's alcoholism (Fewell, 1985; Corrigan, 1980). Women are more likely to be cross-addicted to prescription drugs than men; they are also more likely to suffer from depression, to have marital and family problems, and to have suffered from physical and sexual abuse in the home. Women can be intimidated by men in gender-mixed programs and have difficulty opening up about the problems they experience when men are present. When women are treated with men in "co-ed" programs, the women can also become the targets of sexual harassment, unable to muster the self-esteem to deal effectively with the problem. Further, women's drinking styles differ from those of male alcoholics so that the peer identification needed to penetrate denial and to enhance self-awareness is not easily achieved in gender-mixed programs (Fewell, 1985; Corrigan, 1980).

The elderly may best be treated in special programs for similar reasons. Due to their more conservative views and stereotypes, the elderly have more difficulty in accepting their illness. Identification with others assists in breaking through denial. Elderly clients cannot easily identify with the styles of drinking and drug abuse presented by younger alcohol abusers. Additionally, the elderly are more upset by confrontation and require a gentler approach in treatment. And finally, the elderly may need protection from the noise and leisure activity engaged in by younger people in treatment (Blackmon, 1985).

Minorities also may have special characteristics that must be considered in treatment. Racism and anger in reaction to it may be a major treatment issue for African American alcoholics (Bell & Evans, 1981; Brisbane & Womble, 1985). Native Americans experience high stress due to identity confusion and uncertainty over assimilation into the dominant culture, on one hand, and tribal identification on the other (Gunther, Jolly, & Wedel, 1985). For homosexual alcoholics, it is important for caregivers to be sensitive to homophobia or a lack of self-acceptance among lesbians and gay men (Kus, 1988). Special treatment programs for these subgroups in the population are rare, and even more rare are evaluations of the relative efficacy of these special programs where they do exist. The scarcity of formal treatment programs has given rise to the mutual- and self-help movement for alcoholics.

MUTUAL HELP GROUPS FOR ALCOHOLISM

Organizational Structure: Overview

In no other field of service are nonprofessional fellow sufferers so closely allied with the treatment process as in alcoholism treatment. Alcoholics Anonymous (AA) and Al-Anon Family Groups (AFG) have both literally paved the way for more formal treatment services designed for their respective target populations. AA and other mutual-aid groups for alcoholics are often seen erroneously as a treatment intervention, but are more aptly described as a program of recovery and, for persons treated in formal programs, a frequently recommended follow-up support system. Although AA and Al-Anon are by far the largest and most ubiquitous mutual-aid groups for alcoholics and their families, there are others. Some of those include Women for Sobriety, Secular Organizations for Sobriety (SOS), Mentally Ill Recovering Alcoholics (MIRA), Jewish Alcoholics, Chemically Dependent Persons and Significant Others (JACS), International Doctors in AA (IDAA), Recovered Alcoholic Clergy Association (RACA), National Clergy Council on Alcoholism (NCAA), and Adult Children of Alcoholics (ACOA) (Borkman, 1984). There may be more groups for special populations, but, because of their dominance and centrality in treatment, the following discussion will be limited to AA and Al-Anon.

AA's General Service Office reports 85,270 groups and 1,734,734 members worldwide as of April 1989. Al-Anon Family Groups (AFG) reports over 26,000 groups worldwide. Central to the AA and Al-Anon programs is the Twelve-Step Model, which forms the basis for acquiring a changed life. Although abstinence from alcohol is an objective for AA members, equally important is achievement of other characteristics that represent spiritual progress. Members aspire toward tolerance, honesty, serenity, peaceful interpersonal relationships, and acceptance of the mixed experience of daily life. E. Kurtz (1979; 1982) has identified the fundamental message of AA to its members as they are not God

and, therefore, not in control. For Al-Anon members, the same message converts to giving up the need to control the alcoholism *and* the alcoholic.

Research on Self-Help Groups

Both AA and Al-Anon conduct periodic surveys of their members. The 1986 survey of AA members received responses from a stratified, random sample of the U.S. and Canadian membership (Alcoholics Anonymous [AA], 1989). Results indicated that a member with less than one year of sobriety had a 40 percent chance of going through the next year without drinking; with one to four years of sobriety, these chances went up to 80 percent; and with more than five years of sobriety, the chances went up to 90 percent. The percentage of women in AA increased from 22 percent in 1968 to 34 percent in 1986. Other increases include the number of young people, the number addicted to another drug in addition to alcohol, and the number who cite professional referral as the reason for coming to AA. Their data suggest that about half of the newcomers who attend AA for more than three months will remain sober and active for the coming year (AA, 1980). Another 50 percent of the newcomers will drop out before the three-month point. This indicates a 25 percent success rate over a one-year period for those who attend AA at least once.

Similar surveys of Al-Anon and Alateen members by AFG were taken in 1984 and 1987 (Al-Anon Family Groups [AFG], 1988). Al-Anon members are predominantly middle-aged (35–55 years), female (88 percent), and spouses of alcoholics (72 percent). Figures comparing the 1987 sample with the 1984 sample showed a trend toward younger and more educated members who were more often employed in professional and managerial jobs, more likely to be single, more likely to live in the suburbs, more often in relationships with an alcoholic who was not the spouse, and more likely to be referred by a professional. Unlike AA's, Al-Anon's survey did not attempt to determine outcome of membership. Some Al-Anon groups have been especially developed for adult children of alcoholics (ACOAs); the focus is on resolving patterns of "stuffing" feelings and avoiding enabling behaviors that were learned as survival techniques in the alcoholic family of origin and then reinforced in the current life situation (see Chapter 1). The current situations may or may not involve alcoholic relationships.

Alateen groups, sponsored by AFG, are for children in alcoholic homes who are approximately aged 10 and over, although younger children sometimes attend and benefit. Over half are under 14 years old, 58 percent are female, and 86 percent are in Alateen because of parental alcoholism. Research shows that trends in Alateen between 1984 and 1987 consisted of an increase in minority group members and members with a non-parent alcoholic relative (AFG, 1988; Peterson-Kelley, 1985).

A substantial descriptive and empirical literature on AA supplies many explanations for how AA works to improve the lives of alcoholics. E. Kurtz (1982) contends that both scholars outside the AA program as well as insiders minimize the intellectual significance of AA as a social phenomenon; he goes on to explain how AA ideas parallel existential philosophy through the movement's core concepts of essential limitation and shared mutuality. By accepting one's identity as alcoholic, one accepts not merely a stigmatized identity, but rather the core existential insight of human finitude and the reality of the self-as-is. Further, the concepts of letting go or refusal to will that which cannot be willed are found both in the Twelve-Step philosophy and in the existential understanding of *Gelassenheit,* which teaches that willfulness leads to self-defeating frustration. The "all or nothing" thinking typically found in alcoholics is converted to an understanding of limited control and limited dependence—you can decide not to drink one day at a time; you can depend on others without being totally dependent. From this same analysis comes recognition of the experience of shame and of how shame, in addition to guilt, figures in recovery from alcoholism. AA is, among other things, a therapy for shame. The use of a chemical serves to hide the alcoholic's shame from the inner self. To recover, the alcoholic must be able to confront the reality of self, to give up defensive denial, and to surrender, in this surrender accepting failure to achieve the ideal self (AA, 1976).

Research and Theory

Denzin (1987), Taylor (1977), and Mack (1981) also give thoughtful analyses of how and why AA works, each from differing theoretical perspectives. Denzin's (1987) ethnographic study within a sym-

bolic interactionist framework reveals how the alcoholic acquires an alcoholic self that becomes transformed to a recovering alcoholic self that becomes transformed to a recovering alcoholic self within the context of, first, treatment and, then, the AA group. Denzin (1987) found the mutual support group to be essential to the change process. Treatment involves the dismantling of the alcoholic self-structure, and recovery consists of a rebuilding process. Taylor's (1977) ethnographic study of AA ten years earlier produced similar findings. Using grounded theory, Taylor identified several stages of recovery within AA, starting with an entry or "hitting bottom" stage, through the dry alcoholic stage, and ending with a sober, working-the-program stage that the member remains in for lifetime recovery. Mack (1981) discusses AA's impact on members within a tradition of psychoanalytic theory, self, and social psychology. According to Mack (1981), the alcoholic has lost the ability to control the impulse to drink and is unwilling to give up the belief of being in control. AA interferes with the resulting self-preoccupation and grandiosity of the alcoholic ego and provides a "group conscience," a social structure, or moral community through which the member develops healthy narcissism and restrains the impulse to drink or to take other destructive actions.

Because Al-Anon uses the same twelve steps as AA, many of the foregoing theories and research findings can be applied to it as well. Nevertheless, there is inherent in the qualification for membership a relational dimension to Al-Anon that is missing in AA. One joins Al-Anon because of a relationship with an alcoholic, whether that be a spouse, parent, child, friend, neighbor, or co-worker. The assumption from psychoanalytic theory that spouses of alcoholics are covertly meeting personal, neurotic needs has been largely replaced by theories that view spouse behavior as an ineffective but natural effort to cope with the crises that alcoholism brings to the home (Jackson, 1954; Gorman & Rooney, 1979; Ablon, 1974). Ablon (1974) characterizes Al-Anon as an "education by alternatives" approach to learning practical strategies for coping in an alcoholic relationship (p. 39). These strategies involve "loving detachment," reestablishment of self-esteem, and reliance on a higher power that relieves the spouse of responsibility for the alcoholic.

Bepko and Krestan (1985) add family systems theory to an understanding of the spouse's coping response. They propose that the family system changes when the usually overresponsible spouse joins Al-Anon and begins to focus energy on the self and to detach from the alcoholic. Although they come from a systems framework rather than a basically existential position, they rely on E. Kurtz's (1982) understanding of essential limitation, acknowledgment of vulnerability, and limited dependence as central to their model, and weave the professional intervention together with attendance in AA and Al-Anon. Theoretical explanations of Al-Anon thus add a systems perspective (Steinglass, 1981) to the existential, symbolic interactionist, and psychoanalytical formulations applied to AA.

Outcome Evaluation

Moving from theoretical analysis to outcome evaluation, it is clear that AA has been subjected to more intense scrutiny than Al-Anon. Several extensive reviews of AA outcome research exist (Leach & Norris, 1977; Miller & Hester, 1980; McCrady & Irvine, 1989) and will be reviewed briefly here.

As noted above, AA does its own outcome research through its frequently nonrandom member surveys. Of particular importance is the high dropout rate, which AA acknowledges. For those who do not discontinue attendance, AA estimates a success rate of over 40 percent, a rate that increases as the participant continues attending (AA, 1980). Most researchers note that AA receives acclaim for a success rate that is unwarranted because it has received almost no rigorously scientific study (Miller & Hester, 1980; McCrady & Irvine, 1989). The reasons for this lack of rigorous study are the multiple problems associated with controlled studies of a self-help group; the very use of the term *control* suggests the basic problem. If a researcher controlled the intervention, it would no longer be a nonprofessional self-help group.

Many researchers have found that favorable outcome of other treatments improves if AA attendance occurs upon discharge (Polich, Armor, & Braiker, 1980; L. F. Kurtz, 1981; Miller & Hester, 1980). However, other studies do not confirm these results. McCrady and Irvine (1989) point to two randomized clinical trials, although not good tests of AA effectiveness, in which AA was one of the treatment conditions. Neither found that AA was superior to other treatments, and one of the studies found that AA attenders had the highest treatment dropout rate. The authors clarify that both studies were essentially unfair to AA in that they used involuntary subjects and required minimal attendance at meetings that were only approximations of an AA meeting.

Al-Anon has received virtually no study of outcome and presents even more difficult research problems than does AA, in that a simple outcome measure such as abstinence does not exist for the nonaddicted member. However, the spouse's abstinence has been used as an outcome measure for Al-Anon in some studies. Other possible outcome measures for nonaddicted family members in Al-Anon include communication skills, identification of personal strengths, and finding alternative ways of coping with stress. Bailey (1965) found that couples who both attended their respective programs were most likely to report sobriety for the alcoholic spouse, as opposed to couples where only one attended a group or where neither did. In a study of treatment for wives of male alcoholics, Wright and Scott (1978) found that when wives attended Al-Anon alone or were also involved in other treatment the spouses were more likely to become abstinent. Gorman and Rooney (1979) found that length of time in Al-Anon correlated significantly with reductions in negative coping behaviors by wives of alcoholic men. L. F. Kurtz (1989) has found that frequent Al-Anon attenders report personal change in the form of reduced depression, increased acceptance of self and others, and increased self-confidence.

Combining Self-Help with Other Approaches

The AA and Al-Anon programs have developed extensive materials designed to assist members in their work with professionals and to develop integrated programs within institutions (AA, n.d., a, n.d., b; AFG, 1976). Where sufficient volunteers are available, both mutual help organizations establish beginner groups in treatment centers, correctional facilities, and other institutions to help potential newcomers learn about and begin applying the Twelve-Step program to their own situations. Members also respond to requests for presentations to staff or client groups and volunteer in other ways to assist potential newcomers who might want to attend meetings.

McCrady and Irvine (1989) furnish suggestions for the behavioral therapist who wants to assist clients to integrate the AA and Al-Anon program with behavioral therapy. Behavior therapists should recommend AA only to those whose therapy has an abstinence objective, should become knowledgeable about the program and the diverse nature of local meetings, should have AA and Al-Anon literature available, and should consider accompanying clients to meetings. Clients should be told before attending their first meeting what to expect. McCrady and Irvine point out, as have others (Kurtz & Powell, 1987), that many AA activities and principles contain behavioral and cognitive therapy aspects. For example, typical Twelve-Step slogans, such as "Easy Does It" or "First Things First," can be used to reframe and rethink situations that commonly produce stress and frustration.

L. F. Kurtz (1984a; 1984b; 1985) researched AA and professional relationships in one state's public alcohol treatment centers. This author found that professionals who were ideologically somewhat alike worked well together, while those who differed perceived relationships as more distant, more strained, and less effective in moving the client from treatment to AA for follow-up (L. F. Kurtz, 1984a). Additionally, she found that cooperation improves when there are frequent interactions and appropriate linking strategies, such as employing AA members, having AA volunteers, or having AA meetings in the treatment center, and having professionals visit open AA meetings and attend Al-Anon for themselves (L. F. Kurtz, 1984b; 1985).

In conclusion, research shows that self-help and mutual aid groups are theoretically compatible with most forms of professional *helping,* providing that the treatment objectives are consistent with those of the group. AA and Al-Anon are willing to cooperate with professionals and have established organizational structure to facilitate that process. Additionally, practitioners have evolved linking practices between AA and professional treatment programs that are effective and harmonious and that insure smooth transfer of the client from the treatment center to the AA group. Research shows that, while AA has difficulty holding newcomers as members, those who do continue have increasingly improved chances of successful outcome. Thus, social workers can contribute greatly to successful outcome by doing everything possible to stabilize and lengthen the client's attendance in AA after discharge. Moreover, Al-Anon attendance by the spouse or other significant persons appears to increase the positive effects of outcome for the alcoholic; thus attention to the spouse and to moving the spouse and teenage children into Al-Anon Family Groups is advised.

IMPLICATIONS FOR SOCIAL WORK PRACTICE

Natural support systems of alcoholic clients may be the single most important factor in recovery. Negative interaction patterns in the family, a social life that revolves around alcohol, and workplace drinking cultures can be deadly forces against sobriety for recovering people. On the other hand, stable and supportive family, friends, and co-workers can enhance the alcoholic's success. Therefore, of first importance is the idea that social work practitioners and policymakers can contribute greatly to client success by strengthening the positive forces in the alcoholic's natural environment. Possible means are crisis intervention and counseling for the family, providing alternate social outlets for the alcoholic, and reducing alcoholism and alcohol use in the workplace. Educating clergy, teachers, and family physicians also is essential because research shows that these are the professionals who often first encounter the drinking person who is in trouble.

Secondly, there is research to suggest that counselor skill rather than treatment philosophy is what separates effective from ineffective treatment (Cartwright, 1985). Therefore, educators and administrators must educate, foster ongoing training, and assess the skills of new practitioners along with working to attract and retain those individuals who demonstrate necessary ability. This process will require careful study of the precise qualities needed to facilitate effective recovery and careful planning to improve the treatment work force.

Third, relapse programs are extremely important as part of the formal treatment system. Aftercare and aggressive follow-up by social workers can help the alcoholic and the family to identify and deal with thoughts and behavior patterns that are known to produce stress and lead to relapse. Examples include thinking a mistake means failure and avoiding rather than attempting to resolve conflicts.

Fourth, smoothing the transition from treatment to recovery within AA and Al-Anon or other appropriate mutual-aid groups will give alcoholics and their families a therapy that is structured, cognitive, and behavioral for building a sober life. New leisure activities and friendships will replace those that have been lost through drinking or abandoned due to their nonsupportive features.

NEW RESEARCH PARADIGMS

Along with the practice implications discussed in the previous section, gaps in research technology and focus have been identified. More research is needed, for instance, on cultural factors in treatment for special populations, on the effects of public social policy, on use and abuse of alcohol, and on those factors that inhibit or promote relapse. Social work researchers should continue their research in the area of alcoholism in the workplace and develop programs to build on the findings of that research. Much of the alcoholism research today has a biochemical orientation. Social workers can supplement this important research with knowledge about the social and ecological elements in the alcoholic's life (Donovan, 1988).

In addition to these obvious and ongoing gaps in research on alcoholism, at least two new research paradigms are apparent. One involves the need for naturalistic research on the natural healing process experienced by some recovering alcoholics. The research (direct observations, ethnographic interviews, and self-reports in log or diary form) could be designed to explore the types of clients and environmental situations that contribute to spontaneous or client-system initiated change. It could also clarify the durability of natural healing and show how professionals can identify and build on the apparent client strengths involved. Another new paradigm related to exploration of the natural healing process is research that is initiated and supported by clients as recovering persons. The range of strategies can include both informal and formal research: from the development and analysis of client logs by clients themselves during recovery to classical experiments by helping professionals who are recovering alcoholics themselves. Either of these research paradigms can provide opportunities for operationalizing a strengths perspective in conducting research that is consistent with the profession's values.

CONCLUSION

This chapter has focused on research about treatment within the context of the client's total ecology. An understanding of the alcoholic cannot be separated from knowledge about the person's family, friends, work culture, and recreational settings. All of these can inhibit or reinforce patterns of drinking and must be considered when intervention is planned. Such an approach to practice and the design of research is consistent with the social work frame of reference. Additionally, just as the alcoholic must live within the limitations of an inability to drink alcohol, social workers must plan intervention with attention to the limitations imposed by knowledge from existing research.

REFERENCES

Ablon, J. (1974). Al-Anon Family Groups: Impetus for learning and change through the presentation of alternatives. *American Journal of Psychotherapy, 28,* 30–45.

Al-Anon Family Groups. (1976). *Al-Anon and professionals.* New York: Al-Anon Family Group Headquarters.

Al-Anon Family Groups. (1988). *Who are the members of Al-Anon and Alateen?* New York: Al-Anon Family Group Headquarters.

Alcoholics Anonymous. (n.d.,a). *CPC workbook: Cooperation with the professional community.* New York: General Service Office.

Alcoholics Anonymous. (n.d.,b). *Treatment facilities workbook.* New York: General Service Office.

Alcoholics Anonymous. (1976). *Alcoholics Anonymous: The story of how many thousands of men and women have recovered from alcoholism* (3rd ed.). New York: A.A. World Services.

Alcoholics Anonymous. (1980). *Analysis of the 1980 survey of the membership of A.A.* New York: General Service Office.

Alcoholics Anonymous (1989). *Analysis of the 1986 survey of the membership of A.A.* New York: General Service Office.

Anderson, D. J. (1981). *Perspectives on treatment: The Minnesota experience.* Center City, MN: Hazelden.

Bailey, M. B. (1965). Al-Anon Family Groups as an aid to wives of alcoholics. *Social Work, 10,* 68–74.

Bean, M. H., & Zinberg, N. E. (Eds.). (1981). *Dynamic approaches to the understanding and treatment of alcoholism.* New York: Free Press.

Bell, P., & Evans, J. (1981). *Counseling the black alcoholic client: Alcohol use and abuse in black America.* Center City, MN: Hazelden.

Bepko, C., & Krestan, J. (1985). *The responsibility trap: A blueprint for treating the alcoholic family.* New York: Free Press.

Blackmon, P. (1985). Networking community services for elderly clients with alcohol problems. In E. Freeman (Ed.), *Social work practice with clients who have alcohol problems* (pp. 189–201). Springfield, IL: Thomas.

Blane, H. T., & Leonard, K. E. (1987). *Psychological theories of drinking and alcoholism.* New York: Guilford Press.

Borkman, T. (1984). Mutual self-help groups: Strengthening the selectively unsupportive personal and community networks of their members. In A. Gartner and F. Riessman, *The self-help revolution* (pp. 205–216). New York: Human Sciences Press.

Brisbane, F. L., & Womble, M. (Eds.). (1985). *Treatment of black alcoholics.* New York: Haworth Press.

Brown, S. (1985). *Treating the alcoholic: A developmental model of recovery.* New York: Wiley.

Cartwright, A. (1985). Is treatment an effective way of helping clients resolve difficulties associated with alcohol? In N. Heather, I. Robertson, & P. Davies (Eds.), *The misuse of alcohol: Crucial issues in dependence, treatment & prevention* (pp. 117–134). New York: New York University Press.

Corrigan, E. M. (1980). *Alcoholic women in treatment.* New York: Oxford University Press.

Denzin, N. K. (1987). *The recovering alcoholic.* Newbury Park, CA: Sage.

Donovan, D. M. (1988). Assessment of addictive behaviors: Implications of an emerging biopsychosocial model. In D. M. Donovan & G. A. Marlatt (Eds.), *Assessment of addictive behaviors* (pp. 3–48). New York: Guilford Press.

Donovan, D. M., & Marlatt, G. A. (Eds.), (1988). *Assessment of addictive behaviors.* New York: Guilford Press.

Fewell, C. H. (1985). Psychodynamic treatment of women alcoholics. In E. Freeman, *Social work practice with clients who have alcohol problems* (pp. 172–188). Springfield, IL: Thomas.

Fine, M., Akabas, S. H., & Bellinger, S. (1982). Cultures of drinking: A workplace perspective. *Social Work, 27,* 435–440.

Garbarino, J. (1983). Social support networks: Rx for helping professionals. In J. K. Whittaker & J. Garbarino, *Social support networks: informal helping in human services* (pp. 3–28). New York: Aldine.

Gilbert, F. S. (1988). The effect of type of aftercare follow-up on treatment outcome among alcoholics. *Journal of Studies on Alcohol, 48,* 149–159.

Gorman, J. M., & Rooney, J. F. (1979). The influence of Al-Anon on the coping behavior of wives of alcoholics. *Journal of Studies on Alcohol, 40,* 1030–1038.

Gunther, J. F., Jolly, E. J., & Wedel, K. R. (1985). Alcoholism and the Indian people: Problem and promise. In E. M. Freeman, *Social work practice with clients who have alcohol problems* (pp. 214–228). Springfield, IL: Thomas.

Harper, F. D. (1976). *Alcohol abuse and black America.* Alexandria, VA: Douglass Publishers.

Hawkins, J. D., & Fraser, M. W. (1983). Social support networks in treating drug abuse. In J. K. Whittaker & J. Garbarino, *Social support networks: Informal helping in the human services* (pp. 357–380). New York: Aldine.

Heather, N., & Robertson, I. (1981). *Controlled drinking.* London: Methuen.

Hermos, J. A., Locastro, J. S., Glynn, R. J., Gouchard, A. R., & DeLabry, L. O. (1988). Predictors of reduction and cessation of drinking in community-dwelling men: Results from the normative aging study. *Journal of Studies on Alcohol, 49,* 363–368.

Jackson, J. (1954). The adjustment of the family to the crisis of alcoholism. *Quarterly Journal of Studies on Alcohol, 15,* 562–586.

Kaufman, E. (1985). Family systems and family therapy of substance abuse: An overview of two decades of research and clinical experience. *International Journal of the Addictions, 20,* 897–916.

Khantzian, E. J. (1981). Some treatment implications of the ego and self disturbances in alcoholism. In M. Bean & N. E. Zinberg (Eds.), *Dynamic approaches to the understanding and treatment of alcoholism* (pp. 163–188). New York: Free Press.

Kimball, B. (1978). *The alcoholic woman's mad, mad world of denial and mind games.* Center City, MN: Hazelden.

Kurtz, E. (1979). *Not-God: A history of Alcoholics Anonymous.* Center City, MN: Hazelden.

Kurtz, E. (1982). Why A.A. works: The intellectual significance of Alcoholics Anonymous. *Journal of Studies on Alcohol, 42,* 38–80.

Kurtz, L. F. (1981). Time in residential care and participation in Alcoholics Anonymous as predictors of continued sobriety. *Psychological Reports, 48,* 633–634.

Kurtz, L. F. (1984a). Ideological differences between professionals and A.A. members. *Alcoholism Treatment Quarterly, 1,* 73–85.

Kurtz, L. F. (1984b). Linking treatment centers with Alcoholics Anonymous. *Social Work in Health Care, 9*, 85–94.

Kurtz, L. F. (1985). Cooperation and rivalry between helping professionals and members of AA. *Health and Social Work, 10*, 104–112.

Kurtz, L. F. (1989). [Experiences of family crisis and help from Al-Anon]. Unpublished raw data.

Kurtz, L. F., & Powell, T. J. (1987). Three approaches to understanding self-help groups. *Social Work with Groups, 10*, 69–80.

Kus, R. J. (1988). Alcoholism and non-acceptance of gay self: The critical link. *Journal of Homosexuality, 15*, 25–41.

Leach, B., & Norris, J. L. (1977). Factors in the development of Alcoholics Anonymous (A.A.). In B. Kissin & H. Begleiter, *Treatment and rehabilitation of the chronic alcoholic* (pp. 441–543). New York: Plenum.

Lin, N., Ensel, W. M., Simeone, R. S., Kuo, W. (1979). Social support, stressful life events and illness: A model and an empirical test. *Journal of Health and Social Behavior, 20*, 108–109.

Ludwig, A. M. (1985). Cognitive processes associated with "spontaneous" recovery from alcoholism. *Journal of Studies on Alcohol, 46*, 53–58.

Mack, J. E. (1981). Alcoholism, A. A., and the governance of the self. In M. H. Bean & N. E. Zinberg, *Dynamic approaches to the understanding and treatment of alcoholism* (pp. 128–162). New York: Free Press.

Marlatt, G. A. (1988). Matching clients to treatment: Treatment models and stages of change. In D. M. Donovan & G. A. Marlatt (Eds.), *Assessment of addictive behaviors* (pp. 474–484). New York: Guilford Press.

Marlatt, G. A., & Gordon, J. R. (1985). *Relapse prevention: Maintenance strategies in the treatment of addictive behaviors.* New York: Guilford Press.

McCrady, B. S., & Irvine, S. (1989). Self-help groups. In R. K. Hester & W. R. Miller (Eds.), *Handbook of alcoholism treatment approaches: Effective alternatives* (pp. 153–169). New York: Pergamon Press.

Miller, W. R., & Hester, R. K. (1980). Treating the problem drinker: Modern approaches. In W. R. Miller (Ed.), *The addictive behaviors: Treatment of alcoholism, drug abuse, smoking and obesity* (pp. 11–141). Oxford: Pergamon Press.

Moos, R. H., Finney, J. W. & Chan, D. A. (1981). The process of recovery from alcoholism: Comparing alcoholic patients and matched community controls. *Journal of Studies on Alcohol, 42*, 383–402.

Paolino, T. J., McCrady, B., Diamond, S., & Longabaugh, R. (1976). Psychological disturbances in spouses of alcoholics: An empirical assessment. *Journal of Studies on Alcohol, 37*, 1600–1608.

Pattison, E. M. (1985). The selection of treatment modalities for the alcoholic patient. In J. H. Mendelson & N. K. Mello, *The diagnosis and treatment of alcoholism* (2nd ed.) (pp. 189–294). New York: McGraw-Hill.

Pendry, M. L., Maltzman, I. M., & West, L. J. (1982). Controlled drinking by alcoholics? New findings and a reevaluation of a major affirmative study. *Science, 217*, 169–175.

Peterson-Kelley, A. (1985). Family environment and Alateens: A note on alcohol abuse potential. *Journal of Community Psychology, 13*, 75–76.

Polich, J. M., Armor, D. J., & Braiker, H. B. (1980). *The course of alcoholism: Four years after treatment.* Santa Monica, CA: Rand.

Regan, J. M., Conners, G. J., O'Farrell, T. J. & Jones, W. C. (1983). Services for the families of alcoholics: A survey of treatment agencies in Massachusetts. *Journal of Studies on Alcohol, 44*, 1072–1082.

Rollnick, S. (1985). The value of a cognitive-behavioral approach to the treatment of problem drinkers. In N. Heather, I. Robertson, & P. Davies (Eds.), *The misuse of alcohol: Crucial issues in dependence, treatment & prevention* (pp. 135–147). New York: New York University Press.

Saunders, B. (1985). Treatment does not work: Some criteria of failure. In N. Heather, I. Robertson, & P. Davies (Eds.), *The misuse of alcohol: Crucial issues in dependence, treatment & prevention* (pp. 102–116). New York: New York University Press.

Selnow, G. W., & Crano, W. D. (1986). Formal vs. informal group affiliations: Implications for alcohol and drug use among adolescents. *Journal of Studies on Alcohol, 47*, 48–52.

Steinglass, P. (1981). The impact of alcoholism on the family relationship between degree of alcoholism and psychiatric symptomatology. *Journal of Studies on Alcohol, 42*, 288–303.

Taylor, M. C. (1977). Alcoholics Anonymous: How it works, recovery processes in a self-help group. *Dissertation Abstracts International, 39*, 7532A. (University Microfilms No. 79-13241)

Trice, H. M., & Roman, P. (1979). *Spirits and demons at work: Alcohol and other drugs on the job* (2nd ed.). Ithaca, NY: New York State School of Industrial and Labor Relations.

Tuchfield, B. S. (1981). Spontaneous remission in alcoholics: Empirical observations and theoretical implications. *Journal of Studies on Alcohol, 42*, 626–641.

Vaillant, G. E. (1981). Dangers of psychotherapy in the treatment of alcoholism. In M. Bean & N. E. Zinberg (Eds.), *Dynamic approaches to the understanding and treatment of alcoholism* (pp. 36–54). New York: Free Press.

Vaillant, G. E. (1983). *The natural history of alcoholism:*

Causes, patterns and paths to recovery. Cambridge, MA: Harvard University Press.

Wright, K. D. & Scott, T. B. (1978). The relationship of wives' treatment to the drinking status of alcoholics. *Journal of Studies on Alcohol, 39,* 1577–1581.

SUPPLEMENTAL READING LIST

Al-Anon Family Groups. (1985). New York: Al-Anon Family Group Headquarters.

This volume is the equivalent of Al-Anon's Big Book. It covers the history of Al-Anon, the fellowship's understanding of alcoholism and the plight of the family.

Hester, R. K., & Miller, W. R. (Eds.), (1989). *Handbook of alcoholism treatment approaches: Effective alternatives.* New York: Pergamon Press.

This book is a new volume covering research on motivation to change, primary treatment approaches, and other topics including but not limited to self-help groups, relapse prevention, and family therapy. The editors come from a behavioral psychology background; however, they are able to present a reasonable, scholarly, and balanced overview.

Kurtz, E. (1988). *A.A.: The story.* San Francisco: Harper/Hazelden.

This is a revised edition of *Not-God: A history of Alcoholics Anonymous,* which was published in 1979. The book contains six original chapters detailing the history of A.A., with a new seventh chapter bringing the original history up to date.

Royce, J. E. (1989). *Alcohol problems and alcoholism: A comprehensive survey.* New York: Free Press.

This is probably the best introductory text on alcoholism. Father Royce devotes chapters to the scope of the problem, physiological and sociocultural aspects, the disease concept, the spouse, treatment, self-help groups, special populations, and public policy as well as other topics.

Schuckit, M. A. (1984). *Drug and alcohol abuse: A clinical guide to diagnosis and treatment.* New York: Plenum Press.

A good overview of substance abuse and treatment issues by one of this country's most accomplished researchers in the alcoholism field.

CHAPTER 3

Differential Diagnosis and the Least Restrictive Treatment

Edith M. Freeman
University of Kansas

Toby Landesman
Landesman, Inc.

. . . we know what we are, but know not what we may be.

Ophelia, *Hamlet*

There is growing concern in the alcohol treatment field about how to provide the least restrictive services to each individual with identifiable alcohol problems (Schuckit, Irwin, Howard, & Smith, 1988). While this goal is essential for effective alcohol treatment, the difficulties in achieving it must be acknowledged. One major barrier to the goal is the competition among treatment programs for a limited pool of resources controlled primarily by insurance providers and policymakers. Insurance providers often determine the treatment of choice based on cost containment issues rather than on what is the best treatment for a client (McCrady, Longabaugh, Fink, & Stout, 1986; Kutchins & Kirk, 1988). In other situations, clients may self-select their treatment program. This factor coupled with familial or other social responsibilities can dictate what services are received.

Another difficulty is that the level of knowledge and skills of a facility's treatment providers may not be sufficient to accurately prescribe the least restrictive alternative for clients with alcohol problems. Such prescriptions result from a differential diagnosis highlighting the interacting factors in each client's situation that are relevant to problems with alcohol. Schuckit et al. (1988) indicate that a

differential diagnosis is valuable for additional reasons; for instance, it can "help to predict the clinical course and to select rational treatment approaches" (p. 93) that may vary according to a client's unique circumstances.

McCrady et al. (1986) found that the selection of rational treatment approaches can "allow clients to maintain some job and community responsibilities" (p. 708) with a "lesser loss of freedom" (p. 711). This may be the case when partial hospitalization, rather than inpatient treatment, for example, is indicated as the least restrictive alternative. The goal of this process is to, in Ophelia's words, empower clients to find out "what they may be" as well as "what they are."

These conclusions about the benefits of developing a differential diagnosis in alcohol treatment are consistent with some of the earliest general social work literature. Mary Richmond (1917) coined the term *social diagnosis* to describe the complex and dynamic interrelationship between the person and situation. She emphasized that the diagnosis resulting from an analysis of that interrelationship has no standing by itself except as it clarifies the prognosis for change and the scope of treatment.

Given the importance of differential diagnoses

27

for effective social work treatment, particularly for alcohol problems, this chapter briefly summarizes the process necessary for a general assessment of alcohol problems. That discussion is followed by a description of how the components of a differential diagnosis can enhance the general assessment process. This information can improve the knowledge and skills of practitioners who help with alcohol problems. Finally, race and gender are analyzed as two examples of those components that must be considered in generating a differential diagnosis.

THE GENERAL PROCESS OF ASSESSMENT

A strengths perspective should serve as a guide for all social work practice; this view helps to place emphasis on positive aspects related to clients and their environment (Weick, Rapp, Sullivan, & Kisthardt, 1989). Utilizing a strengths perspective during the assessment makes it more likely that this view will be operationalized throughout the process of helping and that it will be reflected in the assessment tools that are selected.

Operationalizing a Strengths Perspective

When operationalized, a strengths perspective may be observable through a practitioner's flexibility in drawing upon a broad range of theories about the etiology of alcoholism. The selection of an appropriate theory should be determined by identifying theories that encourage an acknowledgment of strengths rather than focusing only on pathology, including anthropological and sociocultural theories (Chaudron & Wilkerson, 1988). (See Chapter 1 for a more detailed discussion of the importance of a comprehensive network of explanatory theories.) The strengths perspective may be evident also when the practitioner uses those theories to help identify strengths during the assessment and helps to build on those strengths in the development and implementation of the treatment plan.

At a more dynamic level, the strengths perspective may be reflected in the quality of the client-practitioner relationship as the latter draws upon a client's assertiveness or a family member's support in resolving a struggle for personal autonomy. Theories of change, such as family systems and crisis

theories, can be utilized to resolve such barriers to recovery. These theories should be critiqued on how well they provide intervention strategies that help the practitioner enhance and add to the strengths in the situation. Another requirement for theories is their linkage with practical procedures for evaluating ongoing changes in a client's situation. The procedures should provide feedback on which strategies are working and which ones are hindering the use of a client's strengths in recovery (Logan, McRoy, & Freeman, 1987). Although this linkage is important during intervention and evaluation, it begins with the careful selection of tools that can facilitate a strengths assessment during initial contacts.

Assessment Tools

Beginning with the assumption that a strengths-oriented assessment sets the stage for an effective helping process throughout, guidelines for the social history, drinking history, and assessment protocols would need to incorporate the same positive perspective. Areas explored with clients for the social history (physical or medical history, employment history, marital and family history, and social functioning) can be assessed to determine the extent of alcohol problems (Blackmon, 1985) and pinpoint those areas of strength that can facilitate recovery. The supervisor who refers a client to an Employee Assistance Program (EAP) or a peer who confronts the client about drinking are as important to note as frequent job changes due to absenteeism or the existence of a neighborhood drinking network.

An assessment of intergenerational patterns is equally important in gathering the client's history, including patterns of substance abuse and dysfunctional relationships (Freeman, 1990). An emphasis on strengths directs the practitioner to more thoroughly explore those relationships by identifying models of abstinence, successfully recovering individuals, and an agreement for family involvement in treatment as supports to recovery.

The drinking history and other assessment procedures should also facilitate a strengths assessment. The drinking history focuses on a client's reasons for drinking and the effects on the life situation, drinking patterns, when drinking began and the circumstances, with whom the client drinks, legal difficulties, and the client's typical methods of coping with stress (Freeman, 1990; Chernus, 1985). As part of the assessment, the effective practitioner helps clients learn about the rewards from drinking, along with circumstances in which they are able to resist drinking or to make the attempt. This exploration points to both negative *and* positive information in the drinking history that is necessary for achieving a balanced assessment.

In a similar manner, other screening procedures such as questionnaires, tests, scales, and cognitive maps can be selected to provide a balanced view of the client's functioning. Most screening procedures such as the Michigan Alcoholic Screening Test (MAST), the *Diagnostic and Statistical Manual III-R* (DSM III-R), the Adolescent Alcohol Index of Severity (AAIS), and the McMaster's Scale of the Minnesota Multiphasic Inventory (MMPI) are useful diagnostic tools (Kutchins & Kirk, 1988; Selzer, 1971; White, & Labouvie, 1989; Blackmon, 1985), but they are not as helpful in identifying the positives in a client's situation. The few existing procedures that are strengths-oriented include the cultural ecomap, the genogram, symptom checklists that contain both positive and negative indicators, and some self-assessment tools (Ziter, 1987; Hartman, 1979). Most of these tools were developed for white male populations. The field should develop minority- and gender-sensitive assessment tools as needed and analyze the effectiveness of existing tools for use with diverse populations. Further, how a worker interprets data from the various procedures also determines whether the assessment is balanced. These general components of a strengths-oriented assessment can be enhanced by a differential diagnosis, which helps the practitioner to consider some of the individual factors in a client's life situation.

DIFFERENTIAL DIAGNOSIS

The term *differential diagnosis* refers to a practitioner's ability to discriminate among a range of unique and individual variables that indicate the extent to which alcohol is a problem for a client and to identify issues that may be maintaining the problem (Freeman, 1990; Chernus, 1985). Specifically, the diagnosis helps the practitioner make distinctions between alcoholism as a primary versus a secondary problem; between the acute versus the chronic nature of the problem; and between the degree of functioning loss versus the degree of functioning

being maintained in the client's life situation; the diagnosis also helps the practitioner recognize the interplay between several components related to human diversity. Thus, a differential diagnosis can refine the general assessment; however, the two processes should be viewed as simultaneous and circular rather than as linear and unidirectional.

Primary versus Secondary Alcohol Problems

The degree to which a problem with alcohol is designated as primary or secondary helps the practitioner determine the major focus of treatment. For instance, Schuckit et al. (1988) believe that the primary diagnosis for a client should be for the problem that appears at the earliest age, while the secondary one is the problem with the later onset. These authors note that this type of distinction is useful when, through a particular screening tool, a client meets the criteria for two or more labels and when a substance abuser has a very complex history. It does not imply that one problem caused the other problem. Nor is it implied that only one problem should be treated and the other ignored; rather the emphasis is on identifying variables that indicate the severity and pervasiveness of each problem relative to the other.

The chronological order of problems is believed to affect the clinical course for the client in response to treatment. Schuckit et al. (1988) indicate that the onset of alcoholism prior to that of a psychiatric disorder, combined with a family history that is negative for psychiatric disorders, supports a diagnosis of primary alcoholism. According to Chernus (1985), in such circumstances "psychological symptoms associated with alcoholism are not the cause of a patient's developing the disease, but rather manifestations or by-products of it" (p. 68). A differential diagnosis will focus treatment on the primary goal of achieving and maintaining sobriety. It will also consider how clients' psychological symptoms can maintain their denial of alcohol problems and block supports from family members and other significant persons that are essential for successful recovery.

In contrast, Turnbull (1988) discusses indicators of secondary alcoholism in depressed women. That author described how secondary alcoholic women (women whose alcoholism is secondary to another dysfunction) may use alcohol as a coping strategy to self-medicate. In these situations, "the superimposed symptoms of alcohol-induced dysphoria mask the features of depression that precipitated excessive drinking" (p. 291). Viewing the depression as only a side effect of alcoholism may obscure the nature of the stress that led to the depression. Without that information and a focus on the source of the depression (a history as an incest victim, for example), the client's response to alcohol treatment may be minimal. Moreover, the loss of cognitive functioning that makes such clients poor historians, along with the role of denial in secondary alcoholic women, means a differential diagnosis and accurate treatment prescription may be even more difficult (Turnbull, 1988).

Acute versus Chronic Alcohol Problems

The treatment prescription can be affected equally by the immediacy of the problem. Some chronic alcohol-dependent or alcoholic clients with external supports may respond more effectively to partial hospitalization or outpatient services (McCrady et al., 1986; Chernus, 1985). These clients may exhibit a readiness for treatment because of the cumulative effects from dysfunctional behavior over a long period of time. Nevertheless, they may have one or more assets in their situation: stable employment, supportive family members, or an openness to the idea that they have lost control over their lives because of alcoholism. Often they may have attempted unsuccessfully to complete treatment programs or recovery on their own. Their problems are usually chronic and serious, but frequently are not immediately life-threatening. Other chronic alcoholic clients with few or no external supports may require inpatient treatment. A differential diagnosis should help social workers to identify these and other facts that indicate the client's motivation and the prognosis for treatment.

Clients in an acute state of need also may be vulnerable or open to help, but only for the period of active crisis. The differential diagnosis can help to identify factors that led to the crisis and highlight how those factors can be utilized quickly to determine the extent of alcohol problems and the prognosis. This information can suggest the type and timing of appropriate treatment, such as immediate crisis management for an acute grief reaction to the death of a significant other. Examples of other acute needs include clients who are suicidal, individuals requiring detoxication, those involved with the legal system for the first time, or clients experiencing a job loss or divorce due to their drinking. It is important for the diagnosis to address how life-threatening the situation is and therefore to prescribe the least restrictive environment in consideration of the potential danger to the client (McCrady et al., 1986). Thus, a client with a suicide plan or one attempting suicide will be identified as needing an evaluation for immediate inpatient hospitalization.

Degree of Functioning versus Degree of Loss

Similarly, a client with a high degree of loss in important areas of functioning might require inpatient hospitalization as indicated by the differential diagnosis. Examples include clients who have lost their emotional stability, personal care skills, significant relationships, income, housing and personal effects, and other social or community supports. The number of losses and the perceived meaning of those losses to clients can affect their hope for change and, realistically, the resources available to initiate and maintain recovery. Therefore, the balance between functional areas and areas of loss helps to determine the prognosis for change and issues to be addressed in treatment, in addition to sobriety. While highlighting these areas, the differential diagnosis must consider also what level of care or least restrictive treatment may be required by the client (outpatient, partial hospitalization, or inpatient services) (McCrady et al., 1986).

Aspects of Diversity

A final area related to differential diagnoses addresses some of the unique needs of clients, each of which should be viewed as it interacts with others in daily life experiences. These factors include a client's age and stage of development, race or ethnicity, gender, principal mode of learning, and orientation to change (Logan et al., 1987). In terms of age, for instance, an adolescent may appear to be a normal alcohol user because there has been only one episode of problem usage. However, White and Labouvie (1989) indicate "that adolescents often encounter problems with alcohol because of a single acute episode rather than as the result of a chronic condition'' (p. 30). While few of them exhibit physical dependence and other chronic symptoms, a differential diagnosis should be sensitive to other factors that can support a diagnosis of alcohol misuse in youth such as fighting with parents or school failure. However, an adolescent's principal mode of learning (visual, auditory, cognitive, and/or emotional) may need to be considered along with age factors in identifying indicators of the problem and prescribing the appropriate treatment.

Similarly, the unique needs of elderly persons may require special attention in the diagnosis. Some individuals may drink to cope with the stresses of the aging process; others may use drinking to cope ineffectively with boredom, loneliness, or loss of self-esteem. Since some factors such as the person's age and health status may be unalterable, the differential diagnosis should concentrate only on aspects open to change and should recommend approaches that can address those areas including the alcohol misuse (Logan et al., 1987). In the same fashion, race and gender need to be considered in developing differential diagnoses. These two components are addressed in more detail in the following sections, based on their relatively greater significance in the life situations of alcoholic clients.

THE EFFECTS OF RACE

Many authors have discussed the importance of culturally sensitive treatment for alcohol problems (Bell & Evans, 1983; Caldwell, 1983). Information that could enhance treatment across different racial and ethnic groups has been almost nonexistent until recently. Logan et al. (1987). Ziter (1987), and Harper and Dawkins (1977) have noted the scarcity of research on minority group alcoholism. In particular, Harper and Dawkins (1977) found, in terms of the minority group receiving the least amount of attention, that only 77 out of 16,000 alcohol studies published during the 30-year period prior to 1974 discussed African Americans. Among the 77 cross-cultural studies, only 11 were focused exclusively on African Americans.

Culturally sensitive treatment is important in that it can demonstrate an appreciation for the characteristics of clients who are culturally different and can seek to empower them in the process of recovery. This applies as much to women as to other minorities. The issue of gender in relation to power will be addressed in another section of this chapter. By developing a differential diagnosis during the assessment, social workers and other helping professionals can attempt to identify the amount of powerlessness and opportunities for empowerment existing in a client's situation, along with tools that may be useful for analyzing the consequences related to alcohol abuse.

Issues of Powerlessness/Empowerment

Similar to individuals in all racial groups, members of minority groups drink for a variety of reasons that can be determined through the drinking history developed during assessment. One factor that can interact with other reasons for drinking in members of minority groups is the emotional energy required for coping with the stress of racism. Often a sense of powerlessness develops when the source of stress remains in spite of efforts to eliminate it. This powerlessness can be manifested by an inability to manage emotions, skills, knowledge, or material resources in a way that performance of valued social roles can lead to personal satisfaction.

As a consequence, some individuals may not be able to develop positive ways of coping with their frustrations about racism and powerlessness. They may use alcohol to manage the depression, sense of failure, and pessimism that often coexist with powerlessness. Ironically, this type of self-medication handicaps the individual and family in their attempts to fulfill valuable family and community roles and in coping with a racist environment.

During assessment and thereafter, focusing only on minority clients' addiction without attempting to help them become empowered is usually viewed by them as irrelevant and useless. Empowerment helps clients to learn specialized problem-solving skills during recovery to alleviate the powerlessness that has resulted from negative valuations (prejudice) and racial barriers (discrimination) by the larger environment. Some clients may possess these problem-solving skills but may be blocked in using them by internal or external barriers, or they may be using them ineffectively. Others may be using the skills but can benefit from support during the assessment process in order to enhance future opportunities for empowerment and recovery.

A differential diagnosis should help practitioners to explore the extent to which these issues are a part of the minority client's misuse of alcohol and the prognosis for change. The focus should be on cultural strengths as well as other assets related to the client and the immediate environment. Strengths might include an individual's racial pride, extended family role models who have had empowerment experiences, racial group support in informal and formal social organizations, and culturally related job opportunities.

Aspects of the larger environment related to racism should also be explored and considered in determining the prognosis for change and the appropriate treatment for helping the client resolve barriers in that environment. Practitioners should be aware that frequently there is greater access to liquor stores in minority communities due to discriminatory city zoning policies. Moreover, health and alcohol treatment resources are less available to some Hispanic, American Indian, Asian, and African American clients. Fewer minority group clients have insurance coverage because of discriminatory employment practices and racial differences in educational opportunities. A smaller proportion of minority group clients utilize available treatment facilities because of the lack of culturally sensitive services in some programs. In other settings, the absence or low percentages of minority staff members is a barrier. A differential diagnosis points to information in these areas that might be maintaining the problem or that might interfere with the recovery of minority clients. These issues are to be considered along with those variables relevant to the general population of alcoholic clients that were discussed in the previous section.

Culturally Sensitive Assessment Tools

An example of a tool that is useful for exploring the role of powerlessness or empowerment in a client's alcohol problems is the cultural ecomap. The guidelines discussed in this section represent an elaboration of a tool described by Ziter (1987) for assessing African American clients that may be useful for other minority group clients as well (Freeman, 1989). As can be seen in Figure 3.1, the cultural ecomap assists the social worker in studying the family as a unit, the family in its immediate environment, and the family in its larger social environment. The goal is to increase the practitioner's and client's understanding of the racial and familial dynamics related to addiction. The outcome is a refined differential diagnosis that is utilized along with the general assessment.

For each of the concentric circles in Figure 3.1, the practitioner assesses how the family unit or individual functions in that area. For instance, the helping professional should assess the following:

1. The family unit: members' abilities to agree on and fulfill functional roles while also meeting individual needs (e.g., conflicts over leisure time or racial identity), and the implications of using alcohol to relieve stress from familial or racial conflicts;
2. The minority group world: the nature and quality of relationships between this world and the family (cultural drinking patterns, cutoffs, or strong positive ties);
3. The interracial world: sources of meaningful personal contacts and exchanges between the white world and the family (the influence of socialization experiences and the larger environment on the quality of and satisfaction with these relationships, within-family differences in the amount of interracial contacts and satisfaction with those contacts, and sources of support and stress in the interracial environment related to addiction and recovery); and
4. The dominant culture or larger environment: sources of powerlessness and empowerment from the mass media, books, laws and social policies, and contacts with social institutions; and differences in the competencies necessary for survival in the minority group culture and in the larger environment (areas of family consensus or conflict in how to cope with these variables and the role of alcohol in the process, survival resources, appropriate steps to take in problem resolution).

Use of the cultural ecomap to facilitate a differential diagnosis (along with the other components discussed previously) can be illustrated by the following case example (see Figure 3.1):

This is an African American family consisting of Jeff (aged 35), his wife, Rae (31), Ted (13) and Judy

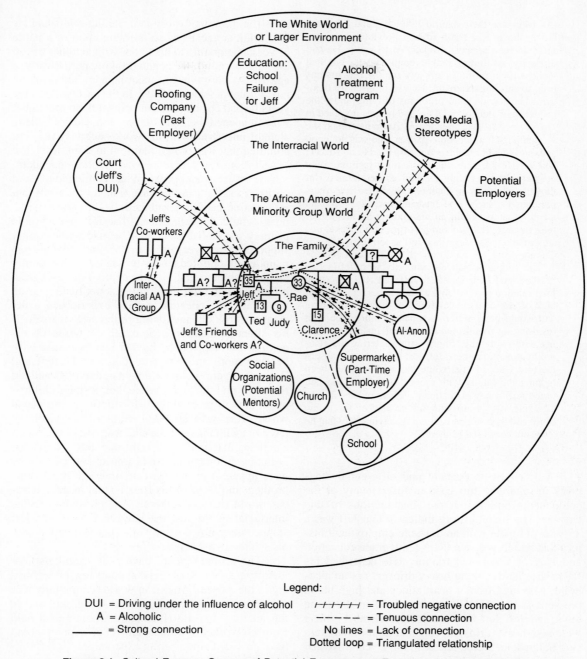

The White World
or Larger Environment

Education:
School
Failure
for Jeff

Alcohol
Treatment
Program

Roofing
Company
(Past
Employer)

Mass Media
Stereotypes

The Interracial World

Court
(Jeff's
DUI)

Potential
Employers

The African American/
Minority Group World

Jeff's
Co-workers

The Family

A

?

A

Inter-
racial AA
Group

A?

A?

35
Jeff

A

33
Rae

A

13
Ted

9
Judy

15
Clarence

Al-Anon

Jeff's Friends
and Co-workers A?

Social
Organizations
(Potential
Mentors)

Church

Supermarket
(Part-Time
Employer)

School

Legend:

DUI = Driving under the influence of alcohol
A = Alcoholic
_____ = Strong connection

⊢⊣⊢⊣⊢ = Troubled negative connection
– – – – = Tenuous connection
No lines = Lack of connection
Dotted loop = Triangulated relationship

Figure 3.1. Cultural Ecomap: Sources of Potential Empowerment Experiences or Powerlessness

(9), who are their natural children, and Clarence (15), who is Rae's son from a previous marriage. Jeff had been a heavy drinker for 15 years. He had difficulty in finding stable employment, but had worked for a roofing company for the few months prior to entering treatment. He was referred for treatment because of legal problems (driving under the influence of alcohol, a DUI), and he was involved in AA as a result. Rae attended Al-Anon meetings; she viewed herself as a people-pleaser who was not good at expressing her feelings but who tried to do so. She had very few friends and was cut off from her only brother and his family as well as her father. Her mother, who was an alcoholic, had died five years previously. Rae's first husband had also been an alcoholic and died in an automobile accident after their divorce. Rae worked part-time as a checker in a supermarket. She described Jeff as too demanding of Clarence and not hard enough on Ted and Judy.

The couple socialized primarily with Jeff's two brothers and their families. Jeff and Rae described their relationship as ''shaky'' due to her jealousy and lack of self-confidence. Jeff was socially outgoing and would have preferred to spend more time with his drinking friends and co-workers instead of visiting with his family. Shortly after entering the alcohol treatment program, Jeff lost his job due to absenteeism. One of his white co-workers had been helping the family with money since then and had urged Jeff to stay in treatment. Jeff attended a mostly all-white AA group with his co-worker for a few times and then stopped attending, saying only that he ''wasn't comfortable there.''

A thorough assessment and differential diagnosis in regard to this case included many of the components outlined in previous sections of this chapter. The social history indicated that Jeff was a 35-year-old male with an unstable employment history that he felt was due to his tenth grade education and lack of vocational training. He described his father as a hardworking heavy drinker, not an alcoholic, who died from a heart attack and high blood pressure at age 51. His mother lived in the same town and Jeff felt they were close. Both brothers were also heavy drinkers. Jeff had high blood pressure but had not seen a doctor in three years. He had accumulated several traffic tickets for speeding in the past five years but had received only one DUI. His marriage to Rae was his first; they had been married for 14 years. This was his wife's second marriage.

The drinking history indicated that Jeff had his first drink at age 13 when he shared part of a bottle of vodka belonging to his father with an older boy in his neighborhood. He began drinking periodically at age 15. At the point of intake he admitted drinking mostly scotch whiskey daily. In the past two or three years he had episodes of not being able to remember what happened the night before. Jeff did not believe alcohol interfered with his work or family life, but admitted that Rae would like him to drink less. The MAST confirmed that he was alcohol-dependent.

If the treatment program had continued to build on its assessment in this case (much of the relevant information had been gathered), a differential diagnosis would have indicated that Jeff had chronic primary alcoholism and that he had some family supports for recovery in his mother and wife. He had maintained a limited ability to function in the family and with some peers. He was appropriate for partial hospitalization after undergoing detoxification as an inpatient. He appeared to have experienced a decrease or loss of functioning in the area of work. If his situation had been analyzed in terms of the cultural ecomap, other, hidden factors would have become more apparent (see Figure 3.1). Jeff and Rae were in conflict regarding parental roles and did not agree on how to discipline their teenage children or on how to prepare them for life in an interracial world. Rae was an adult child of an alcoholic (ACOA) with many of the characteristics of a ''dry'' alcoholic that tended to reinforce Jeff's drinking. Drinking cultures that could impact Jeff's recovery were apparent in the African American world (his brothers and some of his friends) and in the interracial world (his co-workers). Another barrier in the interracial world was the stress created when Jeff stopped attending a mostly all-white AA group with his white co-worker.

The ecomap would have been useful also for identifying sources of racial support for Jeff's sobriety in the African American world (community role models or a more racially mixed AA group) and in the interracial world (financial and emotional help from co-workers). Either source of support could have provided empowering experiences for Jeff during his efforts toward recovery by strengthening his relationships in the African American and interracial worlds.

Jeff had noted that he often drank both before and immediately after job hunting. Perhaps this was an attempt to use alcohol to cope with the stress of applying for work and then being rejected by mostly white employers in the larger environment. The possibility that racial stress and experiences with powerlessness might have been significant in his problems should have been explored further. Helping Jeff to improve his work skills and develop other ways to handle employment discrimination might have resulted in additional opportunities for empowerment.

GENDER ISSUES

Similar to the effects of race, personal and societal gender belief systems influence a practitioner's ability to accurately and effectively assess and treat men and women. Awareness of these belief systems and their impact enables the practitioner to move toward an increasingly gender-sensitive and gender-fair diagnostic process.

Gender-sensitive social workers and treatment programs provide services based on an awareness of how problems can present themselves differently in women and men. They are aware that women's and men's realities are different: that is, the world perceives and treats men and women differently simply because they are male or female. The situations (barriers and opportunities) that people encounter, whether they are perceived as stressful or not, together with the choices people feel they have and therefore their long-term physical and mental health effects, are influenced by being male or female (Barnett, Biener, & Baruch, 1987, p. 7). Gender-sensitive practitioners are knowledgeable about these realities as well as skilled in motivating individuals into treatment and toward improved mental health. Gender-fair assessment involves an openness to finding and accepting any experience in the lives of men and women clients including chemical dependence, incest, depression, acquired immune deficiency syndrome (AIDS), anxiety, eating disorders, aggressive/abusive/violent behavior, homosexuality, heterosexuality, health, strength, hope, and ability.

At the same time that the practitioner recognizes the possible influence of gender, she or he recognizes that people are individuals who will not necessarily "fit" a traditional male or female stereotype. *Ultimately, the goal of a gender-sensitive/fair approach is to treat men and women as individuals influenced by a multiplicity of variables who have a broad range of options and possibilities.*

To be gender-sensitive or gender-fair requires an ongoing awareness of the ways practitioners and clients carry cultural values into assessment and treatment. Every practitioner and client brings a set of beliefs, values, and biases to the helping encounter. These values and beliefs come from personal histories and life experiences and form a filter through which messages are sent and received. These filters create a "mind set" that influences everything a practitioner does (Broverman, Broverman, Clarkson, Rosenkrantz, & Vogel, 1970). How a practitioner thinks, feels, and acts with clients is determined in large part by the practitioner's perspectives, presumptions, and expectations as well as his or her awareness of them and their impact.

Cultural Values and Beliefs

When a client enters a practitioner's office for an assessment, there are a number of ways in which gender values may affect the outcome. These elements are reflected in the diagram of the Client System in Figure 3.2 and include the values and beliefs of the work setting, individual client, family, treatment providers, and the profession of social work. Knowledge of these elements affects the extent to which a differential diagnosis is possible.

The area within the large outer circle reflects the cultural expectations, values, and beliefs of the society (local community, state, country) in which the client and worker are meeting. This includes the history and current realities and attitudes about women and men.

Each generation and culture has standards defining what is appropriate for men and women to do, be, or have. These are reflected in judgments about whether it is permissible and/or valued for men and women to smoke, drink, use drugs, be violent, be abused, have sex, be fat or thin, vote, be married or single, heterosexual or homosexual, adopt children or be employed inside the home as caretaker or outside as construction worker, lawyer, secretary, or doctor. These values and judgments indicate what is prescribed and proscribed. They are evident in local, state, and federal laws, as well as in mores.

The cultural backdrop today includes values about the changing definition of roles for women

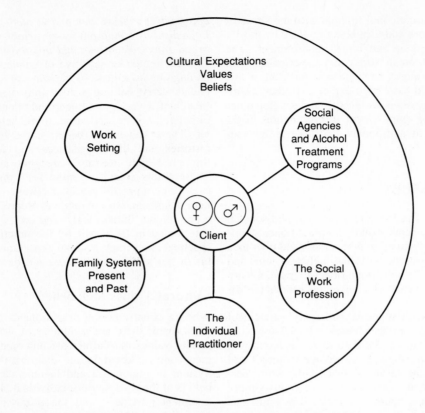

Figure 3.2. Gender Issues and Differential Diagnoses: Elements in the Client System as Individual Enters the Assessment Process

and men in which both can consider broader options in the worlds of work and family life (Freeman, Logan, & McRoy, 1987). Other values are reflected in the lack of social supports for families, the growing numbers of homeless persons, violence against women and children, and the feminization of poverty, as well as the continued disparity of men's and women's salaries.

Violence against women and children, so pervasive in all cultures, requires special attention in this discussion of cultural values. "In the United States a woman is beaten every 15 seconds and each day 4 women are killed by their batterers" (Heise, 1989, p. 45). At least 40 percent of women in chemical dependence inpatient treatment are survivors of incest or other forms of physical or sexual abuse. The high incidence of violence against women reflects a gender value that says it is permissible for women to be abused, and underscores the poten-

tial difficulties for women when confronting the issue of "powerlessness" over a substance. Attitudes, beliefs, and the reality of violence against women influence the diagnostic process and must be taken into consideration throughout the development and provision of services.

Gender values are also reflected in the absence of laws in some states charging first-degree forcible rape by a woman against a minor male. This gender value prevents (1) the reporting of such events, (2) the development and funding of services to help minor males who are raped, and (3) the development of consequences and remediation for women perpetrators.

Society says men and women are different in particular ways. This creates different norms for prescription and use of various substances for men and women. Historically, men have been encouraged more than women to drink alcohol. However,

60 to 80 percent of psychotropic drugs, antidepressants, and amphetamines are prescribed for women (McConnell, 1978). Practitioners need to consider this cultural bias in the assessment process. Simply because society views or treats women or men in a particular way does not mean that way is valid or effective.

Gender values can also influence how soon men and women are identified as having a problem and then confronted about it. Supervisors may not confront a man about work problems or job jeopardy because of his perceived family responsibilities as "man of the house." Women's drug or alcohol problems may be misdiagnosed as personal or emotional problems (Turnbull, 1988). Since "women can't be alcoholics" and "men can't be depressed or have an eating disorder," the right questions are not asked and, thus, accurate diagnoses and interventions are not made. These beliefs and myths also influence the range and type of treatment available (Landesman, 1988).

Sometimes an individual's problem *is* the conflict with cultural norms for men and women. The woman alcoholic, the man who has an eating disorder, the woman who is sole support of her family, the man who cannot hold either a job or his liquor may be misdiagnosed by practitioners who are influenced by personal or cultural values. It is the practitioner's responsibility to diagnose *all* problem(s) within a real world context.

Incorporating Values into the Differential Diagnosis

To illustrate the usefulness of the Client System diagram (Figure 3.2) in facilitating a gender-sensitive and gender-fair differential diagnosis, each of the subsystems within this cultural backdrop is described briefly below. Gender beliefs and values are reflected in the outer circle and in each of the inner circles of the client system. Figure 3.2 includes a focus on gender values in the workplace because work is a significant area of functioning for most employed adults.

Work settings have gender values that are reflected in their policies and procedures, as well as in the ratios of men and women to each other in the organization and at different power and status levels throughout the organization (Landesman, 1988). For example, hospitals generally have 75 percent female staff, yet have primarily male executives.

Gender values also affect insurance and benefits packages (paternity, maternity, or family leave) as well as access to these benefits. A culture that values women as mothers may support maternity leave, but may object to providing paternity leave for fathers. There are far-reaching implications of the gender values inherent in an insurance benefits system that increasingly eliminates long-term, outpatient psychotherapy and other treatment options. Since the majority of people who use these services are women, what does it mean that society is choosing to eliminate accessibility to services for so many women?

Gender beliefs and values are also reflected in the norms established within work organizations related to the use of substances. Drinking among men may be tolerated to a greater extent than is drinking among women (McConnell, 1978; Landesman, 1988). The impact is seen when a woman with alcohol problems is ignored *or* disciplined more harshly for reasons other than drinking. Often it is the supervisor's or company medical department's gender values that prevent them from appropriately confronting the alcoholic man or woman employee. In the Employee Assistance field the observation has been made that supervisors have a hard time believing women use or sell drugs and an even harder time confronting these women. Although it is more acceptable to see men as having a drug or alcohol problem, the diagnosis and intervention may be affected by other gender-related problems. More data are needed to discover how gender influences all the situations described above.

Gender values affect the dollars people earn. Women continue to be paid less than men for the same work. Women's economic status relative to men did not improve between 1959 and 1983 (Fuchs, 1986). "The relative wages of women improved over that period, but women had less leisure time than men, more women were dependent on their own incomes and women's share of financial responsibility for children rose. The net effect of these trends has been that women have 4 to 15 percent less access to goods, leisure time and services, relative to men, than they did in 1959" (Barnett et al., 1987, p. 54).

All these work-related gender value issues should be considered and explored with clients to enhance the differential diagnosis. The practitioner should attempt to determine to what extent these issues affect substance abuse problems that exist or the need and opportunity to diagnose and provide treatment for these and other relevant problems.

Gender values in the Individual Client System also impact the assessment. The client's gender, age, race, religion, and current life situation (including drug and alcohol use and other physical and emotional functioning) must be reviewed. These variables influence the client's perception of what the problem is, what it will take to fix it, and whether it is possible to do so. These variables also influence the client's follow-through once the assessment and differential diagnosis have been completed.

In the previous case study, the practitioner would identify the following relevant variables in Rae's Individual Client System: that she is 33 years old, African American, twice married (one divorce), and the mother of three children (one son from the first marriage). She is the daughter of an alcoholic mother, and both her first and second husbands are alcoholic. She is cut off from her church and her family of origin. Jeff's Individual Client System includes being 35, African American, married, and the father of two. He is an alcoholic. The next step is to investigate how gender and race impact Rae and Jeff's perception of their problems and strengths as well as their real opportunities for change. Understanding the influence of the cultural backdrop and the individual client system, the practitioner would move on to explore the influence of gender on the client's family and significant others.

In the family system, practitioners identify the gender values and teachings of the client's family of origin as well as those within the current family relationships. How does the family define acceptable and valued roles for men and women? How does the family empower female and male members? How are women and men perceived in terms of their relative power and powerlessness? Is there any history of physical violence, sexual abuse, or chemical dependence? How does this influence the client's behavior including the use of substances?

Gender values related to the belief system of the social agency or treatment program must be considered along with the practitioner's personal belief system. These programs exist in the "white world of larger environment" of the cultural ecomap (see Figure 3.1). Gender issues and values are reflected in the models available for assessment and the approach used for treatment. For example, whether separate treatment for women is deemed necessary and therefore made available is a reflection of such values (Turnbull, 1988). Recent research is beginning to indicate that there are differences in the onset and progression of alcoholism in women and men and that there are physiological factors that warrant further investigation (diPadova, Pazzato, Terpin, Baraona, & Lieber, 1990; NIAAA, 1986). These findings will have implications for how alcoholism is assessed and diagnosed in women.

Diagnosis is influenced by the program's and practitioner's views about men and women. Research reflects that, historically, what is defined as healthy adult behavior is the same as healthy male behavior but different from healthy female behavior. For instance, Broverman et al. (1970) asked clinicians to define a healthy adult with sex unspecified and then to apply the definition by judging the healthy male and the healthy female. Clinicians in the study judged healthy women differently from healthy men by saying they were more submissive, less adventurous, more easily influenced, less aggressive, less competitive, more excitable in minor crises, more conceited about their appearance, and less objective. The general and more positive standard of health was applied only to men. Practitioners need to be aware of how belief systems, as indicated by Broverman et al. (1970), can bias their ability to do an effective differential diagnosis.

Other dangers occur when helping professionals generalize from studies of specific populations—for example, from studies of white male alcoholics to females or other minority group alcoholics. As previously noted, most research in the past 30 years or so has been on white males (Harper & Dawkins, 1977). More research is obviously needed on women and minorities.

Other areas needing further data collection and research by the social work profession include the influence of the ratio of men and women staff to men and women clients in substance abuse programs. In a survey of Employee Assistance Program professionals and of substance abuse treatment programs, practitioners reported that women clients in largely male environments were less likely to discuss a history of incest, sexual victimization, rape, or abuse. In another setting where there is largely a male client population and largely female staff, men discuss sexuality and intimacy issues only on the weekends when a male group leader comes in (Landesman, 1988).

More questions to explore include the following: Is the utilization of services affected by gender values? How accessible and effective are services perceived to be for men and women for a broad range of problems such as substance abuse, eating disorders, sexual problems, incest (survivors and perpetrators), physical and sexual abuse, anxiety, and depression? How accessible are those programs to men and women of all races, religions, sexual preferences, and life-styles?

Organizational, cultural, and personal gender values are reflected in a program's literature, orientations to the job, and staff training sessions. What case examples are used? What videotapes and films are used? How are men and women portrayed in these? When the topic of discussion is women in trouble, how often are they portrayed primarily as depressed, while men are portrayed primarily with chemical dependence problems? How often are women portrayed as parents, while men are portrayed as workers?

The area in which a practitioner has the most potential for impact on the differential diagnosis is in the practitioner's own personal value system (Broverman et al., 1970). Practitioners need to ask themselves: What do I believe, value, find acceptable in men and in women? How do those views influence the assessment and diagnostic process? Gender values are visible when practitioners find themselves turned on or off sexually by a client; offended, upset, or uncomfortable with a client or colleague's life-style choices (gay, heterosexual); or annoyed and upset by a person's beliefs (anti-choice, pro-choice, feminist, or chauvinist). Awareness of the gender beliefs reflected in each of the subsystems in Figure 3.2 enables a practitioner to develop and/or select assessment strategies that are increasingly gender-sensitive and effective.

Strategies for Differential Diagnoses

Gender and cultural values are reflected in the questions that practitioners ask to gather demographic data. For example, asking marital status is a reflection of a heterosexual, middle-class value system. Practitioners need to consider how this affects clients. One alternate is to ask if the client is in a relationship at the present time. If so, what kind of relationship is it? If not, has the client ever been? Then, the practitioner might ask if the client has ever been married (Landesman, 1988).

The goal is to eliminate those actions that may limit a practitioner's effectiveness. Collecting data by gender and race will enable the worker to continue to identify and evaluate individual and systemic beliefs and their influence. This includes collecting and comparing data on the people who are served, what problems *they* identify as being of concern, what problems practitioners identify, the recommendations they make, how they follow up or clients follow through, and how clients evaluate the outcomes versus how social workers evaluate them. Data are also needed on the resources that are used for men and women and the possible influence of gender in the process. For example, what is the impact of male versus female practitioners working with either male or female clients, and under what circumstances (Landesman, 1988)?

Another strategy for offsetting the gender and cultural impact is to standardize components of the assessment and follow-up process (Landesman, 1988). For example, when diagnosing clients, have the following areas in mind as possible issues:

1. Personal/emotional functioning
2. Anxiety
3. Loss experiences
4. Depression
5. Important relationships
6. Marital status
7. Family members
8. Client alcohol use
9. Family alcohol use
10. Client other drug use
11. Family other drug use
12. Legal issues
13. Financial status or concerns
14. Day care/elder care
15. Job stress or satisfaction
16. Educational/occupational issues
17. Physical/sexual abuse (self or others—current)
18. Incest survivor
19. Eating disorder
20. Physical health
21. Cultural/social/ethnic context
22. Sexual identity, sexual preference
23. Other

As practitioners evaluate problems with clients, they should notice any tendency to emphasize or omit any of these categories. How easy or difficult is it to ask men about eating disorders or women about substance abuse issues? Notice the frequency with which women complaining of anxiety and somatic symptoms, such as chest pains, are directed to a doctor for a medical exam or to a mental health professional to handle their emotional problems. Women with heart disease sometimes have their symptoms minimized or labeled as psychosomatic (Barnett et al., 1987). Observe the frequency with which men complaining of being depressed are encouraged to seek counseling or are told that they are doing just fine and this will pass. Men's emotional vulnerability is often minimized. The goal is to have a balanced and open perspective that allows for all possibilities with women and men.

To further enhance the quality of the assessment and diagnosis, the social worker can establish some standardized questions that are asked consistently of women and men clients. For example:

1. Does your family use chemicals, medicine, or alcohol and, if so, how are they used?
2. Have you ever been concerned about anyone else's use? Your own?
3. Has anyone ever mentioned concerns about your use?
4. Have you or anyone in your family ever gone for an evaluation, received counseling, or been hospitalized in a psychiatric or chemical dependence program?
5. What do you know about any history of physical or sexual abuse in your family (for yourself or any other family member)?
6. Do you have a personal or family history of problems involving eating, weight, or body image (overeating, eating compulsively, purging, or starving)?
7. How are differences or conflicts handled in your family?
8. How do people in your family express emotions?
9. What do you want to get out of this process?
10. Is there anything else you think it would be important to share in order for you to get help? (Landesman, 1988).

Gender and racial biases are insidious. To un-

cover and address them requires conscious, ongoing attention. Practitioners can further develop their awareness through use of audio- and videotaped sessions and the review of these by colleagues. Very often a practitioner's nonverbal behavior demonstrates the gender and racial values more clearly. Looking for any differences in the ways the practitioner touches, greets, directs, listens to, and talks with women and men clients of different ages, races, religions, and relationship status is useful in discovering the influence of gender and race (Landesman, 1988).

CONCLUSION

If practitioners presume that clients are already "all that they can be," they severely limit their professional effectiveness in developing an accurate assessment and differential diagnosis. Their perceptions or beliefs will determine the outcomes rather than the realities of a client's situation doing so. Those important realities include coping patterns, valued ways of thinking and feeling, and familiar ways of relating to others that affect the development of alcoholism and recovery. Thus, an assessment that is too narrowly focused or that is bound by the practitioner's values does not provide sufficient data for helping the client identify individual needs.

Each client is unique in terms of how those needs should be addressed. The differential diagnosis helps to clarify the client's unique qualities that affect the extent to which alcohol is a problem, and to identify sources of effective treatment. The more clients can be involved in this process in a manner that demonstrates appreciation for their uniqueness, the more they will feel valued. When this type of broad-based differential diagnosis does not occur, clients tend to feel discounted and devalued. They may have less hope that their needs can be met since the assessment has not involved them or captured their perspective about their unique needs.

These outcomes are determined by the practitioner's values and skills in early and ongoing contacts with clients. An awareness and appreciation of the different experiences of alcoholic clients based on age, race, gender, and other factors is an important value for practitioners. Equally important are the skills necessary for utilizing that appreciation of differences in effectively conducting the assessment and differential diagnosis. Skill is necessary also in implementing the specific set of gender-sensitive and culturally sensitive assessment strategies that have been discussed in this chapter. Then, and only then, can practitioners and clients "know what they may be."

REFERENCES

Barnett, R. C., Biener, L., & Baruch, G. K. (1987). *Gender and stress*. New York: Free Press.

Bell, P., & Evans, J. (1983). *Counseling the black client. Professional education, #5*. Minneapolis, MN: Hazeldon.

Blackmon, B. (1985). Assessment in inpatient and outpatient treatment programs. In E. M. Freeman (Ed.), *Social Work practice with clients who have alcohol problems* (pp. 69–72). Springfield, IL: Thomas.

Broverman, I. K., Broverman, D. M., Clarkson, F. E., Rosenkrantz, P. S., & Vogel, S. R. (1970). Sex-role stereotypes and clinical judgments of mental health. *Journal of Consulting and Clinical Psychology, 34,* 1–7.

Caldwell, F. J. (1983). Alcoholics Anonymous as a viable treatment resource for black alcoholics. In T. D. Watts & R. Wright (Eds.), *Black alcoholism: Toward a comprehensive understanding* (pp. 85–99). Springfield, IL: Thomas.

Chaudron, C. D., & Wilkinson, D. A. (1988). *Theories on alcoholism*. Toronto: Addiction Research Foundation.

Chernus, L. A. (1985). Clinical issues in alcoholism treatment. *Social Casework, 66,* 67–75.

diPadova, F. M., Pazzato, C., Terpin, G., Baraona, M., & Lieber, C. S. (1990). High blood alcohol levels in women: The role of decreased gastric alcohol dehydrogenase activity and first-pass metabolism. *New England Journal of Medicine, 322,* 95–99.

Freeman, E. M. (1989). *Culturally-relevant treatment with Black alcoholics*. Paper presented at Cedar Ridge Treatment Center, Shawnee Mission, KS on July 12.

Freeman, E. M. (1990). Assessment of substance abuse problems: Implications for clinical supervision. *The Clinical Supervisor, 8,* 91–108.

Freeman, E. M., Logan, S., & McRoy, R. (1987). Clinical practice with employed women. *Social Casework, 68,* 413–420.

Fuchs, V. R. (1986). Sex differences in economic well-being. *Science, 232,* 459–464.

Harper, F. D., & Dawkins, M. P. (1977). Alcohol abuse in the black community. *The Black Scholar, 8,* 23–31.

Hartman, A. (1979). Diagrammatic assessment of family relationships. In B. Compton & B. Galaway (Eds.), *Social work processes* (pp. 299–309). New York: Free Press.

Heise, L. (1989, November/December). The global war against women. *Utne Reader, 36,* 40–45.

Kutchins, H. & Kirk, S. A. (1988). The business of diagnosis: DSM III and clinical social work. *Social work, 33,* 215–220.

Landesman, T. (1988). [Unpublished study of professionals, clinicians, and professional men and women on gender issues in the workplace.] Chicago, IL.

Logan, S. L., McRoy, R., & Freeman, E. M. (1987). Current practice approaches for treating the alcoholic. *Health and Social Work, 12,* 178–186.

McConnell, H. (1978). Study profiles: Substance abuse by women. *The Journal, 9,* 12–16.

McCrady, B., Longabaugh, J. R., Fink, E., & Stout, R. (1986). Cost effectiveness of alcoholism treatment in partial hospital versus inpatient settings after brief inpatient treatment: 12-month outcomes. *Journal of Consulting and Clinical Psychology, 54,* 708–713.

NIAAA (1986). *Women and alcohol: Health related issues*. Research Monograph 16 DHS Pub. No. Adm 86-1139.

Richmond, M. (1917). *Social diagnosis*. New York: Free Press.

Schuckit, M. A., Irwin, M., Howard, T., & Smith, T. (1988). A structured diagnostic interview for identification of primary alcoholism: A preliminary evaluation. *Journal of Studies on Alcohol, 49,* 93–99.

Selzer, M. L. (1971). The Michigan Alcoholism Screening Test: The quest for a new diagnostic instrument. *American Journal of Psychiatry, 127,* 1653–1658.

Turnbull, J. E. (1988). Primary and secondary alcoholic women. *Social Casework, 69,* 290–297.

Weick, A., Rapp, C., Sullivan, W. P., & Kisthardt, W. (1989). A strengths perspective for social work practice. *Social Work, 34,* 350–354.

White, H. R., & Labouvie, E. W. (1989). Towards the assessment of adolescent problem drinking. *Journal of Studies on Alcohol, 50,* 30–37.

Ziter, M. L. P. (1987). Culturally-sensitive treatment of black alcoholic families. *Social Work, 32,* 130–137.

SUPPLEMENTAL READING LIST

Brisbane, F. L., & Womble, M. (1985). *The treatment of black alcoholics*. New York: Haworth Press.
Overall, this volume includes useful information about variables that make the needs of African American alcoholics unique in terms of assessment, and what constitutes a culture specific treatment approach.

Burden, D. S., and Gottlieb, N. (Eds.) (1987). *The woman client: Providing human services in a changing world*. New York: Tavistock.

Up-to-date information presented in this book about women enables practitioners to use nonsexist approaches to work with women clients (strategies, problems of domestic violence and alcoholism, criminal justice, and health care systems) and special populations (adolescent women, older women).

Daley, D. C. (1987). Relapse prevention with substance abusers: Clinical issues and myths. *Social Work, 32,* 138–142.

This article presents a concise and clear discussion of how clinicians can build in relapse prevention strategies at the point of assessment and treatment planning.

Gunther, J. R., Jolly, E. J., & Wedel, K. (1985). Alcoholism and the Indian people: Problem and promise. In E. M. Freeman (Ed.), *Social work practice with clients who have alcohol problems* (pp. 214–228). Springfield, IL: Thomas.

A good discussion about the interplay of sociocultural variables and governmental barriers that affect practitioners' abilities to engage and assess Indian alcoholics. In particular, the focus on Indian and non-Indian belief systems is enlightening.

McGoldrick, M., Anderson, C., & Walsh, F. (Eds.) (1989). *Women in families: A framework for family therapy*. New York: Norton.

This book addresses the question of how women experience family life from a variety of perspectives. Insights from sociology, cultural anthropology, psychology, and the study of human development form the basis for discussion of clinical assessment and treatment issues.

McRoy, R. G. & Shorkey, C. T. (1985). Alcohol use and abuse among Mexican-Americans. In E. M. Freeman (Ed.), *Social work practice with clients who have alcohol problems* (pp. 229–241). Springfield, IL: Thomas.

A cultural assessment continuum is discussed in this chapter for helping practitioners understand the needs of Mexican-American alcoholics; high-risk subgroups within the population are identified to facilitate assessment.

Rix, Sara E. (Ed.) (1988). *The American Woman 1988–89—A status report*. Women's Research & Education Institute. New York: Norton.

This annual report is prepared by the research arm of the bipartisan Congressional Caucus for Women's Issues; it includes information on the social, economic, and political characteristics of American women.

Wilsnack, S. C., & Beckman, L. J. (1984). *Alcohol problems in women: Antecedents, consequences and intervention*. New York: Guilford Press.

Chapters on therapeutic issues in the treatment of women, multiple substance abuse in women, prevention, antecedents of alcohol problems in women, women's drinking as a cultural preoccupation and a reality, and biomedical aspects of alcohol problems/ alcoholism for women are included in this useful book.

CHAPTER 4

Adult Children of Alcoholics: Uncovering Family Scripts and Other Barriers to Recovery

Patricia A. Pape
Pape and Associates

To survive growing up in an alcoholic family is second only to surviving the Holocaust.

George Vincent

Alcoholism or chemical dependency is a physiological disease that takes an immense toll on its victim. But alcoholism also devastates other victims. Perhaps the greatest effect of alcoholism can be seen in the children of alcoholics (COAs), many of whom grow into adulthood without ever sharing their "secret" or without understanding how having one or both parents with alcoholism has affected them.

According to the National Council of Alcoholism fact sheet (1987, n.p.), the following facts about COAs have been established:

An estimated 28 million Americans have at least one alcoholic parent.

More than half of all alcoholics have an alcoholic parent.

One of three families currently reports alcohol abuse by a family member.

Children of alcoholics are at the highest risk of developing alcoholism themselves or of marrying someone who becomes alcoholic.

Medical research has shown that children born to alcoholics are at the highest risk of developing attention deficit disorders, stress-related medical problems, fetal alcohol syndrome, and other alcohol-related birth defects.

In up to 90% of child abuse cases, alcohol is a significant factor.

Children of alcoholics are also frequently victims of incest, child neglect, and other forms of violence and exploitation.

COAs often adapt to the chaos and inconsistency of an alcoholic home by developing an inability to trust, an extreme need to control, excessive sense of responsibility and denial of feelings, all of which result in low self esteem, depression, isolation, guilt, and difficulty maintaining satisfying relationships. These and other problems often persist throughout adulthood.

Children of alcoholics are prone to experience a range of psychological difficulties, including learning disabilities, anxiety, attempted and completed suicide, eating disorders and compulsive achieving.

The majority of people served by Employee Assistance Programs are adult children of alcoholics (ACOAs).

The problems of most COAs remain invisible because their coping behavior tends to be approval seeking and socially acceptable. However, a disproportionate number of those entering the juvenile justice system, courts, and prisons, mental health facilities, and referred to school authorities are COAs.

These facts clearly indicate the complex set of short- and long-term consequences that can develop

43

when children are reared in families with an alcoholic parent. The costs are not only to the individuals and families, but also to communities and society in general. Treatment, often not utilized until adulthood, is long term and intensive as a consequence, whether or not the individual becomes an alcoholic. This chapter describes in detail the process of treatment with ACOAs in a group modality, the treatment of choice for this population. Preceding that discussion, the problems of COAs are summarized, the dynamics and characteristics of ACOAs are clarified, and guidelines for utilizing this information during assessment and treatment are provided. Some practical assessment and contracting tools are included as well.

THE PROBLEMS OF COAs

According to the National Council of Alcoholism (1987) and the work of Wegscheider (1981), COAs are often victims of fetal alcohol syndrome, the leading cause of mental retardation and birth defects, involving approximately 24,000 births annually. Also, COAs are at four times greater risk than others for alcoholism; 40 to 60 percent develop the disease (National Council, 1987).

Even if COAs escape getting the disease themselves, they suffer retarded social development and severe emotional scars. They grow up with distorted perceptions of themselves and with very little self-esteem. They develop compulsive behaviors to cover up the shame they feel. And they succumb to all kinds of addictions such as food, relationships, gambling, sex, and work (Wegscheider, 1981).

Parents in alcoholic homes are models of inappropriate behaviors—erratic, often violent, controlling, repressing—and often they convey double messages to their children such as, "Come close; go away." According to Wegscheider (1981), COAs become isolated and steeped in denial; they eventually develop survival roles to cover up the pain. They become overachieving family heroes, acting-out scapegoats, lonely lost children, or the clown who must provide the entertainment for an otherwise serious and miserable family.

The problems of most COAs remain hidden because their coping behavior tends to be approval seeking and socially acceptable (Black, 1981). But the human toll is awesome! For every COA whose unhappiness reaches noticeable levels, there are hundreds who suffer silently, repressing the true origins of their pain and asserting that the parental condition "will never happen to me" (Wegscheider, 1981).

The 28 million COAs include 12 to 15 million students (Pilat & Jones, 1984), who are found in every preschool, elementary, and secondary school. At least 1 out of every 4 students lives in a home where there is alcohol abuse or alcoholism. These children are often the victims of abuse and neglect. They show a variety of academic and behavioral problems, which their teachers may not recognize as resulting from living with an alcoholic parent. For example, Pilat and Jones (1984) indicate that COAs are prone to learning disabilities, attention deficit disorders, compulsive over-achievement, and an inability to concentrate in school.

Moreover, these authors assert that COAs bring their family roles into the classroom, roles that allow survival at home but which are dysfunctional in school. For example, superachievers do not allow themselves ever to make a mistake, scapegoats disrupt the classroom by acting out, lost children become so isolated they go unnoticed and often underachieve, and class clowns demand excessive attention.

This society encourages, even applauds, workaholism and all the behaviors associated with that addiction (Pape, 1989b). Unrecovered COAs grow up to be ACOAs, and unrecovered ACOAs take their unfinished issues and survival roles into the workplace, where they set others up to be their "family." This frequently occurs, whether individuals are alcoholic or not, due to the co-dependency effects. While there is little empirical evidence to support self-report data, ACOAs often report similarities between both the dynamics and the feelings produced by their work relationships and the dynamics and the feelings they experienced as children growing up in an alcoholic family system. They may take on the old survival roles they played in their alcoholic family-of-origin, and everything begins to feel familiar again. They continue being treated in the same ways and, in response, they keep acting in the same old ways, until the cycle becomes self-perpetuating. Many have said, "it is as if my boss really is my parent!"

DYNAMICS AND CHARACTERISTICS OF ACOAS

The Adult Children of Alcoholics self-help community has developed its own set of common characteristics that result from having grown up in an alcoholic household. While each person may not exhibit all these characteristics to the same degree, this list has helped individuals identify factors they might not have been able to label and understand previously (ACOA, 1987, n.p.).

Characteristics of Adult Children

We become isolated and afraid of people and authority figures.

We become approval seekers and lose our identity in the process.

We are frightened by angry people and any personal criticism.

We become alcoholics, marry them, or both, or we find another compulsive personality to fulfill our sick abandonment needs.

We live life from the viewpoint of victims and are attracted by that weakness in our love, friendship, and career relationships.

We have an overdeveloped sense of responsibility and it is easier for us to be concerned with others rather than ourselves; this enables us not to look too closely at our faults or our responsibility to ourselves.

We get guilt feelings when we stand up for ourselves instead of giving in to others.

We are addicted to excitement.

We confuse love and pity and tend to "love" people we can pity and rescue.

We have stuffed our feelings from our traumatic childhoods and have lost the ability to feel or express our feelings because it hurts so much. This includes our good feelings such as joy and happiness. Our being out of touch with our feelings is one of our basic denials.

We judge ourselves harshly and have a very low sense of self-esteem.

We are dependent personalities who are terrified of abandonment and will do anything to hold onto a relationship in order not to experience painful abandonment feelings which we received from living with sick people who where never there emotionally for us.

Alcoholism is a family disease and we became para-alcoholics and took on the characteristics of that disease even though we did not pick up the drink.

We are reactors rather than actors.

We guess at what normal is.

We have difficulty following a project through from beginning to end.

We have difficulty having fun.

We have difficulty with intimate relationships.

We take ourselves very seriously.

We overreact to changes over which we have no control.

We usually feel different from other people.

We are extremely loyal even in the face of evidence that the loyalty is undeserved.

We tend to lock ourselves in a course of action without giving serious consideration to alternative behaviors or possible consequences. This impulsivity leads to confusion, self-loathing, and loss of control of our environment. As a result, we spend more energy cleaning up the mess than we would have spent had the alternatives and consequences been examined in the first place.

We tend to look for immediate rather than deferred gratification.

We generally over-react out of fear.

We are either super responsible or super irresponsible.

Robert Ackerman (1987, pp. 27–28) describes eight characteristics of ACOAs that are similar to those found in other studies. These characteristics include the following:

1. Feeling driven and the need for validation; Western culture in general breeds the perfectionism that leads to burnout.
2. A high degree of externalization, seeing all problems as being outside oneself.
3. Passivity and feeling unimportant.
4. The "180-degree people," those who try to portray the exact opposite of what they really are.
5. The conflict avoiders, who spend enormous amounts of time and energy making peace with everyone and therefore avoiding realistic resolutions to problems.
6. Hypermaturity, or accepting responsibility for everything, resulting in high levels of stress and the inability to have fun.
7. Detachment, a behavior type that begins with divesting oneself of one's alcoholic family until one is old enough to leave home (a health trait),

but it can lead to problems in the workplace and in other role responsibilities.

8. The invulnerables, the 10% of ACOA's who are functioning well. Although not invulnerable to pain, they have learned from it and have made it an asset.

Ackerman (1987), in his research on ACOAs, also discovered several important variables that impact on the severity of this population's problems. The major variables he discusses are gender, birth order, and age. This author states that the gender of the alcoholic and the gender of the ACOA are important. In cross-gender addiction (a woman with an alcoholic father), there are greater problems with intimacy, whereas in same-gender addiction (a woman with an alcoholic mother), there are high rates of chemical dependency. He also comments on the fact that males and females do not give the same priority to the issues involved. The age of the child when the parent's active alcoholism occurred is equally important in helping to determine how it might have impacted on the child at that time. Similarly, birth order helps to determine the survival roles that children assume in alcoholic families, according to Ackerman (1987). For instance, the oldest child is more likely to assume the role of family hero and to become an overachiever. During the assessment process with ACOAs, all these three variables need to be analyzed together to clarify the differential effect on the individual.

ASSESSMENT: MAJOR ISSUES

All intakes and assessments, whether for a mental health setting, social service agency, the legal system, or a church-sponsored agency, need to include a detailed alcohol and drug history. The history should focus on alcohol and drug abuse (including prescribed medications) for at least the last two generations. Grandchildren of alcoholics have essentially the same problems as do children of alcoholics (Smith, 1988), so this information is critical for assessment. Untreated ACOAs struggle with several major issues. If social workers are familiar with these issues, they will be able to more effectively diagnose and intervene with the major problem of alcoholism in the family of origin.

Lack of Self-Esteem

The first significant issue is a sense of low self-worth and a lack of self-esteem, often rooted in the tendency for the child to take the blame for a parent's (or parents') alcoholism. This leads to a lifetime of self-blame and feelings of inadequacy (Ackerman, 1987). ACOAs live in constant fear of someone's finding out they are not competent and are "frauds." This leads to perfectionism, workaholism, and overcommitment, especially for oldest siblings who took on the role of "family hero" at an early age. If an ACOA does not relate well to friends or co-workers, the loner automatically assumes the blame.

High Stress/Intensity Levels

A second issue is intensity, preoccupation, and a high level of stress. Unconsciously, the ACOA seems to gravitate toward a stressful environment. If the environment or relationship is not stressful, he or she will create a crisis or a dysfunctional stress to reexperience familiar feelings (Nelkirk, 1986). ACOAs operate extremely well under pressure, often appearing to have a variety of problem-solving skills that are not so apparent when the crisis has passed.

Boundary Difficulties

The inability to set appropriate limits and boundaries is a third issue and is characterized by overinvolvement with people, which can lead to the risk of exploitation by relatives, friends, or employers (Pilat & Jones, 1984). ACOAs often do not have a sense of appropriate self-disclosure with their friends, fellow employees, or dates and thus share too much information about themselves too soon. It is said that boundaries of ACOAs are like zippers, but the zippers are on the outside so that anyone can come along and unzip them! Another result of growing up in a family with erratic boundaries, either extremely rigid or nonexistent, is that ACOAs often take responsibility for the feelings and behaviors of other people. They also find it difficult to say no without feeling guilty even when that answer is in their best interests.

Approval Seeking

A fourth issue is the need for approval and validation. ACOAs tend to equate doing with being, their self-esteem is based on their performance, and a criticism about their behavior is taken as a criticism about their personhood (Black, 1981). This gives tremendous power to the people around them to determine the ACOA's self-esteem. This pattern creates a sense of resentment and of being out of control.

Inability to Trust Others

A fifth issue results from the fact that the ACOA's parents were generally undependable, leading to frequent disappointment and ultimately resulting in the inability to trust others (Wegscheider, 1981). This causes problems in friendships, in intimate relationships, and in the workplace. Many of the other issues to be clarified during assessment are related to this lack of trust. For example, a lack of personal identity, isolation, unresolved grief, unawareness of feelings, and ignoring personal wants and needs for fear of rejection indicate a lack of trust. Other issues are a fear of going out of control if in conflict with authority figures, and unrealistic expectations of self and others. Thus the ACOA typically finds chronic disappointment, which tends to reinforce the lack of trust.

ASSESSMENT PROCEDURES

Some questionnaires have been designed to identify some of the issues that ACOAs experience as problems. Many of those issues were discussed in the previous section. Such questionnaires can be used by social workers in a number of settings as tools in the assessment process. Often they can be self-administered, or the social worker can interview the client and record the data. One such questionnaire is organized into sections focused on cognitions, feelings, and behaviors, with a problem checklist. It can become an aid in setting treatment goals. For instance, "yes" responses to items focused on making harsh judgments about oneself and finding it difficult to have fun suggest that the individual has high stress/intensity levels, an issue discussed in the pre-

vious section. The social worker could then clarify with the client how that issue is handled and experienced and whether the client wants to set a goal for changing the behavior (Pape, 1989a).

The following case examples will illustrate how ACOAs who come into treatment do not do so with a presenting problem of family alcoholism, although that may be the underlying problem:

> George, a 30-year-old Caucasian manager for a computer consulting firm, came in for treatment because his marriage was not good. He was "successful" in many ways: he was handsome, had an excellent income, dressed well, drove a new car, and had a beautiful home; he and his wife were expecting their first child. George started by saying that although he thought he "should be happy and grateful," he had just recently attempted suicide for the third time. He had no friends, and in spite of all of his apparent success he felt inadequate and depressed most of the time. He later understood how this was his own self-induced shame cycle, which he had learned from his family of origin. Nothing he ever did was good enough—for him! George was the oldest child (family hero) of a blaming, critical, unrecovering alcoholic father and an overcontrolling, manipulative, co-dependent mother.

In another example:

> Susan, a 19-year-old secretary who was a self-mutilator, came in because her relationship with her fiancé was not satisfactory. Susan compulsively pulled out her eyelashes and had none at the time when she entered treatment. Her father was an alcoholic who had physically and sexually abused her, although in the initial interviews Susan stated that her childhood had been "fairly normal with some ups and downs." It turned out that her fiancé also was alcoholic, drinking a 12-pack each time they got together. Susan had no idea that this was a problem, and when asked if she thought that twelve beers was a lot to drink she said, "When your dad drinks a quart or more of vodka daily, twelve beers don't seem like much!"

THE TREATMENT PROCESS

Because of the typical sense of isolation and shame illustrated in the case examples above, treatment of ACOA issues is best done in a group modality. The work proceeds faster, it allows for breaking down the isolation that ACOAs have felt, the group enhances the amount of acceptance and support members can experience, and it allows for re-creation of "family-of-origin" issues. In a sense, it can become also the new "family-of-choice." The core issue for ACOAs is the shame that they carry inside as a result of having been reared in a shame-based family system. Much of the current research and writing on the issue of shame indicates that professionally led group therapy, in combination with 12-step self-help groups, is the treatment of choice (Pape, 1989a). Each of these methods will be discussed.

Treatment Groups

The professional treatment model is one currently being used by a group private practice near Chicago that specializes in the treatment of chemical dependency, co-dependency, and Adult Children of Alcoholics. ACOAs spend about 18 to 24 months in treatment, which includes not only ACOA group treatment, but also an education group and family and couple psychotherapy.

The ACOAs groups are small, with six or seven members meeting weekly for one-and-one-half hours. They are a mixture of about one-half men and one-half women. Some members are themselves recovering from their own alcoholism, in which case it is required that the person have two years of continuous sobriety, a solid Alcoholics Anonymous or Narcotics Anonymous (AA or NA) recovery program, and continued attendance at AA or NA meetings. There is a group contract (see Figure 4.1) that group members sign prior to beginning the group. The contract is used to initiate and focus the work in the group. There is variety in the members' family backgrounds and occupations (professionals, white-collar, and blue-collar workers), as well as their ages (from 18 to 70 years old). The major commonality among group members is that they all have grown up in a shame-based alcoholic family system and they want to work on recovering from the effects of that history.

One of the consistent problems for people who have attended AA for some time and who have learned to be responsible for themselves and not to blame anyone else for their problems is the resistance to looking at their childhood. This implies to them that they are "blaming their parents."

1. I will attend group for a minimum of 12 sessions, toward the end of which I will evaluate my continued participation. If I decide to continue, I will either renegotiate for a specific number of sessions or continue to attend with no specific time commitment other than agreeing to give four weeks (sessions) notice of my intent to terminate from group.

2. I will be punctual for all sessions and agree to call my group leader in advance if I cannot attend a session.

3. I agree to keep both the names of other group members and what they say confidential.

4. I will discuss group and/or therapeutic issues with the group, and if for some reason I discuss group issues with other members outside the group, I will be responsible for sharing with group what was discussed.

5. I will adhere to the payment policy for group members. I understand that this requires me to pay at the first of the month for all sessions during a month even though I choose to or cannot attend a session. I further understand that this policy will be waived for two weeks of vacation time, provided I advise the group as a whole prior to my absence.

6. I will participate to the best of my ability and be supportive of others during the sessions.

7. I will maintain 24 hours abstinence from all mood-altering chemicals prior to group.

8. I understand and will adhere to the requirements of my specific group.
Group: _____
Client Name: _____
Date: _____
Address: _____

Figure 4.1. Group Contract

When they go to ACOA meetings, they hear that they are *not* responsible for what happened to them in their childhood, that they were *victims*. Many members have found it helpful to be in their "adult" phase when they go to an AA meeting, self-responsible and not blaming others. But when they go to their ACOA group, they are to go in their "child" phase, not responsible, a "victim" of their own childhood pain. It is this "child" that needs nurturing and healing in order to move on and let go of the past (Black, 1981).

Also, for chemically dependent ACOAs there is a lot of ambivalence and conflicted feelings about their alcoholic parent. They have said they would never be like that! And now they too are chemically dependent! It becomes important for them to look at both the similarities and the differences between their disease and behavior and that of their parent. This begins the separation and differentiation process necessary for individuation and identity formation (Bowen, 1974).

Another major area of treatment in the groups is taking responsibility for oneself and learning to identify feelings and needs. Each group session is begun with a one-minute meditation and centering exercise that focuses on relaxation of the body, deep breathing, various thoughts and letting them go, feelings, and determination of what each person needs from the group during that group meeting. Members then touch base by expressing a one-word feeling in the here-and-now and also by asking for what each person wants or needs. It can take as long as six months for someone to identify and ask for what is wanted or needed.

Some of the group goals are: (1) to create a safe environment where individuals can learn to trust and express their feelings; (2) to allow group members to remember, talk about the past, and reexperience the feelings; (3) to teach new skills for coping with past and present stress; and (4) to talk about the past, both the ''secrets'' and the feelings about these ''secrets,'' which will begin to reduce the shame and also help them to break out of their patterns of isolation.

Problems that need to be addressed by the leader include the tendency to focus too much on family members who are not present rather than on themselves and their feelings. Some members are overly nice, enabling, and afraid of ''hurting someone's feelings'' rather than engaging in the supportive confrontation that is needed. Others focus too much on the negative. Although friendships and getting together outside of group are encouraged, there is an agreement not to have any sexual or dating involvement with other group members. The rationale for this useful rule is that ACOAs have existing problems with intimate relationships that bring them into treatment. Getting involved with this type of relationship with group members before or during the process of working on that issue simply complicates and interferes with their progress.

Individuals set their own specific written goals. Some of these may be: to express anger immediately and directly when it is felt, to talk about feelings toward the alcoholic and co-alcoholic parent, to call someone in the group each week, and to ask directly for what they want.

Some of the issues that are worked on in group are those identified in the section on assessment as important. For example, low self-worth, lack of a sense of personal identity, unclear boundaries, shame, difficulty making friends, lack of an intimate relationship, and isolation are frequent topics. Unresolved grief is a common issue, as well as lack of awareness and expression of feelings, wants, or needs. Fear of going/being out of control, especially related to family-of-origin work, is a recurring theme. The group provides opportunities for giving and receiving feedback. Finally, grieving, forgiving oneself and one's family, and letting go of the past is a progression that each member works through.

In order for ACOAs to change, they must be shown how to develop more realistic expectations of themselves and of others. This helps them to develop appropriate boundaries (Bowen, 1974) and to take appropriate responsibility for themselves and not for others. They can learn how to become more personally powerful and to use that personal power in a healthy way, becoming less dependent on approval and validation from others and more self-approving and self-validating. This allows them to act instead of reacting and provides an avenue for enhancing their self-esteem.

The core of all compulsive behavior is shame, and the core of shame is the lack of control that ACOAs experience. The compulsive behaviors become the mechanisms through which people bind up and manage their shame. Alcoholic family systems, as well as some other rigid, compulsive family systems, are shame based (Steinglass, 1989). Their rules are often inhuman, unclear, perfectionistic, controlling, and steeped in a denial system so that children can never do enough, cannot measure up or be successful enough to feel good about themselves. Guilt has to do with violating one's value system and *doing* something wrong. Shame, on the other hand, has to do with not *being* enough, feeling defective or flawed, and not measuring up, usually to someone else's standards (Pape, 1989a).

Because shame is caused by abusing or neglectful relationships in the past, it is healed through the experience of accepting, respectful, and supporting relationships found in a group. The most important aspect of healing the shame is to externalize it. Telling one's story in the group and talking about what happened in the past are good starting points. Talking about thoughts and feelings in the group and having them affirmed, accepted, and validated is important since those feelings were not validated by the parents. Externalizing the punishing superego and reintroducing a healthier superego involves discovering the critical, shaming messages, both verbal and nonverbal, from childhood (Pape, 1989a). That process helps to discharge safely the rage that accompanies the shame and finally allows for rewriting the "old tapes" and being gentle with oneself. To that end, homework assignments are given to write down the old shaming messages and to write affirmations of oneself. Learning to value and affirm oneself is a major goal of ACOA groups (ACOA, 1987).

Personal identity in general is another issue for homework assignments. Having a "love affair with oneself" is the overall assignment. Examples include assignments to "write down 25 things you like about yourself or 25 things you do well." Mirror work is a similar type of assignment: "Look in the mirror and say out loud something you like about you; then write it down." If the task is done daily, there will be a list of seven things at the end of the week, a list that is then shared with the group.

Learning to play involves a different type of task during treatment. The appropriate work of childhood is play, but when most ACOAs were children they worked! "It's never too late to have a happy childhood!" says a button some of the ACOAs wear. Homework assignments such as taking your inner child to the park to swing, writing twenty-five things you'd like to do for fun, or going to the zoo with a friend help people to begin to allow themselves to have fun. Another favorite assignment is a trip to the big local toy store, letting one's "child" wander around, and buying a special toy and/or a stuffed animal for oneself.

Working through the stages of grief, involving denial, anger, bargaining, sadness, and acceptance, is always the underlying process of treatment. Finally letting go of the hope of ever getting what one needed in childhood from one's family is the ultimate goal. Often this involves several trips back home to visit the family of origin, with many disappointments, in order to relay the truth of this statement to oneself. In some instances, when the family lives in the area, the client and social worker decide how they might come to a session or sessions with the client. Generally this occurs *after* the denial,

rage, anger, and blaming have been worked through. At that point the goal may be problem solving around here-and-now issues, or acceptance of the fact that the family will not be able to meet the client's needs. Individual sessions occur every two months or so. They are useful for reevaluating the client's progress and setting new goals. A rule for these sessions is that clients may not share anything in individual sessions that they are not willing to share with the group, a history of incest, for example. In this way, the work in the group is not subverted.

A Treatment Group Example

A group case history may be helpful to illustrate the dynamics discussed in the previous section:

> This ACOA group has six members, three men and three women. Ages range from 25 to 58 years old. Occupations are varied: a seminarian, a newspaper editor, a manager in an accounting firm, a real-estate sales manager, a secretary, and a construction worker. Two of the group members are "lost children." These members tend to feel unheard and invalidated; they often withdraw into silence. Four of the group members are oldest or only children or "family heroes" who are overachievers, perfectionists; they often try to taken care of or "fix" the other members of the group. Two of the women and one of the men are victims of rape and/or incest.
>
> On several occasions the "lost children" have worked on sibling issues with the "family heroes," and both have gained insight on how it felt to try unsuccessfully to take care of and help a younger sibling and also how invalidating it felt to be constantly taken care of and given unwanted advice from an older sibling. In both cases, feelings of inadequacy and shame were underlying the behaviors of each and could be shared and understood by members of the group.
>
> There has been the opportunity for the three members to talk openly about the rape, sexual abuse, and incest. They were able to share the feelings of anger, rage, and shame that resulted from these traumatic experiences of childhood. The entire group was supportive, understanding, and nurturing, allowing the abused members to work through their shame related to the abuse.
>
> In general, all the group members learned to express their thoughts and feelings. They now under-

stand that even though every member of the group "looks successful," each suffers from feelings of inadequacy, anger, shame, and sadness inside.

By the end of treatment, many of the ongoing goals are beginning to be realized: group members are learning to trust their own feelings and to experience integration of thoughts, feelings, and behaviors. They show evidence that they can affirm and nurture (re-parent) themselves. They have learned to identify and get their needs met, to try new behaviors both with themselves (intrapersonal) and with others (interpersonal). Finally, members know how to find some purpose and meaning in their lives and to have experiences that allow them the freedom to move on in their lives and to feel good about themselves.

Self-Help Groups

In addition to the professionally led psychotherapy groups, ACOAs attend Alanon, Alanon-ACOA, or ACOA self-help group meetings in the community. The 12-step programs are probably the most effective tool for dealing with shame, since they are based on the mutuality and the understanding necessary for recovery (Al-Anon Family Groups, 1988; Kurtz & Powell, 1987; McCrady & Irvine, 1989). Here people can tell their story and no one rejects them. Since part of the shame of the child is related to the total need for the mother, particularly if there is emotional rejection, it is healing to find that the 12-step program assumes and encourages the need for others. Group members are asked to obtain sponsors who are guides or mentors in the 12-step program. Clients learn from them how to work the twelve steps.

The final key to recovery and to reducing the power of shame is spirituality. By the end of treatment, these ACOAs have found and incorporated some sort of "higher power" into their lives. Spirituality is based on a sense of inherent worth, a wholeness, a connectedness with both the higher power and other people. One is encouraged to admit one's powerlessness (step one) and to let go of the need to control (step three) (ACOA, 1987).

The ACOA self-help community has developed what they consider to be the solutions to the problems they have as a result of growing up in an alcoholic family. They suggest that by attending meetings on a regular basis group members learn

how to live in a more meaningful manner. By changing attitudes and old patterns and habits, it is possible to find serenity and happiness (ACOA, 1987, p. 2).

The ACOA community also talks about the promises that become a reality as a result of taking the above actions:

1. We are going to know a new freedom and a new happiness.
2. We will not regret the past nor wish to shut the door on it.
3. We will comprehend the word serenity.
4. We will know peace.
5. No matter how far down the scale we have gone, we will see how our experience can benefit others.
6. That feeling of uselessness and self-pity will disappear.
7. We will lose interest in selfish things and gain insight in our fellows.
8. Self-seeking will slip away.
9. Our whole attitude and outlook will change.
10. Fear of people, and economic insecurity will leave us.
11. We will intuitively know how to handle situations which used to battle us.
12. We will suddenly realize that God is doing for us what we could not do for ourselves (ACOA, 1987, p. 3).

SOCIAL WORK PRACTICE IMPLICATIONS

It is imperative that social workers obtain the necessary education, training, and credentialing in order to work collaboratively with ACOA self-help groups, provide treatment, or refer COAs and ACOAs to appropriate treatment resources. Social workers are already working in the settings where these opportunities exist: schools, workplace, legal systems, mental health agencies, hospitals, and family service agencies. Most social workers are trained in family systems theory and, thus, view problems from this orientation. They are accustomed to working therapeutically with the entire family system and are in a unique position to do case-finding and have access to COAs and ACOAs.

It is estimated that the number of clients with problems related to their own or familial alcoholism runs as high as 70 percent of the average caseload in a typical mental health, hospital, school, or workplace setting (Pape, 1989b). If social work practitioners know what to look for and how to assess for both alcoholism and co-dependent adult children of alcoholics, they can increase the probability of reaching this underserved population.

In addition to professional training needs, two other factors prevent social workers from making appropriate diagnoses and providing relevant treatment. One factor is common to the American culture as well as some others: the tendency to support many of the behaviors characteristic of COAs and ACOAs such as perfectionism, people-pleasing, extreme loyalty, overachievement, personal sacrifice, and caretaking of others. Denial is one of the symptoms of alcoholism, and this culture (including professionals) often denies the severity of the consequences of growing up in a family where there is alcoholism.

The second major factor preventing appropriate diagnosis and treatment has to do with practitioners' personal experiences related to alcoholism. It is estimated that a significant number of health care professionals (doctors, nurses, social workers) are themselves oldest children from families in which there are other addictions or otherwise dysfunctional patterns. If this is true, and if these professionals have not worked through their own issues of denial and emotional pain so that they are in their own recovery, there may be a tendency to overlook these issues in their clients.

The place to begin the preparation for work with this population is with the worker: personal attitudes and feelings about alcoholism and alcoholics. The worker can accomplish this goal by an analysis of the effects of alcoholism and/or other addictions that have been experienced and how this has or has not been addressed.

If the above skills are developed by social workers, and if a self-assessment has been attended to, then practitioners have unique opportunities for intervening with families where alcoholism is or has been a problem. If the worker is in recovery, this can add immensely to the ability to help others recover from their emotional pain. None can take other persons any further than they themselves have

gone. But if one is a "wounded healer" and in the process of self-growth, then one's work with clients will be enriched by the one's own experiences.

CONCLUSION

Adult children of alcoholics are a population at risk. They have an above average probability of developing their own alcoholism or other types of addictions. They will most often marry another ACOA or a person who has alcoholism. This continues the intergenerational cycle of alcoholism, as children inherit the genetic predisposition and/or the learned co-dependent behaviors of their alcoholic and co-alcoholic parents.

ACOAs are also at high risk of becoming involved in other addictive processes. Addiction occurs when something takes over the person's life and leaves him or her powerless. It can be a substance, a person, or a process such as work. When the person begins to feel as if there are no choices, when the substance, person, or process is in control rather than vice versa, the individual is in the addictive process. ACOAs sometimes develop other addictions as well, such as food, sex, gambling, religion, work, and relationships.

It is important to note, however, that much available information about ACOA comes from practice experiences rather than empirical documentation. These direct observations and self-report data have been useful for developing a beginning understanding of the needs of ACOA. Yet it is not clear how ACOAs are similar to and different from children who grow up in other types of problem-filled families. Thus, additional information is needed to ensure that treatment currently prescribed for ACOA is indeed appropriate and effective.

Because it is clear that ACOAs are demonstrating some of the values that this culture condones—overachievement, extreme loyalty, and caretaking—many will remain undiagnosed and suffer silently the emotional scars of growing up in an alcoholic family. It is imperative, therefore, that social workers obtain the knowledge, skills, and willingness to intervene with this vulnerable population. This is critical for stopping the intergenerational family scripts and cycles of addiction!

REFERENCES

Ackerman, R. J., (1987). A new perspective on adult children of alcoholics. *EAP Digest,* 25–29.

ACOA/Chicagoland Area, 1987. Chicago, IL.

Al-Anon Family Groups (1988). *Who are the members of Al-Anon and Alateen?* New York: Al-Anon Family Group Headquarters.

Black, C. (1981). Innocent bystanders at risk: The children of alcoholics. *Alcoholism, 11,* 22–26.

Bowen, M. (1974). A family systems approach to alcoholism. *Addictions, 21,* 3–4.

Kurtz, L. F., & Powell, T. J. (1987). Three approaches to understanding self-help groups. *Social Work with Groups, 10,* 69–80.

McCrady, B. S., & Irvine, S. (1989). Self-help groups. In R. K. Hester & W. R. Miller (Eds.), *Handbook of alcoholism treatment approaches: Effective alternatives,* (pp. 153–169). New York: Pergamon Press.

National Council of Alcoholism (1987). Fact sheet on alcoholic families. Chicago: NCA.

Neikirk, J. (1986). *Is your work working? . . . Adult COAs on the job.* Presented at the Second Annual National Convention on Children of Alcoholics, Washington, DC.

Pape, P. A. (1989a). Chemically dependent and adult COA women in recovery. Part I and Part II. *The Almacan,* March 1989, 18–20, and April 1989, 14–16.

Pape, P. A. (1989b, November/December). Your boss is not really your parent. *EAP Digest,* 37–43.

Pilat, J., & Jones, J. (1984). Identification of children of alcoholics: Two empirical studies. *Alcohol Health & Research World,* Winter, 27–36.

Smith, A. W. (1988). *Grandchildren of alcoholics: Another generation of co-dependency.* Pompano Beach, FL: Health Communications.

Steinglass, P. (1989). *The alcoholic family.* New York: Basic Books.

Wegscheider, S. (1981). *Another chance: Hope & health for the alcoholic family.* Palo Alto, CA: Science & Behavior Books.

SUPPLEMENTAL READING LIST

Beattie, M. (1987). *Codependent no more.* Minneapolis, MN: Hazelden.
Useful information, hope, and guidance are presented in this reference for recovering from compulsive behavior.

Black, C. (1982). *It will never happen to me.* Denver, CO: M. A. C.
This book discusses the effects of family alcoholism on children, adolescents, adults.

Cermak, T. L. (1989). *A primer on adult children of alcoholics* (2nd ed.). Deerfield Beach, FL: Health Communications.
The definition of the disease of alcoholism is provided by the author, along with the characteristics that occur in the adult who grew up in an alcoholic family. The stages of recovery are identified.

Kaufman, G. (1985). *Shame, the power of caring.* Rochester, VT: Schenkman Books.
The author discusses a developmental theory of shame and identity. Also included in the book is a discussion of the therapeutic power of caring in the search for wholeness.

Lerner, R. (1985). *Daily affirmations for adult children of alcoholics.* Deerfield Beach, FL: Health Communications.
This book contains positive, powerful statements that will change the ways individuals think, feel, and behave.

Wegscheider-Cruse, S. (1985). *Choicemaking.* Deerfield Beach, FL: Health Communications.
This reference was designed for co-dependents, adult children, and spirituality seekers to know the difference between "freedom from" and "freedom to."

Whitfield, C. L. (1987). *Healing the child within.* Deerfield Beach, FL: Health Communications.
This book describes how to find and gently heal the child within by resolving inner conflicts.

CHAPTER 5

Multiple-Member Substance Abuse: Exploring the Initiative for Change in Addicted Families

Jerry P. Flanzer
Metropolitan Psychiatric Group

Peter Delany
National Catholic School for Social Services

Every journey begins with a single step.

Anonymous

The intent of this chapter is to sensitize the social work practitioner to issues involved in working with the multiple-member addicted family (MMAF) system. A complex family case is integrated throughout the chapter to illustrate important issues and treatment strategies related to the beginning stages of treatment with this and other families. The implications of family treatment with such families are discussed, highlighting the linkages with social work practice.

Typically, one thinks of only one person in the family having a substance abuse problem with alcohol and/or drugs. In reality, many families have two or more addicted members, often involving more than one generation and more than one type of substance (Stanton & Todd, 1982). Each involved family member may be at differing stages of the disease, actively using or not using the substance of choice, "wet" or "dry." Each involved member may be using at differing rates, often without other members' awareness of the extent or duration. Many multiple-member addicted families also suffer from other emotional or psychological problems that, if they do not predate the onset of the addictive behav-

ior, are intertwined with the existing addictive system (Steinglass, 1989).

BARRIERS TO ASSESSMENT

Assessment and diagnosis of the MMAF are difficult for many reasons but, the authors suggest, two factors are of particular concern. First, many social work practitioners are unable to differentiate between problem use and addiction. Education and training about the important differences are often biased and limited theoretically and practically. Second, addictions continue to be viewed as an individual disorder, diagnosed as either psychological and/or physical. Family dysfunctioning is seen as a consequence of the individual disorder (Steinglass, 1989). Subsequently, treatment focuses on the recovery of the individual with the belief that the family will function better once the alcoholic is in recovery.

Though family treatment has gained increasing acceptance in the last two decades, it continues to be viewed as an adjunct to the primary treatment of medical needs and the recovery process of the individual. The authors argue that family therapy is a viable approach for substance abuse problems. And it is a modality of choice with MMAF when medical problems are not severe enough to require hospitalizations.

CONSEQUENCES OF MULTIPLE-MEMBER ADDICTIONS

The consequences of multiple-addicted family members' behaviors are many. They involve not only each individual family system but the community as well. A major concern for the social work practitioner is the disintegration of internal and external family supports as the family system stabilizes around the addiction and members withdraw from their support networks (Usher, Jay, & Glass, 1982). This leaves the family far more vulnerable to normal family crises than a nonaddicted family system. In addition, one can expect an increased cost to the community as different generations of the family come into contact with various social service and treatment systems (Kaufman & Kaufman, 1979).

Having more than one member of the family drinking or drugging graphically underscores substance abuse as a disease of the entire family. The MMAF typically enters treatment for a problem other than the addiction, whether it is one member's depression, another's deviant behavior, or perhaps a marital disintegration.

By definition the MMAF is a co-dependent, co-enabling system (Usher et al., 1982). All members of the family are engaged in the maintenance of the cycle of chemical dependency. The chosen dysfunctional family behaviors maintain the denial and often serve to deter the social worker from strategies which would help to remove the alcohol from the system. Working with the MMAF system's dysfunctional behaviors as seen by the social worker is certainly more challenging than the seemingly straightforward intervention with individual alcoholics.

The conflict-ridden, straightforward strategies that must be employed to confront the substances used in the system may seem unethical to social workers whose training encourages them to start "where the clients are" rather than "where the

problem is." This professional resistance only increases when a second and, in the case presented below, a third substance abusing member is identified.

THE PATH TO TREATMENT

Johnson, Shontz, and Locke (1984) indicate that the influence of parents' substance abuse on children's use is unidirectional and involves a modeling paradigm. Similarly, Huba, Wingard, and Bentler (1980) reported that as people progress through early adolescence, they appear to become more and more aware of alcohol and other substance use among peers and adults. This and other research (Coleman & Davis, 1978; Huba, Wingard, & Bentler, 1979) document the role of the family in supporting the use of drugs by its members. Consequently, these factors may make it more difficult to help individuals in such families achieve sobriety unless the substance abusing system is involved directly in treatment and recovery for all of its members.

The First family, presented below, was particularly chosen as an example of a multilayered substance abuse problem. Alcohol consumption is the presenting problem. The father is labeled by the rest of the family as a heavy drinker, and they blame his drinking for his sudden aggressive, reactive behavior. He feels increasing helplessness in relation to his spouse, daughters, and general accomplishments in life. The family does not take much notice of the growing drinking problem of the middle daughter, except as an indication of her pairing with her father.

In fact, it was only a matter of timing and agency systems that brought this family to an agency concerned with parental drinking and family violence (Flanzer, Sturkie, & Kinley, 1982). The family might have easily been referred to a youth-oriented agency concerned with teenage alcoholism. For that matter, the Firsts might have been referred to a family service agency had alcohol not been mentioned in the initial contacts. Whatever the stated presenting problem, it indeed leads to different treatment at the hands of different human service systems. The Firsts were also chosen for this example due to the early stages of the alcoholism cycle which they represent.

Moderate to heavy and episodic drinking is often not given as much attention as the drinking patterns of clearly dysfunctional alcoholics are in the alcoholism treatment literature. These problem drinkers are often in danger of not being treated for their drinking (Cocozzelli & Hudson, 1989). Social workers tend to gloss over their drinking levels, preferring the "dramatic" marital and parent-child conflicts they also present. These are the families that most frequently are intact, and their progressive alcoholism is often not acknowledged.

The First case illustrates a phrase that can be labeled *perception is reality*. Each family member's perception of the presenting problem is different. Reality, for the therapeutic intervention, then, must not only take into account these differing perceptions, but also must pay heed to reality as being somewhat within the interaction between members. A structural approach seems to be the most useful for work with the First family. The structuralists are most likely to pay attention to proximity and distance between family members within the family system boundaries, making assessment of the family's place on the enmeshment-disengagement continuum. The structuralists also schematize the hierarchical relationships, alliances, and coalitions, and assess the degree of rigidity-fluidity of the family structure (Usher et al., 1982). They would note the First family's coalitions across generational boundaries and the resultant behavioral identifications of the daughters. The authors clarify these issues as the case is presented below, along with some initial strategies for intervention using primarily the structural theory perspective.

THE FIRST FAMILY: INITIAL IMPRESSIONS

The First family exemplifies the saying: the family that drinks together, stays together. As they present their perspectives, it is clear that the *system* has an addiction problem.

Mrs. First's Version

The First family came into treatment because Mrs. First (aged 47) was worried about Mr. First's (aged 50) behavior. She described a situation wherein her husband was having terrible problems "letting go"

of their daughters (aged 21, 19, 17). Mr. First, she noted, would yell constantly at their daughters, demanding to know their "comings and goings." "Not only that," said Mrs. First, "but he was always after me for sex." Things really blew up when the oldest daughter, Dorothy, announced that she was moving into her own apartment with a girlfriend. This occurred on the same night that Mr. First learned that his wife was covering for the 19-year-old Mary, who had been dating without permission. Mr. First had previously beaten his two daughters to such an extent that neighbors had to rescue them. When Mrs. First had intervened to physically protect the two oldest daughters, she was hit for the first time in 25 years of marriage. Mr. First then went out and "got plastered."

Mr. First's Version

Mr. First added some important information to the case. While he recognized his inappropriate outburst, he did not place blame on himself, but shifted it to his wife's long-term sabotage of his rights as the father and head of the household. Further exploration revealed that Mr. First always had a few beers during the day and frequently enjoyed drinking with his wife after dinner. He noted that he frequently had to put his wife to bed while she was inebriated.

The Daughters' Version

The daughters add yet another dimension. They saw their father as inconsequential in getting what they needed or wanted. Their mother made the key decisions. They saw both parents drinking, but father would more likely stare at the TV, while mother would more likely alternate between screaming at them to take care of their chores, or seeking out details about their dates. The father's recent aggressiveness surprised the daughters. The two other daughters expressed concern over the drinking habits of the middle sibling, Mary.

TREATMENT GUIDELINES

Most social work practitioners have a standard intervention strategy for working with substance abuse problems. They either employ this strategy, ignore the substance abuse, or refer the case to an alcoholism specialist. The MMAF offers something new—

a treatment alternative. Now the social work practitioner has the option of drawing from a broad spectrum of therapeutic techniques from both the substance abuse and family therapy fields. The authors feel that working with the MMAF offers social work practitioners a unique opportunity to use their skills more creatively. There are two "hooks" which the authors hope spark the social work practitioner's interest when working with the MMAF, making them more interesting than the addiction problems of one single member of a family. First, the work is more exciting; and, second, there are more possible points of intervention into the family system than in work with individuals.

The Initial Phase of Treatment

In selecting an appropriate intervention strategy, the authors find it useful to view treatment as a process that moves in phases. The initial phase involves stopping or limiting the drinking among the family members (Davis, 1987). This is true whether there is one member using a substance or many members, though many abusing members make the treatment strategy more complex. The social work practitioner must assist the family system in redirecting the anxiety and irritation that follow when the alcohol is removed from the family system (Treadway, 1989). This is necessary if the family is to achieve some level of success in initial abstinence and be able to move to the next phase of treatment (Berenson, 1976; Usher et al., 1982).

Clearly, the social worker must ascertain the extent of the physical damage to the body caused by the alcohol. This should include, but should not be limited to, physical examinations, laboratory analysis of blood and urine samples, endocrinological workups as well as cognitive assessments. Social workers often forget that alcohol damage may be permanent. Often, cognitive and psychological functioning may continue to be affected long after the abstinence begins.

At this point in treatment, the social worker may observe pseudo-psychiatric symptomatology which may be difficult to differentiate from either undiscovered mental illness or normal recovery symptoms. Assessing family members in the initial phase may be confusing at times. Each member will be physically and emotionally "on edge" while moving through his or her unique stage of recovery

(Usher et al., 1982). For example, a family member who may have previously exhibited a flat affect and lethargy may suddenly exhibit the "four-minute mile" syndrome reminiscent of manic behavior. New conflicts will arise as each family member moves through recovery. The social worker must constantly ask for feedback from each family member to ascertain the member's perceptions of what is happening in the family system.

The social worker also needs to structure the process and often slow it down. In so doing the worker stabilizes the family at each stage of recovery, allowing other members time to move into sync before continuing the treatment plan. At this point, providing reading materials and using self-help support groups such as AA and Al-Anon help to shift blame from one or more family members to a sense of self-responsibility for each member's own recovery (Usher et al., 1982). This has the added benefit of helping the social worker become distanced from the conflict that will emerge within the early abstinence period for the MMAF.

The Second Phase of Treatment

The second phase involves helping the family to identify adaptive behaviors or strengths and assisting them in developing alternative strategies that decrease emotional distance and manage crises. A typical crisis occurs because of a return to substance use by one or more family members (Davis, 1987; Berenson, 1976). Assessment is going on at each phase of treatment. As abstinence continues, the social worker must continually elicit the family members' assistance in analyzing their changing physical and emotional well-being. As members' physical systems detoxify, the worker will be able to determine if there are any other medical or psychological problems previously masked by the substance use. The following section delineates the two phases of treatment in more detail through a discussion of treatment with the First family.

PHASE ONE: REMOVAL OF ALCOHOL AND ANXIETY REDUCTION WITH THE FIRST FAMILY

The social worker's role in the assessment and engagement process is to:

1. make treatment available for the whole family,
2. reframe the problem as a family issue, and
3. *help stress the family system* in ways that increase the family's awareness of the problem, cut through their denial, and increase their motivation to change. (Usher et al., 1982, p. 4).

In this phase of the treatment, the social worker needs to work quickly toward a goal of abstinence within the family system or lose the confidence of the family in the process of treatment (Davis, 1987). The social worker must be acutely aware of the differing medical needs of each member regarding detoxification and withdrawal. The authors agree with Usher et al. (1982) that many alcoholics can achieve abstinence on an outpatient basis. Physician and inpatient referrals should be made, however, if abstinence is not possible or physical withdrawal reactions become significant.

Inpatient recovery programs may present a new problem for the practitioner. Many inpatient alcoholism treatment facilities last 28 to 30 days and some are decidedly biased against any form of simultaneous psychosocial therapy. The authors have found that establishing a working relationship with a specific treatment program and its medical staff and other professionals helps to limit the damage that can be done to the therapeutic relationship and facilitates the return of the referred client to the referring worker.

Once the social worker begins working with the family in an outpatient setting, Berenson (1976) indicates the worker should be more concerned about change in all areas and not just the elimination of drinking. Aside from history taking about alcohol use, that author

> prefers to head for (substantial) changes in drinker behavior—transformational shift or quantum leap— rather than taking a resolute stand on abstinence (certainly a controversial topic). . . . He considers it tactically unwise to take a hard line of abstinence, even though this is usually his ultimate goal. (Stanton & Todd, 1982, p. 386)

As Usher et al. (1982) point out, relapses into previous drinking and patterns of adaptation are to be expected and can often be predicted. In fact, such relapses may be used as evidence to convince family members that drinking must be eliminated if healing is to begin. Frank discussions about drinking as an interference with the recovery process helps both to install confidence and to lower the emotional contagion that often surrounds the issues of substance abuse in the family system (Treadway, 1989). As with the First family, the social worker begins with specific contracting around drinking and any specific behaviors that support the drinking. Members of symptomatic families do not initially require self-understanding of why they drink as much as they require a specific plan for change. The family is "stuck." The social worker must help them "unstick" themselves. This is usually accomplished by initiating a new pattern of behaviors in the family to address what had been the payoffs of drinking.

These new patterns including helping the family develop alternative strategies that reward management of provocative behavior, or in the case of the First family's drinking teenager, changing a disciplinary system so that responsibilities are shifted from an overinvolved parent to the teenager herself. In other cases, the plan may require a number of sequential steps through which the family focus is shifted, for example, from parent to adolescent, to husband-wife, to extended family issues. Regardless of the relative complexity of the plan, however, it is presented to the family in the form of concrete tasks and directives—both within sessions and as homework assignments.

The authors have found the Eriksonian contribution of a "decision destroyer" technique is a helpful way to stop a client from drinking (Bandler, Gordon, & Lebeau, 1985). This cognitive technique is a form of changing one's personal history; it is a key intervention to be used early in the treatment process.

Eriksonians assume that a decision to drink was made earlier on, based upon a rational response to a stressful situation during an earlier time in a person's life. The individual and family continue to respond today "as if" the earlier situation were still true; or the individual and family continue to respond today with the learned response of yesteryear that no longer works in the present. Thus, going back to the earlier time and destroying the decision of the "then" for the "now" can produce quick change. Perhaps earlier decisions to drink were made to gain peer acceptance, to allay anxiety, or to acquire love or admiration from a desired loved one. Such decisions from the past can be quickly de-linked from current decisions. Surprisingly, this type of suggestion—made even without hypnosis or trance work—often redirects positive treatment progress.

How do you get families like the Firsts into treatment, keep them there, and encourage change, particularly with nonvoluntary client families? The social worker must have a way of engaging the total family in treatment, and yet must be aware of the ethical dilemmas involved in coerced treatment. Often the family member who is most open to treatment provides an ethical way "into" the family system. Although treatment of the alcoholic members may be nonvoluntary, the member(s) who are ready for change can be helped to identify their needs in relationship to the behavior of the alcoholic member(s) and the aspects of their own behavior that can be changed. This way of working with other family members in the presence of the alcoholic members may set the stage for the latter's active involvement in treatment. Minimally, the alcoholic members of the unit can be helped to decide how they will respond to the dilemma of being "forced" into treatment and to share their perspective about the situation. In this manner, choices that are open to all members of a family can be revealed: those related to the issue of "forced" treatment and the underlying addiction problems in the family. This type of process provides an opportunity for members to become engaged in treatment as they choose to, but also allows the practitioner to proceed in a skillful yet ethical manner.

The setting or agency, whether public or private, provides another ethical means for engaging the family in treatment. The real life consequences that may be applied by the judicial/correctional system, access to an employer through an Employee Assistance Program (EAP) counselor, or access to a spouse and the possibility of family dissolution often provide the external thrust for keeping a family such as the Firsts in treatment. Once in treatment, other strategies may be useful for maintaining progress in an ethical and competent manner.

The social worker might predict a relapse when the drinking members are not participating in AA or following the prescribed treatment. Thus, if a member drinks, the social worker's predictive power is vindicated. If the social worker is proved wrong, treatment is a success. Another option is to create positive leverage within the treatment session, where the drinking members report their abstinence success to each other. This intervention accomplishes two things. One, the tactic provides family members with a way to support each other and show pride in each other's accomplishments. Two, the tactic acts as what neurolinguistic programmers call an "anchor," associating the treatment setting with positive feelings (Bandler et al., 1985).

The First family members were seen together after the initial phone call by Mrs. First. If the social worker had seen only Mrs. First, a different interpretation of the problem would have occurred. Listening to the story as presented by all five members quickly let the social worker see the numerous concerns that were highlighted previously: the stress of leaving home (Haley, 1980), the changing-needs phase of the family's life cycle, the overinvolved father-daughter relationship, the blurring of the intergenerational boundaries and associated coalitions, and the repetitive, nonproductive problem-solving activity. All of these are noted as important handles for intervention, but of secondary importance to the immediate need to eliminate the alcohol problems of the father, and those of the mother and daughter as well. Family violence is often a corollary to alcoholism (Flanzer, 1980); if present, it must also be stopped at an early stage of treatment, as it was in the case of the First family.

With the First family, the initial phase of treatment was used by the worker to explore how the family organized itself to meet it needs, including obtaining alcohol. This is accomplished by asking members to describe specifically some of their interactions and then by restructuring those patterns:

SOCIAL WORKER: How does your evening together begin? (asking for concrete behavorial sequences)

MRS. FIRST: We come home from work together. We stop at the grocery store, buy some items, and then come home.

MR. FIRST: Yeah, and all the way home she's complaining about how everyone else at work doesn't work to capacity and then she asks what I'm doing at work.

MRS. FIRST: He never tells me.

MR. FIRST: Why should I . . . She'll only tell me I

could do better . . . and how she should have married another guy who became a millionaire. You know, that's 25 years ago!

SOCIAL WORKER (focusing discussion):   What happens when you leave the store?

(DAUGHTER 1) DOROTHY: They come home, Dad takes a beer (a chaser for his bourbon) out of the bag, and puts the rest away in the refrigerator. Mom asks Linda how school was and we all go off to our separate rooms. (Note that Dorothy answers even though the social worker addressed her parents.)

(DAUGHTER 2) MARY: Sometimes I go sit with Dad. Sometimes Dad and I go out together.

(DAUGHTER 3) LINDA: You mean you would go out and "drink" with Dad!

MARY: No one else pays attention to Dad!

MR. FIRST: That's right!

SOCIAL WORKER: Whoa . . . let's back up. Who buys the booze?

MRS. FIRST: I do. My husband usually waits in the car.

SOCIAL WORKER: You know, you two are trying to do the right thing. Mrs. First, you are trying to be a responsible, giving wife, shopping for your husband. And you, Mr. First, are trying to keep the peace by not bringing controversy into the conversation with your wife or at home (noble ascriptions). From now on, Mr. and Mrs. First, how about no one buying booze, and certainly not for each other. Since you both have cars, both of you drive separately to work and on the way back, Mrs. First, you pick up Mary and take her grocery shopping or on other errands for the home front. Mr. First, you take Dorothy and Linda out job hunting every day immediately after work until they both have jobs (a family concern which surfaced in an earlier session).

The social worker ascribed noble intentions to the couple's acts (Stanton & Todd, 1982). This positive interpretation of their behavior helped the marital pair join the social worker, increasing the likelihood that they would heed the directives. The social worker followed traditional sex-linked roles in the directive about doing errands and job hunting, conforming to the family's existing framework. This left opportunity for exploring how to achieve role equity among family members for future development. The social worker also began to reframe the problem. This was not a drinking problem anymore; the problem was now their interaction that provided the behaviorial drinking set. By reframing the drink-

ing as having an interactional purpose, the social worker has changed the working contract within the family and within the therapeutic encounter. By focusing on the spousal pair, apart from the children, the social worker is also allowing the parents to achieve the distance from the children that is necessary to establish a generational hierarchy—restructuring the system's boundaries.

PHASE TWO: STABILIZING INTERNAL CHANGES AND STRENGTHENING THE FIRST FAMILY'S RESOURCES FOR COPING WITH ENVIRONMENTAL ISSUES

At first, the social worker's directives were met with surprise and resistance. In one blow the social worker was asking the family to change their routinized behavior. He did not ask their opinion. He kept the family busy and raised the energy level, thus countering depression and realigning the interaction sequences. In addition, he unbalanced the system. The social worker must be highly directive with multiple-member addicted families, particularly emphasizing elaborate homework schemes that, in this family, simultaneously changed internal performance and blocked external barriers. In one step, the social worker has, in a matter-of-fact manner, raised the issue of alcohol as a focal problem. This creates an environment for changing the drinking patterns and redirects anxiety that can no longer be filtered by the presence of alcohol. The family boundaries are being realigned more appropriately. Now the social worker and the family can work on strategies that stabilize the members' sobriety, a central issue for the second phase of treatment.

Once the alcohol has been removed from the family system, the family needs support to redirect energy toward the maintenance of sobriety. Commonly, a family crisis may erupt when the removal of the alcohol from use by several members does not resolve the underlying problems nor change the dysfunctional behavior that maintained the alcohol addictions.

Usher et al. (1982) suggest four basic types of homeostatic family responses that are possible in their efforts to deal with these crises. The first response is the reintroduction of alcohol into the system. The practitioner may find one or more members will return to drinking. The family is comfortable with this strategy for dealing with problems. Rather than view relapse as failure, the authors' reframe any relapse as a signal to reassess "where family members are." The practitioner needs to be sensitive to the possibility of one or more members being out of sync in the recovery process. A return to drinking is understood as a metaphor signaling that the denial of the drinking member is not being addressed by the family system. This is a normal part of recovery.

A second type of response is the maintenance of sobriety and the splitting or dissolution of the family. Usher et al. (1982) suggest family splitting is seldom beneficial for the individual members. Conversely, the authors find splitting to be destructive for many families that have developed few supportive networks due to the isolation that develops during the addictive process. However, some separations may be called for, particularly when violence has occurred within a family (Flanzer, 1980). Moreover, the issues of spousal violence and of physical and sexual abuse must be addressed openly, and the appropriate authorities must be involved.

In a third type of response the family establishes a new homeostasis without alcohol. This may take many forms. The family may achieve what is known in Alcoholics Anonymous (AA) as a "dry drunk" syndrome—the other dysfunctional behaviors remain the same as when the family was abusing substances but there is no substance use (Steinglass, 1989). This is not to be confused with the physical "dry drunk" syndrome that is a part of normal recovery and that may make it appear that the recovering person is abusing substances. For example, the person may experience depression when no substance has been abused or may have symptoms of a hangover without having used the night before. Another form of homeostasis is the introduction of a new addiction around which the family relates. This may include overinvolvement in AA, Al-Anon, Alateen, or Adult Children of Alcoholics (self-help recovery groups for family members, teenagers, and children of alcoholics) to the extent that the level of family interaction is minimal (Usher, et al., 1982).

An increasing fourth trend noted by the authors is the emergence of a new "addictive behavior"

such as anorexia, bulimia, compulsive gambling, or the like, in one or more family members (Steinglass, 1989). One of the authors, working with a group of recovering persons in a halfway house, found they had begun spending the "free money" (money not marked for rent) on lottery tickets with the hope of hitting the jackpot and establishing their own recovery house. Needless to say, the jackpot was never "hit" and these young men and women ended up without savings and without a place to go when their residency period was up.

Appearing to be agreeable to change, the Firsts were able to confound their social worker initially with their ingenious ability to return to their same comfortable but dysfunctional patterns. The family was more comfortable dealing with their interactional issues as a way of avoiding the "shameful" issues of drinking, creating an effective family denial system. Again, as a note of caution, this is where many social workers lose the abstinence focus necessary to stabilize the family and build the necessary foundation for an effective second phase of treatment. Sticking to the directives gave the First family a sense of "working hard" and helped to block their attempts through external family pressures to maintain the status quo. The social worker refused to become sidetracked by the 25-year-old marital conflict or the explosive sibling rivalry. The shopping trips were designed to help resolve the sibling rivalry and the coalition issues.

The wife's support of her husband's drinking habit was gently exposed. At that point, the wife was in a bind—no matter what she did, the social worker "won." If she chose to let her husband buy his own liquor and thus became disengaged from his drinking-supply behavior, this also would remove her excuse for buying alcohol for the family and force her to face her own drinking issue. If she continued to stay engaged in the husband's drinking-supply behavior, it would be difficult to continue to deny her support of his drinking habit.

Mr. First had the concurrent disapproval of his two daughters, Dorothy and Linda, who were going to be spending more time with him. Helping them find work also helped to indirectly focus on the leaving home part of the family's issues—more "grist for the mill" in the second phase of the treatment process. The daughters, as one might suspect, put up major stumbling blocks to job hunting and other young adult developmental activities.

Now they had to be responsible as budding adults. How could Mary continue to drink in front of her mother, while Mrs. First was helping her to get new clothes (and not hand-me-downs)? This sequence helped Mary differentiate from her two sisters along new dimensions, more appropriate and nondrinking dimensions. This change eliminated the process of triangulation between the siblings and around Mary's drinking.

Notice that the social worker did not prescribe the symptom in this case, but asked for a restructuring of relationships and behavior through directives. The social worker did not ever say it was okay to drink. Prescribing the symptom should not be used in situations such as this one. What if Mr. First physically abused his wife again? The social worker certainly could not give a directive for the client to continue to beat his wife. In the same way, the social worker could not order Mr. First, Mrs. First, or Mary to continue to drink. But the worker could force to the surface the family members' collusion in providing alcohol to all of its drinking members.

By making overt the implicit behaviors that supported drinking, and designating that no one should buy the alcohol for the family, the social worker created control of the supply side of the drinking behavior. This intervention allowed for either (a) rejection of the directive (if a member provided alcohol for him or herself), which would still indicate improvement in the family's previous pattern of collusion, or (b) accepting the directive, which would achieve power over the supply system and begin reshaping the supply line. Either outcome would improve the dysfunctional behavior of the identified drinkers and the dysfunctional alliance within the family unit. These initial changes in structure do not occur overnight. It took three weeks for this to begin to happen with the First family. The process was still fast, considering the years required to develop the rigid patterns that they presented.

IMPLICATIONS FOR SOCIAL WORK PRACTICE

No matter how the family responds, the social work practitioner must maintain a focus on substance abuse as the primary family problem. The authors utilize a psychoeducational approach and devote at least ten minutes of every session to each family member's differing physical, psychological, and social progress in the recovery process. Often physical examinations and lab work are suggested and discussed in the sessions. Progress in AA and Al-Anon is discussed, and strategies that circumvent blocks to investing in these support groups are developed.

Cocozzelli and Hudson (1989), in a thorough review of the literature on the alcohol diagnosis and treatment research, suggested that a paradigmatic shift is occurring in the field of alcoholism. The shift parallels the family focus suggested by these authors. It is a shift from focusing on the individual to one that includes an appreciation for the influence of social and environmental factors. Occupational and family resources, life stressors, and coping skills are viewed as significant determinants. These factors affect the development, treatment, and recovery process from alcohol dependence. Cocozzelli and Hudson (1989) suggest this shift should be encouraging to social work practitioners, especially those in the field of substance abuse. The research is now catching up with the profession's historical emphasis: "on the environmental interactions of individuals and their social systems" (Cocozzelli and Hudson, 1989, p. 46). The traditional linear approach of intake, treatment, and discharge will need to be expanded to take into account the broader treatment issues and the cyclical nature of treatment as noted previously.

Another implication for the practitioner in the 1990s is to help the MMAF develop strategies that will teach and enhance coping skills. With these strategies, individual and family skills are strengthened and become resources to deal with the negative effects of life stressors. Lack of attention to improving these skills can deter the family from establishing a new, more functional pattern that encourages both individual and system responsibility.

The social work practitioner may also find it necessary to advocate for the client in the workplace (at the school or office). This implication means that representing the client may improve the resources within those settings that will encourage client participation as well as abstinent behavior. Advocating may also prevent the workplace from becoming a punitive environment that increases the client's stress level.

CONCLUSION

The authors have presented an approach to working with the multiple-member addicted family. The approach addresses issues of skill in engaging reluctant, coerced family members as well as the values involved. Social workers are in a unique position to offer thorough biopsychosocial interventions. Such interventions focus the work on family system issues, individual needs, issues affecting the family from external pressures such as unemployment, and the role of alcohol in the family. Working with the MMAF builds upon the procedures developed for working with substance abusers in general. The added dimension of several members in the family having a substance abuse problem requires the social worker to be cognizant of the varying stages of recovery. The worker must also consider and address the possibility that multiple-member substance abuse will compound the denial and collusion within the family system. While such barriers to recovery must be recognized early in the process of treatment, the strengths that an MMAF system can bring to bear in achieving and maintaining recovery should also be acknowledged by practitioners. Strengths may range from caring relationships within the family to members' skills and talents to involved support networks. The practitioner demonstrates skill when using the family process to build on such strengths as part of the treatment process.

REFERENCES

Bandler, R., Gordon, D., & Lebeau, M. (1985). *Know how*. San Rafael, CA: Future Pace.

Berenson, D. (1976). Alcohol and family system. In P. J. Guerin (Ed.), *Family therapy: Theory and practice* (pp. 284–297). New York: Gardner Press.

Cocozzelli, C., & Hudson, C. (1989, December). Recent advances in alcoholism diagnosis and treatment assessment research: Implications for practice. *Social Service Review*, 533–549.

Coleman, S. B., & Davis, D. I. (1978). Family therapy and drug abuse: A national survey. *Family Process, 17*, 21–29.

Davis, D. I. (1987). *Alcoholism treatment: An integrative family and individual approach*. New York: Gardner Press.

Flanzer, J. P. (1980). *The many faces of family violence*. Springfield, IL: Thomas.

Flanzer, J. P., Sturkie, D. K., & Kinley, M. (1982). *Alcohol and adolescent abuse*. Holmes Beach, FL: Learning Press.

Haley, J. (1980). *Leaving home*. New York: McGraw-Hill.

Huba, G. J., Wingard, J. A., & Bentler, P. M. (1979). Beginning adolescent drug use and peer and adult interaction patterns. *Journal of Consulting and Clinical Psychology, 47*, 265–276.

Huba, G. J., Wingard, J. A., & Bentler, P. M. (1980). Framework for an interactive theory of drug use. In D. J. Lettieri, M. Sayers, & H. W. Pearson (Eds.), *Theories of drug abuse*. Washington, DC: National Institute on Drug Abuse, U. S. Government Printing Office.

Johnson, G. M., Shontz, F. C., & Locke, T. P. (1984). Relationships between adolescent drug use and parental drug behaviors. *Adolescence, 29*, 295–299.

Kaufman, E., & Kaufmann, P. (1979). *Family therapy of drug and alcohol abuse*. New York: Gardner Press.

Stanton, M. D., & Todd, T. C. (1982). *The family therapy of drug abuse and addiction*. New York: Guilford Press.

Steinglass, P. (1989). *The alcoholic family*. New York: Basic Books.

Treadway, D. C. (1989). *Before it's too late: Working with substance abuse in the family*. New York: Norton.

Usher, M. L., Jay, J., & Glass, D. R. (1982). Family therapy: A treatment modality for alcoholics. *Journal of Studies on Alcohol, 43*, 927–938).

SUPPLEMENTAL READING LIST

Greenleaf, J. (1983, May–June). Co-alcoholic . . . para-alcoholic . . . who's who . . . and what's the difference? *Alcoholism*, 24–25.

A useful discussion of alcoholic family systems in which distinctions are made in multiple-member abuse and co-dependency.

Lassey, M. L., & Carlson, J. E. (1980). Drinking among rural youth: The dynamics of parental and peer influence. *International Journal of the Addictions, 15*, 61–75.

In a high-risk adolescent population in rural areas, the authors of this article found that problem drinking in adolescents was strongly associated with their fathers' drinking.

McDermott, D. (1984). The relationship of parental drug use and parents' attitude concerning adolescent drug use to adolescent drug use. *Adolescence, 29,* 89–96. This article reports a study that confirms the role of parental attitudes (more so than behaviors) in influencing whether their children use alcohol, tobacco, or other drugs.

Smith, A. W. (1988). *Grandchildren of alcoholics, another generation of co-dependency.* Deerfield Beach, FL: Health Communications.

The focus of this book is on the multigenerational transmission process involving grandchildren of alcoholics, some of whom are co-dependent and others who are addicted *and* co-dependent.

CHAPTER 6

Dynamics of Alcoholism and Child Sexual Abuse: Implications for Interdisciplinary Practice

Joanne Pilat
American Telephone & Telegraph
Sara Boomhower-Kresser
Alcoholism-Drug Dependence Program of Lutheran Social Services of Illinois

Soft is the heart of a child

Film, Rogers Film Production

Alcoholism's serious impact on the total family system has been widely acknowledged by most practitioners. Typical estimates indicate that the behavior of each alcoholic affects the lives of four or five significant others. Many of these significant others are children (Reddy, 1977). Child sexual abuse, until recently, has been veiled in the same secrecy that permeates the alcoholic family system. Guilt, shame, and denial are characteristics of both problems. Where alcoholism and child sexual abuse coexist, resolution of one problem may be more difficult because of compounding factors related to the other problem. The emphasis within the family is to maintain its closed, secretive boundaries; this pattern can hinder family members from seeking help and block practitioners who attempt to provide treatment to the system.

Alcohol addiction is often overlooked in child sexual abuse situations for a variety of reasons. One factor is the lack of practical knowledge by social workers about alcohol abuse. This includes knowledge of assessment and treatment of alcoholics and their family members as well as awareness of the role that denial has in maintaining the drinking behaviors.

A second factor is the alcoholic family system's way of functioning as a closed, undifferentiated system (Bowen, 1974). Ideally, family members should experience a level of differentiation, a sense of self as different and separate from others. The opposite of this occurs in alcoholic and other dysfunctional families where members do not have a clear message about individuality. Their fusion is experienced as "feeling stuck together." This dynamic helps the family maintain its secret about child sexual abuse and deflects attention away from the existence of alcoholism in the family.

This lack of differentiation encourages the alcoholic family to remain closed and the alcoholic's drinking behaviors to become the focal point of the family's energy (Pilat, 1982). It is readily apparent that the alcohol eventually controls much of the family's internal functioning: its activities, relationships, emotions, and thoughts (Bosma, 1972).

Third, alcohol may affect the family's external functioning as well. The alcoholic and other family members may develop school, work, health, and social problems. Spouses may escape the family system through extramarital affairs, over-involvement in community projects, or as workaholics. Some children come to the attention of school and court social workers through behavorial and/or academic problems (Chafetz & Blane, 1971; Cork, 1969: Bosma, 1972: Clinebell, 1968). More often, they repress their feelings and attempt to control their inconsistent environment by becoming model students and good children (Black, 1979). These seemingly positive behaviors are survival techniques that also take a major toll on the child and may only surface as problems later in life (Pilat, 1981; Wegscheider, 1981; Whitfield, 1980; Woititz, 1983; Ackerman, 1978). They also make identification and assessment of the underlying problems difficult.

Intergenerational boundaries present a barrier to the identification of children in alcoholic families. Boundaries generally delineate the caretakers, those "in charge," from those who are dependent on them. Lines of authority separating the parent set from the sibling or child set in the alcoholic family system are loose and vague. Children, who should be able to depend on their parents, cannot always do so. Often the children cross these intergenerational boundary lines by becoming confidants and surrogate emotional and sexual (or pseudosexual) partners to their parents, to both the alcoholic and nonalcoholic spouse. This frequent occurrence can mask the parents' inability to function and can make the problem less easy to determine. It creates ambivalent feelings for the children that may surface in childhood or in later adult life. In one example:

> A 16-year-old girl was being seen by a school social worker for behavior problems. The girl's mother was an active alcoholic. Her father would pressure his daughter to go to the movies and to dinner with him. She was able to understand her father's wanting to talk with her, spend time with her, and even take her out for fun (and out of the chaotic household). But she also worried about being "out on a date" with her father and would rather have been out with her boyfriend. At the same time, she did not want to disappoint her father.

These loose intergenerational boundaries, the inconsistent and chaotic functioning, and the family's sense of being "out of control" around the drinking, as well as other behaviors, create an environment where child sexual abuse can easily occur and go undetected. The lack of communication, affection, and sexual relating in the marital dyad, plus decreased inhibitions and lowered impulse control because of the drinking, increase the circumstances and opportunity for child sexual abuse to occur in the family. When the secret of child sexual abuse is added to the secret of the closed alcoholic family system, there are special issues that need to be addressed.

The purpose of this chapter is to identify the incidence of families where alcoholism and child abuse coexist and to discuss the special dynamics that are involved. Treatment issues, especially assessment, interventions, and practice approaches, are described along with the identification of prevention opportunities and appropriate settings for those services. The chapter ends with a discussion of the implications for social work and interdisciplinary practice.

WHEN ALCOHOLISM AND CHILD SEXUAL ABUSE COEXIST

Incidence of the Dual Problem

It is difficult to assess the full extent of this dual problem. Much has been written, studied, and researched in the separate areas of child sexual abuse and alcoholism. One study notes that for every incest case reported, another 25 remain hidden. The Family Violence Research Program at the University of New Hampshire has reported that 19 percent of all American women and 9 percent of men were sexually abused as children (Geiser, 1979; Finkelhor, 1984).

Other researchers have found that more than one-half of the alcoholic parents in their studies had physically or sexually abused their children (Hindman, 1979; Virkkunen, 1974; Spieker, 1978). However, few studies have specifically focused on both of these issues. The literature indicates that authorities in the field often disagree on data that associate alcoholism with sexual abuse (Orme & Rimmer, 1981). Additionally, the shame and guilt that occur in both sexual abuse and alcoholism within families and within the general society, contribute to the lack of collection and reporting of accurate data. The Alcoholism-Drug-Dependency Center (ADD) is a state-funded alcohol and drug residential treatment program of Lutheran Social Services of Illinois. Data gathered there over a six-month period during 1988 indicated that 24 percent of 125 of their adult clients had been victims of child sexual abuse. Of that total (30) 70 percent were female and 30 percent were male. Data from the ADD Center also indicated that 75 percent of all clients treated there during that six-month period had been raised in alcoholic homes (ADD, 1988).

Practitioners in the addictions field also commonly find battering, sexual abuse, and alcoholism present in the same families. In a national study conducted over a period of four years with 409 subjects reared in alcoholic homes and 179 controls reared in normal homes, researchers found that the incidence of child sexual abuse in alcoholic families was twice that in normal homes (Brown, 1988).

Practitioners' anecdotal experiences with alcoholism and child sexual abuse indicate similar connections between the two problems. Many report that convicted incest offenders often indicate that excessive use of alcohol played a role in their incestuous activities. Regardless of what "excessive" means, this implies that alcohol could have altered sexual behavior controls, lowered learned incest inhibitions, and allowed a child in the family to be misperceived as a marital partner (Renshaw, 1982).

Consequences of This Dual Problem

Regardless of variations in the reported incidence of these two problems, there is more consensus on the consequences for victims and their families. Both sexually abusive and alcoholic families are viewed as dysfunctional systems, and both maintain a conspiracy of silence. This need for secrecy exacerbates the isolation, poor communication, and loss of trust of family members, including the inability to trust people outside the family. When the parent-child roles in the system become dysfunctional, the family disintegrates even further. Role confusion and family disruption then follow. As these roles change, members are encouraged to develop compulsive behaviors in an attempt to maintain control over their nonsupportive environments. Members will seek to protect the abuser and maintain the conspiracy of silence about the alcohol and sexual abuse. Both abuses show definite progression, with ever increasing loss of control over behaviors occurring as well as additional boundary infringements. As the abuses progress, more demands are placed on an already overburdened system (Brown, 1988).

Some sexual offenders are imprisoned for long periods while others receive short-term jail sentences; both patterns can often add to the stress being experienced by the family. For some, it may be a great relief to have the perpetrator removed from the home, even if only temporarily. The effects are deep and long-lasting. Family members frequently experience humiliation, shame, and pain that are buried under years of silence. Children of such families tend to repeat the dual cycle of abuse and alcoholism in their own families of procreation (Finkelhor, 1984).

The child victims experience the family trauma as well as individual trauma where sexual abuse and alcoholism coexist. The psychic pain may be so great that the individual "closes down" emotionally. A loss of childhood is a common consequence for many of these individuals: not only the loss of childhood's carefree quality but the loss of innocence as well. The victim's loss of trust in authority figures is one of the most devastating effects of child sexual abuse. Parents are the first adults children learn to trust, and sexual abuse represents the ultimate betrayal of that trust (Geiser, 1979).

These issues related to trust, responsibility, intimacy, and unmet needs for nurturance have long-term consequences for child abuse victims. They can later experience a variety of problems as they seek mature adult relationships. Many victims experience a high level of repressed rage. The anger is directed toward the perpetrator and toward the other parent. A similar dynamic occurs in the alcoholic family as the child often feels as much, and sometimes more, anger toward the nonalcoholic parent because that parent is seen as being ineffective in nurturing and protecting the child. The following case example illustrates this triangulation of feelings:

A 31-year-old recovering alcoholic woman with three years of sobriety was seen by a social worker around issues of self-esteem, child rearing, and depression. Her father was an alcoholic. When she was seven years old she was sexually abused by her male babysitter. She then told her mother, who became angry with her and told her not to tell the father. The mother was afraid the father would kill the baby sitter, leading to additional problems. The non-alcoholic mother had enough on her hands without having to worry about her husband's going to jail. This client was more angry with her mother than with her alcoholic father. At some level she knew her father was out of control and could not be counted on. What she was beginning to struggle with, for the first time, was her mother's inability to meet her emotional needs.

This sense of helplessness and lack of protection from parents sets the stage for being helpless and powerless as an adult (Woititz, 1983). As a consequence, the ability to trust or to make healthy partner choices for themselves is difficult. Some sexually abused individuals cope through alcoholism, abuse of other drugs, prostitution, mental illness, self-mutilation, or suicide. Runaway behavior of teenagers is often due to sexual abuse in the family. Some sexually abused individuals may cope differently than others and thus be affected differently, but all are impacted by the abuse and parental alcoholism. Consequently, the meaning that the particular child gives to these experiences is equally as important as the experiences themselves.

In addition to the consequences for families and child victims, child sexual abuse and alcoholism affect society. Nearly all societies prohibit adult-child sexual contact, but this prohibition is violated fairly often in America. There are two major factors that account for the frequency of this violation: (1) male domination (issues of power and control), and (2) social fragmentation coupled by the increasing isolation of individuals and families (Brown, 1988; Orme & Rimmer, 1981). As more social isolation occurs and less social supervision exists, forms of deviance and inappropriate use of control are likely to increase. At the same time, people may be deprived of socially sanctioned forms of support and intimacy. Understanding and treating child sexual abuse effectively is contingent upon the ability to impact society as a whole, not just the individuals, subgroups, and families that are directly involved (Finkelhor, 1979).

Such an approach recognizes all of the relevant variables and consequences; it is also consistent with an ecological perspective. Traditionally, society has viewed child sexual abuse and alcoholism as moral issues, with little thought given to the effects on the family and society. Families are now acknowledged, for the pain they have endured, and alcoholism is viewed as a treatable condition (*DSM 111-R*, 1987). The long-term effects on society are still an issue. As children in these families become adults, they will tend to repeat this dysfunctional cycle. Society loses through the costs of treatment and incarceration for family members and from their lost potential as emotionally intact and functional adults.

THE ADDICTION PROCESS AND CHILD SEXUAL ABUSE

Given the consequences of the dual problem of addiction and child sexual abuse, it is useful to clarify the *process* of addiction development and child sexual abuse in families. Children of alcoholics often become alcoholic or marry alcoholics; children in sexually abusing homes often become sexual abusers or will have children who become sexually abused. Those who have experienced the coexistence of these problems will unfortunately live out this combination as adults (Virkkunen, 1974). "The majority of sexual abusers are male (97–99 percent) and the majority of victims are female (92–95 percent). Sexual abuse usually begins with episodes of fondling when the victim is five to seven years old. The victims are usually the oldest female child in the family. Fondling continues and can progress to full intercourse when the victim is pubescent.'' (Mayer, 1985, p. 27).

The effects of sexual abuse seem to be less damaging if the abuse is short-term. The literature indicates that the relationship between the child and the perpetrator (the closer the relationship, the more damaging the experience can be) along with the meaning the child gives to the experience are the two most significant factors. These effects can be minimized if other significant adults are supportive to the victim and if counseling is made available (Finkelhor, 1979).

The Addiction and Sexual Abuse Cycle

Parenting is generally difficult for women who were sexually abused as children. Because their own needs were unmet during childhood, they may be unable to nurture their own children and may even feel jealous of the adult attention displayed toward the children. Many resort to chemicals to relieve stress and to enable them to cope with daily problems. A large percentage of alcohol-abusing women were sexually abused as children. ''Over 70% of female drug addicts and prostitutes have a history of sexual abuse'' (Mayer, 1983, p. 64). Due to their own unresolved trauma, some untreated sexual abuse victims may inadvertently repeat the cycle of sexual abuse by marrying someone who will sexually abuse their children (Mayer, 1983).

In these circumstances involving sexual abuse, alcohol is a contributing rather than causative factor (Mayer, 1985, p. 16). Alcohol decreases inhibitions, thus allowing the drinker to act on impulse. As the drinking and sexual abuse behaviors continue, the alcoholic abuser rationalizes the actions and becomes more isolated from family and friends. By this time, the drinking has increased and interferes with many functional areas of the life situation. Guilt and remorse about the sexual abuse become a part of the progression as unsuccessful attempts at restraint and control occur. Promises are made but not kept. False hopes are created, and the cycle repeats itself.

Child victims sense that all is not well but they trust their parents and other adults in the family. The perpetrator misuses this trust, hoping that the child will not disclose the abuse and often threatening the child with undesirable consequences if he or she does tell. Typically, girls do not tell anyone until they are 13 or 14 years old, if they reveal the secret at all. Many ADD Center (1988) clients have carried their secrets into adulthood. Only in the safety of the treatment environment are they finally able to disclose this painful material.

Victims of sexual abuse internalize guilt and blame themselves just as children in alcoholic family systems do. They believe that anything that happens to them must be the result of some problem that they have caused for someone else through their behavior, attitudes, or thoughts.

Common Issues of Alcoholism and Sexual Abuse

It is useful to analyze how this cycle of alcohol and sexual abuse develops out of the common dynamics of the two problems. Both the sexual abuser and the alcoholic tend to deny their behaviors. Both minimize the severity of their behaviors by blaming others, not taking responsibility for their actions, and exhibiting dysfunctional personality changes.

Children from these families learn not to trust their own judgment (Black, 1986). If they question the appropriateness of a parent's behavior, they are frequently told that they are wrong and they are not believed. For instance, if they tell one parent that the other is drunk, that parent usually contradicts them, saying the other parent is sick or depressed. If they tell one parent that the other has sexually abused them, they may be told the abuse did not happen. Therefore, the children learn not to trust their own invalidated perceptions. They are fearful of further abuse and the rejection likely from pointing out contradictions. They are unable to trust their feelings; yet they have much to feel (Black, 1981).

These children can experience a pervasive sense of separateness, being different and apart from others. As adults, they have no sense of who they are, often feeling empty. Their needs were so ignored as children that, as adults, they are unable to determine what their needs are or to feel they are worthwhile. They have difficulty achieving healthy and intimate relationships including sexual relationships (Woititz, 1983).

Vulnerable Individuals and Families

Incest is not linked to social class, to urban or rural populations, or to a particular racial group. Incest, as does alcoholism, occurs among all social classes, in cities and in the country, and among all religious and ethnic populations. Mayer (1985) has noted that authorities do not agree about the effects of social class on the incidence of alcoholism and child sexual abuse. Although available data do not indicate this, some authorities believe that incest may occur slightly more frequently among lower socioeconomic groups due to financial and social stresses and overcrowding. However, other experts believe that these figures merely indicate that incest tends to be disclosed more among these groups due to their involvement with social service agencies (Mayer, 1985).

Certain personality types appear to be high-risk for incestuous relationships. Abusers have been found to have low impulse control, low frustration tolerance, unmet dependency needs, low self-esteem, and a need for immediate gratification of their desires. These traits also apply to the majority of active alcoholics. In addition, sexual abusers frequently have alcohol problems, social isolation, a sense of inadequacy, hypersexuality, and a history of sexual abuse as children (Mayer, 1983; Finkelhor, 1984). Vulnerable children are those who have experienced an illness, handicap, learning disability, psychological problem, stigma, or anything else that may compromise their ability to ask for protection against sexual abuse (Finkelhor, 1979). Vulnerable mothers are those with any type of impairment that affects parenting abilities. Their limitations may reduce the supervision and support available for protecting a child against sexual abuse (Finkelhor, 1984). All of these social and situational factors contribute strongly to the heightened vulnerability of certain individuals to child sexual abuse and alcoholism.

Intergenerational Features

Both child sexual abuse and alcoholism tend to be inter- and intragenerational. A woman who has been molested as a child by her older brother may marry a man who, as a child, was molested by a relative. The husband may then sexually abuse his own children. Moreover, both may have learned that self-medication with alcohol makes it possible to go on living with an alcoholic relative. In such marriages neither partner is to blame but each has sought need-satisfaction in dysfunctional ways. In some situations, women who have experienced difficulties achieving mature emotional and genital satisfaction with an adult male may seek partners who also suffer from sexual dysfunctions. In other cases, men with unresolved needs for nurturance, resulting in unconscious anger, may displace their anger onto helpless victims while seeking affection from those daughters at the same time (Mayer, 1983).

In summary, the process of alcohol addiction and child sexual abuse develops similarly within the same families. "Their interrelated dysfunctions are exacerbated by the similarities of their dynamics: (1) sexual dysfunctions; (2) family-of-origin relationship problems, especially rejection by parents or disruption of parent-child bonding; (3) lowered coping skills, and (4) lowered self esteem" (Brown, 1988, p. 41). These dynamics have implications for the design of effective treatment strategies.

THE INITIAL TREATMENT PROCESS

Families, when alcoholism and child sexual abuse have occurred, usually do not voluntarily seek treatment on their own or acknowledge that they have a problem requiring professional help. Therefore, social workers need to be skilled in engaging resistive families. The discovery of child sexual abuse inevitably creates a crisis for victims and their families. It is important that the professional be aware of the psychological factors involved in the crisis. For instance, it is likely that many parents will feel hostility toward authorities, including the social worker or other helping professional.

It is also possible that the crisis provides the type of disequilibrium that renders the family more open to intervention than at other times when they are "successfully" keeping the system closed. Both criminal and civil statutes govern child sexual abuse. The criminal court has jurisdiction over the perpetrator and the civil system has jurisdiction over the child (Mayer, 1983). Federal and state laws govern the reporting of child sexual abuse. As laws are not the same in all states, social workers need to be aware of current laws governing reporting in their respective states. Most states mandate that professionals report cases of child sexual abuse within a specified period of time. This reporting process protects the child and facilitates the assessment as members adjust and react to the crisis.

Assessment

The clinician must look for common patterns during assessment of the perpetrator and family situation:

1. isolation;
2. historical determinants, (was the perpetrator a victim?);
3. level of harm to the victims;
4. role of confusion;
5. boundary confusion;
6. dysfunctions such as lowered or blocked affective expressions;
7. lowered coping skills;
8. confusion between assertiveness and aggression;
9. overconcern about controlling the interpersonal and family environment;
10. aggressive, hostile, or passive-aggressive attitudes toward women and/or children; and

11. poor impulse control or stress management. (Brown, 1988, p. 46)

Behavioral symptoms of children who have been sexually abused must be assessed similarly:

1. fears of the dark, of being alone, of strangers, and of new situations;
2. regressive behavior such as enuresis, encopresis, thumbsucking, especially of sudden or unexplained origin;
3. personality and behavior changes including depression, anger, withdrawal, school difficulties, secretiveness, chemical abuse (especially in young children), truancy, runaway behavior, seductive behavior, excessive masturbation, and a preoccupation with sex. (Mayer, 1983, p. 98)

A danger in assessment is the ease with which family and individual strengths can be overlooked by practitioners. The child's ability to tell someone about the abuse is a strength. Certainly, previous periods of abstinence by the alcoholic perpetrator are an asset. A mother's resistance to the perpetrator's requests to return to the home before it is safe for the child would be a strength as well as her willingness to get involved in Al-Anon meetings. Similarly, the existence of social supports, the ability to talk about and be introspective about the problem, and a weakening of the denial that alcoholism is a problem or that the sexual abuse occurred, are strengths upon which treatment can be built.

The initial assessment interview should be designed to collect data related to the patterns identified above. The goals of the interview should include the following areas:

1. To discover what has happened
2. To assess the coping style of the parents, and to ascertain the child's safety and the parents' ability to follow through with appropriate actions
3. To determine whether or not either parent has a drinking problem, given the high incidence of alcoholism and child sexual abuse together
4. To provide a sense of the clinician's willingness and ability to help the family to address the identified problems
5. To provide reassurance that change is possible

6. To decide what action needs to be taken (Finkelhor, 1979; Mayer, 1983)

Once the assessment is completed and the relevant issues have been identified, the treatment goal is to establish personal and interpersonal boundaries, impulse control and stress management, and the appropriate expression of both positive and negative feelings. If a drinking problem exists, a thorough drinking history needs to be an integral part of the assessment (see Chapter 2). If the social worker does not have the background to do an alcohol or drug assessment, then a referral should be made. A serious substance abuse problem must be addressed and would need to be a priority for treatment (Pilat & Jones, 1985).

Treatment Planning

To design effective treatment plans, practitioners must look for a pattern, not an isolated incident in both the sexual abuse and the alcoholism. The goal for the perpetrator and alcoholic is to recognize this pattern and its effects. Massive denial will be the main stumbling block.

Recommendations about the circumstances in which family separation should occur are being debated within the profession today. Incarceration or moving the perpetrator out of the home, and hospitalization or foster care for the victim, are some of the possibilities. Decisions need to be based on the solution or combination of solutions that will insure the best conditions for the child's safety and recovery. The child has been victimized during the sexual abuse and by alcoholic dysfunctioning. The treatment should not victimize the child again by overtly or covertly blaming him or her for the perpetrator's leaving the home (Finkelhor, 1979). The plan should include strategies for reassuring the victim about the family's commitment to protection from further victimization.

In order to make these complicated decisions, practitioners need to consider several areas. These areas include the severity and chronicity of the abuse, the age of the child and the child's ability to seek help if the abuse begins again, and the perpetrator's willingness to seek alcoholism treatment as well as treatment for the abuse. Other important areas to be considered are the willingness of the nonabusing parent to stop denying the abuse, to change his or her own behaviors, and to support and protect the child. The availability of support services and extended family support for the child and family, positive behavior change of the perpetrator, and willingness to engage in treatment with all family members should also be considered in whether family separation is indicated (Renshaw, 1982).

Rarely do active alcoholics and/or sexual abuse perpetrators voluntarily enter treatment. The perpetrator is usually pressured into treatment by the legal system. Before being accepted for services, the perpetrator needs to commit to certain requirements of the treatment plan (Mayer, 1983). He must agree not to re-molest the child, to refrain from chemical abuse, to attend appropriate self-help groups such as AA or NA, and to regularly attend all required treatment sessions.

Therapeutic needs vary according to the individual client's needs; thus, a variety of treatment modalities and techniques can be included in the plan. Some of the following may be necessary and/or useful: alcoholism treatment, behavioral management, boundary setting, anger work, self-esteem building, and didactic material regarding alcohol and sexuality. Alcohol education and assertiveness training may be included also.

Perpetrators and spouses who were sexually abused as children need a treatment plan that will help them work through their own blocked feelings of anger and helplessness. Gestalt therapy is often recommended to help them reexperience their own molestation and the feelings associated with their personal trauma (Woititz, 1983; Renshaw, 1982). This can help the perpetrator and spouse gain empathy for the victims. Work with offenders is difficult because it involves both therapeutic interventions and careful monitoring. A relapse of chemical use and/or another act of child sexual abuse should be reported immediately to the legal system. Thus, this stipulation should be included as one of the priority issues identified in the treatment plan (Mayer, 1983).

THE ONGOING TREATMENT PROCESS

Typically, experts in alcoholism treatment and those with expertise in child abuse treatment do not emphasize the biases of their respective approaches.

They frequently debate cause and effect. Those who view alcohol use as only the precipitant of the sexual abuse assume that alcohol treatment will automatically eliminate the sexual abuse. Others believe the perpetrator drinks in order to perform acts of sexual abuse, the implication being that the alcoholic intends the drinking and thus also intends the sexual abuse. A more valuable approach is not to fall into cause-and-effect thinking but to think systemically: to believe that the problems are caused by multiple interacting factors that cannot be analyzed linearly. Most effective would be for practitioners to have expertise in both areas. Interdisciplinary teams may be useful since members can have various areas of expertise related to the client system and its needs.

A systematic approach requires the perpetrator to stop the drinking while working on the sexual abuse issues. If the perpetrator is not drinking, it is easier to diagnose the severity of the sexual abuse dysfunction. It will be clearer how the sexual abuse fits into the overall functioning of the individual and what the client's impulse control is like without the lowered inhibitions of alcohol use (Berenson, 1976).

Treating only the sexual abuse when alcoholism coexists is a setup to never really obtaining a clear picture of "who" is under the mask of the drug. The alcoholism will continue to progress. Perhaps positive steps will be made in the sexual abuse treatment; however, alcohol relapse is likely. Similarly, a relapse to sexual abuse behaviors is likely when only the alcoholism is treated (Brown, 1988).

A systemic approach also recognizes that denial, guilt, shame, and unexpressed feelings of helplessness, anger, and sadness are major treatment issues of the entire family system (Bowen, 1974). The approach helps in viewing the family as a system while also acknowledging the special needs of individual family members. Treatment strategies, then, need to address both the needs of the system and the individual members.

Abused Children

Children in these families need special help for themselves. Education and support can be used to help them understand and emotionally deal with the fact that they are not responsible for the alcoholism or sexual abuse. Nothing they did, not their behavior, their grades in school, nor being a favorite child could cause the caretaker's drinking or the sexual abuse. The children must be helped to realize that they are the dependent ones and deserve to be protected.

Education about alcoholism and its effects on the family (including the linkage with sexual abuse), exploration of feelings in a safe environment, and development of coping skills are needed. These can be achieved through individual treatment, support groups such as Alateen, children's groups, and family therapy (Hughes, 1977). A combination of these strategies is usually most effective. There are some specialized approaches for dealing with the needs of children experiencing parental alcoholism and drug abuse, divorce, violence, and the death of a parent or sibling (Bonkowski, Boomhower, & Bequette, 1985; Pilat & Jones, 1985; Deutsch, 1982). Schools, mental health centers, pediatric and psychiatric hospital units, courts, alcoholism treatment programs, and protective service agencies are all possible sites for these specialized treatments.

Siblings

Treatment for sibling perpetrators must take into account the age of the siblings and whether or not they also have been sexually abused (Geiser, 1979). If they are minors, the legal issues pertaining to adult perpetrators will not be the same. However, in all cases, treatment should deal with many of the same issues as with the child victims mentioned earlier. These are: the sibling perpetrator's own unmet dependency needs, development of coping skills, anger resolution, sex education, and the issues of personal victimization, guilt, and shame.

Nonabused siblings also need help. They are frequently ignored in the treatment process while all the much-needed treatment is geared toward the victim or perpetrator of the abuse. These siblings feel guilt at not having been able to protect their siblings and shame that, because of their fear, they did not *try* to protect them (Mayer, 1985). Their shame can come from being relieved that the abuse did not happen to them, and often they feel anger toward both the abusing and the nonabusing parent. Nonabused siblings are sometimes disappointed at not receiving the attention, presents, and favors that the abused child received. As in many experiences of "survivor's guilt," the feelings mentioned earlier

may be repressed; only through treatment can they surface and be resolved (Mayer, 1985).

The Nonalcoholic Partner

The life of the nonalcoholic partner revolves around the alcoholic and the drinking (Pilat, 1980). Often the partners are themselves children of alcoholics and may have been sexually abused as children. A major treatment issue is the spouse's denial that her child has been sexually abused and also that she was sexually abused as a child. A lack of assertiveness and sense of self, feelings of helplessness, and the minimization of the problems make treatment difficult. The social worker must be gently confrontative, helping the client to face the secondary gains from denial that made it possible for her to survive in the past (Black, 1981).

The client can learn new coping strategies derived from a recognition of her own needs in order to "unhook" from the alcoholic and to protect the children. Al-Anon and other support groups can be excellent adjuncts to formal treatment in which members help each other to stop taking responsibility for their partner's behaviors. Role-playing, communication tasks, homework assignments, and family sculpting are intervention strategies for teaching clients about boundaries and protection (Root, 1964; Reddy, 1977; Steinglass, 1974; Wegscheider, 1981; McCabe, 1978).

The Perpetrator

The majority of perpetrators are males, although it should be acknowledged that females are also perpetrators. Treatment should consider the gender-related dynamics and the special needs of female versus male perpetrators. For instance, women have often experienced a larger number of episodes involving powerlessness and may have fewer alternatives for overt expressions of power due to a gender-biased socialization process. Getting in touch with the impact of that process on their identity and its relationship to the sexual offense can be an important part of treatment. Men, on the other hand, often need help in acknowledging that they have feelings of tenderness and that it is as acceptable to express those feelings appropriately as it is to express anger appropriately (Brown, 1988).

Treatment must involve assessment of the drinking problem and, if necessary, the need for sobriety. The perpetrator needs to remain sober in order to deal with the low self-esteem, isolation, difficulty with relationships, guilt, and impulse control that are part of the problem. Sometimes the abuse is first discovered in alcoholism treatment when family members begin to confront the effects of the drinking. Alcoholism counselors may not want to address this issue because they believe this can cause the newly recovering person additional guilt. *Not* addressing the issue is unethical and likely to lead to ongoing conflict, guilt, and a reason to return to drinking in the future. Insuring the safety of the child and reporting the sexual offense, according to the law and social work ethics, are necessary components of the treatment (Finkelhor, 1984). However, the timing of issues in the perpetrator's treatment is also important. Focus on the drinking problem at the beginning of the treatment, through education and problem-solving, is vital. Ignoring nonattendance at AA or NA, or denying that a return to drinking is significant will make it difficult for the worker to help the client honestly deal with the sexual abuse.

Now that the coexisting problem of child sexual abuse and alcoholism are being recognized more often, some progressive alcoholism programs have included a sexual abuse treatment component. Services are available for family members and the recovering alcoholic either in an outpatient or inpatient setting. Some alcoholism programs form working relationships with sexual abuse treatment programs in the community and then coordinate the separate services that are provided.

Family Treatment

Family therapy, whether in single family or multiple family groups, is especially valuable as a change-producing modality (Bowen, 1974; Pilat, 1980). The intergenerational boundary infringements, dysfunctional emotional cutoffs between family members, and role conflicts can be renegotiated in such sessions. All family members can practice new behaviors through role-playing and communication exercises within a safe environment. Parents are encouraged to rebuild the ''in charge'' position they abdicated in the past; parental decisions are made together, as are plans for how parents will implement their decisions on a consistent basis. Children can be children, perhaps for the first time. Family

members can begin to realize that even though the drinking and sexual abuse have stopped, there are still many problems to be addressed. For instance, members need to struggle with their new roles and the resentment that can develop from their new ways of interacting. Parentified children (those who have assumed parental roles) will not easily give up their hard-earned positions. Parents are sometimes overly authoritative in an attempt to reassume the position they know they had abandoned (Pilat & Jones, 1985). Everyone has to change, and the alteration requires an unmasking, to address the painful feelings that were formerly hidden by the alcoholism and sexual abuse.

Some practitioners believe this is the hardest part of recovery because the alcoholism and sexual abuse are no longer the focus of attention. Now all members are forced to look more closely at themselves and their roles in the system without blaming others. Social workers and others who are trained in understanding family dynamics and also skillful in family therapy are indispensable members of the treatment team during this phase (Pilat, 1980).

To summarize, treatment strategies need to be focused on individual members as well as the system. Often treatment is sequential, with various members being seen individually or in subgroups (the marital pair) first. Then group and family approaches may be appropriate after the initial treatment uncovers feelings and dysfunctional interactional patterns while enhancing the family's coping abilities (Pilat & Jones, 1985).

This treatment process is evident in the following case example:

An eight-year-old girl was brought to the emergency room of a suburban hospital complaining of stomach pains that the mother was calling an appendicitis attack. The child was placed in the pediatric unit for tests to determine the source of the pain. In the emergency room (ER), a hospital social worker asked the mother about family problems as well as about the child's history. The mother denied any family situations that could be contributing to her daughter's stomach problems. The ER medical team did not find any evidence of sexual abuse or other physical violence. The pediatric social worker continued to build on the relationship with the mother that the ER worker had begun. She helped the mother to talk about herself, the difficulty of taking care of her three children, and the fact that her husband's work hours made him unavailable to help her. After three days the tests failed to reveal physical reasons for the stomach pain, so the social worker became more confrontational in exploring information about the family system. The mother admitted that her husband had an untreated drinking problem. A play therapist and the social worker discovered that the father had been touching and fondling the child whenever he came home drunk at night. The mother agreed to participate in a Family Alcoholism Program at the hospital and to attend Al-Anon, while the daughter began child play therapy sessions. The mother, the victim, and the two older siblings met for weekly family therapy sessions. The father was eventually court-ordered to enter an alcoholism treatment program and was ordered to leave the home. He also agreed to follow through with a court-ordered support group for child sexual abusers. After six months, the entire family participated in family therapy sessions at the hospital, although the father did not return home permanently for another three months.

PREVENTION STRATEGIES

Opportunities for prevention exist wherever children and their families spend time. These natural and formal settings include schools, synagogues and churches, hospital pediatric units, day-care centers, outpatient family clinics, alcoholism treatment programs, and others. Education and discussions about sexual abuse and alcoholism can take the power of secrecy away. Families see that this is a problem area that others face, that attention is paid to this problem, and that help is available.

Primary Prevention

Teachers, nurses, and school social workers have a key role in addressing the potential for child sexual abuse at a primary prevention level. They need to be knowledgeable about the problem, its frequency, and its symptoms and dynamics. Educators can provide students with a forum for general discussions about values and goals, and about how to respect their bodies and protect themselves from physical and emotional harm. School prevention programs can more specifically provide information about

1. the fact that abuse can occur;

2. the fact that no one should touch a child's private parts;
3. the range of abusive acts that occur;
4. the need for "yell and tell" techniques;
5. the way to report any abuse; and
6. the fact that children are never at fault.

Some school programs that have attracted national attention include the theme "My body is my property" (Plummer, 1984). Any of these programs focused on children and families can develop screening instruments and curricula about alcoholism as well as child sexual abuse. The Children of Alcoholics Screening Test (C.A.S.T.) is one such instrument that is cost-effective, easily administered, and quickly able to indicate whether a child is living with parental alcoholism (Jones, 1981).

Other Levels of Prevention

When child abuse is suspected in school settings, prevention at a secondary or tertiary level is possible. Some important issues need to be considered in terms of case management strategies. It is especially important for the social worker to interview family members separately from one another and where privacy can be insured (Mayer, 1983). There are usually other children in the home and the worker needs to determine whether or not those children have been abused also. It is best to let the abused child know about the mandate to report the abuse so further trust will not be violated by the practitioner. Responses to questions about the perpetrator's identity and whereabouts, the actual abusive acts, and who the child has told and that person's reactions help to determine what steps need to be taken to prevent the abuse from occurring again. Those steps include placement of the child outside the home, incarceration of the perpetrator, and treatment.

Interdisciplinary Practice in Prevention

Primary school educators, workers in day-care centers, helping professionals who work with children of divorce, and hospital and school social workers know how to tailor programs to fit children's and family's needs. Experts in prevention should team with these professionals to better design programs that will address this area (Bonkowski et al., 1985). Because children of alcoholics and sexually abused children are at risk for repeating this cycle in their own adult lives, special attention must be paid to effective prevention programs that serve adult survivors of sexual abuse and alcoholism as well as the general population.

A well-coordinated, interdisciplinary team has three important components, including those for meeting the physical/medical, the psychosocial, and the legal aspects of the problem. All three aspects are of vital significance and, if neglected, may result in a less than adequate resolution for the child and other family members. The physical and medical aspects involve pediatric social workers, physicians, nurses, and emergency room personnel. The psychological aspect involves social workers, psychologists, psychiatric nurses, counselors, teachers, and school support personnel. The legal aspect involves law enforcement, the courts, court volunteers, and lawyers (Mayer, 1983; Renshaw, 1982). When alcoholism is involved in the family system, the alcoholism treatment network of addiction counselors, rehabilitation programs and self-help groups (e.g., AA and NA) are an additional component to the team approach (Brown, 1988).

If a child or the parents are interviewed by untrained workers who are not attuned to the family's emotional state and needs, neither victim nor parents will cooperate fully and vital legal information may not be gathered. On the other hand, the family that is approached by a qualified interdisciplinary team with sensitivity and patience will be more likely to assist in providing a complete medical history and to report full accurate information to legal authorities. Moreover, they will utilize the services of professional workers more effectively for the long-term follow-up process that is needed for the family and all its members (Mayer, 1985).

SOCIAL WORK IMPLICATIONS

As stated in a previous section, there is a need for practitioners to have expertise in the two problem areas and the knowledge and skills necessary to intervene at the appropriate level. Social work professionals can work more effectively in interdisciplinary teams. For instance, an alcoholism assessment expert might be called in to assist the sexual abuse counselor in determining whether alcoholism exists as a problem in the family. Or the

opposite could occur when the addiction specialist uses the expertise of the sexual abuse counselor to assess and/or intervene with the perpetrator.

Another implication is the danger of ignoring either problem. Because alcoholism is progressive and chronic in nature, allowing it to go untreated makes relapse highly possible. Children and other family members need protection, education, and treatment for themselves. Likewise, if only the alcoholism is treated and the sexual abuse is ignored, lasting progress in treatment will probably not be made. Further sexual abuse incidents are very likely in those situations. All aspects of the impaired system and both problems need attention (Brown, 1988).

Social workers have a systems orientation to intervention and thus can be especially effective in helping the family to handle its isolation and guilt about the problems. This implies that practitioners need an approach that is balanced between confronting denial and demonstrating a caring and nonjudgmental attitude. Moreover, because social workers are experts in identifying and using community agencies, they can be especially useful in modeling how to mobilize resources to assist the family and broaden its social network.

A final implication relates to practitioners and their own issues around alcoholism and child sexual abuse. As helpers and caretakers, many professionals will have countertransference issues regarding these problem areas. Some might have strong negative feelings about the problems and those affected by them; others may have their own unresolved issues around parental alcoholism and/or child sexual abuse. Their denial, enabling behaviors, and suppression of anger and pain can make them ineffective. It is recommended that practitioners work at resolving their own issues through self-help groups and treatment as needed (Pilat & Jones, 1984).

CONCLUSION

The dynamics of family systems in which alcoholism and child sexual abuse occur are similar. Secrecy and denial of the problems and their effects are common denominators. Guilt and shame keep families from asking for help. Practitioners need to develop expertise in the identification and treatment of alcoholism and child sexual abuse. Experts in these two fields can develop expertise by sharing information and working as interdisciplinary teams.

The secrecy surrounding family alcoholism has been explored over the past years, and as a consequence, treatment programs for alcoholics and family members have proliferated. However, the extent of child sexual abuse is only now being acknowledged and explored in society. Knowledge about the problem can be increased through methodologically sound research. The basis for such research can be accurate statistical information provided by community agencies and self-help groups such as Al-Anon, Alateen, Incest Survivors, and Adult Children of Alcoholics. Another value of these groups is their role as adjuncts to treatment and prevention services for which social workers and other professionals are responsible.

The cycle of child sexual abuse and alcoholism can be disrupted, but this outcome will take more consistent laws and additional education for professionals and the general public. An ecological approach will involve increased public awareness, community education, early identification, parenting programs, self-help groups, and improved intervention strategies (Mayer, 1983). These preventative and rehabilitative measures ultimately involve a coordinated and interdisciplinary effort by social workers, health care personnel, public school and day-care staffs, the legal system, and the police. More consistent legislation could take the form of mandated treatment for perpetrators and family members. Laws that will increase society's sensitivity by protecting the children and their need for safety are vital.

REFERENCES

Ackerman, R. (1978). *Children of alcoholics* (pp. 1–48). Holmes Beach, FL: Learning Publications.

Alcoholism-Drug Dependency Center (ADD) (1988). A residential treatment program licensed and funded by the Illinois Department of Alcohol and Substance Abuse.

Berenson, D. (1976). Alcohol and the family system. In C. Guerin (Ed.), *Family therapy* (chap. 15). New York: Gardner Press.

Black, C. (1979). Children of alcoholics, *Alcohol Health and Research World, 4,* 23–27.

Black, C. (1981). Innocent bystanders at risk: The children of alcoholics. *Alcoholism,* 22–26.

Black, C. (1986 February). Alcoholism and family violence, *Alcoholism and Addiction,* 46–47.

Bonkowski, S., Boomhower, S., & Bequette, S. (1985). What you don't know can hurt you: Unexpressed fears and feelings of children from divorcing families. *Journal of Divorce, 9,* 25–35.

Bosma, W. (1972). Alcoholism and the family: A hidden tragedy. *Maryland State Medical Journal, 21,* 34–36.

Bowen, M. (1974). A family systems approach to alcoholism. *Addictions, 21,* 3–4.

Brown, J. (1988, February/March). Common bonds of family tragedy: Alcoholism and child sexual abuse. *Focus,* 18–46.

Chafetz, R., & Blane, H. (1971). Children of alcoholics: Observations in a child guidance clinic. *Quarterly Journal of Studies on Alcohol, 32,* 687–698.

Clinebell, M. (1968). Pastoral counseling of the alcoholic and his family. *Alcoholism,* 189–207.

Cork, R. (1969). *The forgotten children: A study of children with alcoholic parents* (p. 59). Ontario: Addiction Research Foundation.

Deutsch, C. (1982). *Broken bottles, broken dreams: Understanding and helping the children of alcoholics* (pp. 96–106). New York: Columbia University, Teachers College Press.

Diagnostic and statistical manual of mental disorders (1987). *DSM 111-R* (3rd ed. rev.). (pp. 173–175). Washington, DC: American Psychiatric Association.

Finkelhor, D. (1979). *Sexually victimized children* (pp. 109–130). New York: Free Press.

Finkelhor, D. (1984). *Child sexual abuse—New theory and research.* New York: Free Press.

Geiser, R. L. (1979). *Hidden victims: The sexual abuse of children.* Boston: Beacon Press.

Hindman, M. (1979). Family violence: An overview. *Alcohol Health & Research World, 4,* 2–11.

Hughes, J. (1977). Adolescent children of alcoholic parents and the relationship of Alateen to these children. *Journal of Consulting and Clinical Psychology, 45,* 946–947.

Jones, J. (1981). *The children of alcoholics screening test (C.A.S.T.)* (pp. 1–10). Chicago, IL: Family Recovery Press.

Mayer, A. (1983). *Incest: A treatment manual for therapy with victim, spouses and offenders* (pp. 10–134). Holmes Beach, FL: Learning Publications.

Mayer, A. (1985). *Sexual abuse: Causes, consequences, and treatment of incestuous and pedophilic acts.* Holmes Beach, FL: Learning Publications.

McCabe, T. (1978). *Victims no more.* Center City, MN: Hazelden.

Orme, T., & Rimmer, J. (1981, March). Alcoholism and child abuse: A review. *Journal of Studies on Alcohol, 42,* 273.

Pilat, J. (1980). *Multiple family group therapy with*

alcoholic/chemically dependent family systems. Paper presented at 26th International Institute on the Presentation and Treatment of Alcoholism. Cardiff, Wales. 1–11.

Pilat, J. (1981). Children of alcoholics. *Proceedings, 27th International Institute on Prevention & Treatment of Alcoholism* (ICAA). Vienna, Austria, 486–495.

Pilat, J. (1982). Children of alcoholics: Identification in a classroom setting. *Proceedings, 28th International Institute on Prevention & Treatment of Alcoholism* (ICAA). Munich, Germany, 192–204.

Pilat, J., & Jones, J. (1984, Winter). Identification of children of alcoholics: Two empirical studies. *Alcohol Health & Research World,* 27–36.

Pilat, J., & Jones, J. (1985). A comprehensive treatment program for children of alcoholics. In E. M. Freeman (Ed.), *Social work practice with clients who have alcohol problems* (pp. 141–159). Springfield, IL: Thomas.

Plummer, C. (1984). *Preventing sexual abuse: Activities and strategies for working with children and adolescents.* Holmes Beach, FL: Learning Publication.

Reddy, B. (1977). *Alcoholism: A family illness* (pp. 1–3). Park Ridge, IL: Lutheran General Hospital.

Renshaw, D. (1982). *Incest: Understanding and treatment.* Boston: Little, Brown.

Root, L. (1964). Casework with alcoholics. *Selected Papers of the 27th International Institute on the Prevention and Treatment of Alcoholism,* Frankfurt, West Germany.

Spieker, G. (1978). Family violence and alcohol abuse. *Proceedings, 24th International Institute on the Prevention and Treatment of Alcoholism.* Zurich, Switzerland.

Steinglass, P. (1974). Comments on case presentation. *The Family: Center for Family Learning, 2,* 42.

Virkkunen, M. (1974). Incest offenses and alcoholism. *Medicine, Science & The Law, 14,* 124–128.

Wegscheider, S. (1981). *Another chance: Hope and health for the alcoholic family* (pp. 55–84). Palo Alto, CA: Science & Behavior Books.

Whitfield, C. (1980, June). Children of alcoholics: Treatment issues. *Maryland State Medical Journal,* 86–91.

Woititz, J. (1983). *Adult children of alcoholics.* Hollywood, FL: Communication, Inc.

SUPPLEMENTAL READING LIST

Butler, S. (1978). *Conspiracy of silence: The trauma of incest.* San Francisco: New Glide Publications.
This book covers the scope of the problem as well as psychodynamic and social forces. It emphasizes the trauma of incestuous abuse.

Conte, J., & Shore, D. A. (Eds.) (1982). *Social work and child sexual abuse.* New York: Hawthorne Books.
The discussion is well focused on the role of the social worker in addressing the problems of child sexual abuse.

Justice, B., & Justice, R. (1979). *The broken taboo: Sex in the family.* New York: Human Science Press.
The volume covers high-risk families, consequences of incest, and useful treatment strategies.

Kepler, V. (1984). *One in four: Handling child sexual abuse—What every professional should know.* Wooster, OH: Social Interest Press.
The authors deal with investigators and assessment of child sexual abuse, medical and legal management, preventions, and treatment. They include information on training and resources.

Kungman, Kristen, A. (1989). *Healing from childhood sexual abuse: A recovering woman's guide.* Center City, MN: Hazelden Foundation.
A pamphlet for women who were sexually abused as children. It is designed to help them understand the effects of the abuse as well as to offer treatment suggestions for the healing process.

PART II

Addictions to Other Drugs

Practitioners who work in the addictions field typically specialize in one area, leaving few opportunities to explore common aspects of addictions. However, a recent trend in the research literature has been to examine prevalence rates of different addictions in the same populations, of cross or sequential addictions, and the relative effectiveness of particular treatments on different addictions. Part II of this book was designed to allow comparisons of the addiction process for the various drugs discussed in the five practice chapters. Comparisons can be made with other types of addictions in Parts I, III, and IV of the book.

Chapter 7 presents a review of the research literature on community-based drug treatment programs. The chapter summarizes the pertinent findings along with methodological problems in the quality of the research. Barriers to treatment are identified in terms of the special needs of women, particularly those with children, racial minorities, and other diverse groups. Diversity is the focus in Chapter 8 also: individuals who are high-risk casual or recreational drug users. This includes the elderly in their use or abuse of over-the-counter drugs. Theories on the etiology of drug use are related to prevention strategies that are used in a community-based program example. At the other end of the involvement continuum described in Chapter 1 are addicted mothers and their children, the subject of Chapter 9. Medical, legal, social, and emotional consequences are identified, as is the relationship of these consequences to policy initiatives. A model of treatment is presented featuring an integrated informal and formal support network within the context of community change.

Chapters 10 and 11 identify high-risk drug-using populations and the connection between drugs and increased risk behaviors in other areas. These include intravenous drug users and the risks of contracting sexually transmitted diseases including AIDS; and crack cocaine addicts and the pressures of supporting their habits through crimes. Community approaches are heavily emphasized, especially in Chapter 10, on IV drug use and AIDS, in which geographic and racial prevalence data help to identify high priority communities.

CHAPTER 7

Evaluation of Community-based Drug Abuse Treatment Programs: A Review of the Research Literature

William E. Berg
University of Wisconsin-Milwaukee

Improvement counts, no matter how small.

Anonymous

Research on the effectiveness of community-based drug treatment programs tends, as in the case perhaps in all evaluative research, to vary rather widely in the quality of its designs and methodologies. This can be attributed, in part, to the fact that drug abuse is a peculiarly complex problem for both the individual abuser and society as a whole. The recognition of this complexity has led, in turn, to the emergence of a diverse range of programs and modalities, each of which is based upon different models of treatment and each of which includes a broad range of interventions. The existence of multiple programs and multiple treatments represents a problem that, as we shall see, is difficult to overcome.

Although this chapter is concerned with community-based programs and interventions, the relevance and the implications of this research can be assessed only within a comparative framework. Thus rather than limiting the review to community-based programs, the chapter includes research on residential programs as a basis of comparison. In both instances, the research is assessed in terms of what it reveals about the relative success or failure of the programs, about those factors or variables that contribute to success or failure, and in terms of the relative quality of designs and methodologies employed in these studies. The chapter also includes, in addition, a review of the literature on the role of social work and social workers in relationship to these programs and interventions.

STUDIES ON THE EFFECTIVENESS OF DRUG TREATMENT PROGRAMS

The literature on drug treatment programs tends to distinguish between four relatively distinct types of services: residential programs (including therapeutic communities), methadone maintenance, outpatient drug-free programs, and outpatient detoxification (Cole & James, 1975; Craig & Baker, 1984; Lowinson & Ruiz, 1981; Sells & Simpson, 1976; Sobell, Sobell, & Ward, 1980). It also distinguishes between various interventions used within these service arrangements, including vocational rehabilitation, case management, psychotherapy, group therapy, behavior modification, and family therapy.

While these programs and interventions differ from one another, they all share certain commonalities that, in varying degrees, are shared by the broader field of addictions counseling in general (Miller, 1986). These commonalities include an understanding of the addictive process, of the role that treatment plays within this process, and in most cases of the goal of abstinence. They also include certain common designs and methodologies for evaluating the effectiveness of both the programs and the treatments (Maisto & Cooper, 1980).

Studies of drug treatments typically assume one of two forms; that is, they either involve specialized studies of individual programs, or they consist of large-scale outcome evaluations of federally funded programs. There are, as one might expect, differences in the relative quality and in the findings of these studies. Perhaps the least informative studies are case studies of therapeutic communities (Sugarman, 1983; Yablonsky, 1989), while the most useful are large-scale longitudinal studies that provide comparisons across different drug treatments.

Comparison Studies: Residential and Community-based Programs

Two major longitudinal studies on program effectiveness are the Drug Abuse Reporting Program (DARP) and the Treatment Outcome Prospective Study (TOPS). Both studies are based upon relatively large samples (that is, the DARP study's original sample was 4,000), and both attempt to identify the variables that account for observed differences in effectiveness (Hubbard, Rachal, Craddock, & Cavanaugh, 1984; Simpson, 1984; Simpson, Savage, Lloyd, & Sells, 1978). The DARP study was conducted during the 1960s and 1970s, while the TOPS study was initiated in the late 1970s and replicated the designs and methodologies used in the earlier study.

The result of these studies reveal comparable rates of success among both community-based and residential programs. In the DARP study, for example, the proportions of ''highly favorable outcomes'' vary from 24 percent to 28 percent among the methadone maintenance, residential, and outpatient drug-free programs, as compared to 15 percent and 14 percent, respectively, among the detoxification and control samples (Simpson, 1984, p. 32). Similarly, the results for ''moderately favorable out-comes'' vary from 33 percent to 41 percent among the former groups, versus 25 percent and 27 percent among the latter.

These studies also agree, moreover, that the course of treatment is conditional upon a number of factors. Both studies report, for example, a high incidence of psychiatric diagnoses among the samples (Hubbard et al., 1984, p. 56), a finding that is consistent with other studies of substance abuse populations (O'Brien, Wood, & McLellan, 1984; Rounsaville, Tierney, Crits-Cristoph, Weissman, & Kleber, 1982; Wurmser, 1979). They also observe a tendency toward concurrent or multiple drug abuse among the study samples. In the TOPS study, for example, approximately 33 percent of the sample were defined as heavy drinkers during the post-treatment period (Hubbard et al., 1984), a finding that is confirmed by other studies (Sadava, 1984; Wilkinson & LeBreton, 1986). Finally, and perhaps most importantly, both studies observe a strong correlation between the length of stay in treatment (i.e., treatment tenure) and the effectiveness of the program. Thus in the DARP study patients who were enrolled in either community-based or residential programs for fewer than 90 days had recovery rates that were comparable to those found in the detoxification and control groups (Simpson, 1981, 1984).

While these studies suggest that there are only marginal differences in the effectiveness of community-based versus residential programs, these findings need to be interpreted within the limitations of the studies themselves. These limitations include outcome measures that are poorly defined and that provide insensitive scales, baseline and outcome measures that raise questions of reliability and validity, and relatively high attrition rates among post-treatment samples. Although some of these concerns are examined in greater detail in the following sections of this chapter, in terms of attrition rates alone it should be noted that the DARP study reports an attrition rate of 23 percent during the initial posttest period (Simpson et al ., 1978). While some of these 23 percent had died during the period in question (6 percent), it is unclear how the results of the study would have been affected were data available on the 17 percent of the sample who were not located.

In addition to these methodological limitations, both studies lack controls over other variables that may affect the results. For example, the DARP study does not control for any unrelated posttreatment therapies that may have been received by the subjects or for the role that the family or other social groups may have played in determining the course of posttreatment adjustment. Thus, while both studies indicate that each of the major treatments is effective and that effectiveness is related to the length of time in treatment, the psychiatric condition of the client, and the tendency toward concurrent drug use, neither can specify why some patients succeed while others do not (Simpson & Sells, 1983).

Methadone Maintenance Programs

In addition to these two major studies, a number of smaller studies have been conducted on the effectiveness of selected programs. Most of these studies have dealt either with methadone maintenance or with therapeutic community programs. This can be attributed to the fact that these service arrangements have been in existence for relatively long periods of time (i.e., from the late 1950s and early 1960s), and both represent radical departures from an earlier and more punitive approach to drug abuse (Lowinson & Ruiz, 1981).

Methadone maintenance programs are based on the assumption that recovery may be facilitated by substituting a controllable drug (methadone) for an uncontrollable one (heroin or other narcotics) (Dole & Nyswander, 1976; Lowinson & Ruiz, 1981). These programs also specify that the process of recovery must be accompanied by an individualized, planned treatment protocol that incorporates withdrawal, individual counseling, and job training (Dole & Nyswander, 1966a, 1966b).

While the initial studies on the effectiveness of maintenance programs provide support for the approach (Dole, 1972; Martin, Jasinsky, Haertzen, Jones, Kay, Mansky, & Carpenter, 1975; Newman, 1977), later studies raise questions both about their effectiveness and about the conditions or circumstances involved in their implementation. Thus a five-year follow-up program of graduates of a New York program found that positive changes had occurred in only 23 percent of those clients who had remained in the program for more than three years (Kleinman, Lukoff, & Kail, 1977). Studies have also found that maintenance programs have only marginal effects on the level of posttreatment drug use and criminal activities and that clients report an increased level of alcohol use (McGlothlin & Anglin, 1981). Other studies report that nearly one-half of patients who completed a methadone maintenance program were arrested during the year following withdrawal from the program and that only 6 percent of the clients had remained abstinent during this period (Maddux, Desmond, & Esquival, 1980).

These findings are influenced by the fact that, while the original Dole-Nyswander protocols (1966a, 1966b) emphasized the role that counseling and job training play in the rehabilitation process, many of the later maintenance programs have not included these services (Bowden & Maddux, 1972; Desmond & Maddux, 1975). This change has occurred, moreover, in spite of evidence suggesting that these services are highly correlated with treatment effectiveness and that they contribute to stable posttreatment job patterns (Hall, Loeb, & Yang, 1977).

Therapeutic Communities

Similarly, studies on the effectiveness of therapeutic communities vary in their designs, methodologies, and conclusions. These differences may be attributed, in part, to the fact that many therapeutic communities are the products of charismatic movements (Yablonsky, 1989) and, as such, tend to be assessed in descriptive rather than analytical terms (Casriel, 1963; Sugarman, 1983). These variations also reflect the goals of the therapeutic community; they, unlike other types of programs, seek to achieve not only a reduction in drug use, but a "global change in lifestyle reflecting abstinence from illicit substances, elimination of antisocial activities, increased employability, and pro-social attitudes and values" (DeLeon, 1984, p. 69).

Most empirical studies of therapeutic communities have found decreased levels of drug use and criminal activities and increased levels of education and employment training (Aron & Dailey, 1976; Barr & Antes, 1981; DeLeon, 1984). These results have been found, moreover, in spite of the fact that clients who enter therapeutic communities tend to display rather high levels of psychopathology (DeLeon, Skodol, & Rosenthal, 1975) and equally high rates of criminal behaviors (DeLeon, Wexler, Schwartz, & Jainchill, 1982).

Although these results are positive, they need to be assessed within the context of other characteristics of the therapeutic community, particularly the retention rates in treatment. The single most important predictor of success within the therapeutic community is, as with methadone maintenance programs, the length of stay in treatment (DeLeon, 1984, p. 73). Residents who spend fewer than 50 days in treatment tend to display levels of posttreatment functioning comparable to no-treatment control groups (Bale, Van Stone, Kuldau, Engelsing, Elashoff, & Zarcone, 1980). Existing research indicates, however, that the retention rates among therapeutic communities varies between 9 percent and 12 percent (Brooke & Whitehead, 1980; DeLeon & Schwartz, 1984; Sansome, 1984). Thus much of the success observed in studies of therapeutic communities may be attributed to the fact that these studies have, for the most part, involved self-selected samples of clients who remained in treatment for relatively long periods of time. Outpatient programs present a more complex array of variables that impact recidivision rates and study methodologies.

Outpatient Programs: The Special Case of Cocaine Abuse

Much of the existing research on effectiveness of drug treatments has involved programs developed to deal with heroin and other narcotic abuse. The increased rate of cocaine and other stimulant abuse during the previous decade has raised questions concerning the relevance of these programs in the treatment of stimulant abuse (Colliver, 1987).

Current methods of treating cocaine abuse have been based, in most instances, on the assumption that "the basic treatment principles for addiction are consistent, regardless of whether the drug is alcohol, heroin, or cocaine" (Zweben, 1986, p. 245). Most cocaine abuse programs have, as a result, applied the treatments previously used in the treatment of alcohol and heroin abuse without any major changes or adjustments (Gawin & Ellinwood, 1988). This has continued in spite of evidence indicating that the incidence of posttreatment abuse increases dramatically among samples of cocaine users treated through heroin abuse programs and that this incidence exceeds the incidence found among comparable control groups (Kosten, Rounsaville, & Kleber, 1987).

The fact that until very recently there have been relatively few programs developed to deal specifi-

cally with cocaine abuse makes it difficult to draw any conclusions about the long-term effectiveness of existing programs. Those studies that do exist indicate that even in the short term the treatment of cocaine abuse is problematic. Studies have shown, for example, that only 33 percent of cocaine abusers in outpatient programs are able to remain drug-free while still enrolled in the program (Anker & Crowley, 1982; Gawin & Kleber, 1984).

One of the reasons for these findings is that, unlike heroin and other narcotics, cocaine tends to produce few if any dangerous withdrawal symptoms. Most cocaine abuse programs are based, therefore, upon outpatient rather than hospital-based treatment (Kleber, 1988; Rawson, Obert, McCann, & Mann, 1986). Although this has certain advantages for both the programs and the clients, it means that the abuser is constantly subjected to an environment that supports and, in many instances, encourages drug use (Marlatt & Gordon, 1980). In addition, since cocaine abuse is frequently associated with multiple or polydrug use (for example, cocaine combined with amphetamines, barbiturates, or alcohol), the problems of treatment are often more complex than those found with narcotics or alcohol (Mider & Lewis, 1984).

A common treatment approach with cocaine abuse involves the use of pharmacological agents that, like methadone, are designed to substitute a reliance upon nonaddictive drugs such as desipramine and other antidepressants for cocaine dependence (Gawin & Kleber, 1984; Khantzian, Gawin, Kleber, & Riordan, 1984; O'Brien, Woody, & McLellan, 1984). In most instances, these programs follow the Dole-Nyswander protocol (1966a, 1966b) and include not only job training, but a variety of behavior modification and other conditioning treatments (Dews, 1984; O'Brien et al., 1988).

STUDIES ON THE EFFECTIVENESS OF COMMUNITY-BASED INTERVENTIONS

Similar to traditional outpatient programs described in the previous section, the treatment process in community-based programs also includes a relatively diverse range of interventions. Depending upon the underlying treatment philosophy of the program, these may include psychoanalytic psychotherapy, group therapy, behavior modification, vocational rehabilitation, community outreach, individual counseling, and family therapy. The problems involved in assessing the effectiveness of any single intervention are complicated by the fact that most community-based programs utilize multi-method or concurrent interventions (Craig, 1987). These interventions include behavioral techniques, traditional psychotherapies, family therapy, and job training and vocational rehabilitation.

Behavioral Techniques

Community-based programs, by their very nature, seek to address the role that the environment plays in initiating and maintaining patterns of substance abuse behavior (Grabowski & Cherek, 1983; Wikler, 1965). For community-based programs, this means intervening in environments that are characterized by the availability of illicit substances, by peer groups that support and encourage drug use, and by family relationships that may affect whether recovery can be maintained (Robins, Davis, & Gordon, 1974; Thompson & Ostlund, 1965).

Another strategy has involved helping clients to develop patterns of behavior that condition them to exist within their environments without returning to drug use. Many programs have, as a result, relied upon various forms of behavior modification, including contingency contracting, token economies, and contingency management. These interventions have also been incorporated into many methadone maintenance programs, where they provide individualized treatment for clients who typically display widely varying performance levels and therapeutic needs (Bigelow, Stitzer, Lawrence, Krasnegor, D'Lugoff, & Hawthorne, 1980; O'Brien et al., 1988; Stitzer, Bigelow, Lawrence, Cohen, D'Lugoff, & Hawthorne, 1977; Yen, 1974).

Early studies on he effectiveness of these techniques provided favorable results, particularly in relationship to retention rates (Callahan, Rawson, Glazer, McCleaver, & Arias, 1976; Callahan and Rawson, 1980; Cheek, 1976; Cheek, Holstein, Fullam, Aranas, Tomarchio, & Mandell, 1976). However, since many of these studies included small samples with only limited outcome measures, recent studies have sought to address some of these meth-odological problems. Although these studies have produced similar results, they are also often characterized by design problems that raise issues of internal and external validity.

Traditional Psychotherapies

The fact that the levels of psychopathology tend to be relatively high among different populations of drug abusers (Khantzian et al., 1984; Simpson, 1984) has led many community-based programs to incorporate traditional psychotherapies such as psychoanalytic, client-centered, and reality therapy within their treatments. While the causes of these psychopathologies are not apparent, some observers have suggested that drug abuse may be viewed as an attempt at self-medication, that is, as a means for the addict to deal with problems of depression, anxiety, and other related psychiatric symptoms (Wurmser, 1979).

Studies on the effectiveness of psychotherapy with substance abusers have, in general, found that the results are comparable to those found among other, nonaddicted clients (Andrews & Harvey, 1981; Luborsky, Singer, & Luborsky, 1975). Substantial rates of improvement on a variety of post-treatment measures including self-awareness and improved relationships have been found among clients involved in individual therapies (Connett, 1980; Rounsaville, et al., 1982; Woody, Luborsky, McLellan, O'Brien, & Beck, 1983). Similar results have been obtained, moreover, among samples of clients exposed to group psychotherapies (Abrahms, 1979; LaRosa, Lipsius, & LaRosa, 1974; Willett, 1973).

Family Therapy

The role that families and family systems play in relationship to drug abuse has received considerable attention in the literature (Harin & Mazair, 1975; Kaufman, 1987; Seldin, 1972). Studies suggest that the families of drug abusers are often characterized by absent or ineffectual fathers (Fort, 1954; Ziegler-Driscoll, 1979), by mothers who are overly dependent upon the child (that particular child becomes a substance abuser) (Kaufman & Kaufman, 1979), and by frequent reversals in the roles played by that child and the parents (Madanes, Dukes, & Harbin, 1980). Many community-based programs have, as a result, utilized family therapy along with other intervention techniques. While these findings should not be viewed as documenting a causal relationship between family dynamics and substance abuse, they do indicate that family relationships are one of several complex variables that affect treatment outcomes.

Research has found that family therapy generally produces higher success rates than other interventions, particularly when it is used in conjunction with job training and individual and group counseling (Silver, Panepinto, Arnon, & Swaine, 1975). Some studies have found few if any effects from family treatment (Winer, Lorio, & Scrofford, 1974; Ziegler-Driscoll, 1979).

Job Training/Vocational Rehabilitation

Drug abusers tend to also experience substantial problems in work and work-related areas (Nurco, Cisin, & Balter, 1981a, 1981b), and problems that are often associated with criminal activity as an alternative to employment (DeLeon et al., 1975; Inciardi, 1981; James, Gosho, & Wohl, 1979; Johnson & Smeidler, 1981). Most community-based programs have included, therefore, job training and vocational rehabilitation services (Brill, 1977; Caplovitz, 1978; Dole & Wolkstein, 1974, Serban, 1978). Apart from a few case studies (Black, Kase, & Benney, 1980), however, there have been relatively few empirical studies on the effectiveness of these services. While those studies that do exist reveal high correlations between vocational rehabilitation services and posttreatment employment (Dickenson & Maynard, 1981; Friedman, 1978), these results are complicated by the existence of multiple treatment effects and by the fact that in most instances these services have not been systematically integrated within existing programs. Another variable in examining the outcomes of community-based treatment programs is the need to focus on how they address the unique needs of special population groups.

DRUG TREATMENT WITH SPECIAL POPULATIONS

There is a considerable body of literature indicating that the addiction processes of women and of minorities differ from those of white males (Crowther,

1972; Hser, Anglin, & Booth, 1987; Iiyama, Nishi, & Johnson, 1976; Nurco, Ball, & Shaffer, 1986; Tyler & Thompson, 1980). In spite of this considerable evidence, however, there have been few attempts to incorporate these findings into existing treatment programs. As a result, women, minorities, and the elderly are subjected to programs that were developed to focus on the problems of white male addicts (Mondanaro, 1989).

Women Substance Abusers

The major problems that confront women in drug treatment include the need for adequate child care (Rosenbaum, 1979; Mondanaro, 1989), a lack of sufficient economic resources (Reed & Leibson, 1981), the effects of prior criminal activities (Moise, Kovach, Reed, & Bellows, 1982), and pregnancy (Fitzsimmons, Tunis, Webster, Izes, Wapner, & Finnegan, 1986). Some recent programs have been effective in addressing these problems by incorporating the relevant services, but additional research is needed to further document the outcomes of those efforts (Moise et al., 1982; Kerson, 1988).

While most studies that compare men and women in treatment have found few if any differences in either the length of treatment or posttreatment abstinence rates (DeLeon & Jainchill, 1986), other studies indicate that women are less likely to remain in therapeutic communities (Sansome, 1984), less likely to be actively involved in methadone maintenance treatments, and more likely to engage in posttreatment drug abuse (Hser, Anglin, & Chou, 1988). These findings may be influenced by the fact that women in treatment are more likely to include different age cohorts than men, and by the interactions between gender and other characteristics, particularly race (Anglin, Hser, & Booth, 1987; Hser, Anglin, & Chou, 1988; Iiyama, Nishi, & Johnson, 1976). The findings are also influenced by the presence or absence of services related to the special needs of women clients such as child care and employment training. As noted previously, programs that include these services have been more successful than those that fail to meet these needs (Fitzsimmons et al., 1986; Kerson, 1988; Marsh & Simpson, 1986; Reed & Leibson, 1981). Minority group clients are confronted with a similar culturally irrelevant array of services in treatment programs.

Aron, W. S., & Dailey, D. W. (1976). Graduates and splittees for therapeutic community drug treatment programs: A comparison. *International Journal of the Addictions, 11,* 1–18.

Atkinson, R., & Kofoed, L. L. (1984). Substance abuse in old age. *Substance Abuse, 5,* 30–42.

Bale, R. N., Van Stone, W. W., Kuldau, J. M., Engelsing, T. M., Elashoff, R. M., & Zarcone, V. P. (1980). Therapeutic communities vs. methadone maintenance: A prospective controlled study of narcotic addiction treatment. *Archives of General Psychiatry, 37,* 179–193.

Barr, H., & Antes, D. (1981). *Factors related to recovery and relapse in follow-up.* NIDA Research Monograph.

Bigelow, G., Stitzer, M., Lawrence, C., Krasnegor, N., D'Lugoff, B., & Hawthorne, J. (1980). Narcotics addiction treatment: Behavioral methods concurrent with methadone maintenance. *International Journal of the Addictions, 15,* 427–437.

Black, B., Kase, H., & Benney, C. (1980). Vocational rehabilitation. In J. Lowinson and P. Ruiz (Eds.), *Substance abuse: Clinical problems and perspectives.* Baltimore, MD: Williams and Wilkins.

Bowden, C. L., & Maddox, J. (1972). Methadone maintenance: Myth and reality. *American Journal of Psychiatry, 128,* 853–856.

Brill, L. (1977). Historical evolution of the current drug treatment perspective. In A. Schecter (Ed.), *Rehabilitation aspects of drug dependence.* Cleveland, OH: CRC Press.

Brooke, R., & Whitehead, I. (1980). *Drug-free therapeutic community.* New York: Human Sciences Press.

Callahan, E., & Rawson, R. (1980). A behavioral assessment of narcotic addiction and treatment outcome. In L. Sobell and M. Sobell (Eds.), *Treatment outcome evaluation in alcohol and drug abuse.* New York: Plenum.

Callahan, E., Rawson, R., Glazer, M., McCleaver, B., & Arias, R. (1976). Comparison of two naltrexone treatment programs. In D. Julius and P. Renault (Eds.), *Narcotic antagonists.* NIDA Research Monograph.

Callner, D. (1975). Behavioral treatment approaches to drug abuse: A critical review of the research. *Psychological Bulletin, 82,* 143–164.

Campbell, D., & Stanley, J. (1966). *Experimental and quasi-experimental design for research.* Chicago: Rand McNally.

Caplovitz, D. (1978). *The working addict.* White Plains, NY: Sharpe.

Casriel, D. (1963). *So fair a house.* Englewood Cliffs, NJ: Prentice Hall.

Cheek, F. (1976). Behavior modification for addicts on methadone maintenance. *Current Psychiatry, 16,* 223–236.

Cheek, F., Holstein, C., Fullam, F., Aranas, G.,

Tomarchio, T., & Mandell, S. (1976). From heroin to methadone: Social role changes and reinforcement differentials in relation to outcome on methadone. *International Journal of the Addictions, 11,* 659–694.

Cole, S., & James, L. (1975). A revised typology based on DARP. *American Journal of Drug and Alcohol Abuse, 2,* 37–49.

Colliver, J. (1987). *A decade of dawn: Cocaine related cases, 1975–1985.* NIDA, Division of Epidemiological and Statistical Publication.

Connett, G. (1980). A comparison of progress of patients with professional and paraprofessional counselors in methadone maintenance. *International Journal of the Addictions, 15,* 585–589.

Craig, R. (1987). *Clinical management of substance abuse programs.* Springfield, Il: Thomas.

Craig, R., & Baker, S. (Eds.). (1984). *Drug dependent patients: Treatment and research.* Springfield, Il: Thomas.

Crowther, B. (1972). Patterns of drug abuse among Mexican-Americans. *International Journal of the Addictions, 7,* 633–647.

DeLeon, G. (1984). Program-based evaluation research in therapeutic communities. In F. Tims and J. Ludford (Eds.), *Drug abuse treatment evaluation.* NIDA Research Monograph 51.

DeLeon, G., & Jainchill, M. (1986). Circumstance, motivation, readiness, and suitability as correlates of treatment tenure. *Journal of Psychoactive Drugs, 18,* 203–208.

DeLeon, G., & Schwartz, S. (1984). The therapeutic community: What are the retention rates? *American Journal of Drug and Alcohol Abuse, 10,* 16–28.

DeLeon, G., Skokol, A., & Rosenthal, M. (1975). The Phoenix therapeutic community for drug addicts: Changes in psychopathological signs. *Archives of General Psychiatry, 23,* 131–135.

DeLeon, G., Wexler, H., Schwartz, S., & Jainchill, M. (1982). The therapeutic community: Success and improvement rates five years after treatment. *International Journal of the Addictions, 17,* 703–747.

Desmond, D., & Maddux, J. (1975). Reliability and validity of information from chronic heroin users. *Journal of Psychiatric Research, 12,* 95–97.

Dews, P. (1984). Maintenance of behavior by "schedules." In P. Levison (Ed.), *Substance abuse, habitual behavior, and self-control,* Boulder, CO: Westview.

Dickenson, K., & Maynard, R. (1981). *The impact of supported work on exaddicts.* New York: Manpower Research Corporation.

Dole, V. P. (1972). Pharmacological treatment of drug addiction. *Modern medicine, 40,* 19–27.

Dole, V. P., & Nyswander. M. (1966a). Rehabilitation of heroin addicts after blockade with methadone. *New York State Journal of Medicine, 66,* 2011–2023.

Dole, V. P., & Nyswander, M. (1966b). A medical treatment for heroin addiction: A clinical trial with methadone hydrochloride. *Journal of American Medicine Addiction, 193,* 80–87.

Dole, V. P., & Nyswander, M. (1976). Methadone maintenance treatment: A ten year perspective. *Journal of the American Medical Association, 235,* 1117–1126.

Dole, V. P., & Wolkstein, E. (1974). Vocational rehabilitation of patients on the Beth Israel methadone maintenance program. *Mount Sinai Journal of Medicine, 41,* 267–278.

Finalyson, R. (1984). Prescriptive drug abuse in older persons. In R. Atkinson (Ed.), *Alcohol and drug abuse in old age,* Washington, DC: American Psychiatric Press.

Fisher D., & Anglin, M. (1987). Survival analysis in drug program evaluation: Overall program effectiveness. *International Journal of the Addictions, 22,* 115–134.

Fitzsimmons, J., Tunis, S., Webster, D., Izes, J., Wapner, R., & Finnegan, L. (1986). Pregnancy in a drug-abuse population. *American Journal of Drug and Alcohol Abuse, 12,* 247–255.

Fort, J. (1954). Heroin addiction among young men. *Psychiatry, 17,* 251–263.

Freeman, E. M. (1989). The black family's life cycle: Operationalizing a strengths perspective. In S. M. L. Logan, E. M. Freeman, & R. G. McRoy (Eds.), *Social work practice with black families: A culturally specific perspective.* White Plains, NY: Longman.

Freund, G. (1984). Current research directions in alcohol problems and aging. *Alcohol Health and Research, 8,* 11–23.

Friedman, N. (1978). *The wildcat experiment: An early test of supported work in drug abuse rehabilitation.* NIDA Research Monograph.

Gawin, F., & Ellinwood, E. H. (1988). Cocaine and other stimulants: Actions, abuse, and treatment. *New England Journal of Medicine, 318,* 1173–1182.

Gawin, F., & Kleber, H. (1984). Cocaine abuse treatment: An open pilot trial with lithium and desipramine. *Archives of General Psychiatry, 41,* 903–909.

Germain, C., & Gitterman, A. (1980). *The life model.* New York: Columbia University Press.

Gomez, A. G. (1976). Some considerations in structuring human services for the Spanish speaking population of the U.S. *International Journal of Mental Health, 5,* 60–69.

Gomez, A. G., & Vega, D. (1980). The Hispanic addict. In J. Lowinson, & P. Ruiz (Eds.), *Substance abuse: Clinical problems and perspectives.* Baltimore, MD: Williams and Wilkens.

Grabowski, J., & Cherek, D. (1983). Conditioning factors in opiate dependence. In J. Smith, & J. Lane (Eds.), *The neurobiology of opiate reward processes.* Amsterdam: Elsevier.

Hall, S., Loeb. P., & Yang, R. (1977). Improving vocational placement in drug treatment clients: A pilot study. *Addictive Behaviors, 15,* 433–441.

Harin, H. T., & Mazair, H. (1975). The families of drug abusers: A literature review. *Family Process, 16,* 411–431.

Hatfield, B. (1987). Groupwork with users of minor tranquilizers. *Practice, 1,* 53–62.

Hser, Y., Anglin, M., & Booth, M. (1987). Sex differences in addict careers. *American Journal of Drug and Alcohol Abuse, 13,* 231–251.

Hser, Y. Anglin, M., & Chou, C. (1988). Evaluation of drug abuse treatment: A repeated measures design assessing methadone maintenance. *Evaluation Review, 12,* 547–570.

Hubbard, R., Rachal, J., Craddock, S., & Cavanaugh, E. (1984). Treatment outcome prospective study: Client characteristics and behaviors before, during, and after treatment. In F. Tims, & J. Ludford. (Eds.), *Drug abuse treatment evaluation.* NIDA Research Monograph 51.

Iiyama, P., Nishi, S., & Johnson, B. (Eds.) (1976). *Drug use and drug abuse among U.S. minorities.* New York: Praeger.

Inciardi, J. (1981). Heroin use and street crime. *Crime and Delinquency, 25,* 335–346.

James, J., Gosho, C., & Wohl, R. (1979). The relationship between female criminality and drug abuse. *International Journal of the Addictions, 14,* 215–229.

Johnson, B., & Smeidler, J. (1981). *Exploring asymmetries in the hard drug-crime relationship.* Paper presented at Society for the Study of Social Problems, Toronto.

Kagle, J. (1987). Secondary prevention of substance abuse. *Social work, 32,* 446–448.

Kaufman, E. (1987). *Substance abuse and family therapy.* Orlando, FL: Grune & Stratton.

Kaufman, E., & Kaufman, P. (Eds.). (1979). *Family therapy of drug and alcohol abuse.* New York: Gardner.

Kerson, T. (1988). Intensive services for drug and alcohol dependent women. *Health and Social Work, 13,* 302–310.

Khantzian, E., Gawin, F., Kleber, H., & Riordan, C. (1984). Methylphenidate treatment of cocaine dependency. *Journal of Substance Abuse Treatment, 1,* 107–112.

Kleber, H. (1988). Cocaine abuse: Historical, epidemiological, and psychological perspectives. *Journal of Clinical Psychiatry, 49,* 2–6.

Kleinman, P., Lukoff, I., & Kail, B. (1977). The magic fix: A critical analysis of methadone maintenance treatment. *Social Problems, 25,* 208–114.

Knapp, R., & Capel, W. (1979). Drug use among the elderly. *Journal of Drug Issues, 9,* 1–11.

Knight, J., & Bon, M. (1984). Self-esteem and parent-child communication: A comparison of substance-abusing and non-using adolescents. *School of Social Work, 9,* 66–76.

Kofoed, L. (1985). OTC drug overuse in the elderly. *Geriatrics, 40,* 55–60.

Kosten, T., Rounsaville, B., & Kleber, H. (1987). A 2.5 year follow-up of cocaine use among treated opioid addicts. *Archives of General Psychiatry, 44,* 281–284.

Kuncel, E. (1981). Effects of intensive counseling on client outcome in a methadone maintenance program. *International Journal of the Addictions, 16,* 415–424.

Langrod, J., Alksne, L., Lowison, J., & Ruiz, P. (1981). Rehabilitation of the Puerto Rican addict. *International Journal of the Addictions, 16,* 841–847.

LaRosa, J., Lipsius, J., & LaRosa, J. (1974). Experiences with a combination of group therapy and methadone maintenance in the treatment of heroin addiction. *International Journal of the Addictions, 9,* 605–611.

LePantois, J. (1986). Group therapy for children of substance abusers. *Social Work with Groups, 9,* 39–51.

LoSciuto, L. A., Aiken, L., Ausetts, M., & Brown, B. (1984). Paraprofessional versus professional drug abuse counselors: Attitudes and expectations of the counselors and their clients. *International Journal of the Addictions, 19,* 233–252.

Lowinson, J., & Ruiz, P. (Eds.). (1981). *Substance abuse: Clinical problems and perspectives.* Baltimore, MD: Williams and Wilkens.

Luborsky, L., Singer, B., & Luborsky, L. (1975). Comparative studies of psychotherapy. *Archives of General Psychiatry, 32,* 995–1008.

Madanes, C., Dukes, J., & Harbin, H. (1980). Family ties of heroin addicts. *Archives of General Psychiatry, 37,* 889–894.

Maddux, J., Desmond, D., & Esquival, M. (1980). Outpatient methadone withdrawal for heroin dependence. *American Journal of Drug and Alcohol Abuse, 7,* 323–333.

Maisto, S., & Cooper, A. (1980). A historical perspective on alcohol and drug treatment outcome research. In L. Sobell & M. Sobell (Eds.), *Treatment outcome evaluation in alcohol and drug abuse.* New York: Plenum.

Martin, W., Jasinsky, D., Haertzen, C., Jones, B., Kay, D., Mansky, P., & Carpenter, R. (1975). Methadone: A re-evaluation. *Archives of General Psychiatry, 28,* 286–295.

Marlatt, G., & Gordon, R. (1980). Determinants of relapse: Implications for the maintenance of behavior change. In P. Davidson & S. Davidson, (Eds.), *Behavioral medicine: Changing health lifestyles,* New York: Brunner/Mazel.

Marsh, K., & Simpson, D. (1986). Sex differences in opioid addiction careers. *American Journal of Drug and Alcohol Abuse, 12,* 309–329.

McGlothlin, W., & Anglin, M. (1981). Long-term follow-up of clients of high- and low-dose methadone programs. *Archives of General Psychiatry, 38,* 1055–1063.

Meehl, P. (1970). Nuisance variables and the ex post facto design. In M. Radner, & S. Winkour (Eds.), *Minnesota studies in the philosophy of science.* Minneapolis: University of Minnesota Press.

Mider, P., & Lewis, J. (1984). Neuropsychological assessment of polydrug abuse. In R. Craig, & S. Baker (Eds.), *Drug dependent patients: Treatment and research.* Springfield, IL: Thomas.

Miller, W. (1986). *The addictive behaviors.* New York: Plenum.

Mohr, L. (1988). *Impact analysis for program evaluation.* Chicago: Dorsey.

Moise, R., Kovach, J., Reed, B., & Bellows, N. (1982). A comparison of black and white women entering drug abuse treatment programs. *International Journal of the Addictions, 17,* 35–49.

Mondanaro, J. (1989). *Chemically dependent women.* Lexington, MA: Heath.

Morse, R. (1988). Substance abuse among the elderly. *Bulletin of the Menninger Clinic, 52,* 259–268.

Morse, R., Martin, M., Swenson, W., & Niven, R. (1984). Prognosis of physicians treated for alcoholism and drug dependence. *Journal of the American Medical Association, 251,* 743–746.

Newman, R. (1977). *Methadone treatment in narcotic addiction.* New York: Academic Press.

National Institute on Drug Abuse. (1978). *Epidemiology of drug abuse.* Rockville, MD: NIDA.

Nofz, M. (1988). Alcohol abuse and culturally marginal American Indians. *Social Casework, 69,* 67–73.

Nurco, D., Ball, J. C., & Shaffer, J. (1986). A comparison by race/ethnicity of narcotic addict crime rates in Baltimore, New York, and Philadelphia. *American Journal of Drug and Alcohol Abuse, 12,* 297–307.

Nurco, D., Cisin, I., & Balter, M. (1981a). Addict careers: A new typology. *International Journal of the Addictions, 16,* 1305–1325.

Nurco, D., Cisin, I., & Balter, M. (1981b). Addict careers: The first ten years. *International Journal of the Addictions, 16,* 1327–1356.

Nurco, D., Cisin, I., & Balter, M. (1982). Trends in the onset of narcotic addiction. *Chemical Dependencies, 4,* 221–228.

O'Brien, C., Childress, A., Arndt, I., McLellan, A., Woody, G., & Maany, I. (1988). Pharmacological and behavioral treatment of cocaine dependence: Controlled studies. *Journal of Clinical Psychiatry, 49,* 17–22.

O'Brien, C., Woody, G., & McLellan, A. (1984). Psychiatric disorders in opioid-dependent patients. *Journal of Clinical Psychiatry, 54,* 9–13.

Opkaku, S. (1986). Psychoanalytically oriented psychotherapy for substance abuse. *Advances in Alcohol and Substance Abuse, 6,* 17–33.

Pascarelli, E. (1979). An update on drug dependence in the elderly. *Journal of Drug Issues, 9,* 47–59.

Pascarelli, E. (1981). Drug use and the elderly. In J. Lowinson, & P. Ruiz (Eds.), *Substance abuse: Clinical problems and perspectives.* Baltimore, MD: Williams and Wilkens.

Rawson, R., Obert, J., McCann, M., & Mann, A. (1986). *Cocaine treatment outcome: Cocaine use following inpatient, outpatient, and no treatment.* Rockville, MD: NIDA.

Reed, B., & Leibson, E. (1981). Women clients in special women's drug abuse treatment programs. *International Journal of the Addictions, 16,* 1425–1466.

Reifler, B., Raskind, M., & Kethley, A. (1982). Psychiatric diagnoses among geriatric patients seen in an outpatient program. *Journal of the American Geriatrics Society, 30,* 530–533.

Robins, L., Davis, D., & Gordon, D. (1974). Drug use by U.S. Army enlisted men in Vietnam. *American Journal of Epidemiology, 99,* 235–249.

Rosenbaum, M. (1979). Difficulties in taking care of business: Women addicts as mothers. *American Journal of Drug and Alcohol Abuse, 6,* 431–446.

Rosenthal, R., & Rosnow, R. (1985). *Contrast analysis: Focused comparisons in the analysis of variance.* Cambridge: Cambridge University Press.

Rosenthal, R., & Rosnow, R. (1989). Statistical procedures and the justification of knowledge in psychological science. *American Psychologist, 44,* 1276–1284.

Rounsaville, B., Tierney, T., Crits-Cristoph, K., Weissman, M., & Kleber, H. (1982). Predictors of outcome in treatment of opiate addicts: Evidence for the multidimensional nature of addicts' problems. *Comprehensive Psychiatry, 23,* 462–478.

Sadava, S. (1984). Concurrent multiple drug use: Review and implications. *Journal of Drug Issues, 14,* 623–636.

Sansome, J. (1984). Retention patterns in a therapeutic community for the treatment of drug abuse. *International Journal of the Addictions, 15,* 711–736.

Schinke, S., Orlandi, M., Botvin, G., Gilchrist, L., Trimble, J., & Locklear, V. (1988). Preventing substance abuse among American-Indian adolescents. *Journal of Counseling Psychology, 35,* 87–90.

Seldin, N. (1972). The family of the addict: A review of the literature. *International Journal of the Addictions, 7,* 97–107.

Sells, S., & Simpson, D. (1976). *Effectiveness of drug abuse treatment.* Cambridge, MA: Ballinger.

Serban, G. (1978). New approach to the rehabilitation of the hard core drug addict: A pilot community study. *Journal of Clinical Psychiatry, 39,* 111–123.

Silver, F., Panepinto, W., Arnon, D., & Swaine, W. (1975). A family approach in treating the pregnant addict. In E. Senay (Ed.), *Developments in the field of drug abuse.* Cambridge, MA: Shenkman.

Simpson, D. (1981). Treatment for drug abuse: Follow-up outcomes and length of time spent. *Archives of General Psychiatry, 38,* 875–880.

Simpson, D. (1984). National treatment system evaluation based on the drug abuse reporting program (DARP) follow-up research. In F. Tims, & J. Ludford (Eds.), *Drug abuse treatment evaluation.* NIDA Research Monograph 51.

Simpson, D., Savage, L., Lloyd, M., & Sells, S. (1978). *Evaluation of drug treatments based on the first year after DARP.* Rockville, MD: NIDA monograph.

Simpson, D., & Sells, S. (1983). Effectiveness of treatment for drug abuse: An overview of the DARP research program. In B. Stimmel (Ed.), *Evaluation of drug treatment programs.* New York: Haworth.

Smart, R. G. (1976). Outcome studies of therapeutic community and halfway house treatment for addicts. *International Journal of the Addictions, 11,* 143–159.

Sobell, L., Sobell, M., & Ward, E. (Eds). (1980). *Evaluating alcohol and drug abuse treatment effectiveness.* New York: Pergamon.

Stitzer, M., Bigelow, G., Lawrence C., Cohen, C., D'Lugoff, B., & Hawthorne, J. (1977). Medication take-home as a reinforcer in a methadone maintenance program. *Addictive Behavior, 2,* 9–14.

Sugarman, B. (1983). *Daytop village: A therapeutic community.* New York: Irvington.

Thompson, T., & Ostlund, W. (1965). Susceptibility to readdiction as a function of the addiction and withdrawal environments. *Journal of Comparative Physiological Psychology, 60,* 388–392.

Tyler, J., & Thompson, M. (1980). Patterns of drug abuse among women. *International Journal of the Addictions, 15,* 309–321.

Weick, A. (1985). Overturning the medical model. *Social Work, 30,* 310–315.

Wikler, A. (1965). Conditioning factors in opiate addiction and relapse. In D. Wilner & G. Kassenbaum (Eds.), *Narcotics.* New York: McGraw-Hill.

Wilkinson, D., & LeBreton, S. (1986). Early indications of treatment outcome in multiple drug users. In W. Miller and N. Heather (Eds.), *Treating addictive behaviors* New York: Plenum.

Willett, E. (1973). Group therapy in a methadone treatment program. *International Journal of the Addictions, 8,* 33–39.

Winer, L., Lorio, J., & Scrofford, I. (1974). *Effects of treatment on drug abusers and family.* NIDA Monograph.

Woody, G., Luborsky, L., McLellan, A., O'Brien, C., & Beck, A. (1983). Psychotherapy for opiate addicts. *Archives of General Psychiatry, 40,* 639–648.

Wurmser, L. (1979). *The hidden dimension: Psycho-*

pathology of compulsive drug use. New York: Aronson.

Yablonsky, L. (1989). *The therapeutic community.* New York: Gardner.

Yen, S. (1974). Availability of activity reinforcers in a drug abuse clinic. *Psychological Reports, 34,* 1021–1022

Ziegler-Driscoll, G. (1979). The similarities in families of drug dependents and alcoholics. In E. Kaufman, & F. Kaufman (Eds.), *Family therapy of drug and alcohol abuse.* New York: Gardner.

Zimberg, S. (1978). Treatment of elderly alcoholic in the community and in an institutional setting. *Addictive Diseases, 3,* 417–427.

Zweben, J. (1986). Treating cocaine dependence: New challenges for the therapeutic community. *Journal of Psychoactive Drugs, 18,* 239–245.

CHAPTER 8

Recreational or Casual Drug Use: Opportunities for Primary Prevention

Barbara Lynn Kail
University of Texas at Arlington

Habits are at first cobwebs, then cables.

Spanish proverb

At the risk of being the skunk at the garden party, this chapter begins with the cynic's definition of primary prevention as proposed by Bloom (1981):

> Primary prevention deals with problems that don't exist, with people who don't want to be bothered, with methods that probably haven't been demonstrated to be efficacious, in problems that are multidisciplinary, multifaceted, and multigenerational, involving complex longitudinal research designs for which clear-cut results are expected immediately for political and economic reasons unrelated to the task in question. (p. 8)

The rest of this chapter considers why this statement is essentially accurate, and yet why the primary prevention of drug abuse is possible and should remain a crucial goal of our society.

To begin, it is important to consider briefly the extent of the problem and the consequences of illicit drug use. A discussion of some of the major theories of drug use follows, in an effort to explain why so many individuals experiment with illicit substances but fewer move on to regular use. Preventive efforts from both the supply side and the demand side are described, and their effectiveness is considered. Finally, some of the social work skills needed to participate in these preventive efforts are presented.

Throughout, addiction to psychoactive drugs is compared and contrasted with other addictive behaviors.

TO WHAT EXTENT DOES THE PROBLEM EXIST?

Range of Drugs Used and Trends by Age Groups

Based on the National Institute on Drug Abuse 1985 household survey (National Institute on Drug Abuse, 1988), marijuana is the most used of the illicit drugs considered here (see Table 8.1). Fully 32.4 percent of their sample report lifetime use and 9.4 percent report current use (within the past month). Cocaine is the next most widely used psychoactive substance; 11.6 percent report lifetime use and 2.9 percent report current use. The survey reports levels of nonmedical stimulant use that approach those of cocaine (9.2 percent and 1.3 percent). The use of inhalants and hallucinogens is relatively low. Finally, the use of heroin is quite low, although often very problematic for the small percentage who do use regularly; only 1 percent have ever used and .5 percent currently use this drug.

TABLE 8.1. Lifetime Use and Use in the Past Month of Selective Psychoactive Drugs (percentage of respondents reporting use)

Psychoactive Drug	Lifetime Use	Use in Past Month
Marijuana	32.4%	9.4%
Cocaine	11.6%	2.9%
Stimulants	9.2%	1.3%
Inhalants	6.8%	.9%
Hallucinogens	6.7%	.8%
Heroin	1.0%	.5%

Note. Sample consists of a survey of U.S. households, National Institute on Drug Abuse, for 1985.

Trends over time suggest that new users are declining for all the psychoactive substances considered here with the exception of cocaine (National Institute on Drug Abuse, 1988). The use of cocaine appears to have peaked in 1982; however, the 1985 survey preceded the mass introduction of crack-cocaine so that these figures surely underestimate the current use of cocaine in all forms. Some high-risk groups seem to be particularly vulnerable to this drug as well as to other psychotropic drugs.

High-Risk Groups

Males of all ages are more likely to use illicit psychoactive drugs than females. This pattern holds for marijuana, cocaine, and the nonmedical use of stimulants, inhalants, hallucinogens, and heroin. Whites also have higher rates of illicit psychoactive drug use compared to African Americans and Hispanics. Hispanics report generally lower levels of use except for inhalants, of which Hispanics aged 12 to 25 years do use more than African American age cohorts. Those levels are, nevertheless, still lower than those for whites in the same age range.

When age is considered in more detail, some very interesting patterns appear. One pattern reflects the progression of drug use posited by Kandel (1980); the highest rates of use for cocaine and heroin occur among white males aged 26 to 34. There is much less use reported among younger respondents. A second, very interesting pattern occurs among teenagers. Hispanic cocaine use at this age surpasses that of whites and African Americans.

It appears that the young Hispanic female may be particularly at risk.

Overall then, men use more than women, and whites use more than any other ethnic group. Those patterns suggest a progression of drug use from alcohol, cigarettes, and marijuana to cocaine and heroin, as suggested by Kandel (1980). Finally, among the youngest and newest users a different pattern is evident, with Hispanics being at greater risk, especially for cocaine use. The consequences of use are considerable for those who fit these high-risk categories *and* for some casual users.

Consequences of Use

The following consequences of drug use have been fairly well documented:

1. Some but not all casual users go on to regular use. The NIDA (1988) data suggest approximately half of those who ever try a drug have used it within the past month. However, at least based on anecdotal evidence, it appears that a much higher percentage of those who ever use crack-cocaine go on to regular use.
2. Health problems are associated with needles that are not sterile, adulterants in the drugs, the drugs themselves, and the life-style associated with drug use.
3. Truancy, school dropout rates, and absence from the labor force increase with use. For a teenager, heavy drug use may accelerate the teen's premature involvement in adult roles. These adolescents tend to leave school earlier, start work earlier in low-paying jobs, and form families earlier.
4. Entry into other forms of criminal activity is more likely. The drug/crime connection has been well documented especially as it relates to crack-cocaine use.
5. Problems within the family include the loss of family relationships and reversal of roles, such as when a young drug dealer wields the economic power within the family.
6. The potential loss of traditional community institutions is significant, along with the creation of new, deviant institutions such as crack houses and shooting galleries (NIDA, 1988; Inciardi, 1981; Jessor & Jessor, 1977;

Newcomb & Bentler, 1988b; Yamaguchi & Kandel, 1984).

Clearly, then, the need to prevent drug abuse is indeed an issue, especially for the following groups at risk for the consequences listed above: young white males and, among the youngest and newest users, Hispanics. Subsequent discussion of preventive theory and policy in this chapter will, to a certain extent, focus primarily on the adolescent since it is this age group that appears most at risk for problem usage.

THEORIES OF ADDICTION, OR WHY SO MANY TRY DRUGS BUT ONLY SOME GO ON TO REGULAR USE

Biological Theories

Biological theories of drug addiction are among the earliest developed. Lindesmith (1947) posits that addicts continue to use drugs to relieve the physiological stress of withdrawal. Dole and Nyswander (1967) theorize that the use of heroin permanently alters the body and that this metabolic disturbance produces the craving that then leads to continued use. A neurological susceptibility mediates use and addiction. Initial experimentation with drugs is based on normal curiosity; however, those neurologically susceptible individuals experience an altered response to the initial effects of the drugs so that euphoria is produced rather than nausea. Methadone, according to Dole and Nyswander (1967), compensates for this biological change by blocking the craving for the drug.

Theories of the Addictive Personality

Platt and Labate (1976) provide an extensive review of the literature on personality theory, geared to the identification of specific predisposing psychological characteristics in heroin addicts. The idea of predisposing personality factors is exposed to some serious criticism. Those authors believe many of the findings differentiating addicts and nonaddicts may be artifacts, partly because of the failure of the investigator to match the addicted group with the appropriate controls. Furthermore, the nature of the drug use is not always well defined, and definitions differ across studies.

The most important finding appears to be that heroin addicts demonstrate a significant amount of psychopathology, including high levels of anxiety and neurotic and psychotic characteristics. The following personality traits and disorders have also been associated with heroin addiction: a sense of personal inadequacy, an inability to delay gratification, low frustration tolerance, poor self-image, and low self-esteem. The problem is that none of these traits have been documented consistently or used satisfactorily to explain heroin use in *all* addicts. The most reasonable conclusion may be that although many addicts generally exhibit pathologic traits, there is little probability that a common pattern of personality traits is present in all addicts. This is probably even more true for users of many different psychoactive substances.

Social Learning Theories

Sutherland and Cressey (1974) develop a model based on what they term differential association. One learns to be a drug user within a group of peers; the curriculum consists of specific techniques of drug use, and a specified direction of drives, motivations, rationalizations, and attitudes. This process of learning criminal behavior involves all the mechanisms involved in any other form of learning. Differential association with conventional and drug-using friends will determine one's pattern of behavior.

Jessor and Jessor (1977) suggest the likelihood that drug abuse can be predicted by the propensity toward problem behaviors in general. This propensity is in turn determined by the interaction of three systems: behavior, personality, and perceived environment. The behavior system is divided into a problem behavior structure and a conventional behavior structure. Participation in either system serves as an alternative to participation in the other. The personality system is divided into three structures that include a motivation-instigation system, a personal belief system, and a personal control system. The perceived environment is composed of proximal and distal variables. Distal variables include support and controls from parents and friends and the relative influence of parents and friends. The proximal structure includes parent and peer approval for problem behavior.

Stage Theory

Stage theories began as stepping-stone or threshold theories, positing that marijuana was an absolute stepping-stone to heroin use (Kandel, 1980). This theory was widely disseminated and promoted in the 1960s.

In fact, marijuana use often precedes hallucinogen or heroin use, but a good percentage of marijuana users never go on to these other drugs. Kandel (1980) and Yamaguchi and Kandel (1984) report that, based on their longitudinal data, involvement with drugs proceeds through several different stages. Adolescents typically progress sequentially from beer and wine to hard liquor and cigarettes; next, to marijuana and then on to other illicit drugs. Although early involvement does not necessarily lead to use at a later stage, usage at later stages is very unlikely without use at earlier stages.

Theories of Access

Winick (1980) proposes a theory of drug dependence based on roles, access to drugs, and attitudes toward drugs. Drug use is high among those groups in which there is access, an accepting attitude toward drug use, and role strain and/or role deprivation. At points of taking on new roles or being tested for adequacy in a role, adolescents are at particular risk of role strain. Role strain may be caused by incompatible demands within one role or between two roles in a role set, the kind of conformity required by different roles within a role set, the ambiguity of role obligations, or inconsistent role obligations. Once the sources of role strain in society have been specified, it is possible then to specify and predict those role situations that are likely to result in a high incidence of drug dependence. Users will cease use when access to drugs declines, negative attitudes to use become salient, or role strain and deprivation become less prevalent.

Smart (1980) suggests an availability-proneness theory of illicit drug abuse. A drug-prone individual must be exposed to high levels of availability before use will begin. Availability refers to a set of physical, social, and economic circumstances surrounding the ease or difficulty of obtaining drugs, especially in terms of the cost and amount of physical effort needed to obtain them. Availability may also refer to social aspects because drugs are more available in some social groups than others. Availability may be perceived as well as actual. Actual availability takes into account the cost of drugs. Perceived availability is simply subjective estimates of the variables described above. Proneness to drug use may be of many types. Studies suggest opiate addicts have numerous psychological difficulties prior to addiction, including self-image and self-esteem problems (Winick, 1980; Smart, 1980; Inciardi, 1981). Other aspects of proneness may be related to seeking a new life-style (glamour, money, opportunities, excitement).

This model does contain several weaknesses. The concepts of availability and proneness are global concepts with a variety of possible meanings. There are also situations where availability is high but use is very low, such as among farmers who grow opium and cocaine. In those situations, the theory of proneness is not supported. There are also special problems with the concept of availability in that the actual availability of a particular drug for a particular individual is almost never fully known.

Gullotta and Adams (1982) develop a distribution-of-consumption model that suggests drug use in society is distributed in a lognormal fashion: the higher the average consumption, the greater the proportion of heavy users. Therefore, reducing the average consumption is assumed to reduce the proportion of heavy users. This approach has been more widely promoted in the area of alcohol use.

Summary

A review of these theories of drug use generally suggests a number of conclusions. Drug use should be placed within a developmental context, implying that factors that influence drug use evolve as the child matures through adolescence and that the developmental period preceding adolescence and young adulthood should be considered in any primary prevention effort. The theories also suggest drug use may be common for many adolescents and may be part of a larger constellation of behaviors, whether they are labeled problem behaviors, antisocial behaviors, or some other category of behaviors. Drug use must therefore be treated within a behavioral context as well. Many researchers also suggest that drug use may have a functional aspect and that prevention efforts should address this functionality and provide alternative behaviors for drug use rather than trying to suppress any underlying need or reason for drug use. Finally, there is strong support for addressing social-environmental factors in prevention efforts including the effects of modeling, the availability of drugs, and other social factors in the development of drug use.

This chapter suggests that any theoretical framework used as the basis for primary prevention efforts must consider and influence a number of different systems:

1. The individual, including Jessor and Jessor's model (1977) of a personality system with three structures (motivation-instigation, personal belief, and personal control systems) and a behavior system consisting of both conventional and problem/deviant behavior, including drug use; developmental issues of adolescence must also be considered related to how the personality and behavior structures interact.
2. The peer system, including its norms, attitudes, beliefs, involvement in drug use, and availability of drugs at that level.
3. The family system, including its norms, attitudes, beliefs, involvement in drug use, and availability of drugs.
4. The school, work situation, or job training site, including the presence of drug cultures and/or availability of drugs.
5. The community, including the norms, attitudes, availability of drugs and presence of conventional institutions and deviant institutions (e.g., churches, community centers, or crack houses).

The prevention model discussed above has several advantages, the first of which is that it incorporates the often discussed concept of stress. There are at least several different types of stress to consider. One type of stressor is major life events such as a parental divorce or the death of a significant other. A secondary category of stress includes the concept of role strain and everyday life problems that may be related to school adjustment and peer relationships. Yet a third type of stressor includes life transitions and developmental changes at predictable points involving the onset of puberty, for example. Clearly all these types of stress can be thought of as introducing disequilibrium. Primary prevention pro-

grams might consider teaching skills that can help maintain and reestablish the individual's balance.

A second advantage of considering a systems-oriented prevention model is that it incorporates all the systems considered by the varied theories discussed in this chapter, especially the concept of access and the impact of the community. Both these aspects seem to have been neglected in previous models. Again, these gaps clearly have ramifications for the effectiveness of preventive efforts.

Finally, such a model is easily transferable to other forms of addictive behavior. What may be most unique about this model is its consideration of the role of access in the problem of drug abuse. Access may influence alcohol use but perhaps not as much as it does drug use. Everyone has legal access to alcohol at age 21, while some have social access prior to that age. Access may not be crucial for eating, gambling, and sexual addictions as well, since these are not illegal activities to the extent that drug use is in this country. As the cynic's definition of primary prevention suggests, then, any model of prevention is clearly based on a problem that is multidisciplinary, multifaceted, and multigenerational. To what extent is this knowledge translated into policies concerning primary prevention efforts? The cynic replies: with great difficulty and not well.

PREVENTION FROM THE SUPPLY SIDE: INTERDICTION

Policies aimed at prevention from the supply side are based on the assumption that, if the supply and access to drugs are limited, then use will also be limited. In the field of alcohol, this country has experimented with policy from the interdiction point of view; prohibition and age restrictions are notable examples. Policies toward gambling are almost exclusively from the supply side. A unique aspect of policies aimed at stopping the supply of illicit drugs is the international nature of the drug trade and, therefore, the sort of international cooperation needed to address the supply issue.

Perhaps another unique aspect of policies aimed at limiting access to drugs is the extraordinary difficulty of coordinating the more than three dozen federal agencies that claim jurisdiction over drug use policy. Among these agencies there is feuding, duplication of efforts, and conflicting philosophies as described in a recent *New York Times* article (Berke, 1989, September 5). The State Department would like to develop good relations with countries rather than impose penalties on them for not fighting the drug trade. The Justice Department, on the other hand, is geared to arresting and prosecuting drug traffickers. The Pentagon and the Defense Department are reluctant to put money into fighting the drug traffic. The Customs Services and the Coast Guard are known to feud over issues of who should receive credit for drug seizures. Perhaps one of the most serious issues is the coordination of these efforts among agencies that are highly independent and competitive within an atmosphere of increasingly limited resources.

Fully 70 percent of President George Bush's 1989 policy initiative is directed at law enforcement, including stiffer sentences for drug involvement, from occasional drug users to international drug traffickers; a shift in focus from targeting international drug traffic to targeting street traffic; and increased funds for police departments, federal prisons, and military aid to Columbia, Peru, and Bolivia. Specifically the plan includes the following allocations for

1. Corrections (1.6 billion)—the construction of new federal prisons and withholding of funds from states which do not have drug testing for prisoners and parolees.
2. Interdiction (261 million)—military and financial aid to Peru, Columbia and Bolivia.
3. Law enforcement (3.1 billion)—federal assistance to state and local law enforcement. States are also urged to adopt stiffer fines for casual drug users.
4. Court expansion (250 million)—to provide more judges and facilities to expedite drug cases. (Berke, 1989, p. 1)

The current Bush policy faces difficulties on two fronts. The first issue is that of coordination. Robert Martinez, the federal drug policy director, is responsible for assuring the cooperation of agencies. He may not have sufficient influence, however, to carry out the policy and see that agencies spend their funds and deploy personnel in a manner consistent with the goals he has developed. The plan does establish two distinct groups: one deals with supply

and the other with demand. These groups are expected to mediate among the rival agencies.

A second difficulty is in funding. There appears to be some sentiment in Congress that the Bush administration will take credit for establishing the plan to fight drug abuse, while leaving Congress with decisions about which budget cuts will be made to fund the program. State and local officials are quarreling over whether the funds should go directly to local governments. Local governments believe they are fighting the battle on the front lines. State governments argue that funds should go through them to coordinate efforts and to assure that the focus on cities does not neglect other areas of the state. In fact, there is a tradition of states acting as clearing houses for federal funds since the federal anti-drug block grant programs began in 1986. The current federal drug strategy appears to continue this tradition (Berke, 1989).

To what extent are these efforts efficacious? There is no clear-cut way to measure efficacy other than through the pounds of drugs seized or the numbers of dealers arrested and incarcerated. Historical experience clearly suggests that a policy of prohibition without attention to the demand side of the equation is doomed.

PREVENTION FROM THE DEMAND SIDE: TREATMENT

While much of the theoretical literature considers the demand side, current policy appears to place much less emphasis on interventions aimed at primary and secondary prevention than on rehabilitation. One aspect of prevention from the demand side is secondary and tertiary prevention, treating those who are addicted. This reduces their demand and the "spread" of the disease in public health terms. This aspect will be considered only briefly since other chapters in this book deal with the problem of treatment more extensively. Bush's 1989 drug use proposal includes $925 million to expand treatment slots and the range of treatments available. Pregnant women who use drugs are of particular concern (Berke, 1989). (See Chapter 9 for a more detailed discussion of this high-risk population.)

This portion of the current policy has been

criticized on several counts. First, treatment and prevention receive much less funding than efforts aimed at the supply side. While funding for treatment would be increased by 39 percent in 1990 compared to 1989, in reality the plan provides only a modest 10 percent increase over funds already budgeted for 1990.

There are several other issues concerning treatment policy in terms of the new plan. While there is some agreement that the number of treatment slots is insufficient, there is disagreement about the advisability, affordability, and efficiency of creating enough slots for walk-ins, that is, treatment on demand. Another issue is that the type of treatment available addresses the needs of heroin addicts, but the majority of requests for treatment come from cocaine addicts. There is clearly an imbalance in the type of services available. Finally, there is the issue of forced treatment. Courts often include drug treatment as part of an individual's sentence, but enforcement is lax. Moreover, as of 1989, only 19 states had civil commitment laws that allow parents to commit troubled children to drug treatment. When the issue of AIDS is considered, the question of whether forced treatment is appropriate becomes even more complex. It is an issue not only for intravenous (IV) drug users, but also for individuals who are sexual addicts. Some of these problems can be addressed more effectively with primary prevention efforts with population groups in which they are not yet a problem.

PRIMARY PREVENTION: EDUCATING THE YOUNG

The new federal initiative also includes $1.2 billion for education and primary prevention programs. Schools and colleges must have such programs in place as a condition for receiving federal funds. Again, as mentioned earlier, this is a relatively small portion of the total funds that have been allocated for the current drug plan (see the discussion in the section on Prevention from the Supply Side: Interdiction). Here, the content and effectiveness of some of the more popular prevention strategies are discussed within the context of these funding limitations.

Information and Education Programs

Traditionally, drug education programs have been used to provide students with information concerning the health hazards and other consequences of taking drugs. The rationale is that once adolescents are provided with information, they will make the healthier choices. There are numerous difficulties with this approach as outlined by Rhodes and Jason (1988). To begin, there is the assumption that youth begin to use drugs because they are unaware of the potential risks. This is a most simplistic view, as the theoretical frameworks discussed previously suggest.

Developmental research suggests such an approach might work with children and young adolescents who are likely to adopt the opinions of respected adults. Older adolescents and young adults are much more likely to be aware of the cultural inconsistencies in this country toward cigarettes and alcohol use versus drug use. These programs do not address, and perhaps highlight, these inconsistencies. Older adolescents are also more likely to be aware of the contradictory and inconsistent findings concerning immediate and long-term effects of some psychoactive substances such as marijuana. Finally, some of the information presented may contradict the adolescent's own experiences. Evaluations suggest that these approaches have led to increases in knowledge, but they are ineffective in decreasing substance usage or in causing behavioral changes (Rhodes & Jason, 1988).

Skill-based Strategies

Skill-based programs, in comparison to educational strategies, generally seek to enhance the social coping skills or behaviors of youth to offset various influences in the environment and peer group that support drug use. The programs often are based on the concept of psychological inoculation: they expose the teen to some of the natural situations in which there may be pressures to use drugs. Various exercises are conducted such as role-playing, assertiveness training, and cognitive modeling. Some programs use peers as leaders and involve them in peer-led assertiveness training. This focus on skill deficits has led to the development of standardized skill-based programs that can be implemented and evaluated in class settings. The strategies are more broad based than the information and education strategies, but they are derived from similar theoretical roots and utilize similar techniques. Rhodes and Jason (1988) describe three specific types of skill programs: social assertiveness skills training, cognitive-behavioral skills training, and life skills training.

Social assertiveness skills training is based on research within several of the theoretical frameworks discussed in a previous section of this chapter. Research findings suggest a relationship among adolescent substance abuse and the following variables: parent/peer substance abuse; cognitive factors such as low self-efficacy; problem behaviors such as school failure, delinquency, and aggression; stress; and low social support from adults (Bry, 1985; Newcomb & Bentler, 1988a, 1988b; Yamaguchi & Kandel, 1984). From this theoretical base, the programs propose that assertiveness skills training should assist in all of these areas and lower experimentation with and heavy use of drugs. Evaluation does suggest that children who have been through assertiveness skills training do show increased social competence and improved grades.

Schinke and Gilchrist (1984) have developed a cognitive-behavioral skills training program based upon strategies developed originally for pregnancy prevention. Their program is designed to provide adolescents with social coping skills. Strategies are aimed at enhancing such skills as decision making, problem solving, and interpersonal communications. Specific techniques include teaching the steps of the problem-solving process, practicing self-control behaviors, and developing tension-relieving techniques such as relaxation and assertiveness skills. Modeling, feedback, reinforcement, coaching, and behavioral assignments are utilized in the teaching of these skills. Some of these programs have consistently demonstrated that they are effective in diminishing tobacco use. In addition, such an approach has produced improvements in several outcome measures of the skills addressed (Schinke & Blyth, 1981; Schinke & Gilchrist, 1983; Schinke & Gilchrist, 1984).

Botvin (1985) has developed a life-skills training curriculum to teach a wide range of personal and social skills to improve the adolescent's general level of competence. The teenager is taught how to set goals, increase positive self-talk statements, resist persuasive appeals, and use relaxation training and communication skills. Evaluations suggest that

this training appears to reduce drinking and marijuana use as well as produce significant changes in knowledge and attitudes about those substances.

There are several limitations inherent in the three types of skills programs described above, as noted by Rhodes and Jason (1988). First, one weakness is the complexity of these programs. Such a wide range of skills may be included that each may be addressed in a very superficial manner. A second issue is that of cost. Many of these programs require that the school or agency purchase an entire "package" including teacher manuals, student guides, audio-visual aids, and expert consultation for implementing the program. The expense may be prohibitive and an "a la carte" purchase of components may not be offered. A third problem is that dissemination may be impeded more because identifying and training group leaders for such an approach is often difficult. Yet a fourth problem is that these interventions have been developed with white middle-class students and may not be sensitive to the needs of lower socioeconomic status and minority teens. Finally, while coping skills may be important, they do not address many of the other systems involved in the use of drugs (e.g., sources of stress: poor relationships with parents, peers, or teachers, and the lack of resources in a community). Thus, other, more ecological programs may have the potential for addressing some of these other important systems.

Community-based Strategies

In response to some of the problems discussed above, other interventions have been developed, including the family and media. Bry (1985), after exploring the topic, found that family involvement is essential for positive outcomes. When families are included, the risk factors can be reduced. Szapocznik, Santiesteban, Rio, Perez-Vidal, Santiesteban, and Kurtines (1989) describe an innovative prevention program for Hispanic families. Their Family Effectiveness Training consists of didactic and experiential material. Maladaptive patterns of interaction are treated with Brief Strategic Family Therapy. Intergenerational conflict is treated or prevented with Family Development lessons. Conflict due to acculturation issues and racial stress is addressed through Bicultural Effectiveness Training. Flay and Sobel (1983) suggest that some of the well developed media campaigns aimed at reducing heart disease may hold promise for the area of substance abuse as well. They include prevention strategies such as an awareness day in high schools, drug-free dances, and a five-kilometer race, all involving parents, students, and teachers.

Examples of Community Programs

One of the most promising primary prevention programs involves students, the school, the family, and the media in a coordinated approach (Pentz, Dwyer, MacKinnon, Flay, Hansen, Wang, & Johnson, 1989). The experimental program included sessions at school for students as well as homework assignments that involved role-playing with family members and interviewing members about rules concerning drug use. Mass media coverage of the program consisted of the following activities: newspaper articles and television/radio spots, talk show interviews with program staff, and a televised press conference. Findings suggest that those students involved in such programs were indeed less likely to smoke, drink alcohol, or use marijuana compared to those involved in the typical interventions provided within the school system.

Another interesting example of a program is that of a preventive effort that took place in the Dallas/Fort Worth metropolitan area in February of 1990. This media event involved several systems in the community. The CBS, NBC, and ABC television networks each donated two hours of prime time from 8:00 P.M. to 10:00 P.M. on a weekday night, with the program to be broadcast simultaneously on all. It would be hard to miss. Entitled "Texas Crackdown on Drugs," the format represented a variety of approaches. Hosts on each channel introduced representatives from the schools, treatment centers, and law enforcement agencies. Parents and teenagers with drug problems spoke on some of the issues involved. Two hotlines were set up: one for individuals seeking treatment; the other for individuals wishing to report drug dealers. Phone numbers were flashed on the screen at regular intervals. After the local news a "town meeting" was held that invited people to call in and express their views. All the local newspapers carried detailed stories about the event, and one even carried a feature article about the process by which the program was produced. There was also coverage by radio stations;

two local stations translated the program simultaneously into Spanish.

It would appear that prevention programs that involve a number of systems, stemming from the theories and findings cited previously, may have some advantages over other approaches. There are, of course, some drawbacks to these programs. They are expensive to implement. They may involve a "halo" effect and may not be quite so effective once the novelty wears off. Finally, each community will implement the program in its unique way, making evaluation difficult. The approach, however, certainly has merit and is applicable to other addictive behaviors.

A final note on preventive policies aimed at the demand side: The current outcome expected of these policies is absolutely no use of any drugs. A study conducted by Newcomb and Bentler (1988a) suggests that this may not be the optimal goal. For many young people, occasional and nonproblem drug use may be a normal rite of passage. This longitudinal study followed more than seven hundred teens in Los Angeles County for eight years. Those who occasionally used drugs at social gatherings could not be distinguished in later years from teens who abstained totally from drugs. These findings may indicate that the effects of occasional drug use seem benign if the adolescent is adjusting well in school, getting good grades, and participating in extracurricular activities. These findings should be interpreted cautiously. However, as the cynic's definition of prevention notes, there is also a political component to prevention. Anything less than absolute abstention may not be politically acceptable.

SOCIAL WORK ROLES AND SKILLS

Identification of Those at Risk

Clearly, one specific skill social workers need is that of identifying those "at risk." Rhodes and Jason (1988) suggest a multileveled approach that employs the least expensive screening procedure on all students. To begin with, teacher assessments are most often used to identify those youth with behaviors that can be correlated with substance abuse (low academic performance, absenteeism, behavior problems in school). Other more expensive screening procedures can be used to reassess smaller groups of high-risk students (Kandel, 1980; Yamaguchi & Kandel, 1984). Some at-risk teens can be identified by other systems such as the juvenile justice and child welfare systems. Social workers may be involved directly in the school system by identifying those at risk or they may offer training for teachers and professionals in other systems who may identify those at risk.

Treatment Planning: Inpatient versus Outpatient Recommendations

A second skill that may be specific to the secondary prevention of drug abuse is making accurate decisions about whether to refer an adolescent for inpatient or outpatient drug treatment programs. In general such decisions are based on the type and extent of the drugs being used, the physical and mental health of the adolescent, and the adequacy of the support system within the community. Hospital detoxification programs are optimal for those at serious medical risk due to overdoses or withdrawal symptoms. Those clients who require hospitalization usually have long histories of heavy and serious abuse. Inpatient programs of a longer term are for such heavy drug users who need a 24-hour structured program and a controlled environment. Outpatient treatment is appropriate for most adolescent users who have adequate support systems in the community and no substantial underlying psychiatric or medical problems, and no suicide ideations.

Preventive Skills for Individual Work

Bloom (1981) outlines some basic social work skills needed to address the prevention issues outlined above. None of these is unique to prevention, but all must be considered in light of the goals of prevention and the nature of the "problem" addressed—it has not yet occurred. These skills are relevant to social workers who have opportunities to observe youngsters in natural settings including schools, community centers, primary groups, and churches. The skills can be relevant as social workers attempt to get acquainted with these youngsters gradually in order to develop trust and a beginning relationship preliminary to involving the youngsters in prevention programs. They are relevant in individual contacts during the course of those programs and in the group contacts as well.

First, the core skills of warmth, empathy, and genuineness are essential. Regardless of any specific knowledge and skills the social worker may have, the practitioner must be perceived by youngsters as trustworthy.

Bloom (1981) describes empathy within a preventive context as the following:

1. Listening carefully to the content of what the host (teenager at risk in this case) is saying about the situation.
2. Listening carefully to the affect related to content including both verbal and nonverbal cues.
3. Communicating both of these understandings when appropriate to the teenager.
4. Communicating the preventer's hunches about the thoughts and feelings of the teen beyond what has been already communicated. The worker must be careful not to seem too pushy, engaging in active listening without seeming to be inappropriately nosy about inner feelings and ideas of the teens. (p.10)

Warmth and genuineness are the other two aspects of these core skills. Nonpossessive warmth is perceived as unconditional positive regard. The worker must be cautious that this does not descend into nagging and interfering with the teen's responsibility for personal behavior. Practitioners must not be "too right" about how someone else should live. For example, while it is clear that smoking cigarettes may well be a precursor to other forms of substance abuse, the worker must guard against being too righteous. Bloom (1981) discusses genuineness in terms of what Rogers (1979) calls self-congruence. There should be agreement in what the preventer thinks and feels about a situation and the way the preventer acts toward the adolescents on the same point.

Group and Community-Level Skills

Social workers also have basic group and community organizing skills that can be utilized within preventive programs. Within the skills-based prevention programs described in the previous section, family and group techniques are a crucial component of the interventions. One of the most underutilized aspects of the social worker's skills are the community-based ones. Workers might be innovative in assisting residents of a housing project to organize and rid themselves of drug dealers or to close down a crack house located nearby. They might also use community organization skills to assist a community in assessing its own needs to determine whether a prevention program is appropriate and what type of program is likely to be most effective in the particular community. Practitioners can use group skills to mediate differences of opinion or competing organizational interests that may become barriers to implementing such programs.

CONCLUSION

What makes social work unique is its tradition of considering the person in the environment and its emphasis on helping clients to identify and use strengths. A preventive approach aimed at multiple systems is consistent with those theories that consider all aspects of a situation, and with research findings concerning the efficacy of policy approaches on both the supply and demand side. Such an approach also allows for the assessment of barriers to prevention within those various systems with an emphasis on identifying the rich resources that each may also offer. This includes strengths and other resources within the individual as well as those that can be labeled environmental at family, community, and societal levels. Social workers may need to help other decision makers and practitioners in the area of prevention to consider the needs of drug-involved casual and heavy users from this more ecological and strengths-oriented perspective.

REFERENCES

Berke, R. L. (1989, September 5). Disunity is feared as Bush maps war on drug use in U.S. *New York Times*, pp. 1, 9.

Bloom, M. (1981). *Primary prevention: The possible science.* Englewood Cliffs, NJ: Prentice Hall.

Botvin, G. J. (1985). The Life Skills Training program as a health promotion strategy: Theoretical issues and empirical findings. *Special Services in the Schools, 1*(3) (3), 9–23.

Bry, B. H. (1985). Empirical foundations of family-based approaches to adolescent substance abuse. In T. J. Glynn, C. G. Leukefeld, & J. P. Ludford (Eds.), *Preventing adolescent drug abuse* (pp. 115–140).

Rockville, MD: National Institute on Drug Abuse. DHEW# (ADM) 47.

Dole, V. P., & Nyswander, M. (1967). Rehabilitation of the street addict. *Archives of Environmental Health, 14*, 477–480.

Flay, B. R., & Sobel, J. L. (1983). The role of mass media in preventing adolescent substance abuse. In T. G. Glynn, C. G. Leukefeld, & J. P. Ludford (Eds.), *Preventing adolescent drug abuse: Intervention strategies* (DHHS Publication No. ADM 47). Washington, DC: U.S. Government Printing Office.

Gullotta, T., & Adams, G. R. (1982). Substance abuse minimization: conceptualizing prevention in adolescent and youth programs. *Journal of Youth and Adolescence, 11*, 409–424.

Inciardi, J. (1981). *The drugs-crime connection.* Beverly Hills, CA: Sage.

Jessor, R., & Jessor, S. (1977). *Problem behavior and psychosocial development: A longitudinal study of youth.* New York: Academic Press.

Kandel, D. (1980). Developmental stages in adolescent drug involvement. In D. J. Lettieri, M. Sayers & H. W. Pearson (Eds.), *Theories on drug abuse: Selected contemporary perspectives.* NIDA Research Monograph 30 DHHS.

Lindesmith, A R. (1947). *Opiate addiction.* Bloomington, IN: Principle Press.

National Institute on Drug Abuse, (1988). *National Institute on Drug Abuse national household survey on drug abuse: Main findings 1985* (DHHS Publication No. ADM 88-1586). Washington, DC: U.S. Government Printing Office.

Newcomb, M. D & Bentler, P. (1988a). Impact of adolescent drug use and social support on problems of young adults: A longitudinal study. *Journal of Abnormal Psychology, 97*(1), 64–75.

Newcomb, M. D., & Bentler, P. (1988b), *Consequences of teenage drug use: Impact on the lives of young adults.* Beverly Hills, CA: Sage.

Pentz, M. A., Dwyer, J. H., MacKinnon, D. P., Flay, B. R., Hansen, W. B., Wang, E. Y., & Johnson, A. (1989). A multicommunity trial for primary prevention of adolescent drug abuse. *JAMA, 261*, 3259–2366.

Platt, J., & Labate, C. (1976). *Heroin addiction: Theory research and treatment.* New York: Wiley.

Rogers, C. (1979). The case of Ms. Oak. In D. Wedding & R. J. Corsini (Eds.), *Great cases in psychotherapy.* Itasca, IL: Peacock.

Rhodes, J., & Jason, L. A. (1988). *Preventing substance abuse among children and adolescents.* New York: Pergamon Press.

Schinke, S. P., & Blythe, B. J. (1981). Cognitive-behavioral prevention of children's smoking. *Child Behavior Therapy, 3*(4), 25–42.

Schinke, S. P., & Gilchrist, L. D. (1983). Primary prevention of tobacco smoking. *Journal of School Health,* *53*, 416–419.

Schinke, S. P., & Gilchrist, L. D. (1984). *Life skills counseling with adolescents.* Baltimore, MD: University Park Press.

Smart, R. (1980). An availability-proneness theory of illicit drug abuse. In D. J. Lettieri, M. Sayers, & H. W. Pearson (Eds.), *Theories on drug abuse: Selected contemporary perspectives.* NIDA Research Monograph 30 DHHS.

Sutherland, D., & Cressey, R. (1974). *Criminology.* Philadelphia: Lippincott.

Szapocznik, J., Santiesteban, D., Rio, A., Perez-Vidal, A. D., Santiesteban, D., & Kurtines, W. (1989). Family effectiveness training: An intervention to prevent drug abuse and problem behaviors in Hispanic adolescents. *Hispanic Journal of Behavioral Sciences, 11,* 4–27.

Winick, C. (1980). A theory of drug dependence based on role, access to and attitudes toward drugs. In D. J. Lettieri, M. Sayers, & H. W. Pearson (Eds.), *Theories on drug abuse: Selected contemporary perspectives.* NIDA Research Monograph 30 DHHS.

Yamaguchi, K., & Kandel, D. (1984), Patterns of drug use from adolescence to young adulthood: II sequences of progression. *American Journal of Public Health, 74,* 668–672.

SUPPLEMENTAL READING LIST

Newcomb, M. D., & Bentler, P. (1988). Impact of adolescent drug use and social support on problems of young adults: A longitudinal study. *Journal of Abnormal Psychology, 97*(1), 64–75.

This article examines the impact of drug use on the problems of young adults in later life. The regular use of cannibis is associated with increased health and family problems. Alcohol use had no specific negative effects but reduced loneliness in romantic relationships, self-derogation, and family problems. Hard drug use had a wide range of negative effects on health, psychosomatic symptoms, emotional distress, and interpersonal relationships.

Johnston, L. D., O'Malley, P. M. & Bachman, J. (1989). *Drug use, drinking and smoking: National survey results from high school college and young adult populations, 1975–1988.* Washington, DC: National Institute on Drug Abuse.

This report contains findings from the 12-year annual survey of drug use and related attitudes of high school students, college students, and young adults. Each year a representative sample of all seniors in public and private high schools in the United States is surveyed. Students then are followed into young adulthood. This sort of longitudinal data provides unique insights into a population particularly at risk.

Szapocznik, J., & Kurtines, W. (in press). Brief strategic family therapy for Hispanic problem youth. In L. Beutler (Ed.), *Programs in psychotherapy research.* Washington, DC: American Psychological Association.

This study considers the efficacy of Brief Strategic Family Therapy, an intervention developed to achieve the goals of family therapy when it is not possible to have the whole family present. The article further develops another technique aimed at bringing entire families into therapy when there is resistance—the other side of the coin. This technique, Strategic Structural Systems Engagement, is also tested using an experimental design. In both cases, the samples are composed of Hispanic families. Yet a final technique is assessed, Bicultural Effectiveness Training. Such training is hypothesized to reduce intergenerational conflict acculturation and differing cultural alliances. Again an experimental design is used.

CHAPTER 9

Addicted Mothers—Addicted Infants and Children: Social Work Strategies for Building Support Networks

Edith M. Freeman
University of Kansas

Go into your neighbor's house and see the infant child bewitched by the firelight, while the mother is busied at her tasks.

Kahlil Gibran, "On Joy and Sorrow," *Secrets of the Heart*

With the rapid growth of drug and alcohol abuse in the United States among the general population, there has been increased concern about the magnitude of this problem among young women of child-bearing years (Streissguth, Clarren, & Jones, 1985; Wager & Keith, 1981). Concerns have focused on the effects of drugs on mothers as well as their effects on fetal and infant development. The women are at high risk for contracting sexually transmitted diseases and for physical assaults or death through prostitution and drug-dealing experiences. Other consequences are dysfunctional relationships with family members and peers along with employment instability.

For the infants, a broad array of short- and long-term effects have been identified, including prenatal, perinatal, and postnatal complications (Householder, Hatcher, Burns & Chasnoff, 1982). Examples of these short-term effects involve low birth weight, intrauterine respiratory distress, shorter than average labor periods, increased risk of breech deliveries, and severe postnatal withdrawal symptoms from the addiction. Withdrawal complications can develop in babies even when their moth-

ers are involved in a drug treatment program. Infant addiction and withdrawal may result from the mother's drug abuse prior to treatment and from drug maintenance therapy during the program. Householder et al. (1982) found that for mothers enrolled in a methadone maintenance program, "the severity of withdrawal [in the infant] seems to be related primarily to the degree of polydrug abuse by the mother and secondarily to the maternal dosage of methadone" (p. 455). This process has been labeled the neonatal narcotic abstinence syndrome; it occurs from a woman's prolonged or intermittent use of some drugs, while a single episode of using drugs such as cocaine can cause the infant's addiction (Kron, Kaplan, Finnegan, Litt & Phoenix, 1975).

Many of these short-term effects are serious; the long-term effects on addicted infants are noteworthy also. They include attachment problems resulting from the infant's constant agitation and exhaustion and from the challenge to the caregiver's ability to deal patiently and empathically with the infant. Child neglect and abuse in such circumstances are not uncommon due to these dynamics. Another long-term effect can be disturbances in the child's motor and cognitive development, although researchers differ in how long these delays and disturbances might last (Householder et al., 1982; Chasnoff, Hatcher, & Burns, 1982; Streissguth et al. 1985). Finally, these infants require a greater rate of out-of-home placements due to the probability that their addicted mothers will be unable to care for them adequately (Coppolilo, 1975; Miller & Carlton, 1988). The rapid increase in addicted infants is exhausting an already strained child welfare system in terms of the number of placements required and the special needs involved. For example, some of these babies have AIDS or the AIDS-Related Complex (ARC), conditions that require a specific medical regimen and education for dealing with caregivers' natural fears about protecting themselves and their families from contracting the disease (Miller & Carlton, 1988).

The epigraph to this chapter, by Kahlil Gibran (1968), is consistent with the admonition by Householder et al. (1982) that problems and needs of this magnitude demand societal attention. Many authors have noted that fragmented and incomplete information about this dual high-risk population should be integrated. The purpose of this chapter is to integrate current information about the incidence and consequences of this phenomenon for families, communities, and society as a whole. It includes a discussion of the formal and informal networks available for meeting the placement needs of the growing population of addicted infants and appropriate treatment strategies. The implications for social work roles and values are also addressed based on the proposed treatment strategies.

MATERNAL AND INFANT ADDICTIONS

The literature documents the extent to which mothers and their infants are at risk from exposure to both legal and illegal drugs. According to Chisum (1986), "The harmful exposure may be from appropriate use of prescribed, legal drugs or from the inappropriate use of legal and illegal drugs" (p. 89). Some of the most common drugs abused by pregnant women include alcohol, Valium, PCP, cocaine, marijuana, methamphetamines, and heroin

and methadone. All references in this chapter to drug abuse among pregnant women include alcohol use and abuse (along with fetal alcohol syndrome), contrary to the custom of separating alcohol from other drugs in the literature. In addition, although in other segments of the drug-abusing population a distinction is made between casual users and abusers, such distinctions are irrelevant for pregnant women since minimal use of some drugs can produce profound and long-term effects on the fetus. Moreover, many of these women are addicted to several drugs and may use them in combination or in a sequential pattern over time (Finnegan & Fehr, 1980). This section focuses on the dynamics, incidence, and consequences of the addiction for those directly and indirectly involved.

Dynamics Associated with the Addiction

Generally, a woman has developed an addiction prior to becoming pregnant; and although some women attempt to stop their usage during this period, many do not. (Chisum, 1986). Seldom do they come for prenatal care until shortly before or at the point of delivery. Because they are addicted, they often pay very little attention to their bodies so that the symptoms of pregnancy may go unnoticed. Similarly, few addicted women use birth control procedures or protect themselves from sexually transmitted diseases through the use of condoms (Schuckit & Morrisey, 1976; Wager & Keith, 1981). Some of the women are involved in increased sexual activity through prostitution in order to obtain drugs or money. Others who are addicted to crack exhibit the increased sexual activity characteristic of this drug during the quick and intensive "highs" that it produces (Van Gelder & Brandt, 1986). A number of women have experienced rapes and other forms of sexual assault due, according to Hale (1989), to a lack of ability to judge unsafe circumstances while under the influence or while attempting to obtain drugs from dealers. Thus, for a number of reasons these women may be more at risk for pregnancy than other women of childbearing age (*Women, Drugs, and Babies*, 1989).

Moreover, when they are evaluated in medical or drug treatment programs, many fail to provide information that identifies their infants as high risk for addiction or they may not admit they are pregnant (Smith, 1986; Brody, 1989). Addicted mothers can be poor historians simply because they may attempt to hide the magnitude of their usage for legal reasons and because being under the influence makes it difficult for them to remember specific details about their drug use. The phenomenon of denial that is part of the addiction process in all drug users is a factor as well.

Significant family or social relationships may have been severed due to the woman's drug abuse. The fathers of the babies may be either unknown or the women may not wish to have them involved (Hale, 1989). The result is often a series of distant or cutoff relationships and a lack of social supports that tend to reinforce the woman's sense of hopelessness about her addiction and the potential plight of her child. Hale (1989) notes that placement alternatives for the child may be limited as a consequence. All these factors make it difficult to identify strengths within this population, although they often exist, and to provide appropriate services as needed (Kantor, 1978).

Although the dynamics of each woman's addiction problems pose barriers to understanding her needs, some authors emphasize that obtaining even biased information can help in making decisions about the prognosis of drug treatment for the mother and placement alternatives for the child. Kantor (1978) indicates that information about the kinds of drugs used, usage patterns, frequency rates, the period of drug usage, periods of abstinence, and available social supports are vital in clarifying the needs of a particular mother and her baby.

The Incidence and Patterns of Addiction

Information about the incidence of addiction among pregnant women can be useful in a similar way for clarifying the needs of this population in general. Methods for obtaining such information include the rates of calls to drug hotlines; drug histories, life event scales, and urine screenings in treatment programs; studies of drug abusers that include both self-report data and more objective data; and tests on infants born to addicted mothers (Miller, 1989; Van Gelder & Brandt, 1986; Householder et al., 1982). Even when systematic methods for documenting the incidence of drug abuse among pregnant women are used, biases are likely so care must be taken in how such statistics are interpreted and used.

The incidence of drug use in pregnant women varies based on the source of information as well as the drug(s) involved. Estimates from a number of national studies conducted in 1988 indicate that 10 to 11 percent of all births were to mothers who abused drugs. Some 375,000 infants born during that year are thought to have been damaged by drug exposure (Miller, 1989).

These estimates increase when the number of cocaine users is isolated; for instance, according to recent studies conducted in large urban areas, as many as one in 10 babies may have been exposed to cocaine before they were born (Public Health Education Information Sheet, 1989). Further, in large urban areas African American women appear to be among the highest percentage of pregnant users (estimates range from 45 to 65 percent of female abusers) (*Women, Drugs, and Babies*, 1989).

Cocaine appears to be the most common drug used by the pregnant women who have been studied, either singularly or in combination with some of the other drugs identified in the previous section. The incidence of females in general who abuse cocaine has increased also. Among the growing number of cocaine addicts (5 million), one-half are thought to be women. A similar percentage of women may be among the 24 million individuals who have tried cocaine once or who restrict their intake to "party use" (Van Gelder & Brandt, 1986). In 1983, one-third of the 1,000 people who called the National Cocaine Hotline (1-800-COCAINE) daily were women, while in 1986 45 percent of the callers were women. Moreover, a survey of this hotline's users indicated that 80 percent of male callers seek drug treatment after contact, but only 20 percent of the female callers do so (Van Gelder & Brandt, 1986).

Cocaine may be attractive to childbearing women for the same reasons that other segments of the population become physically and psychologically addicted to it. In its beginning or seductive stage the drug is energizing and builds the user's self-confidence. It is called a party or fun drug during this "A" stage of increased sensuality. The "B" stage is one in which the previous funhouse effects are grossly distorted, leading to lethargy and difficulty in concentrating, as well as to loss of the individual's sexual drive (Van Gelder & Brandt, 1986).

In addition to these common reasons for a high incidence of cocaine use, the drug may be more appealing to women in general because of the myth that it is an appetite suppressant and a "clean" casual-use drug. Women of childbearing years may be even more vulnerable to cocaine use because initially it bolsters self-esteem and provides a false sense of status. Developmentally, these women may be intensely aware of the devalued status of women in this society and are likely to be experiencing identity confusion and rapid role transitions—although some studies show the average age of female abusers to have risen from 21 in 1983 to 29 in 1989 (Brody, 1989; Hale, 1989). Crack, the smokable and inexpensive form of cocaine, may have increased the incidence of drug use in this population for similar reasons. Most studies do not separate the incidence of crack abuse from other forms of cocaine use; therefore, according to Van Gelder and Brandt (1986), it is difficult to estimate the number of women who are addicted to crack. Assumptions about crack abuse indicate that because this addiction is more rapid in its development, its incidence is increasing astronomically among this population of women and among other subgroups of abusers.

Alcohol cannot be ignored in any discussion about the incidence of addicted mothers and infants. It continues to be a hidden menace in terms of the problem of fetal alcohol syndrome. Estimates of the number of women alcohol abusers range from 20 to 50 percent of all persons who are addicted (Turnbull, 1988). Evidence shows that the rate of alcohol problems among women in general has been steadily increasing since World War II. Yet in spite of this apparent increase and the increased attention it has received, the rate of women participating in alcoholism treatment has not increased accordingly (Smith, 1986). Turnbull (1988) and Schuckit and Morrisey (1976) found that female alcoholics are more likely to enter the mental health system under a psychiatric label than males (for example, with a diagnosis of depression) and that this factor may contribute to the low incidence of females identified as alcohol abusers in the literature.

In the study of the characteristics of 90 newborns who were born at UCLA between 1983 and 1984 with a history of positive drug exposure, 21 of their mothers had abused alcohol, compared with 48 who abused cocaine (the most commonly used drug) (*Women, Drugs, and Babies*, 1989). Many of these mothers had been polydrug users, so frequently these statistics overlap. Similarly, a study of 14 hospitals (and 915 newborns) conducted by the

C. Henry Kempe National Center for the Prevention and Treatment of Child Abuse and Neglect indicated in 1986 that the frequency of alcohol exposure in newborns was 3.80 percent when compared to exposure to all other drugs. Cocaine, PCP, and heroin were the most frequently used drugs to which the infants had been exposed in utero at 58.06, 10.33, and 7.16 percent respectively (*Women, Drugs, and Babies*, 1989).

Pregnant women and their babies are constantly being exposed to "new" drugs as a reflection of general changes in the drug culture. Currently, for instance, the incidence of methamphetamines such as ice is rapidly increasing, spreading from Hawaii (*Kansas City Times*, 1989). The use of ice is likely to continue to increase, since it provides a more prolonged high (12 to 24 hours) than crack (only 15-20 minutes), and it does not produce the depression that often comes immediately after the use of crack. Consequently, the highest incidence in the use of this smokable drug is expected to occur among those who are addicted to crack, including pregnant women (*Kansas City Times*, 1989). Further, early reports from individuals entering drug treatment programs in the past year in New York indicate that another common pattern of using crack is in combination with smokable heroin (Marriott, 1989). The mixture is considered particularly dangerous because it combines the physical addiction of heroin with the intense high of crack.

Even with these alarming statistics, the incidence of addicted mothers and infants is thought to be undercounted. This fact has been attributed to "maternal denial of drug use, lack of clinician sensitivity to indicators of drug use, and the inaccuracy of toxic screening" (Miller, 1989, pp. 21–22). Undercounting tends to deemphasize the magnitude of the problem as well as the consequences of addiction.

The Consequences of Addiction

As noted previously, there are a number of short- and long-term consequences for both mothers and infants from chronic, maternal drug abuse. The neonatal withdrawal syndrome during and after delivery poses the greatest difficulty for babies if they survive the drug exposure in utero. The consequences prior to delivery are heightened by the differential effects of drugs on the infant when compared to those effects on the mother. With cocaine use, for example, a more potent by-product of the drug called norcocaine remains trapped in the placenta after the initial exposure. This means that once the drug leaves the mother's system within 48 hours, its effects on her are diminished. But for the infant, this same drug exposure continues for four or five days while also the norcocaine is excreted into the amniotic fluid and swallowed by the fetus, thus re-exposing it to the drug and its damaging effects (Brody, 1989).

In general, other consequences for babies can be summarized as complications of labor and delivery, neonatal withdrawal, sudden infant death syndrome (SIDS), newborn lethargy, cognitive and motor disturbances, disturbances of state and feeding, and attachment problems (Householder et al., 1982; Finnegan & Fehr, 1980; Chevez, Ostrea, Stryker, & Smialek, 1982; Herlinger, Kandall, & Vaughn, 1977). More specifically, some of the consequences of addiction for infants based on the primary drug(s) used by the mother can be seen in Table 9.1. The consequences range from short-term withdrawal effects during and after delivery to the long-range cognitive and motor disabilities that have been noted

TABLE 9.1. Short- and Long-Term Effects for Alcohol- and Drug-addicted Infants

Drug	Prenatal Effects	Postnatal and Ongoing Effects
1. Alcohol Fetal-alcohol syndrome from four beers per day or more alcohol consumed on a regular basis.	Growth retardation including microcephaly Mental retardation Genital-urinary defects Heart defects Vision and hearing problems Depressed immune system	Occasional withdrawal Small head size Retardation: mild to moderate Hyperactivity and distractibility a major problem in school
2. Cocaine Any dose can kill or maim a fetus.	Premature separation of placenta from the uterine wall leading to prolonged bleeding, possibly death (spontaneous abortion) Strokes Heart attacks Birth defects including growth retardation, missing limbs, and genital-urinary problems.	Withdrawal At any time during the two- to three-week period after birth: severe irritability, sleeplessness, intolerance to stimuli or change Increased risk of Sudden Infant Death Syndrome (SIDS) By two to five years difficulty with learning, dexterity, social play, and speech
3. Heroin/methadone Any amount addictive to the mother is addictive to the fetus.	Growth retardation Violent withdrawal if the mother withdraws Extremely rapid labor and birth; risk of spontaneous abortions Hepatitis (intravenous drug use in mother)	Withdrawal: can persist up to six months, which interferes with bonding and learning Respiratory distress Sneezing Sweating Convulsions (greater in methadone babies than heroin babies) Five- to tenfold increase in risk of SIDS Speech and language delays Hyperactivity Delayed cognitive-dexterity skills
4. Marijuana Risk is uncertain; increased risks when marijuana is combined with phenocyclidine (PCP).	Growth retardation	Withdrawal symptoms Increased risk of SIDS Decreased neonatal visual responses to light Developmental delays when marijuana is combined with PCP use
5. Methamphetamines Research is limited.	Similar to the effects of cocaine	Similar to the effects of cocaine Optic and respiratory complications Problems frequently not manifesting themselves until after the child is released from hospital

in school-age children at the age of six and seven years. Additional information will no doubt become available through research about more long-term effects as these drug-involved children age (Chasnoff et al., 1982).

In addition to the general consequences shown in Table 9.1, AIDS and AIDS-Related Complex need to be considered for a specific subset of drug-exposed infants and children. As of January, 1987, 410 pediatric AIDS cases and 247 deaths among this population had been reported to the Centers for Disease Control (CDC) with approximately 70 percent of these children being African American or Hispanic (Centers for Disease Control, 1986). For those affected children who survive the effects of this disease after delivery (most contract the disease in utero from a mother who is an intravenous drug user), other consequences are Kaposi's sarcoma, life-threatening opportunistic infections, mental retardation, developmental delays, breathing difficulties, fever, and unexplained enlargement of the liver, spleen, and lymph glands, as well as rapid weight loss (Gurdin & Anderson, 1987). Children with ARC, who may or may not develop full-blown AIDS, often have milder forms of some of these less severe symptoms.

Even in situations where a child does not have AIDS, the consequences for both the babies and their mothers include increased risk of out-of-home placements for the children. This is especially the case when the mother has a personal history of child abuse or neglect, denies her drug involvement, and demonstrates poor impulse control (*Women, Drugs, and Babies*, 1989). In addition, factors such as the presence of health and safety hazards and a lack of preparation for the infant's arrival may be considered in this determination. Kantor (1978) stresses that the presence or absence of a viable support system is another factor. Although some of the mothers abandon their infants at the hospital following delivery and others are unable to bond with their child emotionally, some plan to keep the child with them. For those mothers, the consequence of losing custody of the child is stressful even though objectively placement may be in the best interests of the child (Coppolilo, 1975).

Other maternal consequences include inadequate housing or a lack of housing. According to Hale (1989), many of the women live periodically with relatives, in shelters, or in drug houses night by

night. Others live in abandoned housing where they are at risk for violence and exposure to the cold if the climate is harsh. The lack of employment and an adequate income is another consequence. The cost of maintaining a drug habit, along with the pregnancy, make it unlikely that these women will stay employed; but these factors increase the likelihood that they will become involved in crimes such as prostitution and robbery to support their drug habits (Van Gelder & Brandt, 1986). A final consequence for mothers involves medial complications that often develop from the combination of pregnancy and chronic drug use. These complications are the increased risk of heart attack and sudden death, AIDS, hepatitis, malnutrition, and spontaneous abortion and uncontrolled bleeding (Perlmutter, 1977; *Women, Drugs, and Babies*, 1989). Since these consequences affect a growing number of persons who are directly and indirectly involved, a more comprehensive range of supports is needed at this time.

FORMAL AND INFORMAL SUPPORT NETWORKS

Currently, many of the needs of the children born to addicted mothers are met through a series of complicated and fragmented services. These services include those provided by boarder hospitals in which abandoned babies are kept indefinitely or until they can be placed elsewhere (Brody, 1989). Some of the children in these hospitals, many of them with AIDS or severe neurological and developmental complications, have been in those settings for up to three years (Gurdin & Anderson, 1987). Other children are left with relatives or in regular foster care; a few have been adopted. Some are returned to the natural mothers after the women have completed drug treatment programs and other forms of intensive mental health counseling. Services are not only fragmented; they also lag behind identified needs by several years. Clearly, a more comprehensive set of interacting formal and informal support networks is needed as appropriate resources for addicted mothers and their babies.

Formal Service Networks

A comprehensive formal network of services should range from programs serving mothers prenatally to those serving mothers and infants through early childhood and beyond. The formation and implementation of these networks is in its infancy although some examples do exist (Hale, 1989). An important element of such services is their linkage with informal support networks, with priority being given first to using those natural resources that exist in a community, then to using the existing formal resources, and finally to the development of new resources to fill in the gaps in either formal or informal resources. Figure 9.1 indicates the range of formal services needed and some of their characteristics. It is important to note that linkages exist within the model between health, education, housing, employment, legal, day care, foster care, hospice, drug treatment, and respite programs for mothers and babies.

Within this model of formal services, such a

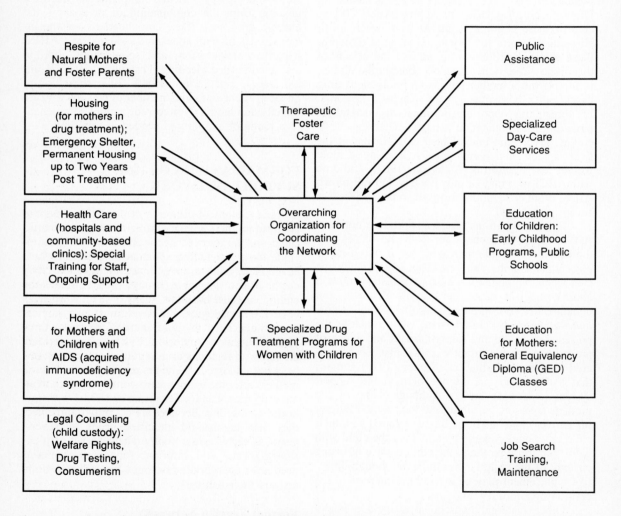

Note: In a fully functioning network, all systems / organizations interact with and have equal access to each other. During an initial phase, the coordinating body is the hub, as illustrated here.

Figure 9.1. Formal Network of Services for Addicted Mothers and Infants

network between programs is vital. One mechanism for facilitating this type of network is to develop an overarching nonprofit organization charged with developing and coordinating all service aspects of the model through the range of subsystems. An advantage is that the coordination can be more effective since the overarching organization plans and develops the component programs and is responsible for operating them on a daily basis (Hale, 1989). Further, this type of organizational model has the capacity to contract with an existing, fragmented set of services and programs to provide more comprehensive resources. An example of this form of the model is Hale House Foundation in New York (Hale, 1989).

An alternative mechanism is the development of a consortium of large systems that implements a coordinating body represented by members from each large system. In this type of organization model described by Gurdin and Anderson (1987), the coordinating body is responsible for advocacy and policy development, but only monitors rather than operates the component services within the formal network. The coordinating body is also charged with running the coordinating or linking system itself (Gurdin & Anderson, 1987). Finally, some form of evaluation research should be involved to document who is being served by the formal *and* informal networks and to what degree of effectiveness. Evaluation should include naturalistic methods as well as the more scientifically controlled methods.

Informal Support Network

Although the informal support network should be the first priority as a resource, the formal network has been discussed first since the latter must be in place in order for professional staff to draw upon the strengths and resources within the informal network. Figure 9.2 illustrates various components of the informal support network within a community that may be operating effectively or that may need to be strengthened. Many of these components typically may not be thought of as strengths and resources, particularly within poor and minority communities (Hale, 1989), although they may be recognizable within the communities of more affluent and majority group drug abusers.

Consequently, it is easy for practitioners to overlook some informal strengths and resources that

may be available for helping addicted mothers and babies in less affluent communities due to stereotypes. For instance, in some families grandmothers are also addicted and are not able to provide alternative placements while mothers are in drug treatment programs or when they abandon their infants. Moreover, grandmothers and significant others who are addicted can pose threats to the mother's continued recovery *after* drug treatment is completed (Hale, 1989). Figure 9.2 helps to broaden alternative solutions to out-of-home placements and to identify natural resources that support recovery within a given community.

In addition, Figures 9.1 and 9.2 indicate how integration of formal and informal support networks can be achieved in each of the need areas addressed in the model. For instance, recruitment and maintenance of foster parents is vital within this model, especially for children born addicted who also have AIDS. Day care can provide support and respite for foster parents. Yet some states have decreed that no children testing positive for the virus can attend daycare or Head Start programs within their jurisdiction (Gurdin & Anderson, 1987); thus there is a need for specialized services in those areas. Natural helpers in communities can be hired as day-care providers in their homes or they can help advocate for having a designated number of beds set aside for special needs children in local day-care centers. According to Hale (1989), they can be trained (by the coordinating body of the formal network in some instances) to become part of the staff of day-care centers to help meet the special needs of these children. The latter strategy is useful because it strengthens the informal network while integrating the work of the formal and informal networks. Coordination between these networks is an important aspect of the treatment approach and the other strategies that are useful for helping the at-risk population.

INTERVENTION STRATEGIES

This integrative model of formal and informal resources is predicated on an underlying strengths perspective and on systems theory. It assumes that although particular drug-abusing women may be more vulnerable to substance abuse than others, all have individual and environmental strengths. Strengths can be enhanced, or in areas where they

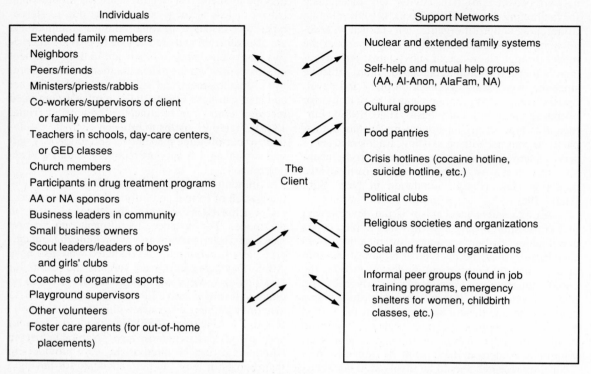

Individuals

Extended family members
Neighbors
Peers/friends
Ministers/priests/rabbis
Co-workers/supervisors of client
  or family members
Teachers in schools, day-care centers,
  or GED classes
Church members
Participants in drug treatment programs
AA or NA sponsors
Business leaders in community
Small business owners
Scout leaders/leaders of boys'
  and girls' clubs
Coaches of organized sports
Playground supervisors
Other volunteers
Foster care parents (for out-of-home
  placements)

The
Client

Support Networks

Nuclear and extended family systems
Self-help and mutual help groups
  (AA, Al-Anon, AlaFam, NA)
Cultural groups
Food pantries
Crisis hotlines (cocaine hotline,
  suicide hotline, etc.)
Political clubs
Religious societies and organizations
Social and fraternal organizations
Informal peer groups (found in job
  training programs, emergency
  shelters for women, childbirth
  classes, etc.)

Note: Natural helpers include individuals and support networks. They feature easy access to people in their natural environments; emotional support, concrete resources, and problem solving; and help is reciprocal. GED= General Equivalency Diploma; AA= Alcoholics Anonymous; NA=Narcotics Anonymous; Al-Anon= Alcoholics Anonymous family groups; AlaFam= Alcoholics Anonymous support group.

Figure 9.2. Informal Support Systems

do not exist they can be developed, through the use of intervention strategies at the community level and those designed to help individuals and families.

Community Strategies

Because of traditional discrepancies in resource allocations to poor and minority communities, this model emphasizes the need for a more effective advocacy and policy development by practitioners serving these communities. Such strategies will need to be used differentially, however, in all communities where services are needed. To begin with, all communities may benefit from prevention programs. One strategy is community education provided through the media and through churches and

other community organizations. Media exposure can include public information announcements on television and radio, entertainment and news programs about addicted mothers and their babies, and letters or direct testimony by individuals who have been affected by the problem (Hale, 1989).

In community education seminars, the focus can be on the incidence and consequences of drug abuse in general with special emphasis on how particular subgroups, such as pregnant women and those of childbearing ages, are at high risk for the problem. The more communities understand how widespread substance abuse is among pregnant women in all circumstances, the less likely they will view it as a problem that affects only inner city and poor communities (Brody, 1989).

Some existing drug abuse prevention programs for teenagers in schools or for the general public in mental health centers are appropriate sites for providing information about the heightened risks to mothers and infants. Specialized drug treatment programs for women provide another useful opportunity for education about such risks (Schuckit & Morrisey, 1976; *Women, Drugs, and Babies*, 1989) as a form of primary prevention for some clients. Programs for preventing and treating the problem of teenage pregnancy should be targeted also for this information. Because the problem is a particularly complex one, education alone may not be sufficient. Experiential strategies can be combined with education, including psychodrama, visits to hospitals to observe addicted infants, and discussions with addicted mothers about the consequences of the problem (Hale, 1989).

Other community-level interventive strategies can involve policy development and advocacy. Practitioners might join natural helpers in a community along with business and civic leaders (Hale, 1989) to form nontraditional coalitions. Joining opportunities can be enhanced by the networking contacts made·possible through the integrative model illustrated in Figures 9.1 and 9.2. These coalitions may be useful in organizing demonstrations to call attention to drug houses in a community, to develop self-help drug prevention campaigns, and to provide testimony before legislative bodies that make policies at local, state, and federal levels.

Practitioners and community residents can work together to pressure hospitals to provide more prenatal services in communities where the incidence of drug abuse among pregnant women is high or is increasing. Hospitals may need assistance from attorneys and helping professionals to develop policies that encourage these mothers to come for prenatal care and to discontinue drug use during pregnancy. There is some controversy about detecting drug abuse during pregnancy and hospitalizing mothers against their will to keep them off drugs. Some mothers whose infants have been born addicted and then died have been prosecuted (Watson, 1990). Sorting out the rights of mothers and infants while educating policymakers about the dynamics of addiction can make advocacy particularly difficult in this area.

Watson (1990) presents a cogent summary of some of the legal issues involved in terms of moth-

ers' and children's rights based on her experience as a social worker, judge, and attorney:

1. The rights of mothers to choose their own medical care including whether to enter alcohol treatment.
2. Whether the fetus' rights can be called into question since a particular debilitating effect for an infant cannot be predicted prior to birth, only assumed if the mother is using drugs.
3. Whether the fetus is a person and whether the mother, therefore, can be legally charged with delivering an addicted child.
4. To what extent helping professionals and others can be charged with failure to report a pregnant woman who uses drugs (under child abuse reporting laws). (pp. 8–9)

Given the current debate about these issues, a number of recommendations have been proposed as interim measures. Watson (1990) has summarized the following possibilities which the courts, social agencies, and hospitals might consider from the least restrictive to the most restrictive:

1. Establish limited guardianship through court action for pregnant women in need of drug treatment who fail to enter treatment voluntarily (forced treatment)
2. Provide intensive family preservation services to pregnant women or mothers and infants in the home to encourage drug treatment, prenatal care, and other significant changes
3. Provide specialized foster care services to pregnant women or mothers and infants that includes drug treatment also
4. Allow the courts to have complete legal jurisdiction and supervision of a child on the assumption that the presence of drugs such as cocaine in the newborn infant constitutes prenatal child abuse

Depending on a particular woman's circumstances, some of these interim suggestions are not feasible; for example, number 2 would not work with homeless women. Number 4 above assumes that resources for placements are adequate or could be improved.

Advocacy could be used to negotiate for placement resources or with drug treatment programs to increase the number of beds set aside for women. Treatment programs might be encouraged to provide child care services to clients after delivery and to those who have other children. In other circumstances, advocacy may take the form of helping a public housing authority to use vacant units for mothers involved in outpatient drug treatment or for those who need housing after completing inpatient treatment.

Strategies for Individuals and Families

The community-level prevention and intervention strategies in the previous section can be augmented with intervention strategies used with individual clients and their families. Similarly, the focus of the latter is on developing or enhancing existing resources and strengths at a small systems, rather than large systems, level. A family systems theoretical approach is useful whether the practitioner is working only with the addicted pregnant woman/mother or with her family and peers as well. Problem-solving approaches and reality therapy are useful also. Intervention strategies include the following:

1. Alcohol and drug education
2. Confrontation about the fact and consequences of addiction related to the mother, infant, and family members
3. Clarification about strengths and barriers in the life situation, including the presence of role models, alternative caretakers, and addiction problems in significant others
4. Provision of emotional support
5. Provision of tangible resources such as housing, child care, and employment
6. Resolution of conflicts and other sources of stress
7. Teaching of communication skills and the handling of feelings more appropriately, and
8. Teaching of specialized problem-solving techniques

The use of these strategies can be demonstrated through the following case example:

An upper-income white couple had used cocaine for two years when the woman became pregnant and decided to stop using until after delivery. After two episodes of false labor, her husband encouraged her to take a "hit" to force the labor. The child suffered a stroke during delivery, causing permanent paralysis on one side. The mother entered drug treatment two months after delivery due to guilt and pressures from her parents. She was able to maintain abstinence for about nine months until her husband's continued use encouraged *her* to return to heavy cocaine usage. During her second attempt at treatment a year later, she was asked to bring her husband for specialized sessions for spouses and partners. Confrontation from other group members who were enablers and users themselves helped to erode denial of his addiction and the effects on his wife. Although child care, housing, employment, and other services were not necessary, emotional support, clarification of strengths and barriers (addiction of peers), and the teaching of communication and problem-solving skills were useful. These interventions facilitated the couple's recovery and enhanced their ability to parent their disabled child.

Moreover, some of the community-level prevention and intervention strategies discussed in the previous section would have been useful in strengthening the natural *and* formal resources in their community. Perhaps many of their peers could have benefited from a drug prevention program and a drug awareness media campaign aimed at their particular community, especially women in childbearing years. Medical personnel and helping professionals serving the community could have been involved in a more specialized staff training program and the development of policies about the handling of newborns addicted to drugs such as cocaine. The rehabilitation of addicted mothers is another area of service that had not been addressed within that community.

In a second example, the circumstances affecting the addicted mother and family as well as the community resources were somewhat different:

A 24-year-old African American woman addicted to crack and alcohol asked a counselor in a drug rehabilitation program for help in getting her baby placed. At intake, Carolyn mentioned the child had been kept in the hospital for a few weeks following its birth due to complications. Later, staff learned that the infant had been held by the hospital because it was born addicted. Carolyn had been brought to

CHAPTER 10

Intravenous Drug Use and AIDS: Community Approaches to Social Work Revisited

Carl G. Leukefeld
National Institute on Drug Abuse

Robert J. Battjes
National Institute on Drug Abuse

An ounce of prevention is worth a pound of cure.

Anonymous

Intravenous drug abuse has played a major role in the spread of the AIDS epidemic. Intravenous drug abusers comprise the second largest group that has contracted AIDS in the United States. HIV infection is spread among intravenous drug abusers primarily through the sharing of drug injection equipment, and it can also be spread between these drug abusers through sexual contact. In addition to HIV transmission among intravenous drug abusers, heterosexual and perinatal spread of AIDS is largely associated with intravenous drug abuse. The purpose of this chapter is to explore community efforts to prevent the spread of AIDS among intravenous drug abusers, their sexual partners, and their children. Due to the rapid spread of the disease and continuing in-

creases in the incidence of heavy intravenous drug use, community approaches offer a more viable resolution to the problem than do more individually focused strategies. A program-level case example is included to illustrate how community approaches can be implemented effectively.

OVERVIEW OF THE AIDS EPIDEMIC

HIV infection has spread at an alarming rate in the United States, and the number of new AIDS cases continues to increase. In 1988 the U.S. Public Health Service (PHS) estimated that one to one and one-half million Americans were infected with HIV (U.S. Public Health Service, 1988). As of May 1989, 94,280 cases of AIDS had been reported to the Centers for Disease Control, and 53,544 deaths had been reported (Centers for Disease Control, 1989b). The annual incidence of new cases has continued to climb, with 17,100 cases in 1986, 25,200 cases in 1987, and 33,454 cases in the one-

The opinions expressed in this chapter do not necessarily represent the position of the National Institute on Drug Abuse, the U.S. Public Health Service, or the Department of Health and Human Services. The chapter was prepared by federal government employees as part of official duties; therefore, the material is in the public domain and may be reproduced or copied without permission.

year period ending April 1989. The PHS has projected that 365,000 persons will contract AIDS by 1992, with 263,000 deaths as of that date (U.S. Public Health Service, 1988).

The AIDS epidemic is expected to escalate for some years. Since most individuals infected with HIV are asymptomatic and do not know that they are infected, the potential for further spread of the disease is considerable. While there is considerable concern about the general population of individuals who are HIV infected or have AIDS, there is growing recognition that new strategies are needed for effective work with the subgroups of intravenous drug abusers in this population.

EXTENT OF THE HIV/INTRAVENOUS DRUG ABUSE PROBLEM

The needs of intravenous drug abusers must be addressed for two important reasons. First, their drug abuse problems are associated with other serious dysfunctions in familial, work, social, legal, and health areas. Their cycle of hopelessness for change and denial of addiction problems is similar to that of all drug abusers in terms of how it develops and how it reinforces dysfunctional behaviors in the five life domains noted above. Secondly, the same cycle of hopelessness and denial encourage unsafe needle sharing and unsafe sex as well as a lack of adequate health care. Thus, the foundation is laid for the development of HIV infection and AIDS. The lack of attention to prevention of the disease is generalized to a lack of attention to treatment once the symptoms develop. Intravenous drug abusers, as a group, are more vulnerable to contracting the disease through their risk behaviors and to dying with little or no medical treatment as a result.

All of these factors provide a context for understanding the interrelated problem of intravenous drug abuse and AIDS. The extent of the problem varies somewhat based on gender, sexual preference, race, geography, and other variables. Twenty-seven percent of all adult cases of AIDS in the United States have occurred among intravenous drug abusers, including 20 percent among female and heterosexual male intravenous drug abusers and 7 percent among homosexual and bisexual men who are also intravenous drug abusers. Among persons

with AIDS who report having used drugs intravenously, 57 percent were heterosexual males, 26 percent were homosexual/bisexual males, and 17 percent were females. Altogether, 25,439 persons diagnosed with AIDS as of April 1989 reported having used drugs intravenously (CDC, 1989a). The importance of intravenous drug use in the heterosexual and perinatal spread of AIDS is also clear. Sexual partners of intravenous drug abusers account for 52 percent of AIDS cases attributed to heterosexual transmission, and 71 percent of perinatal AIDS cases are born to intravenous drug abusers and their sexual partners (Centers for Disease Control, 1989b).

The AIDS epidemic associated with intravenous drug abuse has especially impacted African Americans and Hispanics. African Americans comprise 50 percent of AIDS cases among heterosexual intravenous drug abusers, and Hispanics comprise 30 percent of these cases. Among homosexual/bisexual intravenous drug abusers with AIDS, African Americans comprise 25 percent and Hispanics 15 percent. The impact on minorities of AIDS associated with intravenous drug abuse is also reflected in AIDS cases among heterosexual partners of intravenous drug abusers (77 percent are African American or Hispanic) and in perinatal AIDS cases among the offspring of intravenous drug abusers (86 percent are African American or Hispanic) (Centers for Disease Control, 1989a).

While the racial composition of the general population of intravenous drug-abusers is not known, data on drug abuse treatment admissions, emergency room admissions related to heroin overdose, and medical examiner data clearly establish that intravenous drug abuse disproportionately affects minority groups (National Institute on Drug Abuse, 1983, 1986). Thus, the preponderance of African Americans and Hispanics among intravenous drug abuse associated AIDS cases is, at least in part, due to the overrepresentation of these ethnic groups among intravenous drug abusers. Whether other factors, such as differences in drug use practices, availability of sterile needles, or health status also account for the high concentration of cases among ethnic minorities is not clear at this time. The fact remains that AIDS associated with intravenous drug abuse disproportionately affects African Americans and Hispanics.

Geographically, AIDS associated with intravenous drug abuse has been largely concentrated in the northeastern United States, where the rate of such AIDS cases is 11.2 per 100,000 population, compared with 2.8 in the South, 2.7 in the West, and 1.0 in the Midwest. Rates of intravenous drug abuse associated with AIDS per 100,000 population are particularly high in Puerto Rico (31.6), New Jersey (21.4), and New York (19.2) (Centers for Disease Control, 1989b); yet, all 50 states have reported one or more AIDS cases who also report a history of intravenous drug abuse (Starcher, 1987).

SPREAD OF HIV INFECTION: INTRAVENOUS DRUG ABUSERS

Just as the AIDS case rate among intravenous drug abusers varies substantially across the United States, the rate of HIV infection in this population also varies. For example, 50 to 60 percent of intravenous drug abusers tested for HIV antibody have been found seropositive in New York City, northern New Jersey, and Puerto Rico, while rates below 5 percent have been reported in much of the remainder of the country (Centers for Disease Control, 1987; Hahn, Onorato, Jones, & Dougherty, 1988). A 1984 New Jersey study demonstrated that marked differences in infection rates can exist even within a limited geographic area. Among patients in methadone maintenance and detoxification programs, 59 percent of those within 5 miles of New York City were seropositive, compared with 45 percent 5 to 9 miles out, 24 percent 10 to 25 miles out, and 2 percent 100 miles from New York City (Weiss, Ginzburg, Goedert, Cantor, Altman, Robert-Guroff, Gallo, & Blattner, 1986).

Data on needle sharing among intravenous drug abusers suggest that geographic variation in HIV infection rates may be related to the time when HIV is introduced into a community, rather than differences in risk behaviors. According to their self-report, intravenous drug abusers in communities across the country commonly share needles and syringes, and seldom sterilize their shared injection equipment. For example, a 1985 study in California found that 80 percent of addicts reported sharing their needles (Levy, Carlson, Hinrichs, Lerche, Schenker, & Gardner, 1986). In another study conducted between September 1983 and March 1985,

68 percent of addicts admitted to an inpatient drug abuse treatment program in Dallas, Texas, reported sharing needles, and having shared them during 40 percent of their drug use episodes (Black, Dolan, DeFord, Rubenstein, Penk, Robinowitz, & Skinner, 1986). A study of intravenous drug abusers receiving drug abuse treatment in six areas of the United States (New York City, Baltimore, Tampa, San Antonio, Denver, and Southern California) found rates of needle sharing ranged from 70 percent in New York City to 99 percent in San Antonio (Lange, Primm, & Tennant, 1987).

Another study of intravenous drug abusers entering methadone treatment in five cities (New York City; Asbury Park, New Jersey; Trenton, New Jersey; San Antonio; and Los Angeles) found rates of needle sharing ranging from 76 percent in New York City to 94 percent in San Antonio, while few of those sharing needles reported always cleaning their needles (ranging from 4 percent in Trenton to 13 percent in Los Angeles) (Battjes & Pickens, 1988b). Among San Francisco addicts who acknowledged sharing needles, only 19 percent reported always sterilizing their needles, while another 16 percent reported that they usually sterilized their needles (Chaisson, Moss, Onishi, Osmond, & Carlson, 1987).

While high HIV infection rates in the United States presently appear to be limited to New York City, northern New Jersey, and Puerto Rico, intermediate infection rates are emerging in some areas. For example, in 1985 an HIV infection rate of 10 percent was found among a sample of heterosexual intravenous drug abusers in San Francisco (Chaisson et al., 1987). In 1986 infection rates of 29 percent in Baltimore (Lange et al., 1987) and 24 percent in New Bedford, Massachusetts (Lange et al., 1987), were reported. And 10 percent of intravenous drug abusers in Chicago were found to be HIV antibody positive in a 1988 study (Battjes, Pickens, & Amsel, 1989). Data from New York City and Edinburgh, Scotland, indicate that once HIV is introduced within a community, infection can spread very rapidly. In a New York City study, analysis of stored sera from a hepatitis B study indicated that HIV was first introduced among intravenous drug abusers in 1978. By 1979, approximately 25 percent of addicts enrolled in that study were seropositive for HIV.

More recent data collected to assess the extent of HIV infection among intravenous drug abusers indicate an infection rate of approximately 50 percent in 1985 and approximately 60 percent in the latter part of 1986 (Des Jarlais, 1987). In Edinburgh HIV seropositivity among intravenous drug abusers was approximately 50 percent within two years of the first identified seropositive sample (Robertson, Bucknall, Welsby, Roberts, Inglis, Peutherer, & Brettle, 1986). Thus, the potential for rapid spread of HIV among intravenous drug abusers appears to be considerable and has resulted in a growing number of dually diagnosed individuals.

SPREAD OF HIV INFECTION: SEXUAL AND PERINATAL TRANSMISSION

The U.S. Public Health Service has identified intravenous drug abusers as a major vector for the spread of AIDS to the general population (U.S. Public Health Service, 1986). While the numbers of heterosexual and perinatal transmission cases are small relative to other transmission categories (4,128 cases of heterosexual transmission and 1,233 perinatal cases through April 1989) (Centers for Disease Control, 1989a), the numbers of such cases are not insignificant and can be expected to increase substantially in future years. While the data on the ease of heterosexual HIV transmission are incomplete, there are indications that transmission may occur fairly readily, at least among regular sexual partners of persons with AIDS. For example, 58 percent of 45 spouses of persons with AIDS who reported no other risk factor were seropositive for HIV, and 12 of 14 initially seronegative spouses who continued to have sexual contact with their AIDS-diagnosed partners without using condoms subsequently became infected during the course of one study (Fischl, Dickinson, Scott, Klimas, Fletcher, & Parks, 1987). It appeared that the virus was transmitted with equal ease from men to women and from women to men. Similarly, in a study of regular sexual partners of persons with AIDS or AIDS-related conditions, 48 percent of 100 heterosexual partners with no other risk factors were infected, including 47 percent of 88 female partners and 58 percent of 12 male partners (Steigbigel, Maude, Feiner, Harris, Saltzman, & Klein, 1987).

Many intravenous drug abusers are sexually active. A substantial portion of female addicts and some male addicts resort to prostitution to support their drug habits. For example, in a study of opiate addicts in Baltimore, 35 percent of females and 19 percent of males reported that they had engaged in prostitution, defined as having engaged in sex for money or drugs, in the previous five years (Lange, 1987). In a study of female prostitutes in seven areas throughout the United States, half of the prostitutes had a history of intravenous drug abuse. Use of condoms by these drug-abusing prostitutes was irregular at best. While over 80 percent of these prostitutes had used a condom at least once, only 4 percent reported condom use with each vaginal exposure over the previous five years (Cohen, Wofsy, & Gill, 1987). Thus, the potential for the spread of HIV to nonaddicts is considerable, especially as HIV infection increases among intravenous drug abusers. Strategies for coping with this increasing problem must be multimodal, ranging from community treatment to community prevention efforts.

COMMUNITY INTERVENTION EFFORTS FOCUSED ON CHANGING BEHAVIOR

Focusing on the person in environment is the core of social work practice, and social workers have directed their efforts to providing clinical services for individuals and groups as well as community interventions. The profession is developing a literature focused on the clinical aspects of AIDS (Buckingham, 1988; Leukefeld and Fimbres, 1987). Social workers are also involved with community activities as well as coordinating services for persons with AIDS and have taken initiative to plan and coordinate HIV and AIDS community treatment. In fact, social work has a traditional focus in the community.

The thrust of social work practice includes both individual need and adaptation as well as large scale reforms and community activities. More broadly, social work has been defined as the professional activity of helping individuals, families, groups, or communities to achieve and maintain their optimal psychosocial functioning in relation to various problems of living, in addition to creating societal conditions favorable to this goal (adopted from Inouye, 1986). This overview of social work intervention at

tate entry into drug abuse treatment for those who are willing, and should encourage other risk-reduction behaviors for those who are not. The expansion of drug treatment must be accompanied by an expansion of outreach efforts into all areas where intravenous drug abuse is endemic. Outreach services, using indigenous workers who have credibility and can penetrate drug-abusing subcultures, are an important part of community prevention efforts with drug abusers not in treatment. However, outreach efforts should not rely entirely on indigenous workers; workers with a range of professional expertise and background experiences are needed. In addition to street outreach, outreach should also occur through the use of mobile vans in areas where drug abuse is endemic and through various community sites such as public housing, the criminal justice system, hospital emergency rooms, public health centers, sexually transmitted disease clinics, churches, homeless shelters, and single-room occupancy hotels. Staffs of such organizations should be trained regarding both intravenous drug abuse and AIDS, and AIDS education should be available to intravenous drug abusers within these facilities.

Given the large numbers of intravenous drug abusers who are involved with the criminal justice system, the lock-ups, jails, prisons, and probation and parole offices can provide important access points for AIDS education to encourage behavior change and to facilitate referral to drug abuse treatment. Linkages between the criminal justice system and drug abuse treatment should facilitate initiation of treatment prior to institutional discharge and provide for the ongoing involvement of probation and parole officials to support the drug treatment process.

Outreach programs are needed for the various special target "communities," such as African Americans, Hispanics, women, gays, the homeless. And there is a need to target subsegments of these "communities," such as pregnant women. Homeless drug abusers provide an example of a target "community" that will need an array of supportive social services if AIDS prevention services are to be effective. AIDS-risk behaviors and housing problems are intertwined. The needs of homeless intravenous drug abusers for adequate housing must be addressed if AIDS risk-reduction is to be achieved and maintained. Similarly, for many target groups, health care services play an important role in community AIDS prevention by providing a locus for

interventions and supporting behavior change efforts. Community-based multiservice centers are necessary to provide adequate health care to supplement drug abuse treatment programs in order to meet the health care needs of intravenous drug abusers.

Prevention efforts cannot focus only on intravenous drug abusers, but must also target their sexual partners. As with intravenous drug abusers themselves, prevention efforts aimed at sexual partners must utilize indigenous workers and community agencies that currently are in contact with this group. It is especially important that supportive services for women offer alternatives to unprotected, unsafe sex. Prevention efforts should also target families of intravenous drug abusers, so that family members encourage and support behavior change.

Community AIDS prevention efforts at the primary level must focus not simply on those who are not yet infected, but also secondarily on those who are already infected in order to reduce their risks for transmitting HIV to others. Messages for those infected need to communicate the idea of "Living with HIV infection, not dying from AIDS."

It was also suggested that the distribution of sterile injection equipment to intravenous drug abusers is a possible prevention strategy that at least should be explored. This controversial prevention strategy was also considered by an earlier NIDA-sponsored review meeting that examined issues related to the sharing of injection equipment among intravenous drug abusers (Battjes and Pickens, 1988a).

Finally, major barriers to community interventions were identified. These included the lack of adequate funding for drug abuse treatment and AIDS outreach, community opposition to the expansion of drug abuse treatment services, fragmentation of services, fees for treatment that deter treatment entry, lack of appropriately trained personnel to provide treatment and outreach, lack of leadership at all levels, and the existence of paraphernalia laws that prevent exploration of needle distribution approaches.

Research Strategies

Community research on drug abuse is in its infancy (see Chapter 7 for a more detailed discussion of this topic). Success with community interventions focused on selected health behaviors are encouraging, yet the promise of community approaches in preventing the spread of HIV infection among intravenous drug abusers, their sexual partners, and children is as yet untested. Thus, a rigorous program of research by social workers and other helping professionals is needed to develop effective interventions. The following recommendations touched on the need for data to guide social work interventions as well as outcome research to determine program efficacy.

Research is needed on the incidence and prevalence of HIV infection among intravenous drug abusers and their sexual partners to better define the target populations. Changes in prevalence over time must also be determined to understand the spread of the epidemic.

Research should focus on identifying risk behaviors. What is the prevalence and incidence of these behaviors and what is their meaning? What factors support the maintenance of risk behaviors? How are behaviors changing in response to the AIDS epidemic?

Community or population traits that support or impede behavior change can be clarified through research. What are community attitudes, norms, values, or other cultural characteristics that impact on risk behaviors and efforts to change behaviors? What community support systems and communication patterns impact positively on efforts to change risk behaviors?

Research on community information channels should prove to be useful. What networks, resources, and services have credibility?

At the community level, evaluative research should determine baseline measures of risk behaviors, HIV infection and AIDS, and determine the changes in these measures over time. Community interventions need to be theory-based and adapted to the needs of the specific community through data from developmental research. Project implementation should be designed to permit evaluation of program models, including process evaluation (e.g., availability, acceptability, satisfaction effectiveness) and outcome evaluation (e.g., changes in knowledge and attitudes, risk behaviors, and incidence of HIV infection).

A number of methodological issues impact on the ability to evaluate community interventions empirically. These issues are not unique to AIDS prevention initiatives, but are common to all community prevention research efforts. A major drawback to efforts to "prove" that community prevention approaches are effective may be a lack of appropriate research methods to demonstrate a program effect. Specific methodological issues include the following:

The difficulty in measuring impact: HIV infection, the ultimate measure of program impact, may not be a sensitive indicator, especially in areas where infection rates are initially very low. Measurement of highly personal and illegal risk behaviors, such as sexual intercourse and intravenous drug abuse, must generally rely on subject self-report, which raises issues of the validity of the outcome data.

The use of appropriate control or comparison groups in community research: Randomization of subjects to treatment conditions is seldom possible. Random assignment of communities to treatment conditions does not assure comparability across conditions except in very large studies where a large number of communities is involved. Comparison communities may be used, but comparability between experimental and comparison communities cannot be assured. Change within a community over time might be assessed, but such an historical control is particularly questionable in the rapidly changing AIDS field.

The independence or objectivity of the evaluation: Is the evaluation internal (i.e., conducted by the organization implementing the intervention) or is it external (i.e., conducted by an independent group)? If the evaluation is internal, is there an independent advisory group or some other mechanism to assure the objectivity of the evaluation?

The generalizability of research findings: Interventions may not generalize between high- and low-risk communities or across subgroups of a community. Thus, multisite studies and studies focusing on multiple subgroups may be necessary.

CONCLUSION

This discussion of practice and research implications helps to clarify a common problem facing both program implementation and research, that of defining the "community." To develop effective social work interventions and to demonstrate their effectiveness require clarity regarding the target community. Too often community interventions have a vague sense of community, often defined as residents of a certain geographical area. Even when a community intervention may target multiple communities, the intervention strategies employed must be tailored to the unique needs and strengths of the component communities, and ethnographic research must address program impact on each of these communities. This is an especially critical requirement when the attempt is to resolve problems as complex as drug abuse and AIDS. Such a perspective is consistent with social work values as well as an important axiom for effective community approaches.

REFERENCES

Battjes, R. J., & Pickens, R. W. (Eds.) (1988a). *Needle sharing among intravenous drug abusers: National and international perspectives*. NIDA Research Monograph Series, No. 80. DHHS Publication No. (ADM)88-1567. Washington, DC: U.S. Government Printing Office.

Battjes, R. J., & Pickens, R. W. (1988b). *HIV transmission risk behaviors among intravenous drug abusers*. Poster presentation at Fourth International Conference on AIDS, Stockholm, Sweden.

Battjes, R. J., Pickens, R. W., & Amsel, Z. (1989). Introduction of HIV infection among IV drug abusers in low prevalence areas. *Journal of Acquired Immune Deficiency Syndromes, 2*, 533–539.

Black, J. L., Dolan, M. P., DeFord, H. A., Rubenstein, M. S., Penk, W. E., Robinowitz, R., & Skinner, J. R. (1986). Sharing of needles among users of intravenous drugs (Correspondence). *New England Journal of Medicine, 314*, 446–447.

Brager, G. (1963). Organizing the unaffiliated in a low-income area. *Social Work. 8*, 34–40.

Buckingham, S. L. (1988) AIDS: Bridging the gap between information and practice. *Social Casework, 69* (Special Issue).

Centers for Disease Control (1987). Human immunodeficiency virus infection in the United States: A review of current knowledge. *Morbidity and Mortality Weekly Report, 36* (S-6).

Centers for Disease Control (1989a). *HIV/AIDS Surveillance*. Atlanta, GA: Centers for Disease Control.

Centers for Disease Control (1989b). Update: Acquired immunodeficiency syndrome associated with intravenous-drug use—United States, 1988. *Morbidity and Mortality Weekly Report, 38*, 165–170.

Chachkes, E. (1987) Woman and children with AIDS. In C. G. Leukefeld & M. Fimbres (Eds.), *Responding to AIDS: Psychosocial initiatives*. Silver Spring, MD.: National Association of Social Work.

Chaisson, R. E., Moss, A. R., Onishi, R., Osmond, D., & Carlson, J. R. (1987). Human immunodeficiency virus in heterosexual intravenous drug users in San Francisco. *American Journal of Public Health, 77*, 169–172.

Cohen, J. B, Wofsy, C., & Gill, P. (1987). Antibody to human immunodeficiency virus in female prostitutes. *Morbidity and Mortality Weekly Report, 36*, 157–161.

Des Jarlais, D. C. (1987). [New York State Division of Substance Abuse]. Personal communication.

Des Jarlais, D. C., Friedman, S. R., Sotheran, J. L., & Stoneburner, R. (1988). The sharing of drug injection equipment and the AIDS epidemic in New York City: The first decade. In R. J. Battjes and R. W. Pickens (Eds.), *Needle sharing among intravenous drug abusers: National and international perspectives* (pp. 160–175). NIDA Research Monograph Series, No. 80. DHHS Publication No. (ADM)88-1567. Washington, DC: U.S. Government Printing Office.

Fischl, M. A., Dickinson, G. M., Scott, G. B., Klimas, N. Fletcher, M. A., & Parks, W. (1987). Evaluation of heterosexual partners, children, and household contacts of adults with AIDS. *Journal of the American Medical Association, 257*, 640–644.

Fortmann, S. P., Haskell, W. L., Williams, P. T., Varady, A. N., Hulley, A. B., & Farquhar, J. W. (1986). Community surveillance of cardiovascular diseases in the Stanford five-city project: Methods and initial expertise. *American Journal of Epidemiology, 123*, 656–669.

Gilchrist, L. D. (in press). The role of schools in community-based approaches to prevention of AIDS and intravenous drug use. In C. G. Leukefeld, R. J. Battjes, & Z. Amsel (Eds.), *AIDS and intravenous drug use: Future directions for community-based prevention research* (pp. 150–166). Washington, DC: U.S. Government Printing Office.

Gordon, R. S., Jr. (1983). An operational classification of disease prevention. *Public Health Reports, 98*, 107–109.

Grosser, C. F. (1965). Community development programs serving the urban poor. *Social Work, 10*, 15–21.

Hahn, R. A., Onorato, I. M., Jones, T. S., & Dougherty, J. (1988). *Infection with human immunodeficiency virus (HIV) among intravenous drug users*. Paper presented at the Fourth International Conference on AIDS, Stockholm, Sweden.

Inouye, D. K. (1986, February 25). *Congressional Record*. Washington, DC: Government Printing Office.

Lange, W. R. (1987). [Addiction Research Center, National Institute on Drug Abuse]. Personal communication.

Lange, W. R., Primm, B. J., & Tennant, F. S. (1987). Poster presentations at Third International Conference on AIDS, Washington, DC.

Leukefeld, C. G., Battjes, R. J., & Amsel, Z. (Eds.) (in press). *AIDS and intravenous drug use: Future directions for community-based prevention research.* Washington, DC: U.S. Government Printing Office.

Leukefeld, C. G., & Fimbres, M. (1987) *Responding to AIDS: Psychosocial initiatives.* Silver Spring, MD. National Association of Social Workers.

Levy, N., Carlson, J. R., Hinrichs, S., Lerche, N., Schenker, M., & Gardner, M. B. (1986). The prevalence of HTLV-III/LAV antibodies among intravenous drug users attending treatment programs in California: A preliminary report (Correspondence). *New England Journal of Medicine, 314,* 446.

Litwak, E. & Meyer, H. (1966) A balance theory of coordination between bureaucratic organizations and community primary groups. *Administrative Science Quarterly. 11,* 31–58.

Maccoby, N. (in press). Communication and health education research: Potential sources for education for prevention of drug use. In C. G. Leukefeld, R. J. Battjes, & Z. Amsel, (Eds.), *AIDS and intravenous drug use: Future directions for community-based prevention research* (pp. 1–23). Washington, DC: U.S. Government Printing Office.

Morbidity and Mortality Weekly Report. (1989). Coordinating community programs for HIV prevention among intravenous drug abusers—California, Massachusetts. *38,* 369–374.

National Institute on Drug Abuse. (1983). Data from the National Drug and Alcohol Treatment Utilization Survey (NDATUS): Main findings for drug abuse treatment units. *Statistical Series* (Report F:10), DHHS Publication No. (ADM)83-1284, Washington, DC: U.S. Government Printing Office.

National Institute on Drug Abuse. (1986). Data from the Drug Abuse Warning Network (DAWN)—Annual data 1985. *Statistical Series* (Report 1:5), DHHS Publication No. (ADM)86-1469. Washington, DC: U.S. Government Printing Office.

National Institute on Drug Abuse. (1988, January). *AIDS Community Outreach and Counseling Demonstration Research—Phase II.* Request for Applications. DA-88-03.

Nelkin, D. (1987). AIDS and the social sciences: Review of useful knowledge and research needs. *Reviews of Infectious Diseases, 9,* 980–986.

Network. (1989). NIDA outreach demonstration projects provide insight into drug-use risk patterns. *1,* 1–7.

Newmeyer, J. (1988). Why bleach? Development of a strategy to combat HIV contagion among San Francisco I.V. drug users. In R. J. Battjes & R. W. Pickens (Eds.), *Needle sharing among intravenous drug abusers: National and International perspectives* (pp. 151–159). NIDA Research Monograph Series, No. 80. DHHS Publication No. (ADM)88-1567. Washington, DC: U.S. Government Printing Office.

Robertson, J. R., Bucknall, A. B. V., Welsby, P. D., Roberts, J. J. K., Inglis, J. M., Peutherer, J. F., & Brettle, R. P. (1986). Epidemic of AIDS related virus (HTLV-III/LAV) infection among intravenous drug users. *British Medical Journal, 292,* 527–529.

Starcher, T. (1987). [Centers for Disease Control.] Personal communication.

Steigbigel, N. H., Maude, D. W., Feiner, C. J., Harris, C. A., Saltzman, B. R., & Klein, R. S. (1987). *Heterosexual transmission of infection and disease by the human immunodeficiency virus (HIV).* Paper presented at Third International Conference on AIDS, Washington, DC.

U. S. Public Health Service. (1986). Coolfont report: A PHS plan for prevention and control of AIDS and the AIDS virus. *Public Health Reports, 101,* 341–348.

U. S. Public Health Service. (1988). Report of the second Public Health Service AIDS prevention and control conference. *Public Health Reports, 103* (S-1).

Weiss, S. H., Ginzburg, H. M., Goedert, J. J., Cantor, K., Altman, R., Robert-Guroff, M., Gallo, R., & Blattner, W. (1986). Risk factors for HTLV-III infection among parenteral drug users. *Proceedings of the American Society of Clinical Oncology, 5.*

Zald, M. (1966). Organizations as polities, An analysis of community organization agencies. *Social Work. 11,* 56–65.

SUPPLEMENTAL READING LIST

Battjes, R. A., Leukefeld, C. G., Pickens, I. W., & Herberkos, H. W. (1988). The acquired immune deficiency syndrome and IV drug abuse. *Bulletin on Narcotics, XL,* 21–34.
This article is useful in its analysis of the dynamics of IV drug abuse and responses to the contracting of AIDS in this population.

Hubbard, R. L., Marsden, M. E., Cavenaugh, E., Rachel, J. V., & Ginsburg, H. M. (1988). Role of drug abuse treatment in limiting the spread of AIDS. *Review of Infections Diseases, 10,* 377–384.
The importance of getting IV drug abusers into treatment for both addictions counseling and educating them about the consequences of AIDS is the focus of this article. The latter is presented as the most feasible way to limit the spread of AIDS in this population.

Leukefeld, C. G. (1989). Psychosocial issues in dealing with AIDS. *Hospital and Community Psychiatry, 40,* 454–455.

Some of the important but complex psychosocial issues (related to the AIDS patient *and* significant others) are presented in this article. These issues are critical because they often impact the medical aspects and vice versa.

Maccoby, N., Farquhar, J. W., & Wood, P. D. (1977). Reducing the risk of cardiovascular disease. *Journal of Community Health, 3*, 100–114.

This article presents a useful example of a community health and education approach to the problem of heart disease. The article makes it possible to generalize the strategies to the problem of AIDS and IV drug abuse.

CHAPTER 11

An Ecological Approach to Treatment of Cocaine and Crack Abuse

Sanford Schwartz

Virginia Commonwealth University

. . . tiny prickly feet of ecstasy started dancing through me . . . I felt a superman's surge of power.

R. Beck, *Pimp: Story of My Life*

Cocaine abuse can no longer be regarded as a passing fad that is restricted to status conscious denizens of the entertainment industry. Nor is the growing epidemic of crack use limited to disenfranchised residents of America's inner cities. As knowledge accumulates about the adverse physical and psychological consequences, social work professionals in public and private agencies can expect to confront increasing numbers of clients from a broad range of economic and cultural backgrounds whose health and well-being are jeopardized by sustained use of cocaine and its highly dangerous derivative, crack. As is often the case with drug-related phenomena, a great deal of misinformation about cocaine has been disseminated to the point where a more dispassionate account is necessary if appropriate treatment is to be rendered. Such myths include the supposed nonaddictive nature of the drug and its confinement to well-to-do white males residing in large metropolitan areas for whom treatment facilities are readily available.

This chapter reviews the demographics, etiology, and consequences of cocaine abuse, along with a variety of direct practice interventions for abusing clients and their families. Because of the denial which accompanies chemical dependency and the frequent involvement of cocaine users in the crimi-

nal justice system, particular attention is directed toward social work strategies with resistant, nonvoluntary clients.

THE DEVELOPMENT OF COCAINE ABUSE

Cocaine is a powerful central nervous system stimulant derived from the leaf of the coca bush found primarily in Bolivia and Peru. In the United States the odorless white powder is most commonly injected intranasally through each nostril. Other, more rapid, routes of administration, such as smoking cocaine crystals and injection, are characteristic of compulsive users. Although progression to these types of use is not inevitable, the vast majority of abusers begin taking cocaine intranasally (Dackis, Gold, & Pottash, 1986). From all accounts, clinical descriptions of cocaine's intense euphoric and energizing effects do not do justice to the drug. The seductive nature of cocaine and the tendency for many addicts to relapse is best illustrated by Beck (1969), reflecting on his experiences as an addict: "I felt like the top of my skull had been crushed in. . . . Then tiny prickly feet of ecstasy started dancing through me. I heard melodious bells tolling softly inside my skull. I looked down at my hands and thighs. A thrill shot through me. Surely they were the most beautiful in the universe. I felt a superman's surge of power.'' This passage about inhaled cocaine and its rewards to the addict help to highlight the more intense addiction of cocaine as a smokable substance in the form of crack.

The Crack Epidemic

Crack is the highly addictive, smokable derivative of cocaine that has wreaked havoc with law enforcement and neighborhood groups throughout the country. It is cheap, easy to obtain, highly potent, and increasingly available to persons for whom powdered cocaine was prohibitively expensive. Current estimates place the number of people who have tried crack at 2.4 million with nearly 500,000 regular users (*Washington Post*, 1989b). Although crack can now be found in rural and suburban communities, it appears that most users are economically disadvantaged inner-city residents and teenagers. Some reports suggest an increasing number of young women are being attracted to the drug (White House, 1989). A recent phenomenon (first reported in New York City, but expected to emerge elsewhere) is combining crack and heroin into a smokable mixture (*New York Times*, 1989a). The product, called crank, allows the user to maintain crack-induced euphoria while reducing the intense depression that eventually follows.

Prevalence Data on Cocaine Abuse

The extent of cocaine use in the United States has been the subject of considerable debate. Media accounts of the personal tragedies associated with cocaine and crack abuse, such as the highly publicized deaths of sports stars Len Bias and Don Rogers, probably exert a greater influence on public perceptions than do more comprehensive data collected from a variety of public and private sources. Much of this information is subject to the methodological shortcomings inevitably associated with attempts to gather information about the consumption of illicit drugs (Grabowski & Dworkin, 1985). However, even with acknowledged limitations, some interesting trends are apparent.

An annual survey undertaken by the University of Michigan's Institute for Social Research reports prevalence data from a national sample of high school seniors (Johnston, O'Malley, & Bachman, 1986). From a peak of 13.1 percent in 1986, the proportion of seniors acknowledging any cocaine use in the preceding year dropped to 7.9 percent in 1988. This decline followed a six-year period during which use remained at approximately 12 percent. Follow-up studies of high school students also suggest a leveling off in cocaine use. For example, among college students, the annual prevalence rate is now 10 percent, down from the relatively constant 17 percent figure reported since 1980. For young adults with a high school education, this rate fell from 20 percent in 1986 to 14 percent in 1988.

A comprehensive study of U.S. households in 1988 (*Washington Post*, 1989b) concluded that 21 million people have used cocaine on at least one occasion. An estimated 3 million people use cocaine once a month or more. Most alarming is the one-third increase in cocaine addicts between 1985 and 1988, with nearly 900,000 persons acknowledging cocaine use at least on a weekly basis. Much of this increase has been attributed to the rise in crack abuse.

One interpretive problem with prevalence data from large national samples is the tendency to lose sight of the raw numbers from which composite proportions are derived. A preoccupation with such information often masks the actual damage caused by substance abuse. So while it is encouraging that casual cocaine use may be declining among adolescents and young adults, any celebration is premature and misguided as increasing numbers of persons whose cocaine use is out of control require treatment for their illness.

Since this chapter is designed for social service professionals who are providing treatment to clients, the following incidence, prevalence, and demographic data will focus on persons who are experiencing cocaine-related problems. Data on the involvement of cocaine users in health care systems have been derived from two major sources. The Drug Abuse Warning Network (DAWN) monitors hospital emergency room contacts and medical examiner cases in which cocaine is detected (Adams, Gfroerer, Rouse, & Kozel, 1986). Both measures reflect dramatic increases in cocaine-related emergency visits and deaths from 1984 to 1988 (from approximately 10,000 to nearly 48,000 cases). This proliferation is most noticeable in hospitals serving such urban centers as New York City, Oakland, and

Los Angeles and has been attributed to the infusion of crack into the inner cities (*New York Times*, 1989b). As will be discussed below, a significant number of cases reported by DAWN cite the use of other illicit drugs in combination with cocaine.

The involvement of cocaine abusers in federally funded treatment facilities is reflected in the Client Oriented Data Acquisition Process (CODAP) reporting system. Adams et al. (1986) report that in 1983 nearly one-fifth of all admissions were for clients with either a primary or secondary diagnosis of cocaine abuse. This figure rose to 28.7 percent for the first six months of 1984. Between 1980 and 1983, a hospital-based drug treatment facility reported an increase from three to 52 percent in the proportion of clients with cocaine dependency (Schnoll, Karrigan, Kitchen, Daghestani, & Hanson, 1985). The increasing volume of calls to the National Cocaine Hotline also suggests a worsening of the problem (Washton & Gold, 1986).

Demographics of Cocaine Abuse

Limited descriptive data are available on the characteristics of persons seeking or in treatment for cocaine abuse. One source from which information can be derived is telephone interviews of persons calling the National Cocaine Hotline during three-month periods in 1983 and 1985 (Washton & Gold, 1986). While these data are admittedly skewed with respect to the severity of the problems experienced by clients and the self-report nature of the data collection process, a fascinating and complex picture emerges. Callers reported using cocaine for an average of four years. Women comprised 42 percent of the 1985 sample, up from 33 percent only two years previously. Sizable increases were noted in calls from minority and lower income groups. Similar increases occurred in the use of other drugs to relieve the effects of cocaine and in reported cocaine consumption while at work (68 to 87 percent, and 42 to 74 percent, respectively).

Client data from federal treatment programs confirm that, for their patients, intranasal cocaine use is more prevalent, followed by injection and smoking. Most clients are in their twenties, have completed high school, are not employed, and report multiple drug use patterns (Adams et al., 1986).

Schnoll and his associates (1985) studied 172 cocaine-abusing patients (average age of 30 years) in a combined inpatient–outpatient hospital-based drug treatment program. Most clients were male high school graduates who were employed in a variety of occupations, many at skilled and professional levels. African American and Hispanic client representation was 54 percent. Over 40 percent reported daily marijuana use at the time of admission. Smokers of freebase cocaine were most represented (44 percent), followed by intranasal (35 percent) and intravenous (22 percent) users. One-third of the patients acknowledged using cocaine for at least two years prior to entering the facility. Recent research from private treatment centers serving insurance and private pay clients found similar demographics, and reported significant numbers of alcohol-dependent clients among their cocaine-referred patients (Dougherty & Lesswing, 1989; Miller, Millman, & Keskinen, 1989).

It is apparent that general profiles cannot be readily extracted since demographic composition of cocaine-related treatment populations varies with the type of facility from which samples are drawn. It is also clear that cocaine is becoming an "equal opportunity" drug whose adverse consequences transcend age, gender, ethnic, and socioeconomic boundaries.

Dynamics of Cocaine Addiction

Despite its popularity with socioeconomic groups not usually considered vulnerable to drug abuse, the dynamics of cocaine abuse follow a familiar pattern. "As with all forms of addictive illness, the natural history of cocaine abuse involves a progressive process that begins with recreational use, and evolves gradually to compulsive addiction patterns that encompass and dominate all aspects of the addict's life. Severe cocaine addicts become obsessed with cocaine euphoria, and are subject to frequent and almost irresistible craving" (Dackis, Gold, & Pottash, 1986, p. 8). This pattern is reflected in the decreasing ability to limit, control, or refuse, if offered, the use of cocaine. From all reports, the addiction process is accelerated with the use of crack.

Recreational cocaine consumption without adverse consequences has been reported, although little definitive data exists about this group and how they differ from those persons who become compulsive users (Gawin & Ellinwood, 1988). Two distinctive characteristics of cocaine abuse are a tendency for repeated use over extended lengths of time (binges) and the physical and emotional exhaustion that immediately follow such usage patterns (crash). In order to sustain the intense euphoria associated with the drug, continual readministration of cocaine may occur for up to a week or until such time as one's money, drug supply, or physical energy are depleted. More common duration of a binge ranges from 12 hours to 3 days (Gawin & Ellinwood, 1988). Even more than a pattern of daily use, it has been suggested that binges may be the best indicator of abusive consumption and the need for treatment.

The rapid and frequent mood swings associated with binge use are followed by periods of intense depression, agitation, and anxiety as effects of the drug wear off. Craving for the drug typically wavers during the crash, but often returns within several days (Dackis, et al., 1986). Further binge–crash cycles may ensue, separated by limited periods of abstinence. Restless periods of sleep, depression, general fatigue, and a lack of interest in one's surroundings follow a crash and usually subside within several days. It is not entirely clear whether these withdrawal symptoms associated with abrupt cessation of cocaine use constitute a designation of physical dependence (Gawin & Ellinwood, 1988; Kozel & Adams, 1985). A common reaction to a crash is reliance on alcohol, tranquilizers, or opiates to induce rest and alleviate unpleasant side effects.

CONSEQUENCES OF COCAINE ABUSE

The physical, psychological, social, economic, employment, and legal costs of cocaine abuse are considerable. The specific nature and severity of these consequences will depend upon factors related to the drug (dosage, purity, route of administration) and the user (physical and emotional health).

Physical, Psychological, and Social Consequences

The most commonly experienced physical complications arising from intranasal cocaine abuse include chronic fatigue and insomnia, severe headaches, and weight loss. Other common complaints include nausea and sexual dysfunctioning. Specific medical problems are associated with the manner in which the drug is administered. For example, sustained intranasal use is likely to result in sinusitis, rhinitis, and related damage to the nasal septum. Hepatitis, abscesses, and skin infections are more likely to occur with repeated intravenous administration. Of course, injecting cocaine also places users at increased risk of contracting AIDS. Psychological problems associated with cocaine abuse include the depression, anxiety, restlessness, and irritability that follow cessation of cocaine use.

Similarly, smoking crack poses extremely significant medical and psychiatric risks. In addition to lung damage and assorted respiratory problems, crack users are particulary susceptible to seizures, heart attacks, and strokes (Rosecan, Spitz, & Gross, 1987). Furthermore, the rapidity with which addiction develops often produces emotional volatility that may result in unpredictable behavior and even violence.

Adverse consequences associated with cocaine are not confined to the individual user. It is conservatively estimated that kidney defects are five times as likely to occur in babies born to mothers using cocaine during their pregnancy than in other babies (Chavez, Mulinare & Cordero, 1989). Chasnoff and his associates (1989) recently reported a correlation between maternal cocaine use and both low infant birth weight and neurological complications involving orientation and motor skills. Other studies have demonstrated serious affective and interpersonal problems among babies born to crack-using mothers (*New York Times*, 1989c). Examples include impaired abilities to play with other children and to express emotions.

A recent *National Drug Control Strategy* issued by ex–drug czar William Bennett estimates that 100,000 cocaine babies are born each year. Public hospitals increasingly are confronted with having to care for boarder babies, new-born children of crack-addicted mothers who abandon their infants (*Washington Post*, 1989b). (Chapter 9 presents a detailed discussion on the risks and treatment of addicted mothers and their addicted infants.) Despite inadequate staff, training, and resources, inner-city medical centers are rapidly becoming the primary caregivers for these unwanted babies for months at a time as overburdened child welfare systems struggle to find more permanent substitute living arrangements. In the meantime, the most basic psychological and emotional needs go wanting. Furthermore, babies who remain with addicted parents are no more fortunate, as they are at considerable risk for child abuse and neglect.

The impact of cocaine on persons other than the user is also reflected in the 19 percent of national hotline callers who acknowledged involvement in at least one cocaine-related automobile accident (Washton & Gold, 1986). Nearly three-quarters of the hotline respondents reported using or being under the influence of cocaine at work. On-the-job accidents, thefts from co-workers, and drug dealing were not uncommon.

Crime, the Economy, and Cocaine Abuse

Perhaps as a result of mistakenly viewing most cocaine abusers as economically self-sufficient, little attention has been devoted to examining the connection between cocaine and crime. However, there is some indication that heroin addicts participating in methadone maintenance programs are likely to commit property crimes to the extent that they also use cocaine (Hunt, Spunt, Lipton, Goldsmith, & Strug, 1986). A recent study conducted by the federal Centers for Disease Control found that as many as 75 percent of adult males arrested for serious crimes tested positive for cocaine. Furthermore, the profits generated from the sales of cocaine and, especially, crack have made drug transactions a highly dangerous business for consumers and innocent bystanders alike. Although endemic to many inner cities, this problem is spreading to rural and suburban areas as well. A recent article in the *Washington Post* (1989a) cited the development of a barter system in which drugs are exchanged for guns.

The targeting of poor teenagers and young women by drug dealers is no accident. A cheap (or free) introduction to crack can quickly lead to intense cravings and compulsive use as the euphoric reaction subsides within minutes. The likelihood of addiction may be mistakenly dismissed since the drug is smoked—not injected. Thus, a market of vulnerable users can be created with a relatively inexpensive investment by drug entrepreneurs. The increasing urgency for money to purchase crack may then result in prostitution, street crimes, embezzlement and other white-collar offenses, or recruitment into the drug-dealing business. What may have been initially viewed as an inexpensive, relatively harmless experience rapidly deteriorates into a life-style necessitating considerable financial resources.

TREATMENT ISSUES

Appropriate Settings

Cravings for cocaine's euphoric effects despite a host of concomitant medical and psychosocial complications make abusers a challenging population with which to work. The remainder of this chapter addresses clinical interventions with the abuser. Client assessment and treatment planning, goals, and phases are discussed.

No single method exists for the treatment of cocaine abuse (Washton, 1986). Individual, group, and family interventions have been reported, some in conjunction with pharmacological treatment (Spitz & Rosecan, 1987). Most programs consider cocaine abuse as a dysfunctional reaction to an accumulation of environmental demands by persons who are unequipped to successfully cope with the resultant stress.

While interventions must be tailored to unique client characteristics, several programmatic imperatives can be derived from a consideration of cocaine's distinctive properties. For example, the absence of prolonged, life-threatening withdrawal symptoms minimizes the need for lengthy inpatient hospitalization for many cocaine abusers (Gawin & Ellinwood, 1988; Grabowski & Dworkin, 1985; Rounsaville, Gawin, & Kleber, 1985). Treatment on an outpatient basis is preferred for several reasons. It is less costly, stigmatizing, and personally disruptive for clients. The supportive involvement of family and other members of the client's social network can replace the control and physical confinement inherent in inpatient residential programs. Most importantly, outpatient treatment allows clients to work toward recovery in a realistic ecological context. They can retain the strengths in their environments and, at the same time, begin the challenge of altering the circumstances which helped to precipitate their reliance on cocaine.

The need for hospitalization cannot be dismissed in every instance. Washton (1986) presents the following five screening criteria for determining the appropriate inpatient or outpatient treatment context:

1. How severe is the problem (frequency/duration of use, dosage, route of administration)?
2. Is the patient physically addicted to other substances (e.g., opiates, alcohol, sedative-hypnotics)?
3. Are medical and/or psychiatric problems so severe that hospitalization is required for proper assessment and/or treatment?
4. Is there severe impairment of psychosocial functioning?
5. Has the patient already failed in outpatient treatment? (p. 145)

Several of these criteria characterize the status of many crack abusers. While some persons apparently can maintain recreational use of cocaine without progressing to compulsive abuse, a return to controlled consumption does not appear to be a viable option for those who have passed an abuse threshold. Given the readily available supply of cocaine, clinical interventions must focus on demand reduction strategies. Accordingly, the treatment goals of most cocaine abuse programs are clear and unambiguous: complete abstinence from all mood-altering chemicals. It is only when clients are drug-free that their strengths and deficits can be identified and treatment initiated.

Initial Treatment Considerations

There are two major components to most outpatient cocaine treatment programs. The initial phase focuses on helping clients break binge cycles and abstain from using other chemicals that so commonly are part of the drug-taking life-style. Several meetings are held each week during which clients, and often their spouses, receive education, support, and counseling about the addiction process. Precipitating factors of cocaine use are explored, with specific attention directed toward interpersonal deficits and role conflicts (Rounsaville, et al., 1985). An assessment of client and environmental strengths which can be used to support abstinence also is conducted. Clients are advised to make appropriate changes in their routine behavior to minimize the presence of cues which previously were associated with or sustained cocaine use. For example, changes in leisure time activities and friendship patterns often are encouraged in addition to the removal of all drug-related paraphernalia. Money management responsibilities may shift to the spouse. Social network therapy (Galanter, 1986) uses close drug-free friends and relatives to monitor behavior and provide support when clients experience the urge to resume using cocaine. This kind of intervention is consistent with the ecological perspective.

Central to this initial treatment phase is the client's recognition that the costs associated with continued cocaine use outweigh the benefits of taking the drug. This is an extremely difficult position for most addicts to accept, given cocaine's euphoric effects, the characteristic denial of addictive thinking, and the fact that negative consequences of continued use (for example, threats of job loss or incarceration) often are externally imposed and, thus, not "owned" by the client. A "life consequences" model, wherein the impact of cocaine consumption on one's family, social, employment, health, financial, and legal situations are explored, helps clients to acknowledge, define, and focus on their drug-related problems.

Because most clients, for at least brief periods of time, used cocaine without serious adverse consequences, it is not uncommon for them to view the treatment process as a way of helping them exercise increased control. Thus, while acknowledging cocaine abuse, these clients redefine the problem to one which can be controlled and does not require extensive life-style modifications or complete abstinence. An unwillingness to relinquish past drug-related associations and a tendency to speak in terms of a permanent cure—not recovery—may signal a client's hesitancy to accept the loss of control to cocaine. These forms of self-deceit and resistance can be addressed through educational sessions and later confronted in peer recovery groups. Clients must understand that abstinence from all chemicals is not a goal established for moralistic purposes. Rather, clients should learn about the disinhibiting properties of alcohol and other drugs in order to appreciate their addiction potential and how their use can jeopardize the success of even the most motivated cocaine abuser.

Creating a balance between understanding the etiology of an addictive illness and encouraging client responsibility for change is important and has been the subject of considerable debate, especially among alcoholism professionals. There is concern that, if clients perceive themselves as victims of a disease, motivation for change will be lessened. Cocaine treatment programs operate under the compensatory model where clients are expected to assume responsibility for recovery without being blamed for their condition (Brickman, Rabinowitz, Karuza, Coates, Cohn, & Kidder, 1982). Holding cocaine addicts accountable for initiating life-style changes involves clients acknowledging that "while circumstances—either beyond their control or ability to cope—have contributed to their present situation, they need not detract from their intention or ability to change" (Schwartz & Wood, 1989, p. 13). Accordingly, workers must establish firm limits about what constitutes acceptable behavior, constantly monitor clients' actions, and provide frequent and candid feedback regarding progress. In many respects, the worker's role becomes much like a coach, where the necessary information, encouragement, and skills are provided to clients who ultimately are responsible for their own success.

Frequent, supervised, and random urine testing is a common component of drug treatment programs. It "is an extremely useful treatment tool that helps to counteract denial, promote self-control over drug impulses, and provides an objective indicator of treatment progress" (Washton, 1986, pp. 146–147). Workers should always inform clients of these considerations and be prepared to discuss their reactions. It is important to note that a positive screen should not be viewed as failure. Rather, it should precipitate a mutual reassessment where possible outcomes include a period of inpatient hospitalization, a restructuring of the client's social support network, increasing contact with the worker, or additional life-style modifications/restrictions.

Life-Style Consolidation during Ongoing Treatment and Aftercare

Despite one's best intentions, it is unrealistic to expect clients to restructure their entire lives to avoid any exposure to or temptation for drugs. Thus, the second treatment phase seeks to build upon the stability, progress, and momentum established during the initial abstinence from cocaine. Accordingly, "relapse prevention gradually reduces the external controls that were placed on the abuser during the initiation of abstinence, with the goal of facilitating the development of the abuser's internal controls" (Gawin & Ellinwood, 1988, p. 1177). During this phase, clients become involved in recovery groups where peer support for maintaining the needed life-style changes are offered under the guidance of a professional group leader. Group members typically are in varying stages of recovery. Such heterogeneity allows new participants to use senior members as successful role models while permitting the latter to experience the rewards of helping others and a reminder of their own prior drug-related problems (Wesson & Smith, 1985).

The importance of recovery groups is highlighted by two phenomena: euphoric recall and the Abstinence Violation Effect (Washton, 1986). The first term refers to the tendency for abusers to minimize or ignore their previous cocaine-related problems and instead recall "all the good times." This selective memory and the resultant urge to resume using can be triggered by recurring stimuli with past associations for cocaine (for example, stress, boredom, specific events or people). Reminders of the past negative consequences and testimonials from group members of the hazards associated with relapse can help clients withstand such cravings. In addition, recovery groups can provide the context wherein clients can receive assistance in identifying and rehearsing their responses to high-risk situations and encounters where cocaine may be desired and available.

The Abstinence Violation Effect (AVE) "refers to the predictable defeatist reaction experienced by an abstaining substance abuser after a 'slip' back to drugs" (Washton, 1986, p. 151). A range of client reactions occur such as guilt, pessimism about attaining total recovery, self-blame, and disappointment at having failed the therapist and other group members. Unless clients and family members are forewarned about the possibility of a temporary relapse, the AVE can precipitate premature termination from treatment and a return to sustained chemical dependency. Clients must be taught not to view a "slip" as a discrete, spontaneous event (Wesson & Smith, 1985) but rather as a return to dysfunctional cognitive and behavioral patterns that were characteristic of their pretreatment life-style. Thus, the therapist and group members must help clients examine precipitating factors so that measures can be taken to prevent a reoccurrence.

The Family's Role

Family members play an important role in the rehabilitation of cocaine addicts (Washton, 1986). As a valuable source of information, they can be used to validate a client's statements about their past actions (for example, quantity and circumstances of previous drug use). They also may provide contrary data with which client denial can be challenged. Once a cocaine problem has been acknowledged, family members can reinforce positive steps that maintain client abstinence. In addition, they must learn how to identify and modify their own nurturing behavior that, in the past, may have inadvertently insulated the client from experiencing the negative consequences of drug abuse. Finally, family members "need an opportunity to deal with their own feelings of anger, blame, guilt and victimization so as to minimize family stress and confusion which could itself lead to the patient's early relapse and treatment failure" (Washton, 1986, p. 155).

Self-Help Groups

Following termination from a structured treatment regimen as well as during treatment, cocaine addicts should be encouraged to regularly attend community-based self-help groups such as Cocaine Anonymous. These groups are mechanisms for supporting the previous accomplishments derived from professional treatment. Here, clients receive an unwavering set of principles and unconditional peer support from recovering addicts to assist in fostering a permanent drug-free life-style. Such involvement is especially important for those persons who have abandoned their prior social contacts.

Although consistent with the aforementioned goals of drug treatment programs, self-help groups often receive lukewarm endorsements from professionals who object to a perceived rigidity and a preoccupation with spirituality. Unfortunately, such concerns may reinforce the reluctance of newly recovering addicts to participate in CA meetings. Recovery groups conducted by a treatment professional are ideal settings to explore a member's reasons for discounting self-help programs. With the support of the leader, other members already involved in CA may help to allay fears and misconceptions. The following case study illustrates such a situation.

Kenneth G., a 32-year-old married male Caucasian, was employed as systems analyst for eight years at a large computer manufacturing company. He was referred to an outpatient drug treatment program by his firm's Employee Assistance Program following a noticeable deterioration in job performance and a positive urine test for cocaine. He attributed his situation to casual experimentation with cocaine, but adamantly denied losing control over its consumption. Despite minimizing the hazards of snorting cocaine, he vowed to quit using the drug immediately. Although clearly troubled by recent events, his wife supported Mr. G.'s contention that he was "basically a strong person" and could not possibly be an addict. Mr. G. was superficially compliant during further assessment and counseling sessions until he was apprehended while attempting to steal equipment from his employer. Upon threat of prosecution and termination from his job, Mr. G. acknowledged an escalating pattern of intranasal cocaine use over the preceding eight months. He had hoped to sell the stolen items to support what rapidly had become an expensive habit. Subsequent sessions revealed a pattern of restless sleep and increased alcohol consumption coinciding with his cocaine use. In a tearful encounter, he expressed long-standing feelings of inadequacy regarding his career, which, although financially successful, paled in comparison to his former college classmates and two older siblings. Furthermore, long hours and mounting pressures at work precipitated a need to "unwind and enjoy myself" during his off hours. A complete drug history revealed episodes of alcohol abuse beginning during adolescence.

Outpatient individual and group therapy were initiated with the support and encouragement of Mrs. G. Because of his eight-year record of superior performance, Mr. G.'s employer agreed to allow him to return to work provided he remained in treatment and submitted to regular urine testing.

Initial sessions focused on encouraging the client to further express and clarify his feelings of inadequacy. The dynamics of cocaine addiction were explained, with particular reference to the role it had come to play in his life. With the assistance of his supervisor and of his older brother, Mr. G. was helped to reassess his personal and career accomplishments in a more favorable light.

Following a series of group-based role rehearsals, Mr. G was able to acknowledge his dependency to his nonusing friends and to sever all relationships with his former cocaine-using associates. New social contacts were formed as Mr. G. became more involved with his wife's family and friends. Stress reduction exercises and an accommodating and supportive supervisor helped to relieve job-related pressure. New recreational and other leisure-time pursuits not associated with cocaine use were developed.

Following nine months of treatment, Mr. G. had stabilized his work performance, initiated significant life-style changes, and abstained from using cocaine. To help consolidate Mr. G.'s progress, he was referred to Cocaine Anonymous and Alcoholics Anonymous groups.

Social Work Considerations

As a review of this chapter's references will attest, the social work literature has been notably silent with regard to the profession's clinical role with drug addiction. This deficiency can be attributed, in part, to its reluctance to tackle the issue of working with resistant clients. General guidelines for social workers in addressing resistance among cocaine abusers include the following:

1. Discuss (not necessarily defend) the reasons for mandated client referral by sources such as one's employer, spouse, or the criminal justice system.
2. Explore client's perception of the problem and feelings about involuntary status.
3. Clarify expectations and rationale regarding compliance with treatment regimen and goals, drug-testing procedures, and confidentiality constraints (if any).
4. Acknowledge validity of client reluctance to participate in mandated transactions.
5. Identify opportunities for clients to exert discretion within the context of treatment (e. g., mutual negotiation of behavioral contracts).
6. Consistently use constructive confrontation when assessing self-reported drug use and its impact on client behavior (Reid, 1986).
7. Identify and build on clients' strengths, for example, by helping them to structure leisure time around hobbies and talents, by making strengths such as assertiveness in relationships the focus of work outlined in the treatment plan, and by using them to prevent

relapse as when subcontracts are negotiated with natural supports for assistance during crises.

CONCLUSIONS

For reasons of convenience, political expediency, and pragmatism, the issue of drug abuse in this country has been simplified to the point where universal solutions are sought for what actually is a complex problem. Thus, classroom drug education efforts are viewed by some as *the* answer for all students. The same unrealistic expectations are held by advocates of military boot camps, long prison terms, and 28-day inpatient hospitalization.

To avoid falling into the same trap, it is important to note that the clinical interventions described in this chapter have limited applicability. Most treatment regimens depend upon clients having an existing support network of drug-free friends and family members, a job-related insurance program to finance treatment, and a willingness to consider, use, and incorporate information that argues that a drug-abusing life-style is standing in the way of an otherwise successful and fulfilling existence. To the extent that these assumptions accurately characterize client conditions, the treatment interventions discussed here are appropriate.

But what of the economically disadvantaged crack user? What techniques should be used when working with this population and others for whom the risks of becoming involved with cocaine may be outweighed by perceived psychological and economic benefits? Although it has been asserted that the traditional interventions presented in this chapter are effective with crack abusers (Rosecan, Spitz, & Gross, 1987), no data supporting this contention have been forthcoming. Other obstacles to successful treatment include lengthy waiting lists and inpatient facilities that are primarily designed to treat narcotic—not cocaine—addicts. A community organization approach that builds on community resources and other strengths may be promising; some communities have developed social action campaigns to close ''crack houses'' or have used knowledgeable community leaders to mount public education programs about the symptoms and consequences of cocaine addiction. Some of these groups have been useful in lobbying legislators to increase the monies funded for drug treatment programs in order to reduce waiting lists, and other real barriers to recovery.

A "trickle down" explanation of substance abuse has been used to argue that (1) less educated, lower socioeconomic groups increasingly abuse drugs (especially more dangerous, less costly derivatives such as crack) while mainstream Americans are becoming abstinent or casual consumers as the dangers become publicized. This is reflected by a limited movement toward safer chemical alternatives (e. g., low alcohol beer and wine coolers) by selected segments of the population. Similarly, prevalence data demonstrate a leveling off of recreational cocaine use by high school students and some young adults at the same time that crack use is rising among other groups. (2) This explanation does not clarify, however, why cocaine and crack abuse continues to rise in a subpopulation of heavy users that cuts across all racial, age, and socioeconomic groups, while alcohol use has increased among high school students. (3) The "trickle down" phenomenon and recent cocaine trends argue that the future challenge for social work professionals is to find ways of preventing and treating cocaine abuse among all population groups as well as among our most vulnerable and hard-to-reach populations.

REFERENCES

Adams, E., Gfroerer, J., Rouse, B., & Kozel, N. (1986). Trends in prevalence and consequences of cocaine use. *Advances in Alcohol and Substance Abuse, 6*, 49–71.

Beck, R. (1969). *Pimp: Story of my life.* Los Angeles: Holloway House.

Brickman, P., Rabinowitz, V. C., Karuza, J., Jr., Coates, D., Cohn, E., & Kidder, L. (1982). Models of helping and coping. *American Psychologist, 37*, 368–384.

Chasnoff, I., Griffith, D., MacGregor, S., Dirkes, K., & Burns, K. (1989). Temporal patterns of cocaine use in pregnancy: Perinatal outcome. *Journal of the American Medical Association, 261*, 1741–1744.

Chavez, G., Mulinare, J., & Cordero, J. (1989). Maternal cocaine use during early pregnancy as a risk factor for congenital urogenital anomalies. *Journal of the American Medical Association, 262*, 795–798.

Dackis, C., Gold, M., & Pottash, A. (1986). Central stimulant abuse. *Advances in Alcohol and Substance Abuse, 6*, 7–21.

Dougherty, R., & Lesswing, N. (1989). Inpatient cocaine abusers: An analysis of psychological and demographic variables. *Journal of Substance Abuse Treatment, 6*, 45–47.

Galanter, M. (1986). Social network therapy for cocaine dependence. *Advances in Alcohol and Substance Abuse, 6*, 159–175.

Gawin, F., & Ellinwood, E. (1988). Cocaine and other stimulants: actions, abuse, and treatment. *New England Journal of Medicine, 318*, 1173–1183.

Grabowski, J., & Dworkin, S. (1985). Cocaine: An overview of current issues. *International Journal of the Addictions, 20*, 1065–1088.

Hunt, D., Spunt, B., Lipton, D., Goldsmith, D., & Strug, D. (1986). The costly bonus: Cocaine related crime among methadone treatment clients. *Advances in Alcohol and Substance Abuse, 6*, 107–122.

Johnston, L. D., O'Malley, P. M., & Bachman, J. G. (1986). *Drug use among American high school students, college students and other young adults.* Rockville, MD: National Institute on Drug Abuse.

Kozel, N., & Adams, E. (1985). Cocaine use in America; Summary of discussion and recommendations. In N. Kozel & E. Adams (Eds.), *Cocaine use in America* (pp. 221–226). Rockville, MD: National Institute on Drug Abuse.

Miller, N., Millman, R., & Keskinen, S. (1989). The diagnosis of alcohol, cocaine and other drug dependence in an inpatient treatment population. *Journal of Substance Abuse Treatment, 6*, 37–40.

New York Times. (1989a, July 13). Latest drug of choice for abusers brings new generation to heroin, pp. B1, 3.

New York Times. (1989b, August 6). Emergency room: A crack nightmare, pp. 1, 16.

New York Times. (1989c, September 17). Crack's toll on infants found to be emotional devastation, pp. 1, 26.

Reid, K. (1986). The use of confrontation in group treatment. *Clinical Social Work Journal, 14*, 224–237.

Rosecan, J., Spitz, H., & Gross, B. (1987). Contemporary issues in the treatment of cocaine abuse. In H. Spitz & J. Rosecan (Eds.), *Cocaine abuse*, (pp. 299–323). New York: Brunner/Mazel.

Rounsaville, B., Gawin, F., & Kleber, H. (1985). Interpersonal psychotherapy adapted for ambulatory cocaine abusers. *American Journal of Drug and Alcohol Abuse, 11*, 171–191.

Schnoll, S., Karrigan, J., Kitchen, S., Daghestani, A., & Hanson, T. (1985). Characteristics of cocaine abusers presenting for treatment. In N. Kozel & E. Adams (Eds.), *Cocaine use in America* (pp. 171–181). Rockville, MD: National Institute on Drug Abuse.

Schwartz, S., & Wood, H. (1989). *Clinical assessment and intervention with shoplifters.* Unpublished manuscript.

Spitz, H., & Rosecan, J. (1987). *Cocaine abuse.* New York: Brunner/Mazel.

Washington Post (1989a, June 3). Small towns wrestle with 'the scourge.' pp. A1, 7.

Washington Post (1989b, August 1). Drug abuse said to decline. pp. A1, 8.

Washton, A. (1986). Structured outpatient treatment of cocaine abuse. *Advances in Alcohol and Substance Abuse, 6,* 143–157.

Washton, A., & Gold, M. (1986). Recent trends in cocaine abuse: A view from the National Hotline. *Advances in Alcohol and Substance Abuse, 6,* 31–47.

Wesson, D., & Smith, D. (1985). Cocaine: Treatment perspectives. In N. Kozel & E. Adams (Eds.), *Cocaine use in America* (pp. 193–203). Rockville, MD: National Institute on Drug Abuse.

White House. (1989). *National drug control strategy,* Washington, DC: U.S. Government Printing Office.

SUPPLEMENTAL READING LIST

Erickson, P., Adlaf, E., Murray, G., & Smart, R. (1987). *The steel drug.* Lexington, MA: Lexington Books.

Chapters 1 and 2 present a fascinating historical and multicultural perspective on cocaine.

Gold, M., Washton, A., & Dackis, C. (1985). Cocaine abuse: Neurochemistry, phenomenology, and treatment. In N. Kozel & E. Adams (Eds.) *Cocaine use in America* (pp. 130–150). Rockville, MD: National Institute on Drug Abuse

This article offers a summary of basic neurochemical aspects of cocaine addiction, in addition to survey data and pharmacological treatment issues derived from a sample of National Cocaine Hotline callers.

Lewis, J., Dana, R., & Blevins, G. (1988). *Substance abuse counseling.* Belmont, CA: Brooks/Cole.

The book presents a generalized model for individual, family, and group counseling techniques with substance abusers.

Washton, A. (1989). *Cocaine addiction: Treatment, recovery and relapse prevention.* New York: Norton.

This book, by a well-known clinician, provides an extensive and current overview of cocaine and crack treatment issues.

PART III

Eating Disorders

Much of the current research and practice experience indicates that it is not uncommon for clients to have an eating disorder and chemical dependency or more than one form of eating disorder. Both the interactional effects of these cross addictions and the common aspects require further research. Part III offers some guidelines for treatment of eating disorders, either singularly or in combination with other addictions.

As in the other sections of the book, Chapter 12 as the first chapter in the section is focused on research. It reviews research on the etiology and maintenance of eating disorders; most helpful is the discussion on the categories of the different disorders and their symptoms and consequences.

Chapters 13, 14, and 15 are focused on obesity, anorexia, and bulimia, respectively. Each emphasizes a particular aspect of treatment based on the nature of the disorder; for instance, the importance of mutual goal setting and self-monitoring is highlighted in Chapter 13, given the lifelong need for maintenance activities. Of special interest is the range of common aspects identified as part of the addiction process for all of the eating disorders, and the team approach necessary as a result of the nutritional, psychological, and family issues involved.

CHAPTER 12

Research on the Etiology and Maintenance of Eating Disorders

Betty A. Burrows

DePaul University Community Mental Health Center

The family is the factory, [and] you the adults, are the people-makers.

Virginia Satir

In this society food is abundant for most people and eating has taken on a variety of social and emotional functions beyond nutritional requirements. Along with this change in attitudes toward food and eating, problems with weight and interest in dieting have become an increasing preoccupation, especially among young women. Reports that the incidence of eating disorders is increasing cite changing cultural pressures, especially on women, to be an unrealistic "ideal weight" in order to be successful and attractive (Schwartz, Thompson, & Johnson, 1983). Examples can be seen in advertising on television and in women's magazines. Cultural pressures to be thin, a society in which food is abundant for most people, and the individualized meaning that food and hunger acquire through socialization are important contributing factors to the high number of people spending billions of dollars on the dieting industry. Because the sociocultural pressures for being thin are pervasive, it appears that the reasons some individuals develop serious eating disorders, while others do not, relate to differences in psychological and/or physiological functioning.

It is essential for helping professionals who are working in addictions counseling to be able to recognize, assess, and have an understanding of eating disorders because they are often present with other addictions and are not readily apparent. Among "normal"-weight individuals, eating problems may not be obvious and are often not spontaneously reported due to the shame and secrecy surrounding the disorders. Also, since eating problems are commonly associated with certain addictions (e.g., cocaine), it is important not to regard an eating problem as simply a consequence of the addiction when in fact it may be a separate disorder. From a preventive viewpoint as well as for treatment interventions, early identification of these issues is vital.

This chapter begins with an overview of eating disorders. It then addresses cultural, psychological, and emotional issues associated with the etiology and maintenance of eating disorders based on a review of the research literature. Binge-eating associated with obesity, bulimia nervosa, and anorexia nervosa is presented from a biopsychosocial conceptualization of this literature. Subsequent chapters in this section of the book focus on specific assessment and treatment issues related to obesity, bulimia nervosa, and anorexia nervosa, with a focus on the enhancement of clients' strengths being inherent in the later chapters as well as this one.

OVERVIEW OF EATING DISORDERS

Obesity in Males and Females

Obesity is defined as an excess accumulation of body fat resulting from caloric intake that exceeds energy expenditure. The definition varies, depending on the method of measurement, with the two most common being skinfold thickness and height and weight. A commonly accepted standard for obesity in the research literature, based on its association with increased risk for health problems, is 20 percent over desirable weight for one's height. According to the National Health and Nutrition Examination Survey, 26 percent of adult Americans aged 25 to 70 are obese (Bray, 1989). Estimates of juvenile obesity range from 5 to 26 percent (Weil, 1977), and this problem is increasing among children (Gortmaker, Dietz, Sobol, & Wehler, 1987) as well as adults (Agras, 1987). There is evidence that obesity in childhood has a strong positive relationship to weight status in adulthood, as it is estimated that more than 80 percent of overweight children remain overweight as adults (Brownell & Stunkard, 1978). It is important to note, however, that a high fat cell count during infancy and childhood is predictive of obesity in adulthood only if other factors associated with overfeeding and inactivity persist. Therefore, infancy and early childhood are important targets for the prevention of obesity later in life.

For both children and adults, obesity is associated with health problems and emotional distress. Cardiovascular risk factors, including hypertension and increased cholesterol levels, along with diabetes and respiratory difficulties, are some of the more common health problems associated with obesity. The psychological factors associated with obesity, which are often a consequence of negative reactions by others, include anxiety, depression, and low self-esteem. Stigmatization begins early in life, as obese children are frequent targets of peer abuse and are seen as less popular by their peers than other children (DeJong, 1980; Richardson, Goodman, Hastorf, & Dornbusch, 1961; and Wooley & Wooley, 1980). Adults suffer job discrimination and social ostracism. Being overweight is synonymous with perceived internal character flaws such as weakness, lack of control, and laziness. Given the pervasive preoccupation with thinness and the cultural contempt for obesity, emotional and psychological problems associated with obesity are more likely a consequence rather than a cause of the disorder (Wadden & Stunkard, 1987). The exception to this is obesity associated with binge-eating.

Although binge-eating in the obese is common, it does not characterize all obese individuals. Estimates indicate that binge-eating (at least once per week) occurs in about 50 percent of obese individuals seeking treatment (Gormally, Black, Dastrom, & Rardin, 1982). Binge-eating was first described in obese persons by Stunkard (1959a; Stunkard, 1959b). He noted an eating pattern of irregular "orgiastic" binges, in which large quantities of food are consumed in a short time period. These binges ended in physical discomfort and subjective feelings of guilt and self-condemnation and appeared to be a reaction to stressful situations in his clients' daily lives. Obese binge-eaters differ from other obese individuals in that they more frequently manifest interpersonal, self-esteem, and stress management deficits. Obese binge-eaters have fewer coping and problem-solving skills for stress, exhibit greater social anxiety, and are relatively unassertive as compared to non-binge-eaters (Kornhaber, 1970; Loro, 1984). Also, they report more stress, negative self-statements, and dysphoric moods both preceding and following binges (Fremouw & Heyneman, 1984), Kornhaber (1970) used the term "stuffing syndrome" to describe binge-eating in obese persons. He viewed them as unable to cope with internal or external stressors for both inherited and acquired reasons and felt that internal conflicts that generate anxiety are "stuffed down" by binge-eating similar to the process of stuffing feelings through self-medication with chemical substances. He also suggested that overeating is associated with the feeling of being unloved and that it serves as a defense against "the fear of nothingness" inside (Kornhaber, 1970). Binge-eating is also accompanied by difficulty in making the distinction between negative feelings and hunger. Eating thus becomes a response to emotional distress. Finally, binge-eating has been viewed as a "futile attempt to restock depleted emotional stores" when attempts at doing everything perfectly have failed (Loro, 1984).

Eating Disorders in Young Women

Findings similar to the above are reported in the research literature for anorexics who binge and normal-weight bulimics. However, obese binge-eaters appear to present less psychological disturbance than bulimics and anorexics (Wardle & Beinhart, 1981). Both anorexia nervosa and bulimia nervosa represent extreme attempts to avoid the negative consequences of obesity. These disorders must be viewed on a continuum, however, since fear of obesity among adolescent girls and inappropriate eating behavior are pervasive. It has been estimated that 80 to 90 percent of adolescent and young adult females are dieting or have weight concerns. Actual cases of anorexia nervosa or bulimia nervosa appear to be present in less than 5 percent of young women in high school and college populations. Interestingly enough, unlike obesity, which occurs in both men and women and across the lifespan, 95 percent of cases of anorexia nervosa and bulimia nervosa occur in women in their late teens to mid-thirties. Although preoccupations with food and dieting are common among young women, there are distinct psychological differences between weight-preoccupied women and those who are diagnosed as anorexic or bulimic. How often binge-purge behavior occurs, how out of control a person feels, and how much the eating preoccupation interferes with daily functioning and life adjustment are important factors that distinguish cases of anorexia nervosa and bulimia nervosa from "weight-preoccupied" women. Motivational factors are also important in distinguishing between these groups. Garner, Olmstead, Polivy, and Garfinkle (1984) suggest that chronic dieters may be motivated largely by a desire for physical attractiveness and social approval. For women with "true" eating disorders, dietary restriction and bingeing appear to be related to basic ego and personality deficits, which will now be reviewed.

Anorexia Nervosa. This disorder is characterized by the "relentless pursuit of thinness" (Bruch, 1973), which it is hoped will result in significant weight loss and a sense of mastery over one's body. Most cases occur in adolescent women, and the disorder is viewed primarily as a struggle for identity in those who suffer from a profound sense of ineffectiveness and fears of being unable to control their own impulses (Bruch, 1977). The diagnostic criteria from the *Diagnostic and Statistical Manual of Mental Disorders* (DSM-III-R) include the following:

1. Refusal to maintain body weight over a minimal normal weight for age and height, for example, weight loss leading to maintenance of body weight 15 percent below expected weight; or failure to make expected weight gain during a period of growth, leading to body weight that is 15 percent below that expected
2. Intense fear of gaining weight or of becoming fat even though the person is underweight
3. Disturbance in the way in which body weight, size, or shape are experienced; for example, the person claims to "feel fat" even when emaciated or believes that one area of the body is "too fat" even when she is obviously underweight
4. In females, absence of at least three consecutive menstrual cycles when they are otherwise expected to occur (primary or secondary amenorrhea) (American Psychiatric Association, 1987)

Two distinct patterns of behavior have been distinguished in the research literature among women who are diagnosed as anorexic. The first group, restricting anorexics, typically emaciate themselves by restrictive dieting, refusing food, and excessive and vigorous exercise (Herman & Polivy, 1975). The second group, bulimic anorexics, control their weight level and thinness by vomiting and/or laxative abuse following episodes of binge-eating. It has been estimated that 40 to 50 percent of restricting anorexics develop bulimic behaviors at some time in the course of their disorder (Garfinkel, Moldofsky, & Garner, 1980). Investigations regarding the premorbid and personality differences between the two groups have revealed highly consistent clinical differences that distinguish eating subtypes based on the presence or absence of binge-eating, with binge-eaters consistently exhibiting more psychopathology.

Restricting anorexics are characterized by greater social isolation and many are socially withdrawn. They are also more likely to be sexually inexperienced and often fear and avoid heterosexual dating. They are intensely involved in academic pursuits and are often seen as model students. In contrast, bulimic anorexics display histrionic personality traits and are more socially outgoing and sexually active (Garfinkel et al., 1980). They are more likely to display a variety of impulsive behaviors besides bingeing and purging, including drug and alcohol abuse, stealing, and self-mutilation.

These behaviors reflect a general lack of self-control including a poor mastery of eating behavior and of their sexual and aggressive drives (Garfinkel et al., 1980). Other characteristics include greater body-image disturbances (Button, Fransella, & Slade, 1977), a higher incidence of anxiety disorders (Laessle, Wittchen, Fichter, & Pirke, 1989), and increased depressive symptomatology, along with a greater risk of suicidal behavior (Russell, 1979; Strober, 1981; Casper, Eckert, Halmi, Goldberg, & Davis, 1980; Pope & Hudson, 1984). Finally, bulimic anorexics have greater difficulties with interceptive awareness (the ability to label hunger sensations and affect states) than restricting anorexics (Garner, Garfinkel, & O'Shaughnessy, 1985).

Given the increased incidence of other psychiatric problems, it is not surprising that anorexics who engage in binge-purge behavior have a longer duration of their disorder and a poorer prognosis for treatment than restricting anorexics (Beaumont, George, & Smart, 1976; Garfinkel et al., 1980). These differences indicate that classifications based on weight are less important than the presence or absence of binge-eating. Thus, bingeing, "whether it occurs in obese, normal weight, or anorexic subjects, occurs within the context of weight suppression and may reflect a more homogeneous set of clinical and personality features than is indicated by weight history" (Garner et al., 1985, p. 586).

Bulimia Nervosa. The research literature on bulimia nervosa has been somewhat confusing due to the inconsistent use of different diagnostic labels and criteria. The term "bulimia," literally meaning "ox hunger," is another word for binge-eating. Confusion has existed in the literature because the term "bulimia" had been used to describe both a syndrome and a symptom. From the previous description, it should be clear that bulimic behaviors occur across weight categories. The most recent edition of the *Diagnostic Criteria for Psychiatric Disorders* (DSM-III-R) (American Psychiatric Association, 1987) attempts to eliminate some of the previous confusion in classification by narrowing the definition.

Bulimia nervosa is characterized by cyclical patterns of eating followed by attempts to undo the behavior through purging or restrictive dieting and intense preoccupation with food. DSM-III-R criteria include the following:

1. Recurrent episodes of binge eating (rapid consumption of a large amount of food in a fairly brief, discrete period of time)
2. A feeling of a lack of control over eating behavior during eating binges
3. Regularly engaging in either self-induced vomiting, use of laxatives or diuretics, strict dieting or fasting, or vigorous exercise in order to prevent weight gain
4. A minimum average of two binge-eating episodes a week for at least three months
5. Persistent overconcern with body shape and weight (American Psychiatric Association, 1987)

Demographically, bulimia nervosa occurs in women who are typically single, white, in their twenties, and college-educated. The average age of onset is 18 and the duration of the illness prior to seeking treatment is five years. Bulimic behavior is most commonly precipitated by prolonged periods of restrictive dieting and difficulty in handling emotions. The onset of purging usually occurs about one year after the onset of bingeing (Johnson & Connors, 1987).

Empirical investigations of the eating behavior of bulimics reveal a fairly consistent picture. First, self-esteem and self-regulatory deficits characterize many women with this disorder. Eating fulfills an emotional need and tends to be a solitary and secretive habit (Kirkley, 1986). There is usually a continuous preoccupation with food among these individuals, which often leads to impaired concentration. Depressive symptoms are also prominent, next to the preoccupation with weight and eating. Furthermore, the level of depression usually increases with the severity of the eating disorder (Russell, 1979). Hysterical features are commonly associated with bulimia nervosa, along with minor disassociative episodes during binges. Since bulimia nervosa is such a secretive and shameful syndrome for most women, it is often difficult to assess the antecedents and consequences of bingeing.

Using an innovative time-sampling method, Johnson and Connors (1987) examined the moods and behavior of bulimic women as compared to a group of controls. Subjects were paged by a beeper at random intervals during the day and were asked to fill out a self-report questionnaire regarding their feelings and the situation at that particular time.

Bulimics reported experiencing significantly more dysphoric and fluctuating moods than normal controls. They spent more time alone and engaged in more food-related behavior than the control group. Hunger was often feared and associated with feelings of inadequacy, helplessness, and being out of control. Negative feelings such as disgust, guilt, helplessness, and panic appeared to increase during a binge. For many bulimics who engage in purging, this behavior appeared to offer a sense of relief from the anxiety of overeating. It was also found that purging provided an outlet for feelings of anger, as anger declined during and following purging.

Thus, eating is an attempt to modulate dysphoric and fluctuating mood states in bulimic women in the absence of more adaptive means of coping with intense emotional states. Difficulties in self-soothing or coping with stressful situations have been related to an impairment in the ability to regulate tension (Goodsitt, 1983; Johnson & Connors, 1987; Swift & Letven, 1984) and to interoceptive awareness difficulties (Bruch, 1973; Garner & Garfinkel, 1981; Selvini-Palazzoli, 1985). The same personality factors that place individuals at risk for substance abuse are found in bulimic women. These include an inability to regulate tension and the need to discharge affective experiences through action rather than feeling them or being able to talk about them; the need for immediate gratification; poor impulse control; and a fragile sense of self (Striegel-Moore, Silberstein, & Rodin, 1986; McDougall, 1989).

Despite many similarities among eating-disordered persons, it is important to note that the diagnostic categories of bulimia and anorexia nervosa represent heterogenous personality features and are best viewed on a continuum based on the severity of impairments in the life situation. Johnson and Connors (1987) have described the development and psychological adaptation of anorexic and bulimic behavior across a spectrum of personality functioning (also see Chapters 14 and 15 in this book).

ETIOLOGY AND MAINTENANCE FACTORS IN EATING DISORDERS

The common feature discussed thus far for eating disorders is binge-eating, which occurs across weight categories. In discussing etiological factors in eating disorders, the term "bulimia" will be used in this chapter to describe binge-eating and purging whether it occurs in anorexia nervosa, bulimia nervosa, or obesity. Differences will be highlighted between the disorders only when they are relevant. Due to the complex nature of the disorders described, the research literature indicates it is unlikely that any single, simple explanation can be given to account for bulimia in this very heterogeneous population. Although different theoretical perspectives are proposed in this chapter, they differ primarily in their emphases. There is a consensus among researchers that bulimia is a multidetermined disorder that serves a variety of sociocultural, biological, cognitive-behavioral, familial, and psychodynamic/developmental functions rather than a single set of factors (Johnson & Connors, 1987).

Sociocultural Factors

Sociocultural pressures to be thin are important contributing factors to the increased number of eating disorders in recent years. Despite the fact that the averge weight for most Americans has increased, the standard for women appears to have decreased. Weights and measurements of *Playboy Magazine* centerfolds and Miss America Beauty Pageant winners have decreased over the last 20 years (Garner, Garfinkel, Schwartz, & Thompson, 1980). There has also been a trend for models' shapes to be less curvaceous and more tubular during the past two decades (Morris, Cooper, & Cooper, 1989). These media images create a discrepancy between what is a "realistic" healthy body shape and weight and the perceived "feminine ideal."

These images also promote the cultural message that to be thin is to get ahead and be successful. The high number of young, educated women with bulimia and anorexia nervosa may be seen as evidence that dieting and thinness are an expression of cultural pressures on females to achieve perfection. In the view of Dunn and Ondercin (1981), bulimics have difficulty in integrating new roles for women involving assertiveness and independence with their traditional ideas of femininity. When considerable conflict is generated by a discrepancy between underlying feelings of helplessness, anxiety, and inadequacy, and perfectionistic strivings for achievement, binge-eating can provide a means of escape and avoidance of these intolerable feelings. The pursuit of thinness has been found to be a concrete activity for a woman that results in enhancement of her self-esteem, despite confusing cultural expectations and pressures to achieve success (Johnson & Connors, 1987).

Biological Factors

Biological and genetic factors are also important in both the development and the maintenance of eating disorders. Research has shown that there is a large genetic component to body type; and although environmental factors can modify the effects of heritability, the fact is that weight, the development of fat tissue, metabolism, and how and where fat is stored on the body are heavily influenced by genetics.

Besides the genetic component to obesity, biological factors appear to have an important influence on the development of bulimic behaviors as well. First, the relationship between bulimia and depression has prompted several researchers to claim that many bulimics are suffering from a major affective disorder (Herzog, 1984; Pope & Hudson, 1984). Herzog (1984) found that a major depressive disorder characterized 23.6 percent of bulimic patients and 55.6 percent of anorexic patients. Secondly, there is a high rate of affective disorders and alcoholism reported in first- and second-degree relatives among bulimics (Hudson, Pope, & Jonas, 1983). In one study, bulimics and their families were found to have a significantly higher rate of substance abuse than normal women (Bulik, 1987), and, in another study, one-third of cocaine abusers were found to have bulimia nervosa (Jonas, Gold, Sweeney, & Pottash, 1987). The fact that bulimics were found to have significantly lower and more volatile moods than normal women (Johnson & Larson, 1982) is also seen as evidence of a biological predisposition to affective instability. Finally, metabolic disturbances have been suggested by Wurtman (1988) as a cause of carbohydrate craving in some women. Low levels of the neurotransmitter serotonin have been associated with depressed moods, increased fatigue, and carbohydrate cravings that may lead to bingeing.

Pope and Hudson (1984) endorse a biochemical basis for binge-eating and present research suggesting that the best treatment approach is antidepressant medication. Findings regarding the effectiveness of antidepressant medication, when used alone or in combination with psychotherapy, are promising in that there have been significant reductions in bulimic symptoms for many women (see Johnson and Connors, 1987, for a review of relevant factors).

Further research is needed, however, using better controlled research designs to achieve a further understanding of what medications work best with which type of client characteristics. Johnson and Connors (1987) also emphasize that medication should be viewed as only one possible component of a comprehensive treatment program that includes psychotherapy.

Cognitive-Behavioral Factors

Research concerning the ways in which cognitive-behavioral factors contribute to the development and maintenance of binge-eating focuses on the reinforcing nature of eating behavior. Eating is seen as a means of coping with stressful life experiences and overwhelming feelings, and with both overt (environmental) and covert (cognitions) cues that trigger eating binges. In this research, binge-eating has been shown to occur in response to stressful interpersonal events such as losses, breakups, perceived criticism or rejection, and conflict. Binge-eating is maintained because, although the highly negative consequences (e.g., feelings of fullness, guilt, and weight gain) may outweigh the positive, they are more delayed in time from the point when the actual binge occurs (Loro, 1984).

Immediate reinforcement is provided in the enjoyment of the taste and smell of the food during a binge and in the relief of avoiding the negative consequences of eating through purging. These behaviors also provide relief from negative emotional states such as anger, disappointment, or anxiety by diverting attention from conflict. Eating can also function as an activity that provides relief from boredom by filling unstructured time, even producing feelings of relaxation among overweight individuals (Holland, Masling, & Copley, 1970; Loro, 1984). Finally, bingeing followed by purging not only reduces anxiety related to feared weight gain, but functions as a mood stabilizer. Bulimics report feeling a restored sense of control after purging, thus reinforcing this dysfunctional behavior (Johnson & Connors, 1987). An individual who learns to eat in response to a number of cues may use eating as a way to avoid or relieve aversive experiences later in life and as a way to cope with stress.

Research has been conducted on various theories that have been advanced to explain eating difficulties from a cognitive-behavioral perspective. Externality theory states that overeating is a response to salient information in the environment, such as food cues (e.g., the availability and sight or smell of food) and the perceived time of day (Nisbett, 1968; Schacter, Goldman, & Gordon, 1968). An over-reliance on external cues, then, may contribute to a deficiency in responding to physiological hunger cues and differentiating them from emotions. Self-efficacy (Bandura, 1977), associated with a person's feeling of confidence in being able to resist the urge to binge and purge, has been suggested as another cognitive factor contributing to bulimia. Love, Ollendick, Johnson, and Schleshinger (1985) found that the level of self-efficacy to resist the urge to binge and purge and the perceived efficacy to handle stress and a feeling of having control over life events were the main predictors of bulimic behavior in one of the only studies that applied social-learning principles to bulimic behavior.

Much attention has been focused on the depression that accompanies bulimia. Depressive affect is related to themes of learned helplessness, hopelessness, pessimism, self-hatred, and guilt. Clinical reports suggest that much of the depressive affect is related to cognitive distortions in that bulimics often have unrealistically high, perfectionistic standards for themselves in their eating behavior as they do in all other areas of their lives. They are extremely self-critical when they do not live up to these standards. These cognitive distortions are similar to those frequently seen in affectively depressed clients that have been described by Beck (1970).

Finally, research on restraint theory shows that it takes both cognitive and physiological factors into account. This theory states that binge-eating occurs in response to a disinhibiting effect of some stimulus, such as eating a "forbidden food," experiencing emotional distress, drinking alcoholic beverages, depriving onself of food for long periods of time, and perceiving that one's self-imposed restrictions have been violated (Polivy, Herman, Olmstead, & Jazwinski, 1984). The degree of restraint is a cognitive factor that has been found to be related to bingeing across all weight categories. Restrained eaters diet frequently and maintain a weight

that is biologically under their natural "set point." They restrain their eating by attending to external cues such as how much they are eating, and they are unresponsive to internal cues of hunger and satiation.

Food restriction leads to a physiological imbalance plus a psychological state of deprivation that sets the stage for bingeing. Restrained eaters also exhibit cognitive distortions such as dichotomous thinking. They often classify foods into categories of "good" and "bad" food, and then label themselves as good or bad based on the type of food eaten. Severity of beinge-eating has been related to the degree of dieting concern and preoccupation with maintaining one's weight below the "set point" through restrained eating (Hawkins & Clement, 1980). Given these factors, it is not surprising that periods of restrictive dieting generally precede the initial episode of bingeing for most bulimics (Johnson & Connors, 1987) and that nearly half of all restricting anorexics develop bulimic behaviors some time in the course of their disorder (Garfinkel et al., 1980).

Family Characteristics

Research from a family system perspective demonstrates that anorexia nervosa and bulimia result from two primary problems: the adolescent's difficulty in separating from overprotective and overcontrolling parents, and disturbed patterns of communication within the family. Families of restricting anorexics have been characterized by enmeshment, rigidity, overprotectiveness, lack of conflict resolution, and involvement of the child in parental conflict. Restricting food intake may be the best way the child knows to gain control, act out, or indirectly express anger (Hudson, Pope, & Jonas, 1983).

Families of bulimics have been found to have even greater disturbance in interactional styles than those of restricting anorexics. For example, bulimics view their families as discouraging the open expression of feelings (Ordman & Kirshenbaum, 1984). Humphrey (1983, 1989) examined interactional patterns and perceived relationships among eating-disordered families and found that these parents were highly controlling and constricting toward their daughters and gave them double-binding messages. Another study found maternal depression and paternal impulse disorders and depression to be predictive of greater severity of bulimia (Strober, Salkion, & Burroughs, 1982). More specifically, disturbances in affect, weak internal controls, unmodulated expression of hostile impulses, and the absence of satisfying intrafamilial ties were found in families of bulimics, with the incidence of these behaviors being greater than in families of restricting anorexics. In addition, affective disorders and alcohol and drug usage occurred more frequently in blood relatives of bulimics than in those of restricting anorexics (Strober et al., 1982).

In general, bulimic clients perceive less affection and affiliation in their families than both restricting anorexics and normal controls. Their relationships with their parents are often described as lacking warmth, trust, affirmation, and nurturing. As a result of what appear to be unaffectionate, often critical, relationships with parents, bulimic women seem to adopt similar attitudes toward themselves, according to research. They often feel self-destructive and self-critical; they have difficulty engaging in self-caregiving behaviors (Humphrey, 1989).

Psychodynamic and Developmental Perspectives

Psychodynamic explanations for eating disorders generally include poor early relationships, inconsistent responding from parents (Bruch, 1973; Selvini-Palazzoli, 1985), and failures in parental empathy (Kohut, 1971). These explanations have often been the result of case study investigations, with only a few empirical studies having been done involving such theories. When conflicts occur during early periods of attachment and separation-individuation, they cause impairments in the individual's ability to regulate tension, according to psychodynamic theory. This places them at risk for affective instability in adolescence and adulthood. Both Bruch (1973) and Selvini-Palazzoli (1985) provide a framework for understanding these early developmental failures in eating disorders. They state that during infancy a child presents with needs that are diffuse and undifferentiated. It is the caretaker's responsibility to decode these signals and organize a response (for example, feeding or soothing). To the extent that this occurs, there is an increased ability on the child's part to differentiate inner states.

If food and attention are offered independent of the child's needs, however, and food is offered for a variety of tension states, the child never learns to discriminate among such states. In anorexic and bulimic families the primary caretaker is seen as interpreting whatever the child does as expressing something about the caretaker and not the child. In feeding, for example, refusing food could be equated with criticism and rejection, and eating may be associated with the child's acceptance and love of the parent. Even in nonfeeding situations, control and a tendency to stifle any of the child's own initiatives are thought to occur (Bruch, 1973; Selvini-Palazzoli, 1985). The mismatch between the child's needs and what is provided leaves the child feeling anxious and disappointed in the early relationship.

These early empathic failures often occur in the preverbal period, when the "organizing and anxiety-allaying power of words is unavailable" (Swift & Letven, 1984, p. 491). Later, "a restricted vocabulary or interest in words for communication" is a major consequence of this developmental failure in maternal empathy (Learner, 1983). This, then, is the basis for what Bruch (1973) considers the core deficits in eating-disordered clients:

1. a paralyzing sense of ineffectiveness pervading every thought and feeling,
2. interoceptive disturbances, and
3. body image disturbances. (p. 31)

A "false-self" (Winnicott, 1965) can develop in response to excessive external demands as the child focuses on doing what is perceived as pleasing to others and blocks out personal feelings and wishes. This impairs the development of an internal sense of self and leads to an overdependence on the environment as it is related to the self.

Balint (1968) has described adults who suffer from what he describes as a "basic fault," as appearing extremely needy, as being vulnerable to addictive behaviors, and as experiencing intolerable inner tension and emptiness (cited in Swift & Letven, 1984). For the bulimic, food becomes a means of selectively focusing on the external world in order to avoid anxiety-provoking internal issues and feelings. In other words, bulimic behavior is often a frantic, self-stimulatory activity that functions to drown out states of internal tension and disorganization related to early development failures in terms of this perspective. The bulimic often treats her body as if it were threatening, dangerous, and foreign to herself (Goodsitt, 1983). Denial and undoing are seen as the basic underlying defense mechanisms of the bulimic (Swift & Letven, 1984).

The implications, according to psychodynamic models, are that due to developmental failures in their relationships with others, these individuals are not prepared to cope with the demands of adulthood. Psychodynamic theory provides one explanation for why adolescence and early adulthood are often traumatic times that precipitate the onset of eating and substance abuse problems. Anorexics and bulimics are especially vulnerable to separation experiences and the feelings of loss, helplessness, and depression that accompany them. Early separation-individuation conflicts are reactivated in adolescence when identity formation, autonomy, and developing intimate relationships outside the family are the primary developmental tasks. In the absence of effective internal coping responses that are blocked by the types of developmental failures described here, food and drugs are often used as concrete objects of gratification because relationships cannot be counted on consistently.

AN INTEGRATED BIOPSYCHOSOCIAL MODEL

In summary, research shows that a biopsychosocial model that combines early biogenetic, familial, sociocultural, and psychological factors as contributing to the individual's character structure can best account for the reason bulimia develops and is maintained in some weight-preoccupied individuals and not in others (Johnson & Connors, 1987). This model proposes that biological factors including predispositions to be overweight, metabolic factors, and affective instability make some women especially vulnerable to sociocultural pressures to be thin, and to binge-eating that might result from prolonged attempts at dieting. The character structure of psychologically vulnerable women is such that low self-esteem and affective instability lead to the pursuit of thinness, as thinness is equated with control, discipline, beauty, success, and popularity.

Initially, it has been found that the weight loss is reinforced by others, and the individual experiences an increase in self-esteem. Restrictive dieting soon gives way to binge-eating in an effort to manage stressors, followed by intense anxiety, guilt, and eventually attempts to "undo" the negative effects of overeating with purging behavior. The ritualistic binge-purge cycle that develops is then maintained because it serves a variety of adaptive functions. These include self-soothing, resolving a discrepancy between internal feelings of inadequacy and outside achievement, regulating confusing and dysphoric tension states, and maintaining distance in relationships to avoid expected disappointment and rejection.

IMPLICATIONS FOR TREATMENT AND SOCIAL WORK ROLES

Due to the complex nature of eating disorders, a multicomponent approach to treatment by a multidisciplinary treatment team is recommended. A comprehensive treatment program should include social workers and other helping professionals consistently planning and implementing an ecologically based treatment plan. Techniques for symptom management, as well as a supportive therapeutic relationship with the social worker, can facilitate development of the individual's sense of self and the enhancement of self-esteem. Multimodal approaches to treatment are especially important for bulimics with severe personality disturbance, since they often require a variety of external environmental supports (Johnson & Connors, 1987). A comprehensive treatment program should have the availability of individual, family, and group psychotherapy as well as nutritional counseling and medical consultation with a physician familiar with eating disorders.

Members of the team need to coordinate treatment efforts to maximize client support. Directive interventions should include psychoeducational techniques, nutritional counseling, and self-monitoring to understand the antecedents and consequences of the bulimic behavior. Alternative coping strategies, including the modification of distorted self-perceptions, are needed to help the bulimic deal with her affect and environmental stress. Psychoeducational techniques can occur individually or in group treatment. Group treatment provides opportunities to see situations from others' viewpoints and to allow for sharing of experiences and coping strategies. Social comparison and social support can do much to minimize feelings of aloneness, inadequacy, and the sense of shame that often go along with eating disorders. In addition, other ways to cope with tension and stressful interpersonal situations, and ways to nurture and soothe oneself other than through the use of food, will likely lead to greater self-acceptance and self-awareness. Interventions directed toward factors in the family that inhibit maturation and maintain double-bind communication patterns are equally important. The complex nature of such problems may often require helpers to work in pairs with families rather than alone.

CONCLUSION

Depending on their personality functioning and the severity of depression, many bulimics will require long-term treatment in addition to psychoeducational techniques and other strategies that can be implied from current research on the problem. Moreover, women with eating disorders need to discover their own abilities and inner capabilities for thinking and feeling in more positive, adaptive, and self-supportive ways (Bruch, 1973). Social workers and other helping professionals can help them to develop affect tolerance, learn to use feelings as signals to themselves, and eventually learn to view their feelings as self-limited in duration and intensity. These are important goals for open-ended treatment designed to enhance and build on the strengths of bulimic clients. Another goal should be to continue to explore through future research the antecedents, natural history, consequences, and effective treatments involved in eating disorders as a subset of addictions.

REFERENCES

Agras, W. S. (1987). *Eating disorders: Management of obesity, bulimia, and anorexia nervosa.* New York: Pergamon Press.

American Psychiatric Association. (1987). *Diagnostic and statistical manual of mental disorders.* (3rd ed., rev.). Washington, DC: American Psychiatric Association.

Balint, E. (1968). *The basic fault.* New York: Brunner/Mazel.

Bandura, A. (1977). Self-efficacy: Toward a unifying theory of behavioral change. *Psychological Review, 84,* 191–215.

Beaumont, P. J. V., George, G. C. W., & Smart, D. E. (1976). ''Dieters'' and ''vomiters and purgers'' in anorexia nervosa. *Psychological Medicine, 6,* 617–622.

Beck, A. T. (1970). *Depression: Causes and treatment.* Philadelphia: University of Pennsylvania Press.

Bray, G. A. (1989). Obesity: Basic considerations and clinical approaches. *Dissertation Monographs, 35,* 449–537.

Brownell, K. D., & Stunkard, A. J. (1978). Behavioral treatment of obesity in children. *American Journal of Diseases in Children, 132,* 403–412.

Bruch, H. (1973). *Eating disorders: Obesity, anorexia nervosa, and the person within.* New York: Basic Books.

Bruch, H. (1977). Psychological antecedents of anorexia nervosa. In R. A. Vigersky (Ed.), *Anorexia nervosa,* (pp. 1–10). New York: Raven Press.

Bulik, C. M. (1987). Drug and alcohol abuse by bulimic women and their families. *American Journal of Psychiatry, 144,* 1604–1606.

Button, E., Fransella, F., & Slade, P. (1977). A reappraisal of body perception in anorexia nervosa. *Psychological Medicine, 7,* 235–243.

Casper, R. C., Eckert, E. D., Halmi, K. A., Goldberg, S. C., & Davis, J. M. (1980). Bulimia: Its incidence and clinical importance in patients with anorexia nervosa. *Archives of General Psychiatry, 37,* 1030–1035.

DeJong, W. (1980). The stigma of obesity: The consequences of naive assumptions concerning the causes of physical deviance. *Journal of Health and Social Behavior, 21,* 75–81.

Dunn, P. K., & Ondercin, P. (1981). Personality variables related to compulsive eating in college women. *Journal of Clinical Psychology, 37,* 43–49.

Fremouw, W. J., & Heyneman, N. E. (1984). A functional analysis of binge episodes. In R. C. Hawkins, W.J. Fremouw, & P. F. Clement (Eds.), *The binge-purge syndrome: Diagnosis, treatment, and research,* (pp. 254–263). New York: Springer.

Garfinkel, P. E., Moldofsky, H., & Garner, D. M. (1980). The heterogeneity of anorexia nervosa: Bulimia as a distinct subgroup. *Archives of General Psychiatry, 37,* 1036–1040.

Garner, D. M., & Garfinkel, P. E. (1981). Body image in anorexia nervosa: Measurement, theory, and clinical implications. *International Journal of Psychiatry in Medicine, 11,* 263–284.

Garner, D. M., Garfinkel, P. E., & O'Shaughnessy, M. (1985). The validity of the distinction between bulimia with and without anorexia nervosa. *American Journal of Psychiatry, 142*, 581–587.

Garner, D. M., Garfinkel, P. E., Schwartz, D., & Thompson, M. (1980). Cultural expectations of thinness in women. *Psychological Reports, 47*, 483–491.

Garner, D. M., Olmstead, M. P., Polivy, J., & Garfinkle, P. E. (1984). Comparison between weight-preoccupied women and anorexia nervosa. *Psychosomatic Medicine, 46*, 255–256.

Goodsitt, A. (1983). Self-regulatory disturbances in eating disorders. *International Journal of Eating Disorders, 2*, 51–60.

Gormally, J., Black, S., Dastrom, S., & Rardin, D. (1982). The assessment of binge eating severity among obese persons. *Addictive Behaviors, 7*, 47–55.

Gortmaker, S. L., Dietz, W. H., Sobol, A. M., & Wehler, C. A. (1987). Increasing pediatric obesity in the United States. *American Journal of Diseases in Children, 141*, 535–540.

Hawkins, R. C., & Clement, P. F. (1980). Development and construct validation of a self-report measure of binge eating tendencies. *Addictive Behaviors, 5*, 219–226.

Herzog, D. B. (1984). Are anorexic and bulimic patients depressed? *American Journal of Psychiatry, 141*, 1594–1638.

Herman, C. P., & Polivy, J. (1975). Anxiety, restraint, and eating behavior. *Journal of Abnormal Psychology, 43*, 647–660.

Holland, J., Masling, H., & Copley, D. (1970). Mental illness in lower class normal, obese, and hyperobese women. *Psychosomatic Medicine, 32*, 351–357.

Hudson, J. I., Pope, H. G., & Jonas, J. M. (1983). Family history study of anorexia nervosa and bulimia. *British Journal of Psychiatry, 142*, 133–138.

Humphrey, L. L. (1983). A sequential analysis of family processes in anorexia and bulimia. *Advances in Anorexia Nervosa Treatment and Research*. The Fourth Annual Roth Conference.

Humphrey, L. L. (1989). Observed family interactions among subtypes of eating disorders using the structual analysis of social behavior. *Journal of Consulting and Clinical Psychology, 57*, 206–214.

Johnson, C., & Connors, M. (1987). *The etiology and treatment of bulimia nervosa: A biopsychosocial perspective*. New York: Basic Books.

Johnson, C., & Larson, R. (1982). Bulimia: An analysis of moods and behavior. *Psychosomatic Medicine, 44*, 341–351.

Johnson-Sabine, E. C., Wood, K. H., & Wakeling, A. (1984). Mood changes in bulimia nervosa. *British Journal of Psychiatry, 145*, 512–516.

Jonas, J. M., Gold, M. S., Sweeney, D., & Pottash, A. L. (1987). Eating disorders and cocaine abuse: A survey of 259 cocaine abusers. *Journal of Clinical Psychiatry, 48*, 47–50.

Kirkley, B. G. (1986). Bulimia: Clinical characteristics, development, and etiology. *Journal of the American Dietetic Association, 4*, 468–472, 475.

Kohut, H. (1971). *The analysis of the self*. New York: International Universities Press.

Kornhaber, A. (1970). The stuffing syndrome. *Psychosomatics, 11* 580–584.

Laessle, R. G., Wittchen, H. U., Fichter, M. M., & Pirke, K. M. (1989). The significance of subgroups of bulimia and anorexia nervosa: Lifetime frequency of psychiatric disorders. *International Journal of Eating Disorders, 8*, 569–574.

Learner, H. (1983). Contemporary psychoanalytic perspectives on gorge-vomiting. *International Journal of Eating Disorders, 3*, 47–63.

Loro, A. D. (1984). Binge eating: A cognitive-behavioral treatment approach. In R. C. Hawkins, W. J. Fremouw, and P. F. Clement (Eds.), *The binge-purge syndrome: Diagnosis, treatment, & research* (pp. 183–210). New York: Springer.

Love, S. Q., Ollendick, T., Johnson, C., & Schleshinger, S. (1985). A preliminary report on the predictions of bulimic behavior: A social learning analysis. *Bulletin of the Society of Psychologists in Addictive Behaviors, 2*, 14–21.

McDougall, J. (1989). *Theaters of the body: A psychoanalytic approach to psychosomatic illness*. New York: Norton.

Morris, A., Cooper, T., & Cooper, P. J. (1989). The changing shape of female fashion models. *International Journal of Eating Disorders, 8*, 593–596.

National Institute of Health Consensus Statement. (1985). Health implications of obesity. *Annals of Internal Medicine. 103*, 1073–1077.

Nisbett, R. E. (1968). Taste, deprivation, and weight determinants of eating behavior. *Journal of Personality and Social Psychology, 10*, 107–116.

Ordman, A. M., & Kirschenbaum, D. A. (1984). *Bulimia: Assessment of eating, psychological and family characteristics*. Unpublished manuscript, University of Wisconsin.

Polivy, J., Herman, P. C., Olmstead, M. P., & Jazwinski, O. (1984). Restraint and binge eating. In R. C. Hawkins, W. J. Fremouw, & P. F. Clement (Eds.), *The binge-purge syndrome: Diagnosis, treatment, and research* (pp. 104–122). New York: Springer.

Pope, H. G., & Hudson, J. I. (1984). *New hope for binge eaters: Advances in the understanding and treatment for bulimia*. New York: Harper & Row.

Pope, H. G., Hudson, J. I., & Jonas, M. D. (1983). Antidepressant treatment of bulimia: Preliminary experience and practical recommendations. *Journal of Clinical Psychopharmacology, 3*, 274–281.

Richardson, S. A., Goodman, M., Hastorf, A. H., & Dornbusch, S. A. (1961). Cultural uniformity in reaction to physical disabilities. *American Sociological Review, 26*, 241–247.

Russell, G. (1979). Bulimia nervosa: An ominous variant of anorexia nervosa. *Psychological Medicine, 9*, 429–448.

Satir, V. (1972). *Peoplemaking* (p. 3). Palo Alto, CA: Science and Behavior Books.

Schacter, S., Goldman, R. R., & Gordon, A. (1968). Effects of fear, food deprivation, and obesity on eating. *Journal of Personality and Social Psychology, 10*, 91–97.

Schwartz, D. M., Thompson, M. G., & Johnson, C. (1983). Anorexia and bulimia: The sociocultural context. *International Journal of Eating Disorders, 1*, 23–25.

Selvini-Palazzoli, M. (1985). *Self-starvation*. London: Jason Aronson.

Striegel-Moore, R. H., Silberstein, L. R., & Rodin, J. (1986). Toward an understanding of risk factors for bulimia. *American Psychologist, 41*, 246–263.

Strober, M. (1981). The significance of bulimia and anorexia nervosa: An exploration of possible etiological factors. *International Journal of Eating Disorders, 1*, 28–43.

Strober, M., Salkion, B., & Burroughs, J. (1982). Validity of bulimia-restricter distinction in anorexia nervosa parental personality characteristics and family psychiatric morbidity. *Journal of Nervous and Mental Disease, 170*, 345–351.

Stunkard, A. (1959a). Eating patterns and obesity. *Psychiatric Quarterly, 33*, 284–295.

Stunkard, A. (1959b). Obesity and the denial of hunger. *Psychosomatic Medicine, 21*, 281–289.

Swift, W. J., & Letven, R. (1984). Bulimia and the basic fault: A psychoanalytic interpretation of the binge-vomiting syndrome. *Journal of American Academy of Child Psychiatry, 23*, 484–497.

Wadden, T. A., & Stunkard, A. J. (1987). Psychopathology and obesity. *Annals of the New York Academy of Science, 499*, 55–65.

Wardle, J., & Beinhart, H. (1981). Binge eating: A theoretical review. *British Journal of Clinical Psychology, 20*, 97–109.

Weil, W. B. (1977). Current controversies in childhood obesity. *The Journal of Pediatrics, 91*, 175–187.

Winnicott, D. W. (1965). *The maturational process and the facilitating environment*. New York: International Universities Press.

Wooley, S. C., & Wooley, O. W. (1980). Eating disorders: Obesity and anorexia. In A. M. Brodsky & R. Hare-Mustin (Eds.), *Women and Psychotherapy*. New York: Guilford Press.

Wurtman, J. J. (1988). Carbohydrate craving, mood changes, and obesity. *Journal of Clinical Psychiatry, 49*, 37–39.

SUPPLEMENTAL READING LIST

Bennett, W., & Gurin, J. (1982). *The dieter's dilemma*. New York: Basic Books.
This book discusses setpoint theory, which is the idea that the body has a certain level of fatness that is biologically determined. It helps to explain why diets fail for so many people and gives comprehensive detailed data on the theory.

Boskind-White, M., & White, W. (1981). *Bulimarexia: The binge-purge cycle*. New York: Norton.
A useful book on bulimia in college-age women, easily understood, with a range of case examples. Also it has good chapters on physical complications and the sociocultural context of bulimia.

Chernin, K. (1981). *The obsession: Reflections on the tyranny of slenderness*. New York: Harper & Row.
A beautifully written book on the sociocultural pressures on women to be thin and how this has affected women's relationship to food.

Chernin, K. (1985). *The hungry self: Women, eating & identity*, New York: Random House.
This volume discusses the issues facing young women regarding achievement conflicts and the process of challenging the traditional notions of womanhood, and how these conflicts are played out around food and eating. An excellent description of some of the mother–daughter conflicts involved in the underlying dynamics of eating problems.

Slochower, J. A. (1983). *Excessive eating: The role of emotions and environment*. New York: Human Sciences Press.
A presentation of research findings on binge-eating and its association with the inability to label and differentiate hunger sensations from emotions.

CHAPTER 13

Obesity and Overeating: The Value of Mutual Goal Setting in Social Work Treatment

Steven Perlow
Susan Shrifter
On Track Program for Child and Adolescent Obesity,
St. Joseph Hospital and Health Care Center, Chicago

There is evidence—though not proof yet—from human and animal growth records that fatness in infancy tends to foster obesity for the rest of life.

Benjamin Spock, M.D.

Obesity has been called "the most prevalent and serious nutritional disease in the United States" (Dietz, 1983). During a period when a "fitness craze" is supposedly sweeping across America, people are becoming less fit. Of particular concern is the skyrocketing incidence of obesity among children and adolescents (Gortmaker, Dietz, Sobol, & Wehlen, 1987). Why should serious attention be directed toward this problem? For the obese individual, and especially for those who are superobese, there are a host of significant medical, psychological, and social consequences that impact upon both the individual and society as well. In addition, although losing weight is difficult, maintenance appears to be even more difficult.

Traditionally, the problem of obesity has been quite resistant to long-term change (Brownell & Stunkard, 1978). It is imperative, therefore, that effective permanent treatment strategies be developed, but even more important is the need to shift attention to possibilities of primary and secondary prevention.

The purpose of this chapter, therefore, is to discuss the incidence and consequences of obesity as well as the onset of this condition. The latter is included to highlight the process by which this eating disorder (addiction) develops and the many factors that affect the process. Individualized and multilevel assessment and treatment strategies are discussed, along with factors to be considered in making decisions about inpatient versus outpatient services. Included also is information about the problems involved in maintenance and prevention. The chapter concludes with a description of significant social work roles for the effective treatment of obesity.

THE INCIDENCE AND CONSEQUENCES OF OBESITY

It has been estimated that between 40 and 80 million Americans are obese, depending on the criteria used to define obesity (Stuart & Davis, 1972). Moreover, the Public Health Service has warned that obesity is one of the most prevalent health problems in the United States today. A recent study completed by Dr. William Dietz at Tufts University concluded that the incidence rate of obesity in children and adolescents is truly on the rise and is in fact reaching epidemic proportions (Gortmaker et al., 1987). There are numerous consequences associated with the increasing incidence rates that have been cited.

Medical/Physical Consequences

A broad range of medical problems appear to be associated with obesity. In the Framingham study (Kannel & Gordon, 1979), the development of coronary disease, death from coronary disease, and the likelihood of developing congestive heart failure in men were predicted, based on the degree of obesity. For women, coronary disease, death from coronary disease, stroke, and congestive heart failure were all more likely based on relative body weight. Death from diabetes, digestive disease, and cancer were also found to be related to being overweight (Lew & Garfinkel, 1979).

Increased cardiac output and hypertension are linked to obesity, but they can be corrected with weight loss (Alexander, 1973). Respiratory problems are associated with obesity as well. They include the Pickwickian or hypoventilation syndrome and sleep apnea. The latter is the periodic cessation of breathing during sleep. Some individuals experience breathing difficulties of such severity that they have to sleep in an upright position.

Gallbladder disease has been well documented as being related to obesity (Leijd, 1980). Skin problems such as acanthosis nigricans (darkening of the skin in certain parts of the body) and "stretch marks" have been associated with obesity as well. These dermatologic problems, probably due to their external visibility, cause some youngsters to feel self-conscious about their appearance.

Certain orthopedic abnormalities have been observed in overweight children. Some have slipped capital femoral ephiphysis in one or both hips, while others have back problems or disc disease. Still others demonstrate pes plenus or "flat feet." In addition, premature puberty and rapid gains in height also occur in these children. Youngsters often complain that others treat them as if they are older due to the increase in size and stature.

Psychological Consequences

Although the medical problems associated with obesity are certainly dramatic, among children the psychological effects of being overweight are at least equally important to consider. Whereas nearly all children experience teasing and name-calling at some point during development, those who are overweight are an easy target for others. Anecdotal evidence indicates that obese children believe they are treated differently from those of normal weight.

A study conducted by Richardson, Hastorf, Goodman, and Dornbusch (1961) accurately depicted the social handicap with which the overweight child is burdened. In this study, children were shown four pictures of other children with various physical handicaps, one picture of an obese child, and one picture of a child without a handicap. The children were asked to rank the pictures in term of whom they liked most. Invariably, regardless of gender, race, socioeconomic group, or rural versus urban community of origin, the overweight child was perceived as being the least likable. Similar results were obtained when the study was replicated with adult health-care professionals (Goodman, Richardson, Dornbusch, & Hastorf, 1963).

The authors speculated that the obese child was seen as being responsible for his condition whereas the others were not, and that this led to a lack of popularity among the study participants (Richardson et al., 1961). Some of these children may become shy, isolated, and introverted as a result of such experiences of rejection. They may eventually expect rejection will always happen and become reluctant to initiate conversation or friendships. Thus, their assumption that they will be treated with prejudice may become a self-fulfilling prophecy.

Of course, the problems do not cease once they reach adolescence. At a time when pubescent teenagers are beginning to discover their sexuality, many overweight teens continue to be treated differently than normal-weight peers. Some girls complain they are rarely, if ever, asked out on dates. Boys may fear rejection and become reluctant to initiate dating. Sometimes overweight youngsters are among the last to be chosen for teams in gym class. Both genders have difficulty finding teenage clothes that fit, although more age-appropriate clothing for overweight adolescents is available currently than in the past.

Low self-esteem appears to accompany obesity in many youth. They are often are very body-conscious and have difficulty identifying anything positive about their appearance (Lohman, 1989).

client about the role of heredity in overweight. The date of onset of the obesity is another extremely important factor to assess. If the client's obesity began in early childhood and then continued, the practitioner is likely to be confronting a lifelong pattern of eating and lack of exercise that may then have to be modified. If the client had a more recent onset of the obesity, it may be possible to identify a significant cause or catalyst of the problem. The importance of history can be seen in the following case examples:

> Jane was an eight-year-old female who was recently evaluated at a clinic for treating obesity. Upon initial evaluation, Jane was close to 100 percent over her ideal weight and had gained 50 pounds in the past six months. Upon taking a good history with the client and her mother, the practitioner learned that Jane had been sexually molested by her babysitter and her babysitter's boyfriend. After Jane's parents became suspicious of the abuse, the babysitter was confronted and ultimately taken to court. Because of the lack of solid evidence, the parents were not able to substantiate the abuse. Although the babysitter was no longer involved in the care of the child, Jane would often see her on the streets of their neighborhood. The weight gain continued.

> In another scenario, Jonathan, a 25-year-old man, had been relatively thin most of his life. In the past year or so, however, he had noticed a tremendous increase in his appetite and a driving desire to obtain food. He had gained close to 75 pounds during this period. History revealed no significant emotional trauma or any major transitions or changes in his life. A referral to a physician was made, after which the presence of a slow-growing hypothalamic tumor was detected. This tumor was the cause of the tremendous increase in the client's appetite.

The treatment for each of the above clients was different from that of the typical client who might not have significant medical or emotional factors causing the obesity. The treatment in these two cases was also focused on factors that were maintaining the problem.

Factors that help to maintain the obesity should be evaluated as part of the assessment. A number of factors may be contributory in this regard. The prime source is usually the client's eating patterns. The best way to assess such patterns is by having

clients keep an eating diary as part of the evaluation. The diary not only helps to collect data about eating patterns that might be maintaining the problem, but it also helps to involve the client actively in the goal setting that follows. The information gathered becomes the client's data; it increases commitments and insights into what may be effective goals.

The ideal eating diary is a booklet in which clients are required to write down all of the foods they have eaten, the amount of these foods, the calories for each, when the foods were eaten, and what was occurring at the time or prior to their being eaten that might have contributed to the desire to eat (Brownell & Wadden, 1986) (see Figure 13.1). The diary should be kept for at least three days, but ideally for seven days, as part of the assessment. This gives the practitioner important information as to when, how much, and potentially why food was eaten in order to determine whether any patterns exist in the client's eating behavior.

A second major variable to assess is the client's activity level. Including this information in diary form is also extremely helpful. A simple way of doing this is to include any exercise information on the pages of the eating diary (see Figure 13.1). For a more detailed analysis of activity levels, clients can be asked to summarize their activities hour by hour in order to obtain a sense of their patterns over time (see Figure 13.2). The activity diary should also be completed during assessment for three to seven days.

A sample of the type of information that might be gained from an eating diary involves David, a 40-year-old insurance salesman:

> David's eating diary revealed that he generally skips breakfast and has a doughnut or two at the office with coffee. He then goes out of the office for meetings after which he usually has lunch at a fast-food restaurant. Upon returning home at 6 or 7 P. M. he has a beer and eats dinner with his family. This is then followed by a late night snack of something sweet, such as ice cream, while watching TV. David "doesn't have time to exercise." On the weekend after an argument with his wife, it was observed that David ate a large quantity of sweets following the argument. Weekends, in general, resulted in a lot of snacking, usually in front of the television set. David's behavioral pattern, as obtained from the diary, gave the practitioner and David ample information from which to develop a mutual treatment regime.

Time	Food Eaten with Amount	Calories	Circumstances
			Date: _____

Today's
Exercise _____ How Long?
( )
( )

Figure 13.1. Sample Page of Eating Diary

168

Name: _____ Day, Date _____

Activity Calories		Activity Calories		Activity Calories	
12–1 A.M.		8–9		4–5	
1–2		9–10		5–6	
2–3		10–11		6–7	
3–4		11–12		7–8	
4–5		12–1 P.M.		8–9	
5–6		1–2		9–10	
6–7		2–3		10–11	
7–8		3–4		11–12	

Figure 13.2. Activity Chart

The next major component of the assessment phase is the medical evaluation. No client should be evaluated and treated for obesity without a medical assessment and approval from a physician for participation in treatment. As previously stated, although the numbers are few, some overweight individuals do have a relevant medical condition. This must be ruled out before treatment is to occur. For instance, it could happen that an overweight adolescent female with whom a weight reduction program was producing little success was actually pregnant. In addition to ruling out medical causes for the obesity, obtaining a physician's consent for treatment helps to legally protect the helping professionals (Kannel & Gordon, 1979).

The final element of the assessment phase includes an evaluation of the client's motivation for treatment. This is possibly the most important component of the assessment since it helps to determine if a client will be able to participate in mutual goal setting with the practitioner. Clients who are active participants in goal setting and have hope are more likely to stay actively involved in treatment. However, the social worker or other professional with a client who is unmotivated toward change will become extremely frustrated at some point in the process. Adherence to eating and activity regimes are too simple to undermine, both for children and adults. Clients are usually the only persons who are with themselves 24 hours a day. They need to maintain their behavior changes under a variety of different conditions. If motivation is low, it is unlikely that they will be able to do so (Striegel-Moore & Rodin, 1986).

Assessment of motivation includes an assessment of the client's psychological status. If the client is significantly depressed, psychotic, or mentally deficient, all of these can have major implications for treatment. Some of the children who are treated for obesity have suicidal ideation and some have made suicide attempts. While many obese people exhibit some level of depression, extremely depressed individuals may not be ready initially to work on their weight problem. Other issues such as relationship conflicts may be more pressing for them and will need to be addressed first. The client's identification of priorities along with the practitioner's ability to set mutual goals may, in the long run, provide the energy and motivation for focus on the weight problem as the depression is lifted. In cases involving a psychosis and mental deficiency, the degree of either would need to be assessed. When treatment for obesity *is* appropriate, these clients need a fairly structured approach with external consequences or limits being placed on their behaviors.

For the average obese individual, motivation can be determined in a number of ways. The first and easiest way is to ask if participation in a weight reduction program is their choice. It is not uncommon for an adult to be forced into a session by a spouse or for a child to have been pulled in by a parent. A second measure of motivation is client compliance. This can initially be evaluated quite easily with the use of the eating and exercise diary. Individuals coming in with a completed diary are exhibiting some motivation. A third suggestion made by Brownell and Foreyt (1985) is to have the client lose at least one to two pounds prior to initiating treatment. Most individuals, including children, can do this in one day at the start of treatment. Those not capable of making even this small step may not be ready to make the necessary behavior changes inherent in an ongoing weight reduction regime.

Treatment Planning and Goalsetting

Once the assessment phase of treatment is sufficiently under way, the practitioner and client then have to make some important decisions. If significant medical problems are found, it is even more essential to have permission from a physician to engage the client in treatment. In many cases, the treatment will be the same whether or not the client has a medical condition. In some conditions, such as pregnancy, treatment should obviously not be continued.

Similarly, the assessment may have revealed significant psychological problems. If these do exist, the social worker must then decide along with the client the most appropriate services: (1) treatment for the emotional or family problem first, which can then be followed by treatment for the obesity; (2) no specific treatment for the emotional problem, as it is largely a result of the obesity and should likely be ameliorated through the treatment or program; or (3) specific treatment for the emotional or family problem which can be done concurrent with treatment for the obesity (Striegel-Moore & Rodin, 1986). Even when clients are not able to participate in such decisions, the options and consequences, as well as the rationale for the recommended option, should be fully explained to them.

The next issue to consider in setting up a treatment regime is the severity of the problem. There is a wide continuum of overweight conditions for both children and adults. For those individuals who are only mildly overweight (20 to 30 percent over ideal body weight) or those who have never attempted to lose weight before, it is best to start with an educational approach. This approach is considered a secondary prevention method; it consists of the least amount of (or least restrictive) intervention necessary. This approach assumes that the client has some strengths and that with the benefit of certain educational information the client (and client's parent in the case of a child) will be able to use the information to initiate the necessary life-style changes. The educational approach should consist of helpful articles and didactic information designed to inform the client about significant issues in nutrition and exercise. Many clients can benefit greatly from information about fats, cholesterol, calorie levels of typically eaten foods, nutritional content of fast foods, the four basic food groups, and the rewards of aerobic exercise.

Other clients will need more treatment than the educational approach alone can provide. These are clients who were either unsuccessful with the educational approach alone or with previous weight reduction programs, or those who have a more significant degree of obesity (greater than 40 percent over ideal body weight). Their involvement in goal setting is important for maintaining a commitment to change. Because these clients may see themselves as failures due to prior weight loss experiences or as being incapable of change, they may tend to set unrealistic goals for weight loss and improved relationships. The practitioner's role, in mutual goal setting, is to encourage them to begin with the smallest goal that will signal change and then to revise goals as needed. This prevents a further loss of hope and failure. In addition to goal-setting considerations, treatment for these clients may need to be more intense. They can, nevertheless, be treated generally on an outpatient basis. For individuals in this group who are even more severely overweight (greater than 85 percent over ideal body weight) and who have significant emotional and/or medical problems, it is necessary to consider inpatient treatment to begin the intervention. This triage approach to treatment is illustrated by the treatment flow chart in Figure 13.3.

OUTPATIENT TREATMENT

There are three primary components necessary to provide a thorough outpatient intervention. These include the (1) nutritional, (2) exercise, and (3) psychological elements of treatment (Epstein, 1986;

Stern & Lowney, 1986). The vast majority of clients who seek treatment for obesity would be included in this type of approach. While seemingly separate, these three components all relate to one another. Thus, treatment for obesity should not necessarily be provided compartmentally, but in a way in which the client can see how the different components interact.

Nutritional Component

Nutritional intervention should be provided by a dietitian, nutritionist, or social work practitioner who has obtained sufficient nutritional education, depending on the level of need in each case situation. It is useful to help clients learn how to eat in a healthy manner, a skill which they could continue the rest of their lives. Fasting or modified fasts for children are not realistic in the long-term daily lives of these clients, and they may be harmful as well. Questions about the effectiveness of modified liquid fasts for adults have not been answered adequately. If the long-term empirical data on clients using these products show maintenance of treatment results, this could be an approach worth considering. While the liquid modified fasts do include a refeeding phase, it appears once again that the emphasis is more on weight loss than on teaching healthy eating patterns over time.

On the other hand, lowering the calorie intake for most clients seems more feasible. This approach is not the same as skipping meals, which is a common practice amongst the obese. Breakfast and/or lunch are often skipped by these clients. Many of them choose to skip lunches at school or work because of the embarrassment of eating in front of other people. The intention may be to have others believe that the obesity is not their fault. Skipping meals, however, works against clients. First of all, it makes them hungrier and less energetic. As a result, they do not have the energy to be as active as they need to be; and because they are hungry, they end up eating more than they would have at their next meal. This meal inevitably occurs later in the day when there are fewer opportunities for food to be utilized as energy (Marston et al., 1975). There is also the likelihood that missing meals contributes to a slowing of metabolic rate as the body defends itself against starvation (Goldberg, 1988).

Calorie intake can be reduced in a systematic

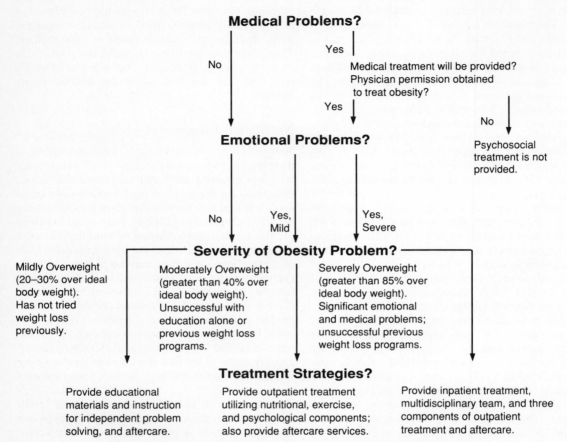

Medical Problems?

No

Yes

Medical treatment will be provided?
Physician permission obtained
to treat obesity?

Yes

No

Psychosocial
treatment is not
provided.

Emotional Problems?

No

Yes,
Mild

Yes,
Severe

Severity of Obesity Problem?

Mildly Overweight
(20–30% over ideal
body weight).
Has not tried
weight loss
previously.

Moderately Overweight
(greater than 40% over
ideal body weight).
Unsuccessful with
education alone or
previous weight loss
programs.

Severely Overweight
(greater than 85% over
ideal body weight).
Significant emotional
and medical problems;
unsuccessful previous
weight loss programs.

Treatment Strategies?

Provide educational
materials and instruction
for independent problem
solving, and aftercare.

Provide outpatient treatment
utilizing nutritional, exercise,
and psychological components;
also provide aftercare services.

Provide inpatient treatment,
multidisciplinary team, and three
components of outpatient
treatment and aftercare.

Figure 13.3. Treatment Flow Chart, Related to Obesity as an Eating Disorder

manner that continues to provide the client with essential nutrients (this is extremely important for the developing child), but not with excess food. The plan should include three meals with planned snacks at times of the day when the client is generally hungry. After school and one to two hours prior to bedtime are common hunger times. The goal is to maintain or increase the quality of the food eaten while decreasing the quantity or portion size. The food diary should be helpful for gathering baseline data (Brownell & Stunkard, 1978).

It is unrealistic to tell clients to avoid certain foods, and it does not lend itself well to the maintenance of treatment effects. If the practitioner tells the client never to have chocolate cake, this will potentially increase the client's desire for such food. The practitioner and client can determine an acceptable amount and frequency for eating certain foods. A mutual goal should be developed for the client to eat only a moderate amount of a high-fat high-calorie food if this is something that is desired. Clients can compensate for this intake by eating less of other foods and saving their calories for the desired food. By helping clients to anticipate wanting to eat a particular food under special circumstances, they can plan to include this food in their nutritional program without interfering with their progress in weight loss (Epstein & Squines, 1988).

The example which follows clearly illustrates this treatment strategy:

A child is going to a birthday party. The child knows that ice cream and cake will be served at the party. Also available might be dishes of candy or chips set out in different areas of the party location. If the child would like to have some of the cake and ice cream, that could be done by taking small portions of each, avoiding the candy and chip dishes, and decreasing the amount eaten for lunch prior to time for the ice cream and cake. In addition, the child could choose to engage in additional exercise later in the day which, if not completely compensating for the additional calories, will at least offset them to some degree. In addition, the exercise can contribute to keeping the client psychologically on track.

Exercise Component

The second major component of the intervention is the exercise or activity element. Brownell and Foreyt (1985) have stated that the implementation of a workable, consistent exercise program is one of the things most highly associated with the maintenance of treatment effects. Unfortunately, the vast majority of Americans do not exercise regularly. This is especially true of obese individuals who are generally less active than people of normal weight; low activity rates have been associated with overweight conditions for individuals across the age spectrum (Ravussin et al., 1988).

The primary goal in the development of an exercise program is to try to make the program realistic for the client. Therefore, the goal must be decided by the practitioner and client together. If the client finds the program too difficult, adherence is likely to become a major problem. Finding activities to which the client can readily have access and in which the client has some interest can significantly increase continued involvement (Brownell & Wadden, 1986).

Generally, some education of clients will be necessary to help them begin an appropriate exercise program. Many clients are under the misconception that "spot reducing" is the best way to exercise. This involves participating in a particular exercise in order to lose weight in a specific area of the body— for example, doing sit-ups to decrease the size of the stomach. In truth, weight loss does not work this way. The body follows its own pattern of where fat deposits are taken from as a result of the need for increased energy. The most effective activity-related method to help decrease the body's fat deposits is

through involvement in aerobic exercise. The latter involves any exercise in which a person performs certain behaviors that result in an increased heart and respiratory rate while performing the activity. Aerobic exercise also provides sweating during effective activity times. Ideally, aerobic exercise should be conducted for at least 20 to 30 minutes continuously. Examples of aerobic exercise include walking, running, swimming, biking, rowing, dancing, and jumping rope. Exercise such as sit-ups or weight lifting will work to tone muscles underneath the fat, but they have little impact on decreasing fat deposits (Goldberg, 1988).

There is no one "perfect" exercise program that is right for everyone. The worker should help the client particularize the exercise plan to individual needs, interests, and daily schedule. The more individualized and mutual the plan is, the more likely the client is to follow it consistently. The helper with little experience in this area would do well to seek some consultation in setting up the exercise program. Likely resources include physical therapists, exercise physiologists, health educators, or the client's physician.

With regard to exercise for children, it is not uncommon for obese children not to be participating in their school's physical education program. This is often at the initiation of their physical education teachers, who are worried that the child might have a heart attack during their class. What is generally needed, however, is not less physical exercise but more activity than they have been getting. A thorough physical exam with a letter from the physician to the gym teacher can usually correct this problem.

Another difficulty that frequently arises for the obese child or adult involved in an exercise program overlaps with the next treatment component: the psychological side of exercise. Many obese individuals are embarrassed to participate in exercise, especially in public. They are frequently afraid that they will look odd and that they might be laughed at. As a result, a common pattern is for the obese client to shun exercise in order to avoid the embarrassment. This pattern usually results in less exercise and skill development. It also promotes a decrease in the individual's perceived competence in this area. Total avoidance of exercise is often the result. Helping professionals who find their clients in this dilemma should work to help them find an exercise plan with which they can feel comfortable. Initially, this might mean exercising in private for an adult or getting permission for a child to wear a full sweat suit in gym instead of potentially embarrassing shorts and a T-shirt.

Finally, a last note about the interaction between psychology and exercise: a consistent finding is that exercise produces a greater sense of psychological well-being for the individual (Brownell & Foreyt, 1985). Stern and Lowney (1986) have pointed out that exercise can contribute to an increase in self-esteem, an improvement in mood, and the alleviation of mild depression. Practice experience also suggests that individuals who are able to continue their exercise regimen on a long-term basis are the individuals who are best able to maintain treatment results.

Psychological/Behavioral Component

The psychological/behavior portion of the intervention again is interrelated with the other major components in order to enhance the overall effectiveness. In addition, it touches on some separate areas which have not yet been addressed.

One of the most important elements of any program requiring behavior change is self-monitoring. Kent (1980) found that this program component was most closely associated with success in his weight reduction program. Self-monitoring literally involves keeping track of one's behavior and one's progress. In the context of the approach described in this chapter, it is strongly recommended that the eating diary be continued both for eating and exercise behaviors. This helps clients monitor progress throughout the day and between days, and it also helps them keep track of what they have or have not yet eaten. Keeping track of exercise helps to make it become more a part of the daily routine.

A second important form of self-monitoring is the maintenance of a graph which shows the client's weight loss progress over time (see Figure 13.4). The graph is particularly useful for helping clients to stay involved in their weight loss and to notice trends. For example, they might see a more consistent or rapid weight loss as they increase participation in exercise from three days a week to four days, or they might notice a gradual weight increase since a new job began. This information is useful for formulating treatment recommendations.

Another significant aspect of this component involves the use of stimulus control techniques in

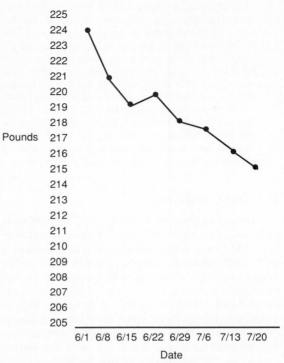

Figure 13.4 Sample Weight Graph

aiding the client. This literally implies an attempt to control stimuli around the client to help promote successful participation in the treatment regime. Examples of stimulus control procedures would include, when at home, eating only in the kitchen to help the client associate eating with that room only. Also, it is helpful not to allow eating and television watching to occur at the same time because of the following issues:

1. TV encourages eating through the airing of commercials,
2. TV watching and eating become associated with each other after repeated pairings, and
3. TV watching encourages "mindless eating" in which clients are not aware of how much they are consuming.

In addition, storing food in opaque containers is useful, as snacks are more likely to be nibbled upon if readily seen. Other tips include: keeping serving trays off the table to discourage "picking" or the taking of second and third helpings, keeping foods out of the house that the client prefers not to eat in order to work toward the programmatic goals, and keeping healthy foods readily available in the house so they can be eaten as snacks (e.g., having a dish of sliced vegetables available in the refrigerator). There are many other stimulus control tactics that can and should be individualized for the particular client's situation.

These strategies may need to be more systemic when it can be recognized that stimuli are initiated by significant others in the environment, as when a spouse expects to be joined in eating in front of the TV. The treatment plan, in those instances, must include the agreement of relevant others to follow stimulus control strategies when they are willing. When they are not, strategies should be aimed at helping the client resist significant others' expectations. This can be accomplished by finding alternative ways to be close that do not involve food, confrontation about the effects of those expectations on the client's efforts to lose weight, and a focus on "unhooking" the client from being responsible for the others' needs. Al-Anon and Overeaters Anonymous (OA) are examples of self-help groups that assist clients in their work on such co-dependency issues and on relapse prevention. The focus on family members, other significant relationships, and self-help work with peers is an important aspect of environmental work. This approach is based on recognition of the impact of these variables on lifestyles and the onset of obesity, which were discussed in a previous section.

Another major psychological intervention involves the use of cognitive techniques to help individuals deal with challenging situations and emotional stress. A significant percentage of obese individuals are emotional eaters—that is, they eat when they are angry, upset, frustrated, sad, or worried. The goal of this intervention is to help the client develop alternative coping mechanisms to replace eating as a stress reliever. Cognitive treatment recognizes that individuals are communicating with themselves all the time. Efforts are made to help the clients revise their self-statements into more adaptive coping statements ("I've had a rough day; I think I'll take a walk to get rid of some of this stress") as opposed to the unhealthy ones that support emotional eating ("A chocolate sundae would make me feel better right now").

Other cognitive techniques involve a recognition of the "sparks" that set off inappropriate eating, and learning how to anticipate and plan for these. Clients can be helped to revise their thoughts about how to react to these events. An example of this might be the overweight client who goes in to buy a doughnut every time he passes a particular doughnut shop because the window display is so tantalizing he tells himself he cannot resist. A cognitive technique might have the client perceive his ability to walk past the doughnut shop without giving in to the doughnut as a challenge. Upon meeting the challenge, the client is to be rewarded in a non-food-related way, often through self-congratulations.

Finally, the helper does need to consider the emotional status of the client. Many clients may be depressed or have some other emotional concern, as indicated previously. The helper must make a clinical judgment, with the client if possible, as to the appropriateness of dealing with these issues directly or deciding if they are actually the side effects of the obesity. Self-esteem is a frequent source of problems for the obese individual. Clients should be encouraged not to "junk" themselves. Obese clients tend to overemphasize the importance of their obesity when taking into account their self-concept as a whole. Because they have this problem they tend to look at their whole person as bad or unworthy. They can be taught to see their obesity for what it is, as only a *part* of their total selves.

Useful self-statements include the following: that they are doing all they can to deal with the problem by being in treatment with the practitioner, and that they should try to recognize their strengths. The diary is a useful tool for monitoring changes in the amount of positive versus negative self-talk which a client includes. The positive self-talk is expected to increase as treatment proceeds, including statements about feeling better or more neutral about the weight or an eating episode, statements that identify personal talents or strengths in other areas, and statements that recognize social supports in the environment that facilitate life-style changes and weight loss. The latter type of resource is an important aspect of strengths that may have been ignored by the client prior to treatment.

Some clients will need psychotherapy either

before, during, or after treatment for the obesity. Others will do fine without additional treatment. Group intervention for obesity often helps to address therapeutic issues as different group members share their common experiences through the weeks of treatment. Children should not be treated without the participation of their parents, as their parents are the ones who will have to actually make many of the household and life-style changes that are necessary.

INPATIENT TREATMENT

Some clients may be more appropriate for inpatient treatment to begin their program than the outpatient treatment that has been described. Inpatient treatment has the benefit of removing clients from the problem-supporting environment and helping them learn new behaviors and see the effects of the behavior change. It also allows the client to be treated for other medical and/or emotional problems associated with or resulting from the obesity. Family members and others significant to the problem situation can be involved in the treatment sessions either concurrently or sequentially.

Criteria for admission to an inpatient treatment program should include a lack of success with previous outpatient efforts. As noted previously, other criteria are significant medical and/or emotional problems of sufficient severity to warrant inpatient treatment, and severe obesity greater than 85 percent above ideal body weight.

Treatment in an inpatient setting can make use of a multidisciplinary team approach in which the social worker can play a key role. In a hospital, the client has the benefit of a physical therapy department, dietary or nutrition department, and possibly a cardiac rehabilitation department that can provide various aspects of treatment. The social worker can provide more intensive individual, family, and group treatment to carry out therapeutic and mutually determined goals. In addition, the presence of the physician and hospital nursing staff assures the monitoring of the client's medical status and treatment for concurrent medical conditions. Another advantage is that inpatient treatment offers an opportunity for the team to handle emotional and physical crises on-the-spot and to provide support in a 12-step self-help program such as OA.

Interventions utilized within the inpatient approach generally incorporate the same goals and philosophy as the outpatient treatment described in the previous section. Both work toward life-style change. The difference between the two is one of intensity and degree of problem severity along with the treatment of complicating medical and/or emotional conditions. Outpatient treatment, or other aftercare services modeled after the format of substance abuse programs, can be implemented after discharge.

MAINTENANCE AND GENERALIZATION

The overwhelming majority of individuals who are treated for obesity do not maintain their treatment gains using traditional approaches. This not only makes the significant amount of effort that the client and helper expend during treatment a waste of time, but is actually harmful to the client. Once the client has lost weight and then regains it, there has been an experience of failure, potentially having significant impact on the client's self-esteem and self-perceptions about being able to be in control.

The most important component of treatment, therefore, is the focus on maintenance and generalization of treatment effects. One cannot assume, because the client was able to make healthy behavior changes during the initial phase of treatment, that these behavioral changes will continue automatically. There are a number of practical interventions, however, that have been shown to be effective in enhancing the maintenance of treatment effects.

Brownell and Wadden (1986) have discussed a variety of factors that enhance treatment effectiveness over time. The first of these is relapse prevention. This is a concept that has come out of the literature on alcoholism, but relates to the way in which the client perceives and responds to her or his own addictive behavior. Basically, the goal of the intervention is to let the client know that people make mistakes, and to identify the cycle or pattern of behaviors that can lead to relapse. These should be seen as momentary lapses, after which the client can get right back on track. If the client perceives the mistake as a total ruination of effort, a relapse will ultimately occur. This relapse is what the client is trying to avoid.

Another helpful intervention to promote maintenance is in-vivo training: that is, trying as much as possible to have the training take place within the clients' actual living arrangements or natural circumstances. This helps clients to actually experience the healthy behaviors within their own context. As an example of this, the practitioner can go out to the homes of clients to help them put their stimulus control procedures in place, and then go with them to their grocery store to discuss food choices and meal planning in that context. This can also help to pinpoint environmental supports *and* barriers to the life-style change.

A third element in maintenance is the implementation of a realistic exercise program. Clients who are able to follow through with exercise on a long-term basis are much more likely to show consistent treatment effects over time. Thus, maintenance is enhanced by a habitual exercise activity.

Again, as previously mentioned, the use of self-monitoring behaviors also promote maintenance. Using an eating and exercise diary and weight graphs are common examples of this technique. The client receives, learns from, and internalizes feedback that reinforces the use of self-monitoring and maintenance activities.

Finally, Christoffel (1986) has stated the benefits of treating obesity on a long-term basis. Research is now suggesting that obesity should be characterized as a chronic disease requiring long-term, regular attention. Individuals who are able to respond to this need for continued attention to changes are more likely to show treatment maintenance and generalization for longer periods of time.

PREVENTION STRATEGIES

The most effective approach is to work on the problem of obesity from a preventative standpoint. As one can see, obesity often requires a great deal of effort to resolve. Time can be much more efficiently spent in teaching young children methods for living a healthy life-style before they become obese adults. Some suggestions for preventative programs might include:

1. education at the high school level for those who will soon be parents;
2. education of young children at the grammar school level for healthy life-styles with some monitoring of their behavior;
3. efforts on the part of schools and society in general to promote a healthy life-style—for example, serving only healthy foods at school, offering quality physical education programs at school, not allowing children to bring food deemed unhealthy into the school environment;
4. efforts on the part of parents to model healthy living behaviors for their children, that is, healthy eating and exercise habits. The importance of modeling effects can be shared with individuals before they become parents when they receive their education at the high school level;
5. putting pressure on the media and food companies to produce healthier foods for children, to label the nutritional and caloric content of their fast-foods, and not to advertise unhealthy foods during children's television viewing hours; and
6. educating mothers during prenatal care about healthy food and life-styles for the family as a whole and especially for infants.

CONCLUSION

Because of social workers' unique orientation toward treating the "person in situation," they are in a key position to be at the forefront in primary, secondary, and tertiary prevention. Social work often focuses on treating the individual not only within the family but also for interactions with other systems. It emphasizes looking at the total picture ecologically instead of merely adopting a "victim blaming" approach. The client's priorities must be considered in this view of the total situation; thus the social worker's role involves insuring that the assessment leads to a mutually determined set of goals and treatment process. Clients whose views and goals are ignored are simply reinforced in their beliefs that they are unworthy and incapable of positive change.

In addition, social workers are based strategically in schools, hospitals, community agencies, and corporations. They are involved also in the shaping of public policy. They are in an excellent position to provide early intervention to high-risk children, adolescents, or adults and to focus on outreach services as well. Furthermore, social workers based in hospitals are in a good position to help advise mothers prenatally of healthy eating, activity levels, and the manner in which food can be used and misused.

Social workers must be concerned with educating American society in general about the high mortality rates and other dangers associated with unhealthy life-styles that lead to obesity. It is part of the social worker's role to disseminate information that the obese child or adult is as much in need of help as, for example, someone with an alcohol problem.

Certainly, in terms of treatment programs, the social worker can serve as an important catalyst on the multidisciplinary team. In adopting a systems approach, staff can be sensitive to the importance of contributions made by all disciplines involved on the treatment team. Social workers are also experts at linking clients with appropriate community resources. This is essential when dealing with secondary prevention issues from a systems perspective.

In years to come, it is hoped that more societal attention will be given to the problem of obesity. In addition, emphasis should be placed on prevention as currently recidivism rates tend to be high. It is an exciting time to be in the field, and social workers can be at the forefront in addressing the needs of this population.

REFERENCES

Alexander, J. K. (1973). Effects of weight reduction on the cardiovascular system. In G. A. Bray (Ed.), *Obesity in perspective, 2* (pp. 233–236). NIH Publication No. 75–708. Washington, DC: U.S. Government Printing Office.

Brownell, K. D., & Foreyt, J. P. (1985 November) Unpublished Obesity Workshop conducted at Association for the Advancement of Behavior Therapy Convention, Chicago.

Brownell, K. D., & Stunkard, A. J. (1978). Behavioral treatment of obesity in children. *American Journal of Diseases in Children, 132,* 403–412.

Brownell, K. D., & Wadden, T. A. (1986). Behavior therapy for obesity: Modern approaches and better results. In K. D. Brownell & J. P. Foreyt (Eds.), *Handbook of eating disorders* (pp. 145–158). New York: Basic Books.

Christoffel, K. K. (1986). Childhood obesity: Treat early

and often. *The child's doctor: Children's memorial hospital, Chicago, 3,* 15–21.

Dietz, W. H. (1983) Childhood obesity: Susceptibility, cause and management. *Journal of Pediatrics, 103,* 676.

Epstein, L. H. (1986). Treatment of childhood obesity. In K. D. Brownell & J. P. Foreyt (Eds.), *Handbook of eating disorders* (pp. 159–179). New York: Basic Books.

Epstein, L. H., & Squires, S. (1988). *The stoplight diet for children.* Boston: Little, Brown.

Goldberg, M. (1988). [Unpublished lectures of On Track Program]. Chicago, IL: Saint Joseph Hospital.

Goodman, J. L., Richardson, S. A., Dornbusch, S. M., & Hastorf, A. H. (1963). Variant reactions to physical disabilities. *American Sociological Review, 28,* 429–435.

Gortmaker, S. L., Dietz, W. H., Sobol, A. M., & Wehlen, C. A. (1987). Increasing pediatric obesity in the United States. *American Journal of Diseases of Children. 141,* 535–540.

Kannel, W. B., & Gordon, T. (1979). Obesity and some physiological and medical concomitants of obesity: The Framingham study. In G. A. Gray (Ed.), *Obesity in America* (pp. 125–163). NIH Publication No. 79–359. Washington, DC: U.S. Government Printing Office.

Keesey, R. E. (1986). A set point theory of obesity. In K. D. Brownell & J. P. Foreyt (Eds.), *Handbook of eating disorders* (pp. 63–87). New York: Basic Books.

Kent, A. (1980). *An evaluation of a cognitive-behavioral treatment program for weight control.* Unpublished master's thesis. Chicago, IL: De Paul University.

Leijd, B. (1980). Cholesterol and bile acid metabolism in obesity. *Clinical Science, 59,* 203–206.

Lew, E. A., & Garfinkel, L. (1979). Variations in mortality by weight among 750,000 men and women. *Journal of Chronic Diseases, 36,* 563–576.

Lohman, T. G. (1989). Assessment of body composition in children. *Pediatric Exercise Science, 1,* 19–30.

Marston, A. R., London, P., & Cooper, L. M. (1975). A note on the eating behavior of children varying in weight. *Journal of Child Psychology and Psychiatry, 17,* 221–224.

Ravussin, E., Lillioja, S., Knowler, W. C., Christin, L., Freymond, D., Abbott, W. G. H., Boyce, V., Howard, B. V., & Bogardus, C. (1988). Reduced rate of energy expenditure as a risk factor for body weight gain. *New England Journal of Medicine, 318,* 467–472.

Richardson, S. A., Hastorf, A. H., Goodman, N., & Dornbusch, S. M. (1961). Cultural uniformity in reaction to physical disabilities. *American Sociological Review, 90,* 44–51.

Roberts, S. B., Savage, J., Coward, N. A., Chew, B., &

Lucas, A. (1988). Energy expenditure and intake in infants born to lean and overweight mothers. *New England Journal of Medicine, 318,* 461–466.

Schacter, S., & Gross, L. P. (1968). Manipulated time and eating behavior. *Journal of Social Psychology, 10,* 98–106.

Segal, K. R., Gutin, B., Albu, J., & Pi-Sunyer, F. X. (1987). Thermic effects of food and exercise in lean and obese men of similar lean body mass. *American Journal of Physiology, 252,* 110–117.

Spock, B., & Rothenberg, M. B. (1985). *Dr. Spock's baby and child care* (p. 91). New York: Dutton.

Stern, J. S., and Lowney, P. (1986). Obesity; the role of physical activity. In K. D. Brownell & J. P. Foreyt (Eds.), *Handbook of eating disorders* (pp. 145–158). New York: Basic Books.

Striegel-Moore, R., & Rodin, J. (1986). The influence of psychological variables in obesity. In K. D. Brownell & J. P. Foreyt (Eds.), *Handbook of eating disorders* (pp. 63–87). New York: Basic Books.

Stuart, R. B., & Davis, B. (1972). *Slim chance in a fat world: Behavioral control of obesity.* Champaign, IL: Research Press.

Stunkard, A. J., Sorensen, T. I. A., Hanis, C., Teasdale, T. N., Chakraborty, R., Schull, W. J., and Schulsinger, F. (1986). An adoption study of human obesity. *New England Journal of Medicine, 314,* 193–198.

SUPPLEMENTAL READING LIST

Brownell, K. D. (1985). The *LEARN program for weight control.* Philadelphia: University of Pennsylvania Press.

A weight reduction manual for adults which can be shared by therapist and client. The manual makes use of research information in a practical way.

Cohen, M., Abramson, L., & Winter, R. (1985). *Thin kids.* New York: Beaufort Books.

An easy-to-read weight reduction guide for parents and children that includes sample menus.

Kirschenbaum, D. S., Johnson, W. G. & Stalonas, P. M. (1987). *Treating childhood and adolescent obesity.* New York: Pergamon Press.

A thorough manual making use of up-to-date research for the clinician.

Norris, W. A., & Fanning, W. L. (1989). *Concepts and strategies for a lifetime of fitness.* Winston Salem: Hunter Textbooks.

An extremely readable and practical guide for the professional or student interested in fitness. It includes usable recommendations for treatment as well as charts and graphs to provide support data.

CHAPTER 14

The Impact of Family Dynamics on Anorexia: A Transactional View of Treatment

Nancy Ellis-Ordway, ACSW

St. John's Mercy Medical Center, St. Louis, Missouri

People condemn themselves to the torture of self-starvation in the futile hope of "deserving respect" and not being despised for being "too" fat.

Hilde Bruch

In a society of wealth and abundance, anorexia nervosa is a baffling and misunderstood response to the overwhelming anxieties of life. A focus on food and eating has long been a natural way for human beings to respond to troublesome or overwhelming emotions. The preparation and consumption of nourishment can serve functions ranging from celebration to grieving. It can bring families closer together and provide a sense of unity for entire communities.

Individuals learn from infancy that food can be used to express love, comfort, soothing, understanding, empathy, and compassion. After infancy, food can be used for other functions such as discipline, scolding, punishment, bribery, power, and distraction (Strober & Humphrey, in press). As individuals grow and develop, they gain more and more control over their own personal eating patterns and also receive mixed messages about the role of food in their lives.

Adults who have healthy interactions with food commonly celebrate successes with steak dinners in restaurants or soothe themselves after a rough day with ice cream. According to Humphrey (1986), dysfunctional relationships with food develop when the individual uses food to avoid unpleasant emo-

tions such as anger, fear, loneliness, or anxiety. The individual learns to reach for food when the real need is for the emotional nourishment that can be found only in close interpersonal relationships. A pattern of compulsive overeating may ensue when an individual responds habitually to overwhelming emotions by focusing on food preparation, food consumption, and the subsequent guilt of going off the diet. The pattern is more subtle in individuals with anorexia nervosa. They use the same focus on food, calorie counting, and restrictive eating to avoid handling thoughts and feelings that are uncomfortable and troublesome (Brownell & Foreyt, 1986).

Anorexia nervosa is a complex and multifaceted illness with far-reaching effects. While much of the conflict that creates and maintains this problem centers on the household in which the individual lives, extended family members, peers, coworkers, and others may also be affected. The problem may mask or exacerbate existing family conflicts (Humphrey, 1986; Strober & Humphrey, in press). It can require considerable energy from others outside the family who are drawn into a caretaking role designed to convince the individual to eat more. As a result, relationships may be damaged, and social withdrawal by the individual often occurs.

This chapter begins with a description of some of the symptoms and consequences of anorexia nervosa. It includes a discussion about the development of the illness, particularly as it relates to family dynamics, and about some of the treatment approaches that have been used effectively. The chapter concludes with a focus on the role of social workers in treatment and prevention. Case histories are used throughout to illustrate the treatment approaches that are discussed.

SYMPTOMS AND CONSEQUENCES
OF THE ADDICTION

The symptoms of anorexia nervosa include a progressively restrictive eating pattern followed by a weight loss of up to 85 percent of the ideal body weight. The individual persists in perceiving a need for more weight loss even as a look of emaciation begins to appear. In women, menstruation generally ceases and the individual may have measurable drops in blood pressure, body temperature, and pulse. Brownell and Foreyt (1986) note that weight loss is sometimes accompanied by obsessional thoughts about food and a preoccupation with preparing food for other people to consume. Many individuals who focus on restrictive eating and lose a great deal of weight also become involved in bulimic type symptoms such as occasional self-induced vomiting, laxative abuse, and excessive exercise (Bruch, 1973). (See Chapters 12 and 15 for discussions about bulimia.) Although symptoms often overlap, most individuals seek treatment because of (1) restrictive eating with weight loss (anorexia nervosa) or (2) normal to excessive eating followed by some kind of purging (bulimia nervosa).

Traditionally, anorexia has been defined as an illness affecting mostly upper middle- and upper-class white adolescent females. In the last decade, anorexia has been seen increasingly in individuals from a wider range of socioeconomic and racial backgrounds as well as in young children, adult women, middle-aged women, and older women (Orbach, 1986). The illness has also been seen increasingly among males, although males are less likely to seek treatment and when they do, they are

more likely to be misdiagnosed (Levine, Petrie, Gotthardt & Sevig, in press).

Medical complications of anorexia nervosa include bradycardia, hypothermia, hypotension, loss of bone density leading to osteoporosis, muscle wasting including heart muscle, kidney damage due to fluid restriction and/or laxative abuse, dry hair and skin, and brittle nails. Although these medical complications may be dramatic and even life-threatening, according to Brownell & Foreyt (1986), it is often the emotional and social consequences of the illness that are more troublesome (Bruch, 1978; Garfinkel & Garner, 1982). Malnutrition leads to impaired cognition, including an inability to concentrate, an inability to think clearly, and an inability to make rational decisions. Increased irritability can complicate interpersonal relations and exacerbate social withdrawal that may have begun as a refusal to attend any social occasions involving food.

For individuals living within a family context, particularly for adolescents, the progression of the illness generally involves an increasing focus by family members on eating patterns and weight. They may argue about the seriousness of the problem and what should be done about it, even as other family conflicts are ignored in order to focus all the energy on one individual (Strober & Humphrey, in press). When the individual or family begins to seek treatment, the focus is generally only on one aspect of the problem. This can delay engagement in the recovery process and allow the illness to become more serious.

Once an individual is engaged in an adequate treatment process, any progress made is at risk for sabotage by the general cultural attitude that only perfection is worthwhile and that beauty always involves extreme thinness (Orbach, 1986). Not only is the individual bombarded with such images on television and in magazines but the family and peer group are receiving the same message. Even when it is acknowledged and discussed, this cultural emphasis on thinness makes recovery very difficult.

THE DEVELOPMENT
OF ANOREXIA NERVOSA

Anorexia nervosa does not develop in a vacuum but rather within a family system. Wooley & Lewis (1989) assume that even when the onset is during adulthood, the conflicts involved can usually be traced back to the family-of-origin. Most persons who enter treatment for anorexia nervosa have a history of significant family dysfunctioning. The most commonly seen style of family interaction is that of enmeshment of one or both parents with each other and with the children. Boundaries are vague if not indistinguishable (Humphrey, 1986). It becomes extremely difficult to tell where one person leaves off and another begins. Boundaries are sometimes metaphorically referred to as being like Velcro. Enmeshed families have a great deal of difficulty in tolerating any movement toward separation and individuation on the part of any member. If one offspring is able to successfully separate from the family, Strober and Humphrey (in press) indicate it often increases the enmeshment between the members who are left behind.

Parent/Child Control Issues

When a parent is overly controlling or intrusive in a child's life, one way that child can take control of herself is with food. The history of an individual with anorexia often reveals a girl who was somewhat overweight as a child and decides during adolescence to lose weight. As she exercises control over her food intake and sees results on the scale, she experiences a sense of being in control of her life that may be new to her. She may or may not be aware of many areas of her life that feel out of control. These can include parental conflict, pressure from peers or boyfriends regarding sexual activity, impending decisions about college or career choices, or any number of other conflicts that are relatively common to the adolescent phase. The future anorexic finds it increasingly comfortable to focus on her control of food and eating as a way to avoid other conflicts in her life that feel out of control (Orbach, 1986; Bruch, 1978).

Physiological Aspects of Anorexia

The traditional view about the development of anorexia nervosa is that the girl is denying her own femininity and adulthood by becoming thin and boyish and by ceasing to have menstrual periods. In light of later evidence, this seems to be an oversimplification. Certainly there is a reluctance to grow up, but this seems to be related to the family's intolerance of moves toward separation and individuation. In addition, there is increasing evidence that the illness at this point becomes biologically driven. A person who is malnourished and underweight becomes physiologically and overwhelmingly hungry in the presence of food. In addition, the metabolism slows to maintain life, if not health, on a progressively decreasing number of calories (Kaye, in press, a).

By this time, the individual is no longer consciously able to recognize her own feelings of hunger but does at some level feel overwhelmed by her desire for food. She sublimates this in various ways, often by obsessively preparing food for others to consume, reading cookbooks, or writing out menus. As the compulsive dieting progresses, weight loss slows and may even stop in spite of the fact that a very minimal amount of food is being consumed. Wooley (1987) found that the individual is convinced that even a few more calories per day will cause her to gain weight although her physiological hunger is overwhelming. She becomes convinced that if she begins to eat again normally, she will not be able to stop and will rapidly gain weight until she is extremely obese. Her relationship with food takes on an almost phobic quality.

In reality, the physiological response to acute starvation is to slow the metabolism to the point that life can be maintained on a very small amount of food. The blood pressure, temperature, and pulse all drop; hair and nail growth ceases; skin becomes very dry; and sometimes lanugo, a soft downy hair, begins to appear in an attempt to keep the body warm. When a person begins eating normally again at this stage, the increased amount of calories is used by the body to restore metabolic functions (Wooley, 1987). It often takes a delayed period of weeks or even months of sustained caloric intake well above normal levels before the individual is able to regain a significant amount of weight. Current research indicates there are additional physiological effects. Neuropeptide levels in the cerebrospinal fluid are dramatically altered in anorexic clients and these levels do not return to normal until ideal body weight has been maintained for a period of time (Kaye, in press, b).

Case Histories: Illustrations of Family Dynamics

The combination of biological, physiological, psychological, and social factors indicate that an innocently begun diet can rapidly become addictive to the individual (Stunkard, 1983). It is no longer simply a matter of deciding whether or not to eat. Why, then, does not every dieter develop anorexia nervosa? Certainly many factors are involved and some family configurations appear with regularity. Garfinkel and Garner (1982) believe these individuals come from a family in which one or both parents are perfectionistic and highly achievement-oriented. Often, there is distance within the parental dyad and one parent becomes overly involved with the at-risk daughter. The following four case histories describe some variations in how these dynamics are manifested:

Angie B. is 14 years old and has been hospitalized twice for anorexia nervosa. Her father is a "fitness fanatic." He works long hours at the office and when he comes home, he almost immediately goes to his health club, where he works out with weights until after the family has gone to bed. Mrs. B. does not acknowledge her anger at her husband for withdrawing this way, but instead focuses her energies on Angie, requiring her to excel at several activities in school as well as maintain a straight A average. She goes over all of Angie's homework and corrects it. In treatment, Angie initially focused exclusively on calorie counting and weight but eventually began to express anger with her mother for her intrusiveness and with her father for his distance. In family therapy sessions, Mr. B. denied any role in the development of the illness and refused to change any of his behavior. Mrs. B. continued to focus on whether or not Angie had gained any weight.

Paula D. is a 30-year-old unmarried woman who has been hospitalized once and is currently in outpatient treatment for anorexia nervosa. Initially, she responded very well to treatment but after discharge had patterns of difficulty in eating. She began to trace these patterns to interactions with her family, and a major focus in her therapy became how her family always denied her perception of reality. She recalled times in her childhood when her father came home drunk and fought with her mother. The next day, both parents denied to the children that anything unusual had happened the night before. Each of Paula's siblings developed some problem with alcohol or depression upon reaching late adolescence or early adulthood, but the parents continued to maintain that they were the "picture-perfect American family." When Paula's eating disorder developed, she was in her late twenties. Her parents refused to become involved in any kind of treatment, alternatively emphasizing their own abilities as good

parents and accusing her of trying to damage the family. Paula's therapy currently focuses on her being able to accept her own perception of reality as valid and to accept the fact that she cannot expect any support from her parents. Nor is she likely to obtain support from her siblings, who help to maintain the family's facade.

Paula's experience with this type of denial is not unusual in alcoholic families. Alcoholism within a parent often leads to particular types of difficulties for children. Typically, a child's perception of reality is denied in an effort to maintain the family's picture of normality.

Jean and Joan D. are identical twins, both hospitalized for anorexia nervosa during early adolescence. They were the youngest of a large number of siblings born to a rural family. Family therapy revealed a strong parental alliance between Mr. and Mrs. D. and a history of normal development for the older siblings. Mrs. D. demonstrated a remarkable capacity for empathy and individual relationships with each of her many children. In spite of this apparently healthy family, both of the twins presented for treatment with an alarming level of illness. Further history-taking revealed that, although inseparable as children, Jean and Joan began to fight with each other as they approached adolescence and became increasingly competitive. When Jean was first hospitalized for anorexia, Joan responded by refusing to eat and it soon became a competition as to which one could be thinner. Additionally, the social worker discovered that when the twins were five years old, an older sister, then age 16, was killed in an automobile accident. The grief-stricken parents had left the twins with a relative while they and the rest of the siblings attended the visitation and the funeral. Apparently it was this unresolved grief that, combined with the separation-individuation struggles of adolescence, predisposed these girls to illness.

Initially, they were both very resistive to treatment and the treatment plan focused on encouraging their separation and individuation. Each girl had a different psychiatrist and they were hospitalized on separate units. A different staff worked with each and, as the girls eventually began to recognize themselves as separate, the competition between them decreased. They maintained follow-up care with their respective psychiatrists for a period of time after discharge, but eventually that was no longer necessary. The mother recently called to tell staff that the girls have started high school and, although they are involved in different activities, had requested a locker together. These ongoing family dynamics, as well as those discussed in the other case histories, indicate that treatment with this client group is often long-term and difficult.

EFFECTIVE TREATMENT APPROACHES

People enter treatment for anorexia nervosa in a number of different ways. Sometimes the individual approaches treatment on her own, but frequently she is encouraged to seek treatment by friends or family members. The younger the individual is, the more likely it is that treatment is sought by parents. This factor can make engagement of the girl and the handling of previously mentioned parent-child control issues more difficult. Therefore, the initial contacts with the family should be handled with these issues in mind.

Initial Client Contacts

The initial assessment process can involve an interview, a physical examination, blood tests, and psychological tests. Family members may also be interviewed to gain an understanding of the family dynamics that influenced the development and maintenance of the addiction. Often, family interviews should be structured to insure input into the problem formulation by each member, particularly the member with anorexia. In some situations, the assessment should also include individual interviews with the anorexic to facilitate her early involvement and to convey that her views of the situation are important. This process allows the practitioner to attend to familial dynamics and their particular impact on the identified client. Appropriate treatment options vary according to the individual and to her own strengths, needs, and resources. Kaye, Enright, and Pesser (1988) note that treatment ideally would include an extensive program involving both inpatient and outpatient care; individual, group, and family therapy; nutritional counseling; meal structure; and follow-up care provided by a specialized eating disorder unit. Such a variety of services is rarely found in one place, particularly in less populated rural areas.

Treatment Options and Models

Although the number of inpatient treatment units has grown greatly in the last decade, there is no standard approach to treatment. Many hospitals offer treatment for anorexia on a general psychiatric unit, while others treat the condition in specialized eating disorder units or even on medical and pediatric units. Treatment models and approaches include strictly behavioral approaches, psychodynamic approaches, and cognitive behavioral approaches as well as the abstinence or 12-step approach. These approaches are used alone or in combination by various programs (Kaye et al., 1988).

Outpatient treatment can range from structured, cognitive-behavioral groups to individual psychodynamically-oriented psychotherapy, to family therapy, to behavioral therapy. Sometimes these approaches are offered in specific eating disorder treatment programs, but often individuals are involved as outpatients with therapists in private practice who may or may not specialize in eating disorders. The approach used in those situations is often individual psychotherapy. Which treatment is effective for which client is affected by many factors. The seriousness of symptoms, their duration, the extent of family support or pathology, and the internal resources of the individual all are significant (Johnson & Connors, 1987; Kaye et al., 1988).

Some individuals require inpatient treatment. Factors to be included in making this decision are a significant level of weight loss, malnutrition, extremely restrictive eating, impaired cognition, fainting, electrolyte imbalance, inability to function in work or school, lack of improvement in outpatient treatment, weight at 85 percent of ideal body weight or lower, worsening depression, chaotic life or family situation that makes improvement improbable, and, of course, suicide risk. Although some clients can improve on a general psychiatric unit, hospitalization on a specialized eating disorder unit is preferable. Length of stay can vary from a few days for medical stabilization to months or even years in some extreme cases.

Barriers to Engaging the Client System

Once the individual agrees to enter treatment with whatever modality or practice approach, there may still be difficulties in actually engaging the individual and family in treatment. Adolescents admitted to a hospital by their parents may be resistive to participating in any kind of treatment. Individuals with a long-standing history of anorexia may express the desire to get better, but may continue to sabotage any development of a treatment alliance. Family members may also have difficulty in engaging in treatment even if they were initially involved in seeking out treatment resources. They often have difficulty acknowledging any role in what they perceive to be someone else's problem, and the prospect of change may be very frightening for them (Levine et al., in press; Strober & Humphrey, in press). The anorexia may be masking long-standing family conflicts that require a change in all of the members.

Illustrations of Effective Treatment Strategies

Different approaches to treatment and how they are suited to family issues and individual problems can be illustrated with the following case histories drawn from a clinical practice in a specialized Eating Disorders (ED) unit offering both inpatient and outpatient care. The approaches included are cognitive-behavioral, psychodynamic, and behavioral. Individual, group, and family therapy were used in these cases based on the individual's and family's needs.

Janet N., 23 and single, sought treatment because of her inability to have menstrual periods. Although she appeared quite thin, she was technically at the low end of her ideal body weight range. In addition to eating restrictively, she ran several miles per day and often participated in marathons. Her percentage of body fat was too low to allow her to menstruate normally, due as much to her exercise as to her dieting. After graduating from college, she had sought employment in a city several hours away from her parents. She entered individual psychotherapy with a private practitioner and had a consultation with a dietician with the understanding that if she did not make progress toward weight gain, she would be hospitalized. Individual psychotherapy was primarily supportive and focused on her adjustment in living away from her parents and perceiving herself as an individual separate from them. She began to idealize the practitioner much as she had idealized her parents. She attempted to please the helper as she had always sought to please her parents.

Janet began to understand that her running was a way of feeling connected to her father, who was also a runner, and she began to run less at the encouragement of the social worker. It was necessary to help her gain awareness of these familial dynamics, while also trying to help her eliminate the self-destructive behaviors. In this way her autonomy was increased, and her control issues decreased. Janet began to eat a wider variety of foods at the encouragement of the dietician but did not actively begin to gain weight until responsibility for her weight was taken over by the dietitian. This was accomplished by having her weigh weekly with her back to the scale. The number was then reported to the dietitian, who agreed to take responsibility not to let her gain weight too quickly. The client no longer weighed herself at all, although she did have a scale at home. As the work progressed, Janet began to feel more independent from her parents and started to focus on more age-appropriate issues such as career choices. It was agreed early in the course of treatment that she would have a specified number of sessions after she had a menstrual period, since that was one of the main goals for treatment. Termination progressed smoothly after her periods resumed.

Some mild cases of anorexia involving only a minimal amount of weight loss in an emancipated adult with considerable internal resources such as Janet can be treated successfully on an outpatient basis. Often, however, issues surrounding food are serious and resistant enough to require more structured treatment.

Sarah A. is a 32-year-old divorced professional woman who was encouraged to seek treatment by co-workers and her supervisor. Although she was normally a responsible and reliable worker, her malnutrition was causing such difficulty in thinking and concentration that she was unable to do her job. Cognition was so poor at that point that she seemed unable to form a treatment alliance with her physician. She was therefore admitted to an inpatient treatment unit for eating disorders that provided a great deal of structure with food. In addition to individual and group sessions with the dietitian, she was placed on a meal plan that included three large meals per day plus supplements.

Even though she was determined to overcome the eating disorder, it still took a great deal of support and encouragement from staff and peers before she was able to eat normally. Once adequate nutrition was restored, her cognition improved. She made an excellent therapeutic alliance with the social worker and was able to talk about many of her difficulties, both in individual and group sessions. Family therapy would have been appropriate in this case because her family history was one of considerable chaos, but the family was geographically unavailable for treatment. Emphasis during Sarah's treatment was on her many strengths, such as her excellent educational and professional background, as well as on helping her to improve interpersonal skills without focusing on any exploration of her early childhood trauma. The focus on interpersonal skills was useful for strengthening her social network of peers and co-workers.

In the treatment of adolescents, unlike the case of Sarah, family therapy is a crucial component (Wooley & Lewis, 1989). Recognizing the particular family dynamics and the impact they have on the individual can often dictate how family therapy can be best used during treatment.

Michelle L., 15, was brought for an evaluation of her anorexia by both of her parents. Mr. and Mrs. L. were divorced and both had remarried. The father and his new wife were expecting a baby. During the course of the evaluation interviews, Michelle adamantly denied any problem, but her parents gave a concise history of worsening difficulties with eating and weight loss. They sat stiffly side by side and at one point Mrs. L. commented that this was the first time in four years that the two of them had been in a room without shouting at one another. Mr. L. then added that they had agreed to put aside their differences until Michelle's eating disorder could be effectively treated.

Over her loud objections, Michelle was admitted to an inpatient eating disorder unit, and a family therapy session was scheduled several days hence. Michelle quickly settled into the routine of the unit and two days later told her therapy group, with a smug smile, that she had succeeded in getting her mother and father back together again. The social worker promptly canceled the family meeting and rescheduled two meetings—one with Michelle, her father, and her stepmother; and another with Michelle, her mother, and her stepfather. Michelle continued to try to exclude her stepparents from sessions and involve both of her parents together. Eventually the father, stepmother, and Michelle were referred to an outside agency for family therapy while the unit social worker continued to see Michelle, her mother, and her stepfather.

In a similar manner, group therapy can serve many functions including support, reality testing, feedback, and confrontation. It provides a setting for the reenactment of familial and other conflicts relevant to the eating disorder. Group process can then be used for addressing and working through common aspects of those family conflicts (Levine et al., in press).

Karen F., a 19-year-old college student, is currently being treated in an outpatient group as a follow-up to inpatient care. Her parents divorced when she was eight and she spent her adolescence living with her mother and stepfather. After high school graduation, she moved to a different state to live with her father and stepmother and to attend college. Although her new situation seemed ideal compared to living with a chronically depressed mother and alcoholic stepfather, her previous eating disorder continued to worsen until she entered treatment.

As the work progressed, several family issues came to the forefront that were more appropriate for group rather than individual sessions. Her family conflict had left her with a pervasive sense of never fitting in. Whether she is with one family or the other, at school or at work, she always perceives herself as being on the outside and excluded from whatever is going on. When she began to perceive herself as being excluded from her treatment group, the issue was brought vividly into focus and members helped her to recognize how she herself does the excluding. Another important issue for her is her inability to trust her own perception of reality. Her stepfather consistently ran his household based on the idea that his perception of reality was the only accurate one. Karen was constantly told that her ideas, thoughts, and feelings had no validity. She has been able to use the treatment group, not only to help her understand how abusive these family interactions are, but also for having her perceptions validated so that she can increase her own reality testing.

Just as anorexia is multifaceted and complex in cases such as Karen's, an adequate treatment approach needs to be capable of addressing many different issues. This can include helping the client to create a different family network to aid in recovery from family conflicts.

Amy B. was 16 when she was hospitalized for the first time for anorexia on a behavioral medicine unit for adolescents. She was assigned an individual social worker and had to earn time with her in small increments by gaining weight. Suffering from an underlying obsessive compulsive disorder, Amy was quickly able to organize herself in order to gain the weight to see her social worker. Her family was involved in treatment only to the extent of being educated about the illness. Her condition deteriorated markedly immediately following discharge, and her parents brought her to a psychodynamically oriented treatment program for further care. At that time Amy had a great deal of difficulty eating normally and tolerating any kind of weight gain because she perceived weight gain as leading directly to abandonment by treatment staff. She obsessed continually about calories and food intake, repeatedly asking staff, ''Is this O.K. for me to eat?'' Family therapy revealed a significant degree of pathology involving an alcoholic father, a co-dependent mother, a depressed sibling, and an aggressive sibling. The parents, initially very concerned, became resistive when it was suggested to them that they needed treatment individually and as a couple. During treatment in the behavioral program, Amy's underlying obsessive compulsive disorder was exacerbated. The strength of the second program was its focus on the family therapy approach for resolving underlying family issues.

Often, when an individual enters treatment, different issues are dealt with one at a time in different ways. A multifaceted treatment program can provide a variety, a menu so to speak, of different treatment modalities.

Chris C. entered treatment at the age of 25 while she was living away from home and attending school. She was admitted to an inpatient eating disorder unit due to feelings of panic, anxiety, and the sense of being out of control, as well as malnutrition. The family history revealed that her parents, who had lived out of state, were emotionally unavailable to her and always had been. One brother, who lived locally, was very supportive and interested in being involved in treatment. The initial feelings of panic

continued to escalate after Chris was admitted and she was unable to eat. Privileges such as visitors, phone calls, and passes were contingent upon eating and weight gain. While she remained a voluntary patient, eating was so difficult for her that eventually clothes were taken from her, and she was required to dress in surgical scrubs.

At this point, she began to rage at the staff, who were able to tolerate her rage and encourage her to continue to express her anger. Encouragement of appropriate expression of emotion was very therapeutic for Chris, and she began to talk about some of her conflicts with her family as she began to eat. Upon discharge, she remained in outpatient treatment for about two years, utilizing both group and individual sessions as well as one additional hospitalization when her panic again became overwhelming.

Family therapy sessions with her brother helped validate her perceptions of her family and their dysfunctional interactions. With the support of her brother and of her peers in the treatment group, she was able to make more appropriate career decisions for herself and was increasingly able to eat adequately without the structure of the inpatient unit. She eventually terminated treatment, married, and seems to be comfortable in a life-style involving a less stressful job and a happy marriage. In a recent follow-up interview she revealed that, although she is still occasionally plagued with feelings of being fat, she is able to continue to eat normally and to talk about her feelings with her husband. Even the recent stress of a death in the family did not cause her to revert to her former dysfunctional eating patterns.

Although a wide variety of treatment approaches and modalities were used in the case of Chris, some other individuals are not able to utilize these resources as effectively as needed. This is often due to an underlying personality disorder that does not become apparent until the individual enters treatment for help with the eating disorder.

Alicia A. was brought to inpatient treatment when she was 17 from a rural area by her parents who could not find adequate treatment for her near their home. A very engaging and appealing young woman, Alicia initially made an excellent treatment alliance with her psychiatrist and with the other treatment staff. As treatment progressed and the staff found itself embroiled in arguments over decisions regarding this patient, it became apparent that she was suffering from a borderline personality disorder. Her inability to see anything in terms other than perfection or worthlessness extended to the treatment staff. Some staff were idealized while others were devalued, and which staff members fell into which category could change at any moment.

She continued to eat restrictively and ritualistically and her body image distortion was dramatic. Family therapy revealed a well-meaning but ineffectual mother and a father with a borderline personality disorder of his own. Alicia remained in treatment long enough to allow the staff ample time to try various treatment approaches including behavioral; cognitive-behavioral; family, group, and individual psychodynamic treatment; expressive therapy; and intense nutritional support. Each change in approach brought about a temporary improvement followed by a worsening of symptoms. The staff repeatedly recommended to the family that they consider hospitalizing her in a facility that is designed to take care of long-term psychiatric patients, and eventually they did.

Many people with eating disorders never enter treatment at all but find some level of functioning that they can maintain without getting either better or worse. There is very little material available as to the long-term physiological effects on the individual or the indirect effects on the family. Although the underlying dynamics of anorexia tend to preclude the development of healthy relationships, a number of these women are able to marry. It is not unusual for some of these women with a history of anorexia to become mothers, especially where the severity of the illness fluctuates. It is only recently that treatment professionals have begun to notice some of the long-term effects that this can have on the children of anorexic mothers (Orbach, 1986; Humphrey, 1986).

Melissa W. entered treatment for bulimia and depression at the age of 19. She was the eldest of four children born to a high-achieving professional and his wife. Her academic record was excellent but she quit college at the end of her first semester to enter treatment. Family therapy revealed that the family presented a facade to the world of being perfect, but it was in reality emotionally cold and impoverished. The father worked long hours and spent very little time with the family. When he did, he consistently praised his wife as being a perfect role model for his daughters. Melissa's mother, an exceedingly thin woman, had never worked outside the home but was very involved in charity work. She ate very little herself but she consistently stocked her family pantry with such huge amounts of food that Melissa's bingeing went unnoticed. Mrs. W. continued to deny that she had anorexia or in fact any emotional problems of her own. Melissa is currently in treatment struggling with trying to control her bulimia while living in the family household with its emotional impoverishment, its overabundance of food, and an anorexic mother.

SOME PREVENTION STRATEGIES

While the case histories and descriptions of treatment in the previous section have highlighted barriers to treatment and effective treatment approaches, less is known about prevention of anorexia. Although much is said about the importance of prevention, there is little evidence to indicate that any particular approach or tactic is effective. Education about eating disorders in the school systems does not seem to be effective in preventing the development of the disorders (Rosen, 1988) and may, in some cases, actually provide ideas to girls who are at high risk for the problem. Education of the general community certainly increases the chances that others will encourage the individual to seek treatment after the illness becomes noticeable. However, this approach does not seem to contribute to the prevention of the development of the problem. There are no specific developmental factors yet identified that can be used in predicting high-risk individuals or families.

Many of the contributing factors to the development of anorexia nervosa are so pervasive in our society that it is impossible to protect individuals from them. The cultural preoccupation with thinness and fitness affects not only the at-risk adolescent but also her parents, her peers, her teachers, and in fact anyone with whom she comes in contact (Orbach, 1986). It is not uncommon for girls with anorexia to have parents who are chronic dieters and/or excessive exercisers. The majority of Americans, however, seem to be chronic dieters and many are involved in exercise programs without developing problems. In addition, the media present confusing and conflicting information about nutrition and good eating patterns. While the national craze for health and fitness may have contributed to a decrease in cholesterol levels and blood pressure, it has also certainly contributed to the increase in eating disorders and other dysfunctional weight preoccupations (Wooley, 1987).

A cultural focus on perfection, achievement, and an ideal outward appearance tends to de-emphasize the warm, human, empathic, and creative aspects of individuals. Even when parents concentrate on building good self-esteem at home, a child is still faced with a school system, a peer group, and media that value people for what they do and what they look like rather than for who they are.

While there are no clear-cut strategies for prevention at this time, adequate education increases the likelihood of early diagnosis and treatment before the emotional and physical symptoms become severe. Education of parents and school personnel can help increase recognition of the illness, but it is also vital to educate health and mental health professionals so that the illness will be correctly diagnosed. Education of the general community is equally important in that it decreases the stigma felt by people who seek treatment.

SOCIAL WORK IMPLICATIONS

The participation of physicians, nurses, social workers, dieticians, psychologists, and other mental health professionals is essential for adequate treatment for the individual with anorexia nervosa. However, the social worker is uniquely qualified, by virtue of training, to recognize how the affected individual is influenced by the dynamics not only of her family but also of her peer group and of society in general. While the individual's internal conflicts are being dealt with in one-on-one sessions, conflicts of the external world still affect her. Part of the social worker's role is to point out this perspective for the entire treatment team. Individual insight is going to be of little use to a young woman who, after discharge, returns to a conflictual and enmeshed family, a highly competitive academic schedule, a part-time job in a bakery, and a cheerleading coach who insists that each member of the squad be a size 7 or smaller.

Understanding family dynamics is invariably a vital part of recovery from anorexia. It is helpful for the social worker to advocate for having family members involved in treatment, and it is especially important when the individual still lives with the family-of-origin. Even if family members are unwilling to change or understand, family therapy can enable the individual to understand and accept that fact and move on alone toward her own recovery (Wooley & Lewis, 1989). Other staff can be encouraged to take a neutral stance toward the recovering person, without blaming either her or the family for the anorexia or for barriers to treatment. Increasing staff's understanding of family dynamics also aids in the exploration of strengths and decisions about how to build on such resources. The social workers were able to accomplish those tasks with Sarah and Chris, two of the cases that were discussed in this chapter.

A third important role for social workers in the treatment of anorexia nervosa is the traditional one of helping the client find resources through brokering and linking strategies. This is becoming increasingly difficult in recent years as insurance companies tighten their requirements and limit their coverage. The social worker may be involved in exploring insurance possibilities as well as appealing unfavorable decisions by insuring companies. If private insurance is not available, then the social worker becomes involved in trying to locate and develop government or United Way-sponsored resources. While some state medical insurance carriers cover specialized treatment in private hospitals, others do not. Community mental health facilities offer general psychiatric care but rarely have specialized treatment approaches for anorexia and other eating disorders.

CONCLUSION

While much has been learned about the etiology, development, and treatment of anorexia nervosa in the last decade, there remains much more knowledge to be uncovered. There are many pieces to the puzzle: biological, physiological, social, cultural, familial, emotional, and psychological. The social worker, as a treatment professional, is uniquely qualified to help put all of the pieces of the puzzle together until the picture can be seen as a whole. The work does not end there, for a thorough family-focused assessment is merely a beginning step. The practitioner must skillfully involve the young woman in identifying the implications of the assessment, and other family members must be involved also when the young woman still lives at home or the family is accessible. Data can be gathered from what is said and done in these initial contacts as well as from how members interact during the process.

The family-focused assessment helps the practitioner to effect a skillful treatment process, whether on an inpatient or outpatient basis. The focus cannot be solely on more appropriate eating patterns and weight gain. The familial dynamics must be addressed even when family members are not involved directly in treatment, as in the case of Janet, whose compulsive running was modeled after her perfectionistic father's behavior. Support for changes may involve co-workers or a sibling, as illustrated by other cases in this chapter. Creating changes in family-of-origin relationships or in how the anorexic views such dynamics is an important pathway for eliminating the eating disorder and improving family-of-procreation and peer relationships.

REFERENCES

Brownell, K. D., & Foreyt, J. P. (1986). *Handbook of eating disorders: Physiology, psychology, and treatment of obesity, anorexia, bulimia.* New York: Basic Books.

Bruch, Hilde. (1973). *Eating disorders: Obesity, anorexia nervosa, and the person within.* New York: Basic Books.

Bruch, Hilde. (1978). *The golden cage: The enigma of anorexia nervosa.* New York: Basic Books.

Garfinkel, P., & Garner, D. (1982) *Anorexia nervosa: A multi-dimensional perspective.* New York: Brunner-Mazel.

Humphrey, L. L. (1986). Structural analysis of parent-child relationships in eating disorders. *Journal of Abnormal Psychology, 95,* 395–402.

Johnson, C., & Connors, M. (1987). *The etiology and treatment of bulimia nervosa: A biopsychosocial perspective.* New York: Basic Books.

Kaye, W. H. (in press, a). The psychobiology of bulimia: Possible relationships between binging and vomiting behavior and disturbances in mood and neuroendocrine function. In B. Spring, J. Chiodo, & J. Silas (Eds.), *Diet and behavior.* New York: PMA Publishing.

Kaye, W. H. (in press, b). Disturbances of neurotransmitters in anorexia nervosa: A review of CFS studies. In B. Blinder & R. Goldstein (Eds.), *Modern concepts of the eating disorders: Research, diagnosis, treatment.* New York: PMA Publishing.

Kaye, W. H., Enright, A. B., & Pesser, S. J. (1988). Characteristics of eating disorder programs and common problems with third-party providers, *International Journal of Eating Disorders, 7,* 4–7.

Levine, M. P., Petrie, T. A., Gotthardt, J., & Sevig, T. D. (in press). A professionally led support group for males with eating disorders. In A. E. Anderson (Ed.), *Males with eating disorders.* New York: Brunner/Mazel.

Orbach, S. (1986). *Hunger strike: The anoretic's struggle for survival as a metaphor of our age.* New York: Norton.

Rosen, J. (1988). *Working with secondary schools in the prevention of eating disorders,* Paper presented at the Seventh National Conference on Eating Disorders, Columbus, Ohio, October 5–7, 1988.

Strober, M., & Humphrey, L. L. (in press). Family contributions to the etiology and course of anorexia nervosa and bulimia. *Journal of Consulting and Clinical Psychology.*

Stunkard, A. J. (1983). *Eating and its disorders.* New York: Raven Press.

Wooley, S. C. (1987). Psychological and social aspects of obesity. In A. E. Bender, & L. J. Brookes (Eds.), *Body weight control: The physiology, clinical treatment and prevention of obesity,* (pp. 163–175). London: Churchill Livingstone.

Wooley, S. C., & Lewis, K. G. (1989). The missing woman: Intensive family oriented treatment of bulimia. *Journal of Feminist Family Therapy, 1,* 61–83.

SUPPLEMENTAL READING LIST

Bauer, B., Anderson, W., & Wyatt, R. W. (1986). *Bulimia: Book for therapist and client.* Indianapolis: Indiana Accelerated Development.
Overview of issues pertaining to nutrition, exercise, dieting and depression, personality dynamics, and various aspects of therapy.

Bemis, K. M. (1985). "Abstinence" and "nonabstinence" models for the treatment of bulimia. *International Journal of Eating Disorders, 4,* 407–437.
Evaluation of the strengths and drawbacks of 12-step and non-12-step approaches to treatment.

Bennett, W., & Gurin, J. (1982). *The dieter's dilemma: Eating less and weighing more.* New York: Basic Books.

Explanation of the "set point theory" as well as social and historical perspectives on dieting and weight.

Garner, D. M., & Garfinkel, P. E. (Eds.) (1988). *A handbook of psychotherapy for anorexia nervosa and bulimia*. New York: Guilford Press.
Comprehensive and systematic review of psychodynamic behavioral, cognitive, family, and group therapy approaches to treatment.

Schwartz, H. (1986). *Never satisfied,* New York: Free Press.
An extensive history of the perceptions of food and weight throughout human culture.

CHAPTER 15

Bulimia: Interdisciplinary Team Practice from a Normative and Developmental Perspective

Mary E. Connors, Ph.D.
Community Coordinator–ABtec Unit, Chicago

Happiness is not the absence of conflicts; it is the ability to cope.

Anonymous

The treatment approach described in this chapter focuses on the functions that the bulimic symptoms serve for the client. While the client may experience her urge to binge and purge as a mysterious and uncontrollable occurrence, it can be demonstrated to her that her bulimia is instead a response to the physiological and psychological deprivation induced by chronic dieting as well as a means to cope with painful affective states. Treatment must focus on management of the symptomatic behavior through behavioral and cognitive behavioral techniques while also exploring intrapsychic and interpersonal issues. This exploration is best done utilizing a psychodynamic approach informed by self-psychology, wherein the bulimia is seen as an effort at self-soothing in an individual who lacks internal resources for managing affects due to faulty self-object experiences.

Four different points of intervention with the symptomatic behavior are described. A section on prevention discusses the necessity of ceasing dieting behavior, normalizing eating, and correcting cognitive distortions relating to a drive for thinness. Interventions at the pre-binge point are described, oriented toward identifying the particular mood state that is triggering the binge, such as anger, loneliness, boredom, or anxiety, and finding more appropriate coping strategies, so that a client may be taught to use more assertive behavior when angry rather than bingeing. At the post-binge period the primary goal is to restrain from purging. Here the client learns how to tolerate the anxiety that eating induces. Finally, at the post-binge-purge point, the focus is on relapse prevention, so that the client will learn to eat her next regular meal and get "back on track" after a binge, rather than allowing herself to feel so defeated by a binge that she continues with another binge.

The multidisciplinary team approach is included in its utilization of a variety of intervention modalities. Depending on the needs of the client, they may include antidepressant medication, marital or family therapy, nutritional counseling, group therapy, and self-help 12-step groups. The heterogeneity of clients who experience bulimia is discussed, with an emphasis on tailoring interventions to the particular client, taking into account each person's general level of psychopathology, degree of separation from family, weight range, sex, and interpersonal resources.

DEFINING BULIMIA

Bulimia is a complex, serious, and relatively widespread disorder, as Chapter 12 made clear. A comprehensive treatment program must recognize the biopsychosocial nature of the disorder (Johnson & Connors, 1987) and the heterogeneity of the patient population. Because bulimics are predominantly female, with males comprising only around five percent of the population, this chapter emphasizes the treatment of bulimic women.

The *DSM-III-R* definition of bulimia nervosa states that binge-eating followed by purging must have occurred at least twice a week for three months in order for the diagnosis to be made *(Diagnostic and Statistical Manual,* 1987). However, many women who are distressed by their eating behavior do not meet these criteria. Those who binge but do not purge are usually referred to as binge-restrictors if they alternate between bingeing and dieting. This group may also be referred to as compulsive overeaters, especially if they gain significant amounts of weight. An additional group purges normal meals without bingeing. Others do binge and purge but at a lesser frequency. Finally, some bulimics may also be diagnosed as having anorexia nervosa if they have lost enough body weight. For the purposes of this chapter all of these individuals having some involvement with bingeing and/or purging will be loosely referred to as bulimic. The treatment program which is described includes components that specifically address each behavior.

The Symptoms of Bulimia

The symptoms of bulimia have such grave physical and psychological consequences that a neutral stance on the part of the therapist is not appropriate. Bulimia can be life-threatening because of such physical concomitants as electrolyte imbalances and gastric dilatation. Less dangerous but still problematic consequences include dental erosion, swelling of the parotid glands, and attenuation of the gag reflex. The psychological consequences of bulimia are also severe, with intense shame, self-disgust, and self-despair about their behavior being common reactions. Bulimic symptoms do not tend to remit spontaneously without treatment nor do they remit

with any regularity in treatments that do not specifically address them. Numerous clients have reported previous therapy that helped them feel significantly better in many ways with no impact on their bingeing and purging. The symptomatic behavior can acquire a life of its own, and as long as it is present many continue to feel very distressed by it, with continued low self-esteem and self-hatred.

By the time a bulimic seeks treatment, she generally feels very out of control of her behavior. While the average age of onset for bulimia is about 17, bulimics usually struggle with the symptom alone for several years before finally concluding they cannot manage it on their own (Johnson, Stuckey, Lewis, & Schwartz, 1983). At this point a woman may be bingeing and purging many times per day. Some bulimics continue to eat and at times keep down normal meals, but others have restricted their involvement with food to bingeing and purging only. The great majority of the bulimic's time and energy is devoted to eating and weight concerns; whenever she is not eating she is planning to eat, worrying about eating, or concealing her latest binge. She is preoccupied with warding off fat and may be weighing herself several times a day, exercising compulsively, and scrutinizing her body mercilessly.

Initial Considerations

Helping professionals must appreciate the magnitude of this type of obsession. Empathy can be conveyed only if the social worker can demonstrate a willingness to speak the client's language and connect around food-related issues. In the initial consultation individuals should be encouraged to provide detailed information about their weight history and their eating behavior, including weight fluctuations and their correspondence to other life events, family eating attitudes and weight status of family members, the events surrounding the onset of bingeing and of purging, and a microscopic exploration of the frequency, circumstances, consummatory behavior, and subjective experience of bingeing and purging. This will not only provide the helper with vital information but will also convey to the client that this is a person who can understand what her real life is truly like behind the mask she wears in public. The social worker can appreciate the desperate need that has driven the client to arrive at this particular adaptation, while at the same time conveying that more constructive means of caring for oneself must be sought. The therapeutic stance is thus one of balance rather than neutrality.

When an individual first presents for treatment she may have absolutely no idea why she is bulimic. She may experience the urge to binge and purge as something that descends on her "out of the blue"; her bulimia is an uncontrollable mysterious force before which she is helpless. Here the practitioner can provide a badly needed educative function. Helpers can convey their appreciation for the fact that the behavior seems senseless and uncontrollable, but that actually it is helping the client to meet some very important needs. The therapeutic task is to identify those needs and begin to address them in alternative ways. Often clients are only focusing on the self-destructive aspect of their symptoms, and their self-hatred can diminish somewhat if they are helped to appreciate that they have been attempting to care for and nurture themselves, albeit in a problematic fashion. Many will also want to know "why me?" in terms of the development of bulimic symptoms; they can benefit from a discussion about their underlying biological vulnerability to difficulties in mood regulation (Pope, Hudson, Yurgelun-Todd, & Hudson, 1983) as well as issues related to their own development within a particular family environment and sociocultural climate (Johnson & Connors, 1987).

THE DYNAMICS OF BULIMIA

Clients must modify some general attitudes and behaviors about eating and weight before much reduction in bingeing and purging is possible. The onset of bulimic symptoms tends to be preceded by a period of dieting, and most bulimics are chronic and obsessive dieters. They split the world of food into "good foods" and "bad foods," with good foods comprising a limited list of "diet" foods such as yogurt and salads and bad foods being everything else. Binge foods usually include foods from the "very bad" list such as ice cream, cookies, and potato chips. These are high fat and/or high sugar

carbohydrates that the client will never permit herself to eat when she is not bingeing.

Just as the world of food is split, so is the self; an individual feels "good" when she is starving herself and eating only small quantities of diet foods. However, even one bit of a "bad" food can be enough to turn the self-experience from good to bad. If a person already feels herself to be bad ("I've blown it"), she reasons that she might as well "go all the way" and binge and purge, planning to resume the diet tomorrow. There is often a feeling that this is the last meal before deprivation once again sets in, so one should compulsively cram in as much food as possible and also rid the house of fattening foods that might tempt one in the future. The frenzied eating induces terrible guilt in these women, which they attempt to assuage by purging and recommitting themselves to stringent dieting the following day. Once the cycle is activated, it resembles some aspects of the addiction cycle associated with other substances such as alcohol and cocaine and that of addictive relationships.

Those with bulimia must be taught that a significant degree of their preoccupation with food stems from deprivation. They are suffering physical deprivation from insufficient caloric intake on a regular basis and psychological deprivation from never allowing themselves to eat nondiet foods or considering them to be legitimate. The more clients try to stay away from food, the more they are driven compulsively to binge. It is helpful to acquaint them with research findings on starvation and restrained eating (Keys, Brozek, Henschel, Mickelson, & Taylor, 1950; Herman & Mack, 1975) that suggest that normal people experience intense preoccupation with food when being underfed and that chronic dietary restraint is followed by counterregulatory binge-eating. The practitioner must stress that the young woman will stop bingeing only when she stops dieting and feeds herself regularly with a variety of foods.

NORMALIZING BULIMIA

Most persons will need a good deal of help in translating this principle of normalization into action. They may state that they have no idea when they are hungry or full, what constitutes a portion size, or what normal meal choices are. The social worker may have difficulty believing that such topics are the proper realm of psychotherapy, but it is imperative to respond to the need for appropriate structure in an area where the woman feels totally lost. There are many ways in which practitioners can help the client keep a food diary in which she records all normal eating, bingeing, purging, and any feelings she may have been aware of prior to a binge. They can examine the diary together after a week or two. The helper will now have data to support the notion that the client is depriving herself by skipping meals or eating too little, and can point out particular problem areas. Then they can work together on helping the client normalize her eating in a gradual fashion. It is important that practitioners understand how difficult these changes are and that they maintain empathy for each person's level of anxiety. Most of these women are not going to be eating three normal meals a day for some time, and they need to know they can proceed at their own pace.

The Importance of Small Successes

Early in treatment, clients really need to have some experiences of success in changing and controlling their eating. Their tendency to think in all-or-nothing terms means they conceive of their recovery as an abrupt cessation of bingeing and purging, and they often vow to themselves that they will never binge again. When they cannot maintain this vow of abstinence, they conclude that they will never recover. Some of them feel a tremendous sense of relief and hope upon being told that their recovery will be a gradual process composed of small steps. This principle of taking recovery one day at a time is consistent with the philosophy of 12-step programs and the approach toward recovery from other addictions.

Setting concrete goals for themselves that they can successfully meet promotes a sense of mastery and counteracts feelings of helplessness and lack of control. Early treatment goals usually revolve around adding a meal where it is typically skipped or experimenting with a broader range of foods. For example, a person who does not eat normal meals may set a goal of eating a small breakfast one day during the week. One who typically eats only a salad for lunch can try adding a bagel. Individuals who are a bit farther along with their eating may experiment with adding previously identified binge foods to their normal meal eating. However, the practitioner must help them structure the experience to ensure success. For instance, someone who often binges on ice cream would not be advised to bring a half gallon of her favorite flavor into the house and try to eat one bowl. Instead, she can go to an ice cream parlor with a friend, order a cone, and then take a walk with the friend to structure herself during this anxiety-provoking time.

Eliminating Self-defeating Goals

The primary obstacle to normalizing eating is the client's compulsive drive for thinness. While bulimics do not usually experience the body image distortion characteristic of anorexia nervosa, they do have a great degree of body dissatisfaction. They may believe that being thin is the most important thing in the world, that they are nothing if they are not thin, and that fat equals failure. Our sociocultural milieu promotes such distorted notions that bulimics have rigidly internalized. The helper should adopt a questioning attitude toward the current cultural standards for thinness and educate clients about how norms have vacillated historically rather than being engraved in stone. The social worker might also discuss the economics of the multibillion dollar diet industry which manipulates women into thinking they are not acceptable as they are but they can be transformed after they purchase the diet product. They can be encouraged to reject this manipulation and to prioritize health over thinness. All of these interventions can help the client recognize there is something wrong with the prevailing cultural standards rather than with herself.

The social worker must be prepared to confront women about their view of an ideal weight, which is usually significantly below their actual weight. Often clients will agree that the helper's ideas about normalizing eating make sense, and that they will start the new plan as soon as they lose ten pounds. It must be stressed to them that trying to lose weight will sabotage any efforts to stop bingeing, and that normalizing eating must come first. Often some of them will lose weight gradually as their eating becomes more regular and the bingeing diminishes, but this must be a by-product, not a goal by itself.

Often clients choose an ideal weight that is biogenically too low for them. Information on set point theory may be useful; it suggests that humans and animals have a biogenetic predisposition to maintain certain levels of body fat and that attempts to deviate from one's appropriate level induce metabolic changes designed to restore the preferred level (Nisbett, 1972). Dieting induces a lowering of the metabolic rate and an increased propensity to restore weight in the form of fat rather than muscle tissue. Thus, one must learn to live with the weight that one's body wants to be. Individuals typically react to this news with rage and frustration. It is a narcissistic blow not to be able to control this aspect of oneself; it also runs counter to typical American beliefs that one can do anything with sufficient willpower. Many clients experience despair as they begin to realize that their ideal weight may be unobtainable. However, there is often some relief from feelings of failure and the shame about lacking willpower when clients realize they have been fighting their own biology. They can also be told that because their eating has been so chaotic it might be unclear what their set point is and that research suggests that regular exercise can have an impact on set point by regulating metabolic efficiency. Moreover, frequent weighing amounts to self-torture; clients should be advised to discontinue weighing themselves.

THE DEVELOPMENT OF BULIMIA

Once there has been some normalization of eating, clients are in a better position to explore the psychological concomitants of bingeing. The food diary again can be a great help with this, as they begin to record the circumstances surrounding each binge.

Early Need Deprivation

Generally some patterns emerge rather quickly and it becomes apparent that the bingeing is being utilized to help clients cope with painful tensions and affective states. They may binge when they are angry, anxious, depressed, lonely, empty, or bored, depending on the individual. Bulimics seem to experience more dysphoric moods and more mood fluc-

tuations than the "normal" population (Johnson & Larson, 1982), and are constantly struggling with the problem of regulating these moods. Self-psychology offers a useful perspective for understanding these deficits in affect regulation. They can be viewed as the result of inadequate provision by parents for the young child's needs for feeling part of an admired other with whose strength, power, and calmness one can merge (Kohut, 1971, 1978). If these needs are not adequately met by the child's self-object milieu, the gradual internalization of such psychic functions as self-soothing, cohesion, vitalization, self-esteem regulation, and tension regulation will not occur.

Often bulimics' early environments appear to be deficient in attending to mirroring and idealizing needs. Bulimic families are characterized by high levels of hostility, belittling, and blaming, with little display of affection or support (Humphrey, 1989). Bulimics often have difficulty recalling occasions where they felt their talents were appreciated and encouraged by family members or being allowed to feel special. Childish grandiosity was quickly squelched with unfavorable comparisons to siblings and cautions about being conceited. Many bulimics become desperately compliant people-pleasers in their efforts to find something about themselves to which others will respond favorably. A feeling of never being truly loved, appreciated, or wanted by parents is common, with vividly recalled descriptions of how the parent really wished for an altogether different type of child.

Parents in bulimic families tend to have such disorders of the self in their own right that they have great difficulty allowing a child to internalize adult strength and calm. They often are depressed, feel overburdened and resentful of the needs of others, and may have an eating disorder or a substance abuse problem themselves. The child is used to meet the needs of the parent for a confirming self-object or for the perfect child whom they can merge with and display to others. The child is forced into precocious development as the parental caretaker and assumes a "false self" (Winnicott, 1965) of competence and pseudomaturity. Parents may utilize the child as a confidante or otherwise make it clear whose needs matter, while blurring the issue of who is the parent and who the child. The child's anger or distress is experienced by the parents as threatening because it may stimulate their own rage and depression. The child is likely to be attacked rather than soothed during an emotional outburst, as can be seen in the following case.

> For instance, a client remembered that as an adolescent she called her mother on the phone sobbing about a rejection from a boyfriend, and her mother snapped, "Stop crying! You'll get wrinkles!" Thus a single comment conveyed that her mother had no interest in helping her manage her feelings and that the most important thing is one's appearance.

Food as a Source of Self-validation

The bulimic therefore is left with deficits in the functions of self-confirmation and self-validation from faulty mirroring and deficits in self-soothing and self-calming from failures of idealization. Bulimia represents an attempt to replace the missing structures with a relationship to a new self-object: food. Having found that the interpersonal world is deficient in meeting her needs, and lacking the psychic structure to deal with them internally, she turns to a substance. The self-object quality of the bulimic's relationship with food is vividly illustrated in comments such as, "It feels like my best friend" and "I know it's always there for me and it calms me down." Food is experienced as infinitely more reliable than people; one can stock the cupboards and know that one will be surrounded by the needed substance and that even if it runs out, the 24-hour grocery store is near. The bulimic can control her food as she was never able to control her parents' responses to her.

Turning to food represents an effort to obtain wholeness by a restoration of mother and child synchrony; but as Kohut (1977) states, it is not really the food that the individual craves, but the experience of the food-giving empathic mother in tune with the child's needs. Attempts to evoke such soothing as did occur with the mother are apparent in bulimics' descriptions of favorite binge foods and their associations with them. One client with numerous siblings and an alcoholic father binges on pastries and recalls that her mother spent her one day off from work baking and how as a child she treasured that day. Another young woman binges exclusively on ice cream, which her family ate every night. Indeed, the theme of food as an evoker of the caring maternal presence is widespread in our culture generally, with such notions as chicken soup as a panacea and "comfort foods" for the blues.

Other Sources of Validation

The bulimic's vulnerabilities in self-regulation lead her to turn not only to food but to external sources of validation. Her inability to confirm herself and regulate her self-esteem internally impel her to seek the approval of others and to look for concrete standards against which she can measure herself. Weight regulation provides the perfect opportunity to achieve the almost universally desired goal of thinness and to know whether she has achieved it by the number on the scale. Additionally, parents of bulimics are very clear in communicating what they *do not* admire in their children. Fat is considered to be repulsive by these parents, who often have eating and weight disorders of their own, and the child learns at least one concrete aspect of avoiding parental disapproval.

Co-dependency Aspects

Two additional aspects of the bulimic's adaptation will be important in assessment and intervention. Because her parents had so much difficulty in responding to her needs, she will experience guilt and uncertainty about meeting them, and will be easily destabilized or fragmented by internal and external events. Many bulimics fit the description of co-dependency whether or not they grew up in a substance-abusing home. They put others' needs before their own, take responsibility for others' feelings, and in general act as caretakers. Although as a result they may be conscious of feeling resentful and deprived, they defend against risking further rejection after their painful early experiences with people and turn to food instead. The wish to obtain something for oneself is expressed only in bingeing, with the experience of unentitlement being the rule.

Faulty meeting of the child's needs for soothing result in an overburdened self (Kohut & Wolf, 1978) who has repeatedly suffered the trauma of unshared emotion. Powerful emotions, even positive ones, are experienced as overwhelming the self and threatening it with fragmentation. An angry thought, a slight rebuff, or a concern about some new demand assumes major importance in the client's mind, and she feels both that she is a bad person and that she is falling apart. The predictable experience of bingeing and purging provides a soothing ritual, allows the young woman to take in something for her depleted self, and provides distraction from the upsetting experiences that preceded it.

TREATING AFFECTIVE DYSREGULATION

The weakness in the bulimic's self-image and the symptomatic behavior that is the result must both be addressed in treating the client's difficulties with her affective states. The relationship with the practitioner is primary, in that the therapist becomes a new self-object for the client. Healing and soothing is provided by the focused empathic understanding of the helper who explores the negative self-object experiences of the past and affirms the legitimacy of the child's wishes. Gradually the client becomes more able to turn to the helper to share her upsetting feelings, although she may resist her dependency needs for some time, fearing further humiliation. The building of the client's psychic structure occurs through internalization of the therapist's self-object functions (Elson, 1986).

Psychic Restructuring

Structure building can be enhanced by the practitioner's provision of active strategies for dealing with painful affects and situations. The individual can be taught to try to figure out what she is feeling when she wants to binge and to consider alternative activities. If the client frequently binges when she is angry at someone, the practitioner can initiate a discussion of assertive behavior. The client may then be able to behave assertively with the appropriate person when angry. If this feels impossible, she may write an angry letter and not send it, conduct an imaginary conversation, or let off steam with physical activity such as exercise or punching a pillow. A client who binges when lonely can be taught to initiate contact with someone. Being with or calling a friend at these times is reported as consistently satisfying by those who have some positive relationships. For more isolated individuals, group support is helpful. Others may need a feeling of connectedness with the social worker through a phone call or the use of a transitional object such as a tape of the worker's voice, a handwritten note, or a journal shared with the worker.

Those who binge when feeling depleted and overwhelmed can be taught a variety of self-organizing and self-nurturing strategies. Often clients binge when they feel overwhelmed with responsibilities and decisions that need to be made, all of which they believe must be perfect. Challenging their cognitive distortions around perfectionism and catastrophizing can be very helpful. They might also need to learn decision-making skills such as prioritizing and listing the pros and cons of any decision. They should be encouraged to discover ways of nurturing themselves that do not involve food. Clients need to spend some time thinking about what would feel pleasurable to them. Frequently used strategies are taking a bubble bath, buying oneself fresh flowers, taking a walk, enjoying favorite music, reading a magazine, or shopping and getting oneself a small gift.

Handling Transitions and Rituals

That bulimics have difficulty with separations is no surprise, considering the inadequate early environment. The onset of bulimia often occurs around the time a young woman is graduating from high school and undergoing a major transition into college or work. However, much more minor separations and transitions can also feel highly disruptive. The daily transition of leaving work and returning home is often very difficult to manage, leading many bulimics to binge upon returning home to help them shift gears and ease into leisure time. Merely pointing out her sensitivity in this area can be helpful to an individual, who can then be on the alert for problematic situations. The ritual quality of a binge and purge is very anxiety-reducing, and clients can be taught to construct new rituals to handle transitions. For instance, upon returning home from work a client could open her mail and sip some tea rather than binge. One young woman reported that getting a puppy that she had to feed and walk after work obviated the need to binge at that time.

Additionally, the social worker needs to be particularly sensitive to the impact of any separations or disruptions in the continuity of treatment, however minor they may seem.

One client had just begun treatment with this author, who after three sessions had to cancel one because of a family emergency. She saw me on the street a few days after the canceled session and hurled herself into my arms. I was a bit surprised at the desperation she felt for contact with me so early in treatment, but later came to understand the magnitude of her difficulties with separation and what an eternity that few days seemed to her.

It must be stressed to clients that at first probably nothing will address their feeling state in quite as satisfying a way as bingeing and purging. New relationships, hobbies, and other pursuits will become gratifying over time. For a long time the client may have difficulty substituting an alternative for bingeing. The practitioner can point out that even delaying a binge can be helpful in demonstrating that painful feelings need not be done away with immediately. Individuals can gradually build up their tolerance.

Advocacy Strategies

The social worker must always be mindful of the client's need to merge with the practitioner's strength or calmness in order to manage anxiety. At times this may need to extend beyond the usual in-session explorations of the client's feelings to more active help with crisis management.

One young woman who was fragmenting under extreme stress was being pressured by a group facilitator to join her group, and the client felt quite unable to tell the staff person that she felt uncomfortable with her and did not wish to join. Under most circumstances it would be appropriate to encourage the client to struggle with her issues of self-assertion. However, because the client was so overwhelmed, the present author suggested she tell the group therapist that her individual therapist did not think the group was a good idea at the present time and she could approach me if she had questions about that. The client expressed great relief and immediately became more organized.

THE PURGING PROCESS

When clients first discover purging they feel euphoric. At last they have found a way to eat all they wish and still not gain weight. However, because purging removes the natural consequences of overeating, namely, painful fullness and increased weight, the bingeing becomes much more chaotic. Many now feel there is no reason to curb themselves and they may binge and purge for many hours each day. Purging may come to be more than simply undoing the consequences of the binge; in fact, for some it is the purging rather than the bingeing that is most satisfying. They will eat in order to purge rather than vice versa. Most bulimics find purging to be extremely effective in reducing anxiety. Not only is the fear of weight gain removed, but they report feeling "cleaned out" and relieved at being able to "start over."

Purging seems to help shift the self-representation from bad to good again. It also may represent a repudiation of wishes for merger with and comfort from the maternal self-object. The client feels relief that indeed she can manage all of her needs on her own. Some individuals report feeling pleasantly empty following a purge, which probably relates to experiencing themselves as free from needs. This is in contrast to the distressing state of inner emptiness often reported by bulimics, resulting from a depleted self that lacks psychic structure and good internal objects.

Bulimics must be taught that the more they allow themselves the "out" of purging, the more they will binge. They need to begin committing themselves to abstaining from purging whether or not they have binged. Needless to say, this is intensely anxiety-provoking, and will not occur without a good deal of trust in the helper. Clients have a variety of cognitive distortions about gaining ten pounds from a single binge, becoming hugely fat, and having the food in their stomachs sitting there and then going directly to fat deposits. They need help in correcting these distorted cognitions. It is true that gastric emptying seems to be slowed down in bulimics, but the clients can be reassured that this will normalize as purging ceases. If an individual is not able to avoid purging entirely after a binge, she should be asked to delay it for longer and longer periods and gradually increase her ability to tolerate the anxiety.

Those who purge through laxative abuse tend to be more disturbed than those who self-induce vomiting. The use of laxatives appears to represent a more primitive and masochistic adaptation. Laxative abusers should be educated about the fact that laxatives are very ineffective in ridding the body of calories. Only about 12 percent of calories eaten can be eliminated through the use of laxatives (Bo-Linn,

Santa Ana, Morowski, & Fordtran, 1983), with the primary loss to the body consisting of water. Occasionally some individuals will purge by using the emetic ipecac. This is extremely dangerous, as this product is cardiotoxic and could kill when the proper toxicity level is reached. Clients must be sternly warned about this practice. If further purging with ipecac occurs after receipt of this information, the activity should be treated like a suicide attempt.

RELAPSE PREVENTION

Bulimia tends to be an episodic disorder. Many will continue to struggle with occasional bingeing and purging even after a great deal of progress has been made. It is vital for the social worker to prepare the client to cope with periodic episodes, while also stressing that some people do recover completely with time. The first binge-purge episode after a period of abstinence represents a crucial point. The individual is likely to be so discouraged and full of self-hatred for bingeing again that she will feel back to square one and become resigned to further bingeing and purging. She must be taught to regard the episode as a learning experience, a cue or signal that she is being overstressed and must attend to the source of the recent disruption. Many are often vulnerable to renewed bingeing following a loss or rejection in a relationship, when they feel both depleted and compelled to be thinner in order to be loved. The other typical cause for renewed bingeing is stringent dieting. Two clients who had become symptom-free in a group treatment both relapsed a few months after the group stopped when they went on a liquid diet.

Clients must be taught to give themselves credit for their binge-free period, rather than feel it is all destroyed because they eventually did binge. They must commit themselves to eating their next meal and getting back on track following an episode, with quick recovery from an episode rather than complete avoidance being the goal. They should come to regard the symptomatic behavior as a potentially positive avenue of awareness about their own feelings rather than as an adversary lying in wait for the unwary. Unacknowledged needs will press for recognition, and the symptom appears in order to remind them to pay attention to themselves.

A MULTIDISCIPLINARY TEAM APPROACH

The multidimensional nature of bulimia demands that in many cases optimal treatment requires the involvement of several professionals. In institutional settings and in private practice, the social worker may want to have the participation of an internist, psychiatrist, psychologist, and/or a nutritionalist. Often the social work role involves helping other team members to take a more ecological, wholistic perspective and to serve as the case manager or key person in the formal network of services. Also considered for use may be adjunct treatment modalities, including group therapy, family or marital therapy, and self-help groups.

Medical Considerations

The physical consequences of bulimia demand medical attention. If a woman is purging with any regularity and has not had a complete physical within the last year, a medical examination can be made a condition of treatment. It is helpful for the social worker to make contact with a few internists who specialize in treating eating disorders. They can monitor the electrolyte levels and consult with the practitioner about their findings, which the practitioner can then use in helping the client formulate treatment goals. Under no conditions should a nonmedical person assume responsibility for the client's physical condition; ethical practice requires referral if there is the slightest health risk.

Antidepressant medication has been shown to be very effective in the treatment of bulimia (Pope et al., 1983). It is not yet clear which clients are most responsive to medication. The social worker might consider referral to a psychiatrist for a medication evaluation whenever a client is significantly depressed or is symptomatic at least several times per week. Again, it is helpful for the social worker to develop a relationship with a psychiatrist who specializes in eating disorders.

Psychological and Nutritional Consultation

The social worker might consider referring a woman to a psychologist for psychological testing when a clearer understanding of the client's dynamics and ego resources is desired for the purposes of treatment planning. When a client's knowledge of basic nutrition is very limited and she seems to need a good deal of help in many aspects of normalizing her eating, referral to a nutritionist for a consultation or some ongoing work may be very helpful, and it will give the social worker more time for other work in psychotherapy.

Family Work

Some practitioners conceive of bulimia as a family systems problem, and utilize family therapy as the treatment of choice (Schwartz, Barrett, & Saba, 1985). However, since most bulimics are living as independent adults by the time they present for treatment, individual therapy may be more appropriate. Even though the family may not be seen in treatment, the social worker should always be aware of the family system and the fact that there are external and interpersonal issues to be addressed as well as internal ones. If a client is younger and particularly enmeshed with her family, or if her symptom appears to be serving a current function in the family, family therapy is probably indicated. Couple or marital therapy should be considered any time there is significant distress in the couple relationship. Even if ongoing intervention is not indicated, a few meetings with the spouse or significant other together with the client may be helpful in aiding the couple's interactions around bulimia.

Group Work

Group therapy can be beneficial to a large number of bulimics. They tend to experience great relief at coming to know and like other bulimics, because their usual secrecy about themselves does not have to be maintained. They can also see that these other women are appealing rather than disgusting, so perhaps they are too. In the safety of the group setting they can begin to rely on others for support with less fear of rejection. They can also feel like part of the human community rather than outcasts whose shameful behavior would disgust anyone who knew them. In the group setting clients can also share strategies about what has worked for them in terms of normalizing eating and becoming less symptomatic. Group members can be particularly helpful in modeling how one stabilizes in an appropriate weight range after the cessation of purging. Hearing about others' experiences and seeing that they do not

continue gaining indefinitely is usually much more salient to a client than reassurances about weight stabilization from the practitioner.

Twelve-Step Self-Help Groups

Clients can benefit a great deal from 12-step and other self-help groups as well as from professionally led groups. However, when there is no professional to intervene, the group members must make sure they are not caretaking a few more disturbed group members at their own expense. Many clients also experience some confusion about being in psychotherapy and an Overeaters Anonymous group at the same time, since abstinence is the goal of OA. Powerlessness over food is also accepted in OA, whereas the assumption of control may be stressed in therapy. An abstinence model is more appropriately applied to substances like alcohol that can be eliminated from one's life entirely. Eating food requires making choices multiple times per day. However, the group support in OA can be tremendously helpful for members, and can provide them with a level of structure and contact with others that is simply not possible with psychotherapy alone. Bulimics seem to do best with OA when they define abstinence in a way that has meaning for them, which might include abstinence from purging or from eating certain foods that are consistently problematic.

Bulimics who are also alcoholics or drug abusers must become abstinent from their other substance abuse before progress on the bulimia is possible. Rehabilitation programs as well as involvement in Alcoholics Anonymous or Narcotics Anonymous may be necessary. Since a large number of bulimics grew up in alcoholic homes, groups for Adult Children of Alcoholics are especially helpful to them.

RESPONSE TO TREATMENT

Bulimics are a very heterogeneous group both in terms of their symptom picture, as detailed earlier, and regarding their psychological functioning. Bulimics may be grouped along a continuum of psychological disorder. At one end there is a group of relatively high-functioning individuals who might be considered neurotic or identity-conflicted. These individuals tend to have positive stable relationships and clear goals for school and work performance, with just enough self-esteem vulnerabilities to have gotten carried away with dieting. Their symptomatic behavior is very ego dystonic, they are highly motivated, and often are able to cease most bingeing and purging after a relatively brief intervention.

In the middle of the continuum is a group with disorders of the self of moderate severity. These clients generally are quite depressed and have little sense of their own needs and affects. They usually have difficulty in establishing intimate relationships because of anxiety and fear of rejection. Faulty mirroring in the early environment has also led to an inability to assess their talents and pursue realistic goals, so they may be confused or paralyzed about career pursuits. Individuals in this group often can make use of symptom-focused interventions relatively early in treatment, but may need many months of these interventions and the therapeutic relationship before becoming asymptomatic or nearly so.

Finally, there is a group of borderline bulimics whose functioning may be very low. They may be polyaddicted, using alcohol or cocaine in addition to the bulimia. This group is more masochistic, often purging by means of laxative abuse. Difficulties with impulse control may be severe, and they may engage in self-mutilation, suicidal gestures or attempts, and frequent compulsive shoplifting. Symptom-focused treatment is usually not very effective with this group, as they rely upon bingeing and purging to ward off severe fragmentation. Long-term individual psychotherapy aimed at building psychic structure is the treatment of choice for them. Because they are so needy and can easily provoke negative countertransference reactions, the practitioner would do well to utilize the team approach and recommend a 12-step or other support group to which the client can turn for support.

CONCLUSION

Bulimia is a complex disorder that must be addressed with a multidimensional treatment program. Doing psychotherapy with a bulimic may warrant more involvement with the client's physical condition and symptomatic behavior than the social worker is accustomed to. Reliance upon a multidisciplinary team to ensure that the client's needs for physical care, medication, and nutritional informa-

tion are met can enable the practitioner to conduct psychotherapy and other interventions without being overburdened. Bulimics are individuals whose needs while growing up were ignored, deferred, or derided. It is incumbent upon the social worker to provide an atmosphere where their needs for acceptance, confirmation, sharing, and empathic understanding can at last be met.

REFERENCES

Bo-Linn, G. W., Santa Ana, C. A., Morowski, S. G., & Fordtran, J. S. (1983). Purging and calorie absorption in bulimic patients and normal women. *Annals of Internal Medicine, 99,* 14–17.
Diagnostic and statistical manual (3rd Ed. rev.) (1987). New York: American Psychiatric Association.
Elson, M. (1986). *Self psychology in clinical social work.* New York: Norton.
Herman, C. P., & Mack, D. (1975). Restrained and unrestrained eating. *Journal of Personality, 43,* 647–661.
Humphrey, L. L. (1989). Observed family interactions among subtypes of eating disorders using the structural analysis of social behavior. *Journal of Consulting and Clinical Psychology, 57,* 206–214.
Johnson, C., & Connors, M. E. (1987). *The etiology and treatment of bulimia nervosa: A biopsychosocial perspective.* New York: Basic Books.
Johnson, C., & Larson, R. (1982). Bulimia: An analysis of moods and behavior. *Psychosomatic Medicine, 44,* 333–345.
Johnson, C., Stuckey, M., Lewis, L., & Schwartz, D. (1983). Bulimia: A descriptive study of 509 cases. In P. L. Darby, P. E. Garfinkel, D. M. Garner, & D. V. Coscina (Eds.), *Anorexia nervosa: Recent developments* (pp. 159–172). New York: Alan R. Liss.
Keys, A., Brozek, J., Henschel, A., Mickelson, O., & Taylor, H. L. (1950). *The biology of human starvation, Vol. I.* Minneapolis: University of Minnesota Press.
Kohut, H. (1971). *The analysis of the self.* New York: International Universities Press.
Kohut, H. (1977). *The restoration of the self.* New York: International Universities Press.
Kohut, H. (1978). *The search for the self: Selected writings of Heinz Kohut: 1950–1978* (Vols. 1–2). P. Ornstein (Ed.). New York: International Universities Press.
Kohut, H., & Wolf, E. (1978). The disorders of the self and their treatment. *International Journal of Psychoanalysis, 59,* 414–425.
Nisbett, R. E. (1972). Eating behavior and obesity in men

and animals. *Advances in Psychosomatic Medicine, 7,* 173–193.

Pope, H., Hudson, J., Yurgelun-Todd, M., & Hudson, M. (1983). Bulimia treated with imipramine: A placebo controlled, double blind study. *American Journal of Psychiatry,* 140, 554–558.

Schwartz, R., Barrett, M. J., & Saba, G. (1985). The family therapy of bulimia. In D. M. Garner & P. E. Garfinkel (Eds.), *A handbook of psychotherapy for anorexia nervosa and bulimia.* New York: Guilford Press.

Winnicott, D. W. (1965). *The maturational process and the facilitating environment.* New York: Basic Books.

SUPPLEMENTAL READING LIST

Hudson, J. I., Pope, H. G. & Jonus, J. M. (1983). Family history study of anorexia nervosa and bulimia. *British Journal of Psychiatry, 142,* 133–138.
These authors present family histories analyses to illustrate the etiology and dynamics of the two eating disorders; their comparisons of anorexia and bulimia are particularly enlightening.

Humphrey, L. L. (1989). Observed family interactions among subtypes of eating disorders using the structural analysis of social behavior. *Journal of Consulting and Clinical Psychology, 57,* 206–214.
This is a useful article on interactional patterns of families with a member who has an eating disorder. The author attempts to identify several subtypes based on these interactional patterns among various eating disorders.

Streigel-Moore, R. H., Silberstein, L. R. & Rodin, J. (1986). Toward an understanding of risk factors for bulimia. *American Psychologist, 41,* 246–263.
The authors present a productive discussion on risk factors related to the individual, family, and general culture. This process of clarifying risk factors has significant implications for prevention efforts with the population before the problem is manifested or at early warning stages.

PART IV

Other Addictions

A state-of-the-art issue is the difficulty of finding a method of categorizing the addictions that works consistently. Thus, the addictions included in this section of the book involve behaviors, relationships, *and* substances. Some similar addictions have not been included because not enough information about them is available currently; spiritual or religious addiction is one example. Others that have been included in this section could fit more than one category. For example, the nicotine in tobacco is recognized as an addictive chemical; yet there is a lack of consensus about whether it should be placed in the same category with crack or heroin. This dilemma provides a rationale for developing this fourth section of the book.

Love and sexual addiction are the subject of Chapter 16. The types of addiction and how they differ from sexual dysfunctions are made clear. Included are guidelines for structuring the treatment based on the process of addiction.

The focus of Chapter 17 is tobacco addiction with emphasis on high-risk male youths and the sociocultural variables that heighten their vulnerability. Since impacting the peer group is essential, a school-based prevention program is described in the chapter.

A similar stance is taken toward impacting the families of compulsive gamblers in Chapter 18, the final chapter of the book. The chapter discusses the national enabling behaviors that encourage social gambling, and thus undergird the development of compulsive gambling in high-risk individuals. The discussion details how the family support network and self-help groups facilitate formal treatment.

PART IV

Other Additions

CHAPTER 16

Overcoming Sex and Love Addiction: An Expanded Perspective

Sadye M. L. Logan
University of Kansas

Your task is not to seek love, but merely to seek and find all of the barriers within yourself that you have built against it.

F. Vaughan and R. Walsh

In American society where a double standard still influences love and sexual behavior, most people cannot imagine such behavior as a compulsion or obsession. However, others can identify not only with destructive or desperate love, but also with the low self-esteem, aimlessness, apathy, and escapism that are associated with the problem. In many ways our culture subtly encourages love and sexual excess as a sign of healthy sexuality ("The Heat Is On," 1989). This attitude is connected to the message of the early 1970s that conveyed the notion of "guilt-free uninhibited sex." The "new morality" or "sexual revolution" sanctioned sex and love without emotional commitment. It was also during this period that love and sexual addiction surfaced as psychological problems. Prior to the 1970s these problems were virtually ignored in the literature of sexual behavior, despite the increasing number of men and women affected by the problem. During the mid-1980s, due to increasing awareness of serious sex-related diseases such as AIDS and herpes, a more concentrated focus has been directed toward this problem.

Historically, sexism prevented serious consideration of sexual addictions in the literature. The problem was viewed mainly as a woman's problem,

although it was unacceptable for women to discuss excessive sexual behaviors due to the prevailing double standard (Orford, 1985; Quadland, 1985). Not unlike sexual addictions, love or interpersonal compulsion has, in recent times, received substantial attention in the popular and professional literature (Forward, 1986; "Hooked on Love?" 1988; Norwood, 1985; Russanoff, 1983). However, as Peele (1975) points out, it is the least recognized form of addiction. This lack of recognition is, in part, related to the myth that anything done in the name of love must be good. Additionally, the interpersonally or sexually addicted are unlikely to reveal their problems to friends and relations or to seek professional help. From another perspective, the highly personal nature of sex and love dictates anonymity. For example, the preamble of the Sex and Love Addicts Anonymous Self-Help Group reads: "We need to protect with special care the anonymity of every SLAA member. Additionally, we try to avoid drawing undue attention to SLAA as a whole from the public media" (*Sex and Love Addicts Anonymous*, 1985, p. 2).

Available evidence profiles the sex and love addict as economically comfortable, but socially dependent. Sexual orientation or gender are viewed as irrelevant. In essence, these individuals experience a sense of inner emptiness and a fragile sense of self. They report a lack of control over their sexual behavior or chronic dependence on another person. These symptoms persist despite repeated physical and/or emotional abuse. The result of such destructive behavior impacts negatively on employment or careers, family life, and self-respect. Self-reports detail the lives of many men and women who felt powerless to end destructive relationships. Some expressed their addiction through frequenting unsafe areas or ''pick-up'' bars despite the fear of discovery by family members or the danger of contracting a sexually transmitted disease (STD). Others speak of engaging in compulsive solitary acts such as voyeurism, exhibitionism, masturbation, obsessive fantasy, and romantic intrigue (*Sex and Love Addicts Anonymous,* 1985).

Available evidence suggests a great deal of overlap between these two addictive behaviors; therefore, love addiction will be discussed in the same context as sexual addiction. The rationale for this approach is that it provides an extended and more complete view of the issues. Further, sex is often viewed as an expression of commitment in a love relationship. According to Quadland (1985), the literature on sexual behavior has focused exclusively on sexual inhibition as opposed to sexual compulsion. As a result, there is a more comprehensive understanding of the etiology and treatment of sexual dysfunction. Likewise, the social work literature has been more concerned with sexual dysfunction than sexual addiction. With this recognition, it is the intent of this chapter to examine within a broad-based context the dynamics of love and sexual addictions and the implications for intervention that range from prevention to treatment. More specifically, a framework will be established for viewing the problem by defining the main issues, discussing theories related to the development of these addictions, and identifying strategies of intervention.

DEFINING THE ADDICTIONS

Although uncontrollable sex and love have been frequently described as addictions, other common terms associated with the conditions include compulsion, obsession, and excess. Regardless of the terminology, however, both conditions are viewed

as progressive illnesses which cannot be cured but which can be arrested (Nakken, 1988; Peele, 1975; Quadland, 1985). Characteristically, the conditions may take several forms that include the compulsive need for sex or sexual gratification, extreme interpersonal dependency, and/or chronic preoccupation with romantic and related fantasies.

It is important to define clearly what is meant by sex and love addiction in order to be able to distinguish between what is considered ''normal'' enjoyment in sex and ''normal'' attachments in love. The key distinction between these addictions and healthy love and sex is the matter of experiencing the behavior not only as unacceptable, but beyond control. More specifically, an interpersonally addicted person engages in behavior that has the following qualities according to Hunter (1988), Peele (1975), Schaeffer (1985), and *Sex and Love Addicts Anonymous* (1985):

1. Experienced as disgusting, demeaning, and against their better judgment
2. Ritualized, obsessive, and the cause of great distress if interrupted
3. Joyless and pleasureless, without being concerned with true intimacy or individual growth

Additionally, there is a pattern of negative consequences connected to the sexual behavior. For example, these consequences may be social, emotional, physical, financial, and legal in nature. Social issues may include loss of family due to preoccupation with extramarital affairs and isolation from outside activities. Another consequence may be the loss of friends due to sexualizing relationships. Emotional concerns may include depression, suicidal thoughts, lack of assertion, self-hatred, fear, and guilt about disgusting behavior or behavior against one's values (for example, same gender sex, lying about the frequency of acts, and abortion).

Physical consequences can include STD, partner- or self-inflicted bruises or other abrasions, and complications due to abortions or pregnancies. Injuries may occur due to the frequency or type of sex or masturbation. Substance abuse or misuse is common as a method for enhancing or justifying sexual or interpersonal relationships.

Financial costs involve fines, fees for retaining a lawyer due to an arrest, relocating due to breakup of relationships, and being fired for behavior on the job. There may also be costs associated with pornography or prostitution.

Legal consequences are closely related to financial ones. Being arrested and jailed or imprisoned for sexually related crimes such as rape or voyeurism can occur. Some individuals steal money for drugs, love, or sexual reasons leading to incarceration.

Due to the common tendency to associate addictions with physiological or chemical addiction, many people have difficulty applying the concept of addictions to sex and love. However, available evidence shows that it is not only possible but very common for individuals to be addicted to one or more persons in love and/or sexual relationships (*Sex and Love Addicts Anonymous*, 1985). According to Peele (1975), addiction is not a chemical reaction, but an experience that grows out of an individual's ritualized subjective response to some object or person. Moreover, an individual finds security or special meaning in this experience, and believes it to be indispensable to existence. To further substantiate this point, several studies on drug addiction cited by this author have demonstrated convincingly that the addicting element is not the substance, that is, alcohol, cocaine, or tobacco, but is in the person who is addicted (see Peele, 1975, 1985). Such evidence offers an alternative view of how addictions develop, and, accordingly, how they can be arrested or treated.

THEORIES RELATED TO THE ADDICTION PROCESS

A major assumption undergirding nearly all theories of human development is that within the first year of life infants develop a strong attachment to their caretaker. According to Bowlby (1971), attachment behavior (crying, clinging, following) assures the growth and survival of the infant. There are three major conditions associated with the form and intensity of attachment behavior:

1. The condition of the child:
   —fatigue
   —hunger
   —ill health
   —pain
   —cold

2. The whereabouts and behavior of caretaker:
   —caretaker absent
   —caretaker departing
   —caretaker discouraging of proximity
3. Other environmental conditions:
   —occurrence of alarming event (e.g., death)
   —rebuffs by other adults or children (p. 313)

These conditions create attachment behavior of a very high intensity in the child, and require more than a light touch or a reassuring glance to terminate the behavior. Although attachment behavior never disappears completely, it diminishes with age. Essentially, the behavior becomes less activated as the child matures and experiences on an ongoing basis a safe and secure environment. Mahler (1968) describes the stages of child development or the psychological birth of the child as autism, symbiosis, individuation, and rapprochement. It is important to note that these stages are not clearly demarcated, but overlap. Mahler (1968) and Mahler, Pine, and Berman (1975), through extensive research on children and their families, use these stages to further highlight the importance of attachment and to explain the etiology of thwarted attachment in the child.

According to Mahler (1968), the newborn infant strives to maintain the balance experienced in the mother's womb. Therefore, from birth to two months, the newborn is totally preoccupied with personal well-being and feels no differentiation between self and the caretaker. Mahler views this *autistic phase* as normal, and explains that if the child's needs are adequately met during this time, the child moves naturally to the *symbiotic phase*. This phase extends from two months to one and one-half years of age. During this stage, the child is dimly aware of the boundary between self and the caretaker. Mahler describes this period between the child and mother as one of mutual physical and psychological interdependence.

The very critical stage of *separation-individuation* begins around 16 months and extends to three years. This period sets the stage for a separate development of self. Through practicing a series of games such as hide-and-seek, and through simply saying, "No" to the caretaker's request, the child tests the environment and the caretaker for consistency and availability. Through this process, the child learns to function autonomously. With support and encouragement from the caretaker, the child develops a strong sense of self and positive feelings about functioning independent of the caretaker.

At about age two, the child moves into a *rapprochement phase* where attachment behavior is less frequently or less intensively activated. The child's sense of self consolidates, and longer periods away from the primary caretaker can be tolerated. This healthy transition between child and primary caretaker is illustrated in Figure 16.1a, where a positive transaction assures the realization of the infant's survival and growth needs. The child feels safe and secure due to consistent nurturance, thereby experiencing a sense of trust in self and others.

A different picture will emerge, however, if the caretaker is overprotective or overcontrolling, or if the conditions that activate attachment behavior are present during this phase-specific stage of development. For example, during the separation-individuation process, the caretaker may feel rejected by the child's refusal to cooperate or tendency to run away; the caretaker may then withdraw support. As a result, the child may become overly dependent to assure the caretaker's continued support or withdraw due to fear of being engulfed by the caretaker.

More specifically, if during the autistic phase the infant's development is blocked within the first few days of life by ill health, hunger, or inadequate nurturing, the infant may experience the primary caretaker as unavailable and become locked in a symbiotic state. Psychosis occurs if the child is unable to move into the individuation phase, and neuroses may develop if movement through the individuation phase is blocked. The psychotic child, though locked in the symbiotic stage, has only a dim sense of self. The neurotic child, on the other hand, has a greater sense of self, but wavers between maintaining the sense of separateness from the safe, secure feelings of the symbiotic phase. Figure 16.1b illustrates this process. The transaction between the child and the primary caretaker is conflicted for reasons discussed earlier. As a result, the child's needs may be met on a continuum that includes tenuous care, conflictual care, or the absence of care.

(a)

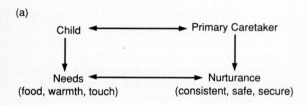

(b)

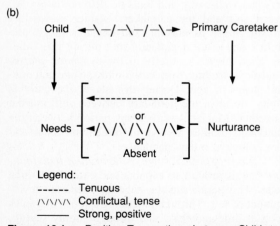

Legend:
```
------    Tenuous
/\/\/\    Conflictual, tense
          Strong, positive
```

Figure 16.1 *a.* Positive Transactions between Child and Caretaker during Early Stages of Attachment (Birth to Three Years) *b.* Nonnurturing Transactions between Child and Caretaker: Basis for Addictive Sex and Love

Memory of these processes becomes a permanent part of one's experiences, although children and adults sometimes consciously or unconsciously suppress painful memory traces associated with growing-up experiences. It follows that the roots of addictive behavior begin at birth. Individuals learn in early childhood the basic tenets of survival. In other words, certain behaviors will guarantee that needs are met. On those occasions when others were not there for children, they attempted to care for themselves. As a result, their needs were not always consistently met in the way they desired. Therefore, on an unconscious level, individuals continue to search for the ultimate need-gratifying object. This process extends from childhood into adult relationships. Because of unmet childhood needs, some people seek individuals or external experiences designed to meet unfulfilled dependency needs and to give direction to their lives.

On another level, these unmet needs perpetuate feelings of low self-esteem and inadequacy. People may become convinced that their needs do not count; that it is safer not to trust anyone; or that getting close is hurtful, unsafe, and suffocating. The paradox is that some people search for relationships or things to meet their unfulfilled needs, but they select people who fit their unconscious beliefs about their unworthiness and end up feeling more needy and unsatisfied.

According to other researchers, drug addiction develops from unresolved childhood conflicts about autonomy and dependence (Chein, 1969; Lasagna, Mosteller, von Felsinger, & Beecher, 1954; Winick, 1961). The perspective can be applied similarly to love and sex addictions. Within the framework of a social-psychological theoretical perspective, it is believed that the addictive process involving love and sex starts with these memory traces from early childhood in which tapes about low self-worth and unworthiness have been recorded. Addicted persons view life as an unenjoyable ordeal. They are pessimistic and feel incapable of impacting the environment in a positive way. They are cut off socially and emotionally and cannot establish a meaningful relationship to their environment as a whole. They believe that survival is impossible without outside support. As a result, their lives evolve around a series of chronic dependencies in relationships and/ or substances related to family, school, work, drugs, and social functioning.

In essence, the addict becomes locked into a downward spiral that results in a total breakdown, as illustrated in Figure 16.2 (Nakken, 1988). At this stage the addict has lost total control over the rate, frequency, or duration of bottom-line behavior. This loss of control always leads to negative, self-destructive consequences that can be financial, legal, or physical. For example, the bottom-line behavior may involve a large consumption of alcohol, extensive viewing of pornographic material, driving and being arrested while under the influence of alcohol, being arrested for visiting prostitutes or for displaying addictive sexual behavior in public places, persistently pursuing the object of a love addiction despite legal restraining orders, and being abusive to the body by not practicing safe sex or by attempting suicide (*Sex and Love Addicts Anonymous,* 1985). It is usually at the point of breakdown that many of these individuals seek outside help. The help may be of a professional or nonprofessional nature.

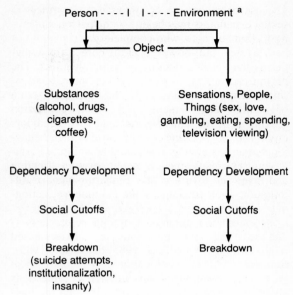

^a The person is in search of the inner self (an integrated being). When the person is cut off from the environment, the search leads to addictions such as *substances* or *sensations, people,* or *things.*

Figure 16.2. The Addiction Process

ASSESSMENT OF SEXUAL AND LOVE ADDICTIONS

It is generally recognized that addictive aspects such as wanting to feel needed and feeling close exist in many relationships. This awareness is important throughout the helping process. Halpern (1982) indicates that such aspects put individuals in touch with the best in themselves, and are self-affirming by adding strength and delight to relationships. Recognition of this common need and emotionally bonding process can encourage the practitioner to be empathic with clients who have not been able to achieve such relationships.

Sex and love addictions can be viewed on a continuum, reflecting relationships with one's spouse or companion, with a stranger, or with numerous familiar or previously unknown partners.

The use of successive or simultaneous partners in sexual encounters may be due to the person's inability to find someone who completely accepts him or her. Without fail, however, at the core of the addiction is the person's feeling of incompleteness. The person, according to Peele (1975), uses relationships compulsively to seal off the inner self from a frightening environment. The client population seeking help for addictive sex and love behaviors reports not only feeling out of control of their behavior, but also engaging in acts that are entirely unsatisfying. For many, there is a split between affection and love, and love and sex. Embarrassment or humiliation often accompany the compulsive, acting-out behavior.

A common agreement among researchers is that sex and love addictions are anxiety-based (Halpern, 1982; Quadland, 1985; Schaeffer, 1985). Some theoreticians view the anxiety as ontological in nature, stemming from individuals' questions about the purpose and meaning in life and the feeling of being incomplete in themselves (Laing, 1965). Others view it as related to faulty upbringing, while others see it as a combination of both (Peele, 1975). It has been shown, however, that this search for purpose and meaning is intimately connected to messages from important social institutions and significant others such as the family about self-worth, self-identity, and confidence in self and others. The goal of the person feeling this incompleteness is to find some way to achieve wholeness. The sex or love addict seeks to achieve this completeness by becoming symbiotically attached to the object of the addiction. This symbiotic attachment may also be viewed as merging with the other person. To gain a better perspective on the role of anxiety and the dynamics involved in assessing the sex and love addictive process, several factors should be considered in assessment including the client's family, environment, and quality of other intimate relationships.

The Role of the Family

It is a generally accepted tenet in this society that families provide for the physical, cognitive, emotional, and spiritual needs of their members. This not only includes financial security but also the maintenance of a household, the provision of food, and the feeling that individual members are valued and loved. Additionally, the family is expected to provide a foundation for the individual's development of social and emotional ties at work and in the community (Logan, 1989). Obviously, families have a great impact on how children develop and experience their world. Take, for example, the situation of Audry and her girlfriend Jane:

> Audry's parents were middle-income professionals who were forever attempting to "keep up with the Joneses." Audry had to have the best of everything and would associate only with "the right kind of people." Not only was she overindulged with material things, but she was overprotected and never allowed to think for herself. She had two best friends: Jane, of whom her parents did not quite approve, and Reggie, a young man from a background similar to Audry's. Jane's was a low-income family. Jane's father's job kept him away from the family, while her mother, in addition to working split shifts at a factory, assumed both parenting roles for Jane and her younger brother. Jane described her mother as a nag who made her assume nearly total care of her younger brother. Reggie was the middle child of three brothers. His parents constantly talked about the importance of excelling and being the best at whatever a person chooses. The family is very achievement-oriented. His older brother is considered the family's "brain" and one day will be a medical doctor. Inadvertently, Reggie is compared to his brother. As a result he feels pressured either to be as good as or to go beyond his brother's achievement.

One could easily conclude that the parents in these families want the very best for their children, but in each instance the children are being deprived of their sense of autonomy and a strong sense of identity and confidence. In essence, a child's view of the world is generally a reflection of the parents' attitudes, beliefs, and values. Numerous case studies, including the example described above, have revealed that parental attitudes and/or the home atmosphere are common factors in the addiction process. In completing assessments with clients, it is important to view these factors in combination with other childhood traumas such as death and divorce, sexual or other forms of abuse and neglect, how an individual copes with love or sexual addictions in significant others, sibling rivalries, and special treatment of one child over the others by parents.

In providing their social histories, clients may not be aware that these childhood experiences are shared by other families and that they are endemic to the general culture of today. Furthermore, the impact of advanced technology has resulted in families being more isolated from natural supports such as extended family members. Workers should assess the extent to which clients' families have been able to overcome their isolation or to cope with it in functional ways that increase children's nurturing and autonomous experiences. If a client's parents have tended to orchestrate their children's lives in ways that do not allow the children to explore their world with a sense of joyous wonderment or to be free from fear and anxiety, the client may have grown up being distrustful and anxious as an adult. Such individuals are more likely to view their strengths and lives as being controlled by a force outside themselves, setting the stage for love and sexual addictions if such patterns are not addressed early.

The Role of the Environment

The individual's environment is an all-encompassing concept that incorporates several levels of complex functioning such as the (a) social-cultural, (b) physical, and (c) social networks (see Figure 16.3). These elements have the potential for being nurturing or nonnurturing (Germain & Gitterman, 1980), depending on the balance between debilitating social issues such as family violence, AIDS, adolescent and adult substance abuse, crimes and adolescent parenthood, and more positive environmental forces.

It is suggested that something very valuable was lost in society's transition from a preindustrial era to a modern era. This valuable possession is described as an internal (inner) strength—a strength that comes from a belief in the connectedness between the individual and the environment. This belief was the foundation for a joyous and competence-based existence. In essence, people took pleasure in the simple acts of sharing with friends and relatives, in work and play, and in being alive. This view also included an existence that reflected the ability and confidence of people to master or change their environment in ways that were beneficial to themselves and others.

To escape the current empty and constricting existence that some individuals experience, they seek solutions outside themselves. It follows that the sources of sex and love addictions can be found in various aspects of the environment, that is, schools, the neighborhood, significant others, and the individuals themselves, as noted in the following situation involving love addictions:

Frank is a 35-year-old graduate student, studying art. He had never been married. He has a younger brother (32 years old) who was married, and a sister (29). Their father was a builder-contractor whose business was not the success he had envisioned, but it served to support the family. He was a mistrustful, angry man. Everything had to be done in a prescribed, perfectionistic way. Although he was a procrastinator, he demanded that his children do things on time and in a certain way. Frank's mother was sickly and no one ever talked about the cause of her illness. She relied totally on her husband. Although she experienced his behavior as frustrating, she stifled her feelings and resorted to silence. She also encouraged the children to submit and not to question their father.

The family lived a fairly isolated existence. There was no contact with extended family members. Involvement in community activities was nearly nonexistent. The children were also encouraged to keep friends at a minimum. Frank grew up in a very controlled environment. He was nonassertive and approached his life in a task-oriented, organized way. He never considered challenging any form of authority. He was easy to get along with and was liked by peers. He dealt with differences and his father's bickering by retreating within himself, into his room, or to the solitude of a small neighborhood park.

Frank graduated from college, but immediately joined the U.S. Army to avoid going into his father's business as was expected. He discovered his love for painting while in the army, but also came close to a dishonorable discharge for going on drinking binges. This was one of the ways he dealt with anxious feelings. Upon discharge from the army, he never seemed to connect with anything of substance. He wandered from job to job and from addictive relationship to another. Frank's brother was dubbed ''Mr. Love-Them-and-Leave-Them.'' He was considered outgoing, charismatic, and the successful one in the family. His sister suffered from being sporadically depressed for most of her adult life. She had never been involved in a serious relationship. It is suspected that she was sexually abused over a period of time by her father.

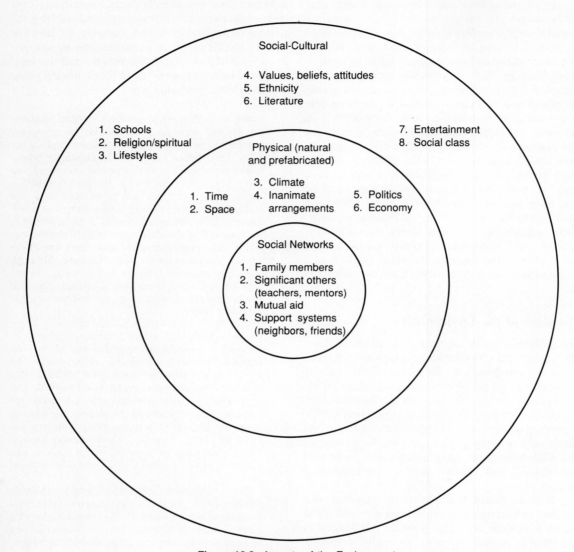

Figure 16.3. Aspects of the Environment

The dynamics illustrated in the above situation reflect not only the impact of the environment on the potential for sex and love addiction, but focus attention on those critical factors that must be considered in the assessment process. It is important to note that many of these influences on Frank's intense attachments to current partners are subtle.

With regard to the influence of the environment on addicted behavior, it is implicit in Frank's situation that, at a minimum, children need an open, supportive family environment in which to grow and develop into autonomously functioning adults. An active and supportive social network enriches the overall functioning of the family. In the case of Frank's family, the support of extended family members, that is, grandparents, uncles, aunts, and

ship, who ends it, and who was the dominant partner. This process serves to bring to the surface insight and awareness about patterns that are overlooked or minimized. Frank begins the relationship review by chronicling his life experience. The major revelation of this process for Frank was related to the types of women that he selected for partners (strong and assertive). He also learned about his inevitable breaking off of the addictive relationships because of what he describes as their "bitchiness" that made him feel "less than a man." These women were the direct opposite of his mother. In general, the life review is complemented by a relationship log which Frank was asked to keep. Support between sessions is provided through a singles group. Frank felt that the singles group would be more appropriate to his needs than an SLAA support group.

The Role of the Social Worker

Working with love and sexually addicted individuals is a unique challenge. On one level, the challenge is related to the diverse pattern of behaviors presented by this group. For example, the presenting concerns may include a wife who compulsively lives for and through her husband and children; a husband who finds it impossible to refrain from involvement in extramarital affairs; a college student who shares her apartment with a man she believes she cannot live without (a man who comes and goes as he pleases, humiliates her in front of her friends, and demands that she not see anyone except him); or a young writer whose sexual acting-out has forced him to frequent the most dangerous pick-up places, and who is fearful that he may contract a life-threatening STD or be arrested.

On another level, the challenge may be related to the worker's level of competence. Sex and sexuality are not an area of practice in which many social workers have expertise (Gochros, 1972). Additionally, to work with interpersonally or sexually addicted clients, the social worker must not only be self-aware, but possess the capacity to observe self by standing back and questioning the meaning of what is going on within the work with the client. This quality is useful in helping the worker to maintain a balanced perspective about personal fears about closeness, separateness, or the expression of feelings and needs (Schaeffer, 1985).

The practitioner must guard against the treatment becoming a substitute addiction. Essentially, this substitution is similar to an individual's switching from one form of drug or food addiction to another as a means of attempting to break the addictive cycle. It is also similar to a person's becoming a dry drunk; the drinking is stopped, but the person does not recover from the accompanying dysfunctional communication and relationship patterns. Although this dependence on the practitioner is viewed as necessary for the client's movement toward growth, Halpern (1982) points out the worker's ethical role in eliminating the dependence as the client's sense of self-worth and personhood are restored.

It is evident from the foregoing that the social worker is dealing with complex and sometimes entrenched behaviors. Therefore, it is important to recognize those persons who are suffering from a sexual dysfunction rather than an addiction or those who are in the breakdown stage of the addiction (see Figure 16.2). In the first instance, the worker may simply not have the necessary skills for dealing with a sexual dysfunction; and in the second instance, the person is simply not yet available to treatment. Hospitalization or inpatient treatment may be the treatment of choice in these cases. In both instances, a referral to a more specialized service is required.

OPPORTUNITIES FOR PREVENTION

Throughout this chapter, addiction has been described as a process. In this context, patterns of behaviors are shaped by social and cultural forces including especially the mass media. Therefore, any attempt to support or sustain non-addictive lifestyles requires educational and recreation programs and activities that not only address individual change but society and its major institutions (Peele, 1975). For example, social agencies, schools, and religious organizations may develop educational growth programs that enhance self-esteem and identity development. The media can address the topic through public awareness *and* entertainment programs. Likewise, families may also need to be supported in their natural tendencies to affirm individual members' independence, sense of competence, joy, and confidence in experiencing life to its fullest. The essential focus in creating an environment in which healthy relationships exist is on building individual inner strengths and a sense of purpose. This focus must be encouraged and nurtured. It is "only through working hard at learning to do something well, something which is important to us and to other people, that we can generate the competence and self-possession that will make a difference in our lives" (Peele, 1975, p. 228).

CONCLUSION

Sex and love addictions are complex problems. They stem, in part, from a variety of forces within the environment. Many of these forces foster an empty and joyless existence. Some relate to the individual, the family, societal pressures, and cultural norms evident in the emphasis that the mass media place on immediate, physical pleasures in isolation of caring relationships. The journey out of sex and love addictions is equally complex. It is a process that requires time, effort, faith, and commitment. It involves the assumption of responsibility for self and the development of confidence and competence in terms of abilities and self-worth. The social work practitioner has much to contribute to this self-affirming process that involves many of the principles that guide recovery from other addictions. In addition, interventions must be focused on the object of the addiction, which in this case may be the reinforcer of the client's dysfunctional cycle of addiction. Available treatment approaches, including behavior modification strategies and group process, provide support and guidance on this personal journey to healthy relationships.

REFERENCES

Bowlby, J. (1971). *Attachment and loss.* (Vol. 1, Attachment). New York: Penguin Books.
Chein, I. (1969). Psychological functions of drug use. In H. Steinberg (Ed.), *Scientific basis of drug dependence* (pp. 13–30). London: J. & A. Churchill.
Forward, S. (1986). *Men who hate women and women who love them.* New York: Bantam Books.
Fromm, E. (1956). *The art of loving,* New York: Harper.
Germain, C. B., & Gitterman, A. (1980). *The life model.* New York: Columbia University Press.
Gochros, H. (1972). Social work's sexual blinders. In H. Gochros & L. Schultz (Eds.), *Human sexuality and social work* (pp. 85–92). New York: Association Press.
Halpern, H. M. (1982). *How to break your addiction to a person.* New York: Bantam Books.
The heat is on: Sex, romance, love and lust in the '90s [Special issue]. (1989, May). *Ms., XVII.*
Hooked on love? (1988). *Essence, 19,* 140–143.
Hunter, M. (1988). *What is sex addiction?* Center City, MN: Hazelden Foundation.
Laing, R. D. (1965). *The divided self.* Middlesex, England: Penguin Books.
Lasagna, L., Mosteller, F., von Felsinger, J. M., & Beecher, H. K. (1954). A study of the placebo response. *American Journal of Medicine, 16,* 770–779.
Logan, S. (1989). Diversity among Black families: Assessing structure and function. In S. Logan, E. Freeman, & R. McRoy (Eds.), *Social work practice with black families* (pp. 73–96). New York: Longman.
Mahler, M. (1968). *On human symbiosis and the vicissitudes of individuation: Infantile psychosis.* New York: International Universities Press.
Mahler, M., Pine, F., & Bergman, A. (1975). *The psychological birth of the human infant: Symbiosis and individuation.* New York: Basic Books.
McGoldrick, M., & Gerson, R. (1985). *Genograms in family assessment.* New York: Norton.
Nakken, C. (1988). *The addictive personality: Roots, rituals, and recovery.* Center City, MN: Hazelden Foundation.
Norwood, R. (1985). *Women who love too much.* New York: Pocket Books.
Orford, J. (1985). *Excessive appetites: A psychological view of addictions.* New York: Wiley.
Peele, S. (1975). *Love and addiction.* New York: Taplinger.
Peele, S. (1976). *Love and addiction.* New York: Signet.
Peele, S. (1985). *The meaning of addiction: Compulsive experience and its interpretation.* Lexington, MA: Lexington Books.
Quadland, M. C. (1985). Compulsive sexual behavior: Definition of a problem and an approach to treatment. *Journal of Sex and Marital Therapy, 11,* 121–132.
Russanoff, P. (1983). *Why do I think I am nothing without a man?* New York: Bantam Books.
Schaeffer, B. (1985). *Is it love or is it addiction?* Center City: MN: Hazelden Foundation.
Sex and love addicts anonymous. (1985). Boston: The Augustine Fellowship, Sex and Love Addicts Anonymous, Fellowship-Wide Service.
Sex and love addiction: 40 questions for self-diagnosis. (1985). Boston: The Augustine Fellowship, Sex and Love Addicts Anonymous, Fellowship-Wide Service.
Vaughan, F., & Walsh, R. (Eds.). (1983). *Accept this gift* (p. 90). Los Angeles: Jeremy P. Tarcher.

Winick, C. (1961). Physician narcotic addicts. *Social Problems, 9,* 174–186.

SUPPLEMENTAL READING LIST

Anderson, A. K., & Ream, J. K. (1986). *Struggling for wholeness.* Thomas Nelson, Publishers.
This book is written by twin sisters who talk about their vulnerability and strength in a series of subjects including sexuality, assertiveness, friendship, and change. This is a book for everyone; it is a true story about being human.

Beck, A. T. (1988). *Love is never enough.* New York: Harper & Row.
Beck examines the hidden as well as obvious problems in relationships: negative thinking, idealization and disillusionment, rigid rules and expectations, life-changing decisions not discussed, and anger and hostility that can develop from miscommunication.

Gordon, B. (1979). *I am dancing as fast as I can.* New York: Harper & Row.
This book painfully details both Gordon's relationship with a misogynistic lover and her encounters with ineffective professionals from whom she sought help.

Lerner, H. G. (1986). *The dance of anger.* New York: Harper & Row.
The book explores the causes and pattern of anger and provides a helpful guide to understand and reduce anger in important relationships.

Tschirhart, L. F., & Donovan, M. E. (1985). *Women and self-esteem.* New York: Penguin Books.
An excellent and comprehensive look at how society and family interact to damage female self-worth and emotional well-being.

CHAPTER 17

Tobacco Addiction: Correlates, Prevention, and Treatment

Michael S. Moncher

Steven P. Schinke

Gary W. Holden
*School of Social Work,
Columbia University*

The pharmacologic and behavioral processes that determine tobacco addiction are similar to those that determine addiction to drugs such as heroin and cocaine.

Robert E. Windom, M.D.
Assistant Secretary of Health

Tobacco use, including both smoked and smokeless tobacco, continues at unacceptably high rates in the United States, despite strong nationwide prevention efforts begun more than 20 years ago. As with other addictive behaviors, attempts at both prevention and treatment have fallen short of initial expectations. Examining prevalence rates alone does not clearly indicate why patterns of usage have increased in high-risk groups or the complex factors that are associated with heavy usage. These questions support the need for a more thorough analysis and wholistic perspective about those phenomena. Accordingly, this chapter reviews prevalence rates and patterns of tobacco usage in the general population and in certain high-risk groups. Morbidity and mortality rates as well as other consequences are included. The process of addiction and appropriate prevention and treatment strategies are discussed, while a program example is used to illustrate those strate-

gies. A final section focuses on the role of social workers in such programs.

TOBACCO USE IN AMERICA

Prevalence Rates

Although population prevalence rates have been declining, in 1987, 32% of all males and 27% of all females reported current use of smoked tobacco. More than 8 out of 10 smokers begin before age 21. Further, the proportion of heavy smokers has been increasing within the smoking population, even as the total number of smokers decreases (Schwartz, 1987).

Smoking rates are particularly troublesome among women and African Americans, with recent data indicating that women under 23 years of age represent the fastest growing population of smokers, and African American men and women currently smoke at higher rates than whites (32% versus 29%, and 25% versus 24%, respectively). Among Hispan-

---

Preparation of this chapter was supported by the National Institute on Drug Abuse (DA 03277) and the National Cancer Institute (CA 29640; CA 44903).

ic females, smoking prevalence rates range from 24% for Mexican-American and Cubans, to 30% for Puerto-Ricans. Rates for Hispanic males are higher, ranging from 40% to 43%. Northern plains Native Americans have higher reported prevalence rates across gender, ranging from 42 to 70%, while southwestern Native Americans report rates lower or comparable to other racial groups (Kellie, 1989).

Smokeless tobacco rates are equally disquieting, indicating a trend toward increased incidence of use. In the 1985 National Institute of Drug Abuse (NIDA) National Household Survey, males reported lifetime prevalence rates almost seven times those of females (20% and 3% respectively). Rause (1989), interpolating from that sample, estimates that 11.1% of the population has tried smokeless tobacco at least once, with 2.9% engaging in daily use. Whites reported higher lifetime prevalence rates (12%) than African Americans and Hispanics (9% and 5% respectively). Especially troublesome are high and increasing rates among northwestern Native American youth, reported by Hall and Dexter (1988) and confirmed by the present authors' research (Moncher, Schinke, Holden, & Aragon, 1989). Age is also an important factor in usage rates. In a recent study involving over 1900 subjects in five states (46% female; mean age 10.3), 48% of males and 26% of females reported ever using smokeless tobacco (Rause, 1989).

Smokeless tobacco is either sniffed, chewed, or held in the cheek pouch. Produced and sold in snuff and smokeless tobacco forms, smokeless products are primarily used by young adults, in part, it is believed, because they lend themselves to clandestine administration.

Snuff, a finely ground tobacco, is distributed in small pouches or in loose powder form. The snuff user either places a "pinch" between the gum and lip area, or inhales the power intranasally. Chewing tobacco is a coarsely cut tobacco sold in loose, plug, or pouch form. The tobacco is usually gathered up and placed in the cheek area next to the teeth and gum, where it is sucked. If purchased in the "plug" form, the tobacco is chewed (Christen, 1980).

Excessive salivation occurs in users of both forms of smokeless tobacco, necessitating repeated spitting (although many chewers swallow the saliva). Nicotine and other chemicals in the tobacco are absorbed into the body through the nasal or oral mucosa. The snuff or smokeless tobacco may be kept in the mouth for several hours before it is replaced. The tobacco product may, in some cases, remain in the mouth for up to 24 hours. Many users report daily use of the product for decades or more (Jones & Moberg, 1988; Christen, 1985).

In recent years, as requirements surrounding smoked tobacco have become more stringent, tobacco companies have greatly increased smokeless tobacco promotion targeted at youth. Not only are certain products packaged specifically for this market (e.g., Skoal Bandits), but also the tobacco may contain numerous chemical additives to increase sweetness and enhance flavor to make the product more appealing to the youthful consumer. Federal reporting requirements for additives in smokeless tobacco products are not as rigorous as those for smoked tobacco, making it difficult to ascertain which of the potentially thousands of additives are present in a given smokeless product.

The Surgeon General, in the most recent Report (Department of Health and Human Services, 1988a), highlights the following broad trends:

> The overall prevalence of smoking in the United States decreased from 36.7% in 1976 (52.4 million adults) to 30.4 percent in 1985 (51.1 million adults). In 1985, the mean reported number of cigarettes smoked per day was 21.8 for male smokers and 18.1 for female smokers. Smoking is more common in lower socioeconomic categories (blue-collar workers or unemployed persons, less educated persons, and lower income groups) than in higher socioeconomic categories. . . . An estimated 18.7 percent of high school seniors reported daily use of cigarettes in 1986. The prevalence of daily use of one or more cigarettes among high school seniors declined between 1975 and 1986 by approximately 35%. . . . Since 1976, the smoking prevalence among females has consistently been slightly higher than among males. The use of cigars and pipes has declined 80 percent since 1964. Smokeless tobacco use has increased substantially among young men and has declined among older men since 1975. An estimated 8.2 % of 17–19 year-old men were users of smokeless tobacco in 1936. (p. 16)

Morbidity and Mortality

Warner (1989), reporting findings from a recent study by the American Cancer Society, indicated that 390,000 American deaths—20% of all disease-related deaths in 1985—were attributable to smoked tobacco. Chronic obstructive pulmonary disease (COPD) was the largest single cause of smoking-related mortality (82 percent of all cases of this disease), followed by cancer, coronary heart disease, and stroke. Of additional concern are complications of hypertension, reproductive disorders, and gastrointestinal disorders. Moreover, rates of chronic bronchitis, chronic sinusitis, emphysema, arteriosclerotic heart disease and peptic ulcer disease are higher among smokers than nonsmokers (Schwartz, 1987).

Smokeless tobacco is also associated with numerous health risks and the literature documenting these consequences is extensive (Blachley & Knochel, 1980; Greer & Poulson, 1983; Squier, 1984; Shah, Sarode, & Bhide, 1985; Schroeder & Chen, 1985; Bernstein, 1986). Nicotine, an addictive substance contained in smoked and smokeless tobacco, may also lead to physiological dependence.

Use of smokeless tobacco has been linked to various cancers. Hall and Dexter (1988) note:

> Many epidemiological studies have found a close correlation between the use of smokeless tobacco, and the frequency of oral, esophageal, and pharyngeal cancer. . . . Oral cancer, in 1984, reported to be the 7th leading type of cancer in the United States, is found to be a greater risk among smokeless tobacco users than among smokers. In one study, the increased risk of oral cancer among long term users was reported to be reaching 50%. (p. 2)

Leukoplakia, a white thickening of the oral mucosa, is commonly found among smokeless tobacco users (Greer & Poulson, 1983). Leukoplakia has been found to convert to squamous cell carcinoma. Found even among the youngest of snuff and smokeless users, leukoplakia may signal the onset of oral cancer.

Additionally, snuff and smokeless tobacco use are associated with tooth loss and gum disease (Greer & Poulson, 1983; Squier, 1984). The act of placing the tobacco in the cheek pouch in contact with teeth and gums erodes the gum, causes inflammation, weakens the tooth structure, and causes tooth loss. Inflammation of the gum and exposure of the tooth root contribute to the discomfort and the pain. Further, such flavoring constituents as sodium and sweeteners that are added to smokeless tobacco may lead to hypertension, poor glucose control, and dental caries (Hampson, 1985; McPhaul, Punzi, Sandy, Birganelli, Rude, & Kaplan, 1984).

Mattson and Winn (1989) conclude that, to date, there is no commonly accepted estimate of the percentage of oral cancers associated with smokeless tobacco use. Thus reliable mortality projections are not yet possible. None of the existing literature discusses the effects of smokeless tobacco on the nasal mucosa. It is assumed, however, that similar damaging effects to those documented for other inhaled substances (e.g., cocaine) are likely.

Other Consequences

While morbidity due to smoking has been well documented in the literature, what is less often discussed are the economic consequences. In a review of findings from a number of studies (Schwartz, 1987), estimates that losses in 1976 resulting from such factors as lost production, direct health care costs, and fire totalled 27.5 billion dollars. In 1980, the overall cost was projected to be $47.5 billion. Estimates of the additional sick leave used by smokers when compared to nonsmokers have ranged from 23 percent to 50 percent. To the authors' knowledge, no such estimates are available for smokeless tobacco use.

Additionally, familial and societal consequences of passive smoke should be noted. Negative health consequences among children and spouses of smokers include higher rates of bronchitis, pneumonia, and heart disease; impaired pulmonary function; and increases in frequent coughs (Byrd, Shapiro, & Schiedermayer, 1989).

Schwartz (1987) notes that numerous studies have documented disturbances in nonsmokers from smoke in the workplace. *The Surgeon General's Report on the Health Consequences of Involuntary Smoking* (Department of Health and Human Services, 1986) concluded that mere separation of smokers from nonsmokers was not likely to eliminate harmful consequences. Tobacco smoke contains numerous carcinogens and other toxic agents that may be hazardous to nonsmokers who are regularly and randomly exposed, with decreased lung function noted as a potential consequence (Collishaw, Kirkbridge, & Wigle, 1984). Investigators, examining acute effects of environmental tobacco smoke, have noted that from 30 to 70 percent of indoor carbon monoxide and other noxious agents in the workplace were due to tobacco smoke, 25 to 40 percent of employees were bothered by second-hand smoke, and a similar percentage suffered from eye irritation in the workplace (Weber, 1984; Eriksen, 1986). It is clear that the consequences discussed in this section affect users as well as other individuals in their environments. These consequences make it important to clarify and increase understanding of the process whereby tobacco addictions develop.

THE ADDICTION PROCESS

Addiction has come to be more broadly defined in recent years. The present authors take the position that both smoked and smokeless tobacco use may lead to addiction due to repeated exposure to nicotine, an addictive substance. Nicotine addiction does not differ significantly from any other addiction in terms of etiology, progression, and treatment. Certainly there are substance-specific addictive consequences that require differential emphases in treatment, just as would be the case between, for example, marijuana and cocaine addiction. Further, the licit nature of tobacco use and the attendant advertising must, as with alcohol, also be considered in assessment and treatment.

Evidence of Dependence and the Abstinence Withdrawal Syndrome

Any earlier debates regarding the generally addictive properties of tobacco seem to have been put to rest convincingly by the most recent Surgeon General's Report, entitled *Nicotine Addiction* (Department of Health & Human Services, 1988b):

1. Cigarettes and other forms of tobacco are addictive. Patterns of tobacco use are regular and compulsive, and a withdrawal syndrome usually accompanies tobacco abstinence.
2. Nicotine is the drug in tobacco that causes addiction. Specifically, nicotine is psychoactive ("mood altering") and can provide pleasurable effects. Nicotine can serve as a reinforcer to motivate tobacco-seeking and tobacco-using behavior. Tolerance develops to actions of nicotine such that repeated use results in diminished effects and can be accompanied by increased intake. Nicotine also causes physical dependence characterized by a withdrawal syndrome

that usually accompanies nicotine abstinence. (p. 215)

This position is further reinforced by the DSM-III-R (American Psychiatric Association, 1987), which classifies nicotine as a substance whose use may result in dependence, in the same fashion as do substances such as alcohol, amphetamines, cocaine, sedatives, opioids, and others. Both nicotine dependence (305.10) and nicotine withdrawal (292.00) are detailed in the diagnostic system and a comparison of the requisite classification criteria shows only substance-specific differences.

While DSM-III-R provides a diagnostic nosology for assessment of the presence or absence of nicotine dependence or withdrawal syndromes, it is less useful in terms of providing a framework for treatment. In the authors' view, assessment and treatment of addictive behaviors (as is the case for all social work related treatment activities) are reciprocal processes. The social worker working with client systems uses each component to inform the other. Thus, assessment is a continuous monitoring process leading first to initial contracting and treatment planning. In such a system, treatment will be responsive to data gathered by the clinician in the ongoing assessment process, just as data gathering will be guided by treatment goals, objectives, and results.

Further, the DSM-III-R classification system does not provide the practitioner with the fully balanced, biopsychosocial perspective that is a requisite for the extensive and broad-ranging data-gathering techniques likely to provide the most relevant and efficient formulation of initial and continuing treatment stratagem. Donovan's (1988) definition of addiction is especially useful to the practitioner in conceptualizing both assessment and treatment:

"Addiction" is seen as a complex, progressive behavior pattern having biological, psychological, sociological, and behavioral components. What sets this behavior pattern apart from others is the individual's overwhelmingly pathological involvement in or attachment to it, subjective compulsion to continue it, and reduced ability to exert personal control over it. (pp. 6–7)

From this theoretical perspective, addiction may be viewed as the result of a process in which multiple variables interact over time in such a way as to foster the initiation, progression, and maintenance of a behavior. A number of antecedent and consequent conditions may prompt and maintain use, including physiological elements such as genetic predilection, tolerance, and withdrawal; cognitive elements such as positive expectancies regarding future use of the substance and rationalizations about using substances; affective states such as depression and hopelessness; sociological forces including varying levels of community modeling of the behavior and, in the case of tobacco, widespread promotional campaigns; and external systems (e.g., family, social network, workplace, community). The frequency, duration, and pattern of substance abuse behaviors, as well as types and quantities of substances consumed, may depend on some or all of these factors (Bauman, Koch, & Lentz, 1989).

Acquisition Patterns and Associated Characteristics

Smokeless tobacco use is typically a male phenomenon that tends toward highest prevalence among 12 to 25-year-olds. Generally, white males use more often than African American or Hispanic males. Western Native American males appear to use at exceptionally high rates, and among certain Native American groups, adolescent female use rates surpass male use rates in the population at large (Moncher, Schinke, Holden, & Aragon, 1989).

The authors' work with northwestern elementary and junior high school populations of mixed ethnic/racial backgrounds leads to the impressionistic conclusion that, as noted above, smokeless tobacco use likely begins at an earlier age than smoked tobacco. This is especially the pattern among high-risk, lower socioeconomic status males in rural settings where its use is more normative. While data regarding age of onset are conflicting, the issue of varied geographic norms has received some support from data about weekly use during the past year, collected by NIDA in its 1985 National Household Survey. These data indicated that 1.6 percent of respondents residing in large metropolitan areas used smokeless tobacco weekly, compared to 2.7 percent and 5.1 percent in small metropolitan and non-metropolitan areas, respectively (Department of Health and Human Services, 1988a).

While researchers have attempted to specify psychosocial correlates and provide onset data and

use rates regarding smokeless use, to date the literature does not seem to provide a coherent, generalizable model. This may be due to several factors. First, because interest in smokeless prevention and treatment is a fairly recent phenomenon, and prevalence rates are substantially lower than are noted for smoked tobacco, research to date does not allow the formulation of conclusions that are salient across populations. Second, given the predominant research focus on high-risk groups, the lack of uniformity of variables studied, and the general absence of replication studies within and across populations, all but the most tentative conclusions are suspect (Jones & Moberg, 1988; Edmundson, Glover, Alston, & Holbert, 1987; Ary, 1989; Schinke, Schilling, Gilchrist, Ashby, & Kitajima, 1989).

However, certain factors that have been identified seem worthy of mention, in part because they are supported by more general theories of acquisition that cut across substances, including smoked tobacco (Holden, Moncher, & Schinke, in press; Moncher, Holden & Schinke, 1989; Newcomb, Maddahian, Skager, & Bentler, 1987; Kandel, 1982; Oettling, Beauvais, & Edwards, 1988). Smokeless users have been found to be more reserved and less socially outgoing, more conforming, and less sentimental than nonusers (Edmunson, Glover, Alston & Holbert, 1987). In addition, being white, living in a non-two-parent home, using cigarettes and alcohol at higher rates, performing less well in school, engaging in more delinquent and deviant behavior, and having higher levels of team sports participation appear to be associated with smokeless use (Jones & Moberg, 1988).

Smoked tobacco initiation has been more exhaustively researched, allowing some generalizable conclusions to be drawn. Early and midadolescents have reported that situations where they felt pressured to smoke or started smoking often occurred in the home and involved other individuals, primarily peers. Further, persistent youthful experimental smokers have reported initial smoking experiences as significantly more pleasurable (physiologically and emotionally) than minimal experimenters. The persistent experimenters were also more likely to have planned to smoke in advance and to accept offered cigarettes with no hesitation (Friedman, Lichtenstein, & Biglan, 1985).

The most recent high school senior survey sponsored by NIDA found that the initiation of daily smoking typically occurs in junior high school.

Fifty-seven percent of high school seniors who smoke daily began before age 14. Factors that seem to differentiate among high school seniors who smoke include geographical location, intentions regarding higher education, and academic standing. Among students smoking a pack or more daily, 95 percent reported having used an illicit drug. This group of smokers was 13 times as likely as nonsmokers to use an illicit drug other than marijuana. Further, this group of smokers was 11 times more likely than nonsmokers to use alcohol daily (Johnston, Bachman, & O'Malley, 1988).

A number of studies have reported characteristics of youth at high risk for experimentation and ongoing use of smoked tobacco. As noted above, many of these characteristics are applicable to the use of smokeless tobacco as well. In a large, longitudinal study that was representative, Chassin, Presson, Sherman, Corty, and Olshavsky (1984) note that:

> They are relatively nonconventional, have higher attitudinal tolerance for deviance, are more external in locus of control, have lower expectations for attaining academic success, and have family and peer environments that are relatively lower in personal controls. Moreover, these adolescents are in environments with more smoking models, and they overestimate the extent of smoking by adults and teenagers. Finally, these high risk adolescents have stronger intentions to smoke and more positive attitudes towards smoking. (p. 238)

Across virtually all age groups, more of those reporting cigarette use in the past month also reported use of other psychoactive substances than did nonsmokers.

PREVENTION AND TREATMENT ISSUES

Given the licit nature of tobacco use, and a traditional social work mandate to focus on client-defined problems, areas in which social workers are likely to be engaged in active intervention programs to curb tobacco use are limited. There is virtually no likelihood, for example, of a social worker's being involved with a mandated client around smoking or smokeless tobacco cessation issues. Consequently, the focus in this section is on those aspects of practice where social workers are likely to come in contact with clients who either desire to stop using tobacco and/or whose medical condition proscribes continued use.

Opportunities for Focus on Tobacco Use

There may be a number of situations where the social worker might be involved in delivering a smoking cessation intervention when, for example, an agency, EAP (Employee Assistance Program), hospital, or other organization decides to offer smoking cessation programs to its constituents. Alternatively, larger scale community health programs (e.g., Stanford Heart Disease Prevention Program or Minnesota Heart Health Program) may contain smoking cessation components. In either case, the natural role for the social worker would involve the design and implementation of intervention.

Too, workers may come in contact with clients in inpatient or outpatient settings for whom continued tobacco use poses a more significant, even a grave, threat to health. Cardiac patients, those suffering from hypertensive and respiratory disorders, and, more recently, those clients who suffer compromised immune systems resulting from diseases such as HIV infection, ARC, or AIDS are examples where intervention should be explored, even in the absence of an initial desire on the part of the client to consider habits regarding tobacco use as problematic. Similarly, workers in a variety of settings including hospitals, clinics, agencies, mental health centers, EAPs, and HMOs (Health Maintenance Organizations) may be involved in pregnancy counseling for women from various age and racial/ethnic groups. In such settings, workers may provide direct client services, including education and group or individual work, toward cessation efforts on behalf of the client and her unborn child.

In such cases, depending upon the treatment setting, the worker will act either as a collaborator, an advocate, or both, working with or engaging other members of the client's health care team toward cessation efforts. As Schwartz (1987) has noted:

> Physician advice and counseling do encourage many patients to attempt to break their cigarette habit. The number who succeed in quitting after a brief warning is small, but the yield is large. When physicians give a stronger message, give tips on how to quit, or provide support, results improve. Quit rates for patients with pulmonary or cardiac disease who are

told to stop smoking are substantial. Approximately 38 million smokers in the United States visit a doctor each year. If all doctors counseled all of their patients who smoked on how to stop and were successful with just 4 percent, the yield would approximate 1.5 million ex-smokers. (p. 127)

In many of these cases, the social worker may need to view the physician as a client. Until recently, physicians were not likely to confront patients about smoking. Some of the factors affecting physicians' behavior in this regard may have been their low self-efficacy regarding counseling ability, a lack of knowledge about relevant techniques, their perceptions of clients as resistant to change, the absence of incentive (in the form of reimbursement) for provision of such services, and the lack of positive reinforcement gained from quickly visible results, unlike the more traditional therapies physicians typically provide (Schwartz, 1987). Moreover, medical training most often does not include significant components dealing with prevention, or the utilization of cognitive and behavioral techniques for the amelioration of health problems. While some positive change is taking place within the medical profession, much work is needed and the social worker as advocate, educator, or collaborator may do much to further this movement.

In schools and adolescent treatment settings, workers may explore individual and group interventions in the service of smoking and smokeless tobacco cessation. Such treatment modalities are atypical today, in part due to a lack of funding and demonstrably effective cessation interventions for this age group. The adolescent smoker, as noted above, is often more recalcitrant than are the nonsmoking peers. Given the characteristics often noted for this stage of development, including poor impulse control and a tendency toward feelings of immortality, this population is particularly intractable to cessation efforts. Efforts must therefore be doubled to reach adolescent tobacco users before habituation becomes entrenched due to the interaction between the reinforcing nature of nicotine and the vulnerability of this population to a variety of pressures to initiate tobacco use.

The Assessment Process

Given that the presenting problem will not often be tobacco use cessation, the issue may emerge only as assessment and treatment progress. Regardless of when cessation becomes relevant in the worker-client dynamic, comprehensive assessment is an issue that cuts across many of the treatments potentially available to worker and client.

The critical nature of the assessment process relative to the identification, treatment, and follow-up with those exhibiting nicotine addiction cannot be overemphasized. This is especially true given the differential nature of settings. To the extent that assessment is unsystematic, inaccurate, inappropriate, or incomplete, unfounded conclusions may be drawn, with corresponding inappropriate treatment plans, negative client labeling, client resistance, and, finally, failure of the intervention. The worker may be tempted to label the client as noncompliant, assume some personal responsibility for the failure, or both. Often this is the result of the nature of the setting or the mandates of funding sources, requiring that clients be labeled with particular diagnoses for purposes of reimbursement. Just as frequently, however, failure seems to be the result of inappropriate stereotyping on the part of the worker, either due to a particular clinical orientation or a particular set of personal experiences.

The assessment model that promises to be most useful in work with addiction is the "sequential assessment model" developed by Cone and Hawkins (1977) and Skinner (1981), which presents a "behavioral assessment funnel" providing a three-stage assessment typology.

Stage 1, at the top of the funnel, is a very *broad assessment* that serves as a brief screening. Its purpose is the identification of general problem areas used to determine the more precise procedures incorporated at the *second stage,* referred to as *basic assessment.* Here, two functions are involved. First, if an addictive problem is identified during phase one, the initial definition of the extent and nature of the addictive behavior is noted in descriptive, functional, and diagnostic terms. Tentative decisions are made concerning the need for treatment, the general type of intervention (e.g., inpatient, outpatient, group, family, self-help, or a combination), and about available treatment programs to which the client might most appropriately be referred.

Second, inferences are formulated concerning the more specific factors across biological, psychological (cognitive and behavioral), and social dimensions that may foster maintenance of the behavior, as well as those factors likely to be instrumental in overcoming the problem.

Stage 3, specialized assessment, is the most precise. A more thorough, specific, and detailed set of information is gathered, often pursuing inferences generated at the preceding level. Specific aspects of the addictive behavior across the dimensions discussed above are pinpointed as targets of the intervention. More specific decisions are made about the exact nature of these interventions.

Once the client has begun treatment, the worker must continue to monitor. The point at which the decision is made concerning the appropriate type of treatment represents the first stage and the beginning of the second stage, or the base of the behavioral assessment funnel. The focus of assessment during the course of treatment is on changes in the specified target behaviors associated with the addiction, progress toward the specified goals of the intervention, and changes in other areas of general life functioning.

As treatment continues, there should be a dynamic interplay between assessment and treatment processes to provide feedback for both client and worker. This process facilitates movement to the action stage of change. This phase of assessment corresponds to the initial portion of the ''neck'' of the behavioral assessment funnel, corresponding to the continuation of phase 2 and the beginning of phase 3.

Posttreatment maintenance (relapse prevention) requires a continuation of assessment for a variety of reasons, including issues of potential or actual relapse, shifting support systems, the need for additional support, and other psychological and environmental determinants associated with the recovery process. With what will the addiction be replaced? How will clients develop alternatives for dealing with unanesthetized pain? What is going on within the rest of the systems in the client's environment? Assessment here corresponds to *stage three* of this assessment model.

Treatment Roles and Skills

A variety of smoking cessation interventions have been tested. We have included Schwartz's (1987) summary of the results of these outcome studies in Table 17.1. In general, combinations of treatments tend to be more effective over longer periods of time than do individual interventions. An example, as noted in the table, is nicotine gum. When used alone, the median quit rate at 12 months or greater is 11 percent. When used in combination with behavorial treatment or therapy, however, the quit rate increases to almost 30 percent.

It can be seen from Table 17.1 that only one cessation intervention restricted to a specific subset of tobacco users (physician intervention with cardiac patients) demonstrated a median success rate greater than 40 percent at a one year or longer follow-up. A number of other, less population-specific interventions, however, hold promise. The Surgeon General's Report (DHHS, 1988b) notes that ''interventions that hold promise and deserve additional attention are low-aversion directed-smoking strategies, skill-training treatments, interventions that enhance the self-attribution of treatment success, and interventions that train individuals to obtain and use social support resources'' (p. 517).

While the specifics of particular interventions are beyond the scope of this chapter, social work practitioners from various theoretical orientations have important roles to play in both individual and group interventions. Further, the traditional role of the social worker as a systems negotiator is of particular relevance in the development of training and educational programs, as well as in the establishment of relevant and accessible social support networks.

Social workers must also be sensitive to differences among various components of the population. Although to date no specific guidelines have been set forth for intervening differentially with minority and other specific groups, sensitivity toward particular cultural characteristics and related social and environmental factors will be critical to positive outcome and to the development of new, more effective strategies.

PREVENTION: LIFE SKILLS AND COMPETENCY ENHANCEMENT

In a recent discussion of prevention (Moncher, Holden, & Schinke, 1989), it was noted that:

> The traditional separation of prevention and treatment activities today has fused into a perspective that considers these two activities as different only in timing. The competency enhancement rationale emphasizes skills building, both to keep problems from

TABLE 17.1. Summary of Follow-up Quit Rates (percentages) of 416 Smoking Cessation Trials, by Method, Reported 1959–1985

Intervention Method	At Least 6-Month Follow-up			At Least 1-Year Follow-up		
	Number	Range	Median	Number	Range	Median
Self-help	11	0–33	17	7	12–33	18
Educational	7	13–50	36	12	15–55	25
Five-day plan	4	11–23	15	14	16–40	26
Group*	15	0–54	24	31	5–71	28
Medication	7	0–47	18	12	6–50	18.5
Nicotine gum	3	17–33	23	9	8–38	11
Nicotine gum and behavioral treatment	3	23–50	35	11	12–49	29
Hypnosis—Individual	11	0–60	25	8	13–68	19.5
Hypnosis—Group	10	8–68	34	2	14–88	—
Acupuncture	7	5–61	18	6	8–32	27
Physician advice/ counseling	3	5–12	5	12	3–13	6
Physician intervention/ more than counseling	3	23–40	29	10	13–38	22.5
Physician intervention Pulmonary patients	10	10–51	24	6	25–76	31.5
Cardiac patients	5	21–69	44	16	11–73	43
Risk factor	—	—	—	7	12–46	31
Rapid smoking	12	7–62	25.5	6	6–40	21
Rapid smoking and other procedures	21	8–67	38	10	7–52	30.5
Satiation smoking**	11	14–76	38	12	18–63	34.5
Regular-paced aversive smoking**	13	0–56	29	3	20–39	26
Nicotine fading**	7	26–46	27	16	7–46	25
Contingency contracting**	9	25–76	46	4	14–38	27
Multiple programs**	13	18–52	32	17	6–76	40

Note: Median not calculated for less than three trials. Caution: Quit-rates provided suggest overall trends. Most quit rates were based on self-reports. Some quit rates were recalculated to include all subjects, but most quit rates were based on reports by investigators. Some quit rates omitted subjects who did not complete treatment or persons who did not reply to follow-ups. Definitions of follow-up may vary between trials.
*3 group trials had 5-month follow-ups.
**Other procedures may have been used, and some trials may have included more than one method.

occurring (prevention) and to solve or resolve problems after they have occurred (treatment). The goal of this prevention approach is providing cognitive and behavioral skills to help groups of people anticipate and cope with potential problems. (p. 149)

Overview of Prevention Issues

Given the limited cessation success rates noted above, coupled with the estimate that 90 percent of the 41 million former smokers in the United States quit without aid of formal intervention, it can be concluded that for a number of reasons, not the least of which is the strong addictive qualities of nicotine, tobacco use prevention programs may be more cost-effective in the long term (Department of Health and Human Services, 1988a). Thus, advocacy for and provision of prevention services offer promising roles for social workers.

Tobacco use prevention programs have a long history in the United States, due to the impact over the past 20 years of the Surgeon General and funding efforts by the National Institutes of Health, primarily through the National Cancer Institute and the NIDA. These programs have been broad-ranging and the subject of much empirical research as the country moves forward toward the goal of a "smoke-free" America by the year 2000. Interestingly, and consistent with the similarities across addictions noted previously, many of the interventions originally developed around tobacco prevention have been extended to other drugs of abuse. The view of adolescent substance abuse by Bell and Battjes (1985) provides a succinct summary of the issue:

> Public concern over the issue of drug abuse among children and adolescents has stimulated a major effort on the part of researchers and clinicians to identify effective ways of deterring or delaying onset of this behavior. Traditional health education approaches had proven largely unsuccessful in reducing rates of drug abuse. Thus, new approaches were sought to address this problem. Encouraging results have been reported from research studies based on psychosocial models of behavior. Originally applied to the prevention of tobacco use, these interventions are currently being adapted to other drug abuse behaviors (e.g., alcohol and marijuana use), and preliminary findings are most promising. (p. 1)

Much of the developmental work toward effective prevention programs has focused and continues to focus on the identification and conceptualization of antecedents and correlates of tobacco use. There is much in common among these approaches, most of which are conceptualized in cognitive-behavioral, or behavioral terms. Interventions focusing largely on developing and enhancing social skills, generally referred to as life skills training, have been a major focus of the present authors' work (Schinke & Gilchrist, 1984; Botvin & Wills, 1985; Moncher, Holden, & Schinke, 1989). These methods will be discussed for the remainder of this chapter.

Useful Prevention Techniques

Other prevention approaches that have been found useful, elements of which we have incorporated in more recent interventions, include social inoculation training concentrating on enhancing resistance to peer and other social influences (Evans, 1976; Flay,

1985), and cognitive-developmental training focusing on physiological reactions to smoking experimentation (Glynn, Leventhal, & Hirschman, 1985). While each of these approaches has a number of variants, an examination of the more recent applications of the life skills model will provide an overview of the current state of tobacco prevention generally, in a form that is particularly well suited for effective utilization by social workers.

The life skills approach uses a number of techniques. True to its cognitive-behavioral roots, they include modeling; role play and behavorial rehearsal; didactics; values clarification exercises; self-management procedures including self-talk, progressive muscle relaxation, breathing exercises, and delaying tactics; problem-solving and decision-making strategies; and enhanced interpersonal communications emphasizing the development of assertion-refusal skills.

At the core of the model are practice and homework assignments, necessary for skills development. Further, the assignments foster utilization of techniques in situations outside of the training sessions, providing necessary contextual or environmental reinforcement. Too, as clients practice what they have learned, they develop a sense of skills ownership and are more likely to apply them automatically. This has obvious implications as the client moves temporally farther away from the training sessions. Finally, more recent work emphasizes an environmental support component in which families and significant others are involved in various ways to further enhance the prevention ideology and requisite skills. Where culturally and age-appropriate, entire communities may become involved in endorsing efforts toward prevention. A number of projects involving American Indian youth have augmented skills training with community-level interventions (Schinke, Botvin, Trimble, Orlandi, Gilchrist, & Locklear, 1988). In these situations, workers wili often act as community advocates.

The Follow-Up Process

Postintervention booster sessions, during which obstacles to skills application are discussed and potential solutions are examined and practiced, also add strength to the overall intervention by allowing the client opportunities to shore up areas of weakness. They can also apply skills to individual situations that may have developed subsequent to the initial training sessions. Thus, for example, a client newly involved in a relationship with a tobacco user may learn more direct ways to assert the desire not to smoke.

Summary

Given the generic nature of the skills involved, the model is highly flexible. It can be modified to fit a wide range of client variables including race/ ethnicity, socioeconomic status, gender, age, and geographic location. Work across a variety of populations has shown its efficacy (Schinke & Gilchrist, 1985; Schinke, Botvin, Trimble, Orlandi, Gilchrist, & Locklear, 1988; Schinke, Moncher, Palleja, Zayas, & Schilling, 1988; Schinke, Orlandi, Gilchrist, Schilling, & Locklear, in press). Further, although the model has been traditionally applied in prevention efforts, the reader will note that each of the techniques has its genesis in cognitive-behavioral theory. Thus, although the authors have not directly tested the notion, it would seem that life skills training might be generally applicable to cessation interventions as well.

SKILLS TRAINING IN PRACTICE: A PROGRAM EXAMPLE

To illustrate the model in practice, one of the authors' school-based prevention programs is described in this section. A recently completed longitudinal outcome study undertaken in a number of Pacific Northwest elementary and middle schools is discussed in the context of the various program components. The population served by the majority of these schools ranged from lower-middle to middle-class youth, with a mean age of just over 12 years at the time of initial program. In the particular school focused on here, prevention strategies were provided primarily by social work interns over a 15-week period. The program was composed of 15 50-minute sessions.

The first component involved providing information regarding the negative health consequences of tobacco use and the typical reasons for smoking onset among youth. In interactive discussions, perceived versus actual prevalence of tobacco use was examined. Studies have noted that high-risk youth

tend to overestimate smoking rates among teenagers and adults. The influential role of advertising in encouraging youthful tobacco use was also examined. Subjects were asked, as a homework assignment, to find various examples of tobacco advertisements and bring them to school. Counter-advertising messages were then developed and videotaped by the students. The point of this cognitive dissonance strategy was to begin a process of inoculation—that is, to make youth more aware of and resistant to pro-tobacco influences.

Next, the trainers used brainstorming techniques to model a problem-solving process. The students identified typical age-appropriate problem-solving situations and discussed potential solutions. Typical situations included peer and sibling pressures to smoke. Potential solutions to these problems were then generated and rank-ordered according to practicality and desirability. Individually, students chose particular solutions most comfortable for them. These solutions were then role-played with the worker acting as the individual encouraging use. Feedback was provided by both worker and classmates regarding the efficacy of each solution. Further role-plays then incorporated skills refinement.

To enhance further the students' conceptual understanding of problem solving, a cognitive model was introduced based upon the acronym SODAS. The five steps of this model were practiced in the face of problem situations. First, the students were taught to *Stop* in order to combat the impulsive behavior often seen in this age group. Next, and consistent with brainstorming, potential *Options* were examined. Youth then reviewed these options to *Decide* which of them would be most appropriate. The chosen decision would then be *Acted* upon and self-talk techniques were employed as the students engaged in *Self-praise* for well-made decisions. Self-praise is important, given that appropriate external reinforcement might not be available in the natural environment for the chosen decision.

The third major program component involved modeling appropriate methods for both overt and covert coping in stressful situations. Relaxation and deep-breathing exercises were taught and practiced, providing students with alternatives to the use of tobacco. Brainstorming was used to generate a list of potential situations where youth might be placed at high risk for tobacco initiation. Group members were encouraged to discuss these situations in terms of anticipation and avoidance. For example, students were taught how to avoid situations where known smokers might pressure them to use tobacco.

Coping skills, including assertive communication and appropriate refusal, comprised the next module, toward development of effective means for dealing with unanticipated and/or unavoidable situations where tobacco use might be encouraged. Through modeling, behavioral rehearsal, and examination of performance using videotape and feedback from peers and workers, verbal and nonverbal skills were honed.

As with the other components in the model, workers sought to ensure that youth had acquired the necessary basic skills and had refined their performance through practice. Concomitantly, students' self-efficacy regarding skills application in future high-risk situations was emphasized. The importance of self-efficacy and self-praise in the prevention of tobacco use cannot be overemphasized. The process builds and enhances the strengths of the participants by providing them with the opportunity to develop internal sources of satisfaction. Similarly, youngsters in the same peer group are helped to strengthen their support networks since self-efficacy in individuals may increase the network's sense of efficacy and mutual support. As should be clear, each aspect of the prevention program employed standard cognitive-behaviorial techniques.

Efficacy of the Life Skills Model regarding both smoking prevention and cessation has received some support. Botvin and Wills (1985), by example, provide a review of earlier findings regarding this model and conceptually related interventions. Longitudinal analysis of programs begun in the mid-1980s are still in progress. Further, transfer of these technologies across minority populations at high risk for smoking initiation and/or maintenance are currently underway.

CONCLUSION

There is no doubt that tobacco use remains a major health problem among diverse populations in the United States, despite long-standing, intensive nationwide efforts toward cessation and prevention. While inroads have been made in some populations, morbidity and mortality rates resulting from both smoked and smokeless tobacco abuse remain unacceptably high.

Not unlike other addictive behaviors, tobacco use has been most resistant to traditional cessation and prevention efforts. Research and practice must come together toward continued development, implementation, and evaluation of sound, empirically based interventions.

Social workers are in a unique position to influence this effort. As practitioners, they must work within their settings to critically evaluate interventions. They must learn more about what works and what does not. As advocates, practitioners must work on a number of levels to influence local, state, and national policies regarding legislation directed at further restricting dissemination of tobacco products, and to assure continued support for implementation and empirical evaluation of new and innovative prevention and cessation programs.

From a cost-benefit perspective, prevention continues to provide the greatest potential for efficient and effective interventions. Certainly, workers will be involved in cessation efforts, and this work is of great importance. It is with the generations to come, however, that prevention holds the most promise. As more is learned about the correlates of tobacco use, it will become possible to accurately target populations at high risk for use and to generate interventions more likely to achieve success among them.

REFERENCES

American Psychiatric Association (1987). *Diagnostic and Statistical Manual of Mental Disorders* (3rd ed. rev.). Washington, DC: American Psychiatric Association.

Ary, D. V. (1989). Use of smokeless tobacco among male adolescents: Concurrent and prospective relationships. In G. M. Boyd & C. A. Darby (Eds.), *Smokeless tobacco use in the United States* (NIH Publication No. 89–3055). Washington, DC: National Cancer Institute.

Bauman, K. E., Koch, G. G., & Lentz, G. M. (1989). Parent characteristics, perceived health risk, and smokeless tobacco use among white adolescent males. In G. M. Boyd & C. A. Darby (Eds.), *Smokeless tobacco use in the United States* (NIH Publication No. 89–3055). Washington, DC: National Cancer Institute.

Bell, C. S., & Battjes, R. J. (Eds.) (1985). *Prevention research: Deterring drug abuse among children and adolescents* (NIDA Research Monograph No. 63. p.

1). Washington, DC: U. S. Government Printing Office.

Bernstein, M. J. (1986). Health applications of smokeless tobacco use. *Journal of the American Medical Association, 255,* 1045–1048.

Blachley, J. D., & Knochel, J. P. (1980). Tobacco chewer's hypokalemia: Licorice revisited. *New England Journal of Medicine, 302,* 784–785.

Botvin, G. J., and Wills, T. A. (1985). Personal and social skills training: Cognitive-behavioral approaches to substance abuse. In C. S. Bell, & R. J. Battjes (Eds.), *Prevention research: Deterring drug abuse among children and adolescents* (NIDA Research Monograph No. 63, pp. 8–49). Washington, DC: U. S. Government Printing Office.

Byrd, J. C., Shapiro, R. S., & Schiedermayer, D. L. (1989). Passive smoking: A review of medical and legal issues. *American Journal of Public Health, 79,* 209–215.

Chassin, L., Presson, C. C., Sherman, S. J., Corty, E., & Olshavsky, R. W. (1984). Predicting the onset of cigarette smoking in adolescence: A longitudinal study. *Journal of Applied Social Psychology, 14,* 224–243.

Christen, A. G. (1980). Tobacco chewing and snuff dipping. *New England Journal of Medicine, 302,* 818.

Christen, A. G. (1985). The four most common alterations of the teeth, periodontium, and oral soft tissues observed in smokeless tobacco users: A literature review. *Journal of the Indiana Dental Association, 64,* 15–18.

Collishaw, N. E., Kirkbridge, J., & Wigle, D. T. (1984). Tobacco smoke in the workplace: An occupational health hazard. *Canadian Medical Association Journal, 131,* 1199–1204.

Cone, J. D., & Hawkins, R. P. (1977). Introduction. In J. D. Cone & R. P. Hawkins (Eds.), *Behavorial assessment: New directions in clinical psychology, xiii-xxiv.* New York: Brunner/Mazel.

Department of Health and Human Services (1986). *The health consequences of involuntary smoking: A report to the surgeon general* (DHHS Publication No. CDC 87-8398). Washington, DC: U. S. Government Printing Office.

Department of Health and Human Services (1988a). *NIDA national household survey on drug abuse: Main findings 1985* (DHHS Publication No. ADM 88-1586). Washington, DC: U. S. Government Printing Office.

Department of Health and Human Services (1988b). *The health consequences of smoking: Nicotine addiction. A report of the surgeon general* (DHHS Publication No. CDC 88-8406). Washington, DC: U. S. Government Printing Office.

Donovan, D. M., (1988). In D. M. Donovan & G. A. Marlatt (Eds.), *Assessment of addictive behaviors* (pp. 6–7). New York: Guilford Press.

Edmundson, E. W., Glover, E. D., Alston, P. P., & Holbert, D. (1987). Personality traits of smokeless tobacco users and nonusers: A comparison. *International Journal of the Addictions, 22,* 671–683.

Eriksen, M. P. (1986). Workspace smoking control: Rationale and approaches. In W. B. Ward (Ed.), *Advances in health education and promotion, 1,* JAI Press.

Evans, R. I. (1976). Smoking in children: Developing a social psychological strategy of deterrence. *Prevention Medicine, 5,* 122–127.

Flay, B. R. (1985). What we know about the social influences approach to smoking prevention: Review and recommendations. In C. S. Bell & R. J. Battjes (Eds.), *Prevention research: Deterring drug abuse among children and adolescents.* (NIDA Research Monograph No. 63, pp. 67–112). Washington, DC: U. S. Government Printing Office.

Friedman, L., Lichtenstein, E., & Biglan A. (1985). Smoking onset among teens: An empirical analysis of initial situations. *Addictive Behaviors, 10,* 1–13.

Glynn, K., Leventhal, H., & Hirschman, R. (1985). A cognitive developmental approach to smoking prevention. In C. S. Bell & R. J. Battjes (Eds.), *Prevention research: Deterring drug abuse among children and adolescents* (NIDA Research Monograph No. 63, pp. 130–152). Washington, DC: U. S. Government Printing Office.

Greer, R. O., & Poulson, T. C. (1983). Oral tissues alterations associated with the use of smokeless tobacco by teenagers. *Oral Surgery, 56,* 275–284.

Hall, R. L., & Dexter, D. (1988). Smokeless tobacco use and attitudes towards smokeless tobacco among Native Americans and other adolescents in the Northwest. *American Journal of Public Health, 78,* 1586–1588.

Hampson, N. B. (1985). Smokeless is not saltless. *New England Journal of Medicine, 312,* 919–920.

Holden, G. W., Moncher, M. S., & Schinke, S. P. (in press). Substance abuse. In A. S. Bellack, M. Hersen, & A. E. Kazdin (Eds.), *International handbook of behavior modification and therapy* (2nd ed.). New York: Plenum.

Johnson, L. D., Bachman, J. G., & O'Malley, P. M. (1988, January 13). Summary of 1987 drug study results. *University of Michigan News and Information Service Press Release.*

Jones, R., & Moberg, P. (1988). Correlates of tobacco use in a male adolescent population. *American Journal of Public Health, 78,* 61–63.

Kandel, D. (1982). Epidemiological and psychosocial perspectives on adolescent drug use. *Journal of the American Academy of Child Psychiatry, 21,* 328–347.

Kellie, S. E. (1989). Tobacco use: Women, children and

minorities. In E. M. Blakeman & A. L. Engelberg (Eds.), *Tobacco use in America conference: Final report*. Washington, DC: American Medical Association.

Mattson, M. E. & Winn, D. M. (1989). Smokeless tobacco: Association with increased cancer risk. In G. M. Boyd & C. A. Darby (Eds.), *Smokeless tobacco use in the United States* (NIH Publication No. 89-3055). Washington, DC: National Cancer Institute.

McPhaul, M., Punzi, H. A., Sandy, A., Birganelli, M., Rude, R., Kaplan, N. M. (1984). Snuff induced hypertension in pheochromocytoma. *Journal of the American Medical Association, 252*, 2860–2862.

Moncher, M. S., Holden, G. W., & Schinke, S. P. (1989). Primary and secondary prevention. In M. Hersen (Ed.), *Innovations in child behavior therapy*. New York: Springer.

Moncher, M. S., Schinke, S. P., Holden, G. W., & Aragon, S. (1989). Tobacco use prevalence, incidence, and influences among American Indian youth. *Journal of American Medical Association, 262*, 1469–1470.

Newcomb, M., Maddahian, E., Skager, R., & Bentler, P. (1987). Substance abuse and psychosocial risk factors among teenagers: Associations with sex, age, ethnicity and type of school. *American Journal of Drug and Alcohol Abuse, 13*, 413–433.

Oetting, E. R., Beauvais, F., & Edwards, R. (1988). Alcohol and Indian youth: Social and psychological correlates and prevention. *The Journal of Drug Issues, 18*, 87–101.

Rause, B. A. (1989). Use of smokeless tobacco by age, race and gender in ten standard metropolitan statistical areas of the Southeast United States. In G. M. Boyd & C. A. Darby (Eds.), *Smokeless tobacco use in the United States* (N. I. H. Publication No. 89-3055). Washington, DC: National Cancer Institute.

Schinke, S. P., Botvin, G. J., Trimble, J. E., Orlandi, M. A., Gilchrist, L. D. & Locklear, V. S. (1988). Preventing substance abuse among American-Indian adolescents; A bicultural competence skills approach. *Journal of Counseling Psychology, 35*, 87–90.

Schinke, S. P., & Gilchrist, L. D. (1984). *Life skills counseling with adolescents*. Austin, TX: Pro-Ed.

Schinke, S. P., & Gilchrist, L. D. (1985). Preventing substance abuse with children and adolescents. *Journal of Consulting and Clinical Psychology, 53*, 592–602.

Schinke, S. P., Moncher, M. S., Palleja, J., Zayas, L. H., & Schilling, R. F. (1988). Hispanic youth, substance abuse, and stress: Implications for prevention research. *International Journal of the Addictions, 23*, 809–826.

Schinke, S. P., Orlandi, M. A., Gilchrist, L. D., Schilling, R. F., & Locklear, V. S. (in press). Tobacco use

by American Indian and Alaska Native people: Risks, psychosocial factors, and preventive intervention. *Journal of Alcohol and Drug Education.*

Schinke, S. P., Schilling, R. F., Gilchrist, L. D., Ashby, M. R., & Kitajima, E. (1989). Native youth and smokeless tobacco: Prevalence rates, gender differences and descriptive characteristics. In G. M. Boyd & C. A. Darby (Eds.), *Smokeless tobacco use in the United States* (NIH Publication No. 89-3055). Washington, DC: National Cancer Institute.

Schroeder, K. L., & Chen, M. S. (1985). Smokeless tobacco and blood pressure. *New England Journal of Medicine, 312*, 919.

Schwartz, J. L. (1987). *Review of smoking cessation methods: The United States and Canada, 1975-1985* (U.S. DHHS, NIH Publication No. 87-2940). Washington, DC: National Cancer Institute.

Shah, A. S., Sarode, A. V., & Bhide, S. V. (1985). Experimental studies of mutagenic and carcinogenic effects of chewing tobacco. *Journal of Cancer Research & Clinical Oncology, 109*, 203–207.

Skinner, H. A. (1981). Assessment of alcohol problems: Basic principles, critical issues, and future trends. In Y. Israel, F. B. Glaser, H. Kalant, R. E. Popham, W. Schmidt, & R. G. Smart (Eds.), *Research advances in alcohol and drug problems*. (Volume 6, pp. 319–369). New York: Plenum.

Squier, E. A. (1984). Smokeless tobacco and oral cancer: A cause for concern? *CA-A Cancer Journal for Clinicians, 34*, 242–247.

Warner, K. E. (1989). Smoking and health: A 25-year perspective. *American Journal of Public Health, 79*, 141–143.

Weber, A. (1984). Annoyance and irritation by passive smoking. *Preventive Medicine, 13*, 618–625.

SUPPLEMENTAL READING LIST

Bandura, A. (1986). *Social foundations of thought and action: A social cognitive theory*. Englewood Cliffs, NJ: Prentice Hall.
Provides an overview of a broad theory of human behavior that can be useful for the practitioner in conceptualizing addictive behaviors from both etiological and treatment perspectives. Some research has been done employing components of this theory in the treatment of addictive behaviors.

Department of Health and Human Services. (1988). *Bibliography on smoking and health* (1987). (DHHS Publication No. CDC 88-8399). Washington, DC: U. S. Government Printing Office.
This well-organized reference volume provides a comprehensive, annotated bibliography on research about

tobacco-related issues including smoking prevention, intervention, and cessation methods. Pharmacological and physiological issues are also highlighted.

Kazdin, A. E. (1986). The evaluation of psychotherapy: Research design and methodology. In S. L. Garfield & A. E. Bergen (Eds.), *Handbook of psychotherapy and behavior change* (pp. 23–68). New York: Wiley
This chapter provides a detailed examination of research issues in assessing addiction treatment outcomes. While geared toward researchers, Kazdin presents an excellent overview of evaluation issues for the clinical practitioner.

Peele, S. (1989). *The diseasing of America: Addiction treatment out of control.* Lexington, MA: Lexington Books.

Provides a provocative exposition of addictive theory in which the medical model of addiction is critically examined. This work will be useful to practitioners in a number of settings, as it calls into question the dominant paradigm under which some current treatment models have been developed.

Warner, K. E. (Ed.) (1989). Tobacco and Health (Special Issue). *American Journal of Public Health, 79.*
This special issue provides the clinician with the most recent research concerning smoking patterns in a number of special groups with emphasis on minorities. Of particular interest to clinicians are articles focused on a prenatal self-help cigarette cessation program in an HMO setting, and the evaluation of a restrictive smoking policy in a general hospital.

CHAPTER 18

Compulsive Gambling: Reframing Issues of Control

Ronald Gaudia

*Westchester Jewish Community Services,
Hartsdale, New York*

We're on the last throw—the one that really counts.

Ugo Betti

The gaming industry in the United States has the majority of Americans as its customers. A popular activity, gambling has been romantically depicted in films and novels, and it has been a source of entertainment for people since the beginning of history. For most people, placing a bet in the many ways legitimately open to them is one of several forms of pleasure. They are the social gamblers. A decade ago, the American Psychiatric Association (1980) recognized that some individuals cannot control their gambling, and pathological or compulsive gambling was accepted as a disorder of impulse control. Lesieur and Custer (1984) state that the acceptance of compulsive gambling as a psychiatric disorder helped replace the moral view of the addicted gambler as a sinner or weak-willed person to one of a person with an illness. Treatment, rather than moral judgment, was needed.

There are no accurate statistics on the number of compulsive gamblers in the United States. The Commission on the Review of the National Policy Toward Gambling (1976) estimated that there were 1.1 million "probable compulsive gamblers" in the population and 3.3 million "potential compulsive gamblers." Nadler (1985) critically reviewed the methodology of the Commission's study and thought that both figures should be combined. Nadler's conclusion is supported by the claim of

Gamblers Anonymous (GA) (1989) that up to 4.2 million Americans may be addicted to gambling. In addition, considering Lesieur and Custer's (1984) estimate of between 10 and 15 persons directly affected by a typical compulsive gambler, the actual number of individuals caught in the net of a gambler's addiction is staggering. Blackman, Simone, and Thomas (1986) reported the average debt of gamblers at their treatment program was $54,662. Money is the substance compulsive gamblers use to fuel their habit, and money can be begged, borrowed, or stolen from spouses, children, parents, other relatives, friends, gamblers, and employers.

Gaudia (1987) has described the devastating consequences for the compulsive gambler and family members resulting from the disease. Virtually no area is left untouched. Money for essentials is not available, threats from loan sharks are common, social ostracism is prevalent especially from family creditors, constant financial and emotional stress leads to physical problems, family relationships are strained and dysfunctional, and crimes committed to obtain money for gambling may lead to jail sentences or criminal records.

Relatively little is known about the children of compulsive gamblers. Custer and Milt (1985) believe that serious levels of emotional problems and dysfunctional behavior may exist in these children.

The gambler's winning phase leads to excessive spending on the children; and when losing sets in, the gambler neglects the children and pushes them away. Younger children exhibit behavior and academic problems at school, develop anxieties and phobias, suppress angry feelings, and may develop sleeping and eating disorders. Adolescents may react by running away from home, abusing drugs, using alcohol or gambling, developing psychosomatic illnesses, or becoming lethargic and depressed. No data are available on the adult children of compulsive gamblers.

As the various states have legalized lotteries, casinos, on- and off-track betting, numbers, and other forms of gambling, an increased number of compulsive gamblers have sought help. Kaplan (1984) notes that the availability of gambling opportunities is recognized as conducive to abuse. State policies toward lotteries have changed from prohibition to acceptance as a means to increase revenues. Many forms of gambling that were previously illegal have been made legal. Corruption and crime have always been associated with gambling, especially in casino cities such as Atlantic City and Las Vegas. The lure of bigger casino jackpots, multi-million dollar lottery wins, and the recent prospect of a gigantic federal lottery prize, are serious forces increasing the chances of vulnerable individuals becoming addicted.

This chapter presents compulsive gambling in the framework of the addictive disease model, with some of the common factors in alcohol and drug addiction. The course of the gambling disease is described, and available data on the incidence of compulsive gambling in various groupings in the population are provided. A treatment program and a case illustration are described as well as the importance of the self-help group as part of an integrated program for recovery. Finally, a challenge is issued to the social work profession to encourage more commitment and participation in meeting the needs of the compulsive gambling family.

THE ADDICTION PROCESS

From the first settlers in this country to today, risk taking has been an important and prevalent value. To raise revenues, lotteries were initiated in the thirteen original colonies. Frontiersmen were ad-mired for chancing danger to claim land or to hunt for gold. Today, adventures in business undertakings and stock market investing are supported as ways to "get ahead." Compulsive gamblers can become players in the stock market by risking money on uncertain events. The October 17, 1987, crash of the stock market brought to the surface gamblers addicted to transactions involving stock and commodities options—the fourth preference for compulsive gamblers, coming after horse racing, sports, and casinos (National Council on Compulsive Gambling, 1987). Strange (1986) depicts the Western financial system as resembling a vast casino. The players use the latest advances in electronics to play a choice of games. They are hooked on what might be called "electronic morphine."

Scandals involving inside traders have highlighted an essential attraction for compulsive gamblers. Millions of dollars can be made, more than any horse player could imagine, in a split second of action. The action was readily available, as near as a phone. When caught, the inside traders puzzled many people. Why would they take such chances when they already had so much money? Compulsive gamblers knew they were in it for the action, for the thrill and the excitement.

The present state of knowledge has not provided a final explanation of compulsive gambling. Theoreticians have advanced models, the major ones being the medical, social learning, sociological, genetic, psychological, and economic models. Blume (1988) has concluded that the medical model is presently the preferred conceptualization because it is conducive to the fostering of treatment techniques, encourages funding for treatment and research, and provides a useful framework for formulating social and legal polices related to the disorder. The success of GA can be largely attributed to the group's following the disease concept as Alcoholic Anonymous has done with alcoholism. GA believes compulsive gambling is a progressive illness that can never be cured but can be arrested. The disease model enables compulsive gamblers to free themselves of irrational guilt. The compulsive gambler is not held responsible for having the disorder but is responsible for doing all that is possible to arrest the course of the illness, including full restitution of all money owed. Its deficits include the risk of holding to one model while restricting investigation and learning from other models. Biological and genetic factors may be given undue attention while minimizing the significance of both psychosocial and environmental factors in the development of the problem.

Common Symptoms of Addictions

The American Psychiatric Association (1987) has revised its criteria for pathological or compulsive gambling. Now conceptualized as an addictive disease, the criteria are very similar to those for alcohol or drug dependence. Similarities include a preoccupation with the abusing behavior, abusing larger amounts over longer periods of time than intended, the need to increase the behavior to achieve the desired effect, repeated efforts to cut down or stop the behavior, social or occupational activity given up for the behavior, and continuation of the behavior despite social, occupational, or legal problems. Hard evidence does not exist to document whether compulsive gamblers experience withdrawal symptoms. Although the DSM-III-R lists restlessness as a criterion for compulsive gambling, this does not compare with the characteristic withdrawal syndromes described in psychoactive substance use disorders (American Psychiatric Association, 1987). But it is known that the absence of a dramatic withdrawal syndrome in cocaine users does not make the drug less addictive. The fact that there are a number of physical manifestations associated with alcohol and drug ingestion has made it easier for individuals and clinicians to accept the disease model. Compulsive gamblers do not show the signs that clearly point to their problem; it is an "invisible illness."

There are additional common factors found in the three addictions. All three will produce states of pleasure, excitement, and depression. Each is initially socially acceptable. Gambling has the distinction of also being sponsored and promoted by government and religious bodies. Media advertisements urge individuals to catch the spirit by "being in it to win it" while helping to support education, the aged, the handicapped. Churches, synagogues, and civic organizations invite everyone to take a chance and support a worthwhile cause. Gamblers have not been warned that gambling may be detrimental to their health. Finally, what all addicts do to maintain their habit, what they do in their quest for excitement, will eventually erode ethical considerations.

Perhaps the success of 12-step programs such as Alcoholics Anonymous, Gamblers Anonymous, and Narcotics Anonymous is the realization that ethical values need to be returned to the individual. The three groups follow a "spiritual" program, and each group stands for abstinence. They view addictions as a family disease and make provisions to assist family members.

The Phases of Compulsive Gambling

The medical model postulates that a disease runs a course similar to the course for compulsive gambling as described by Custer and Milt (1985). Compulsive gamblers are caught up in a progressive and chronic disorder in which they are unable to resist impulses to gamble. In the first, or winning, phase gambling is experienced as enjoyable, stimulating, and pleasurable. Employing good skills, gamblers succeed in winning initially. Cognitive abilities are utilized as they develop techniques and methods to increase their winning potential. Beginner's luck supports a false optimism about the ability to win. When a bet is lost, the encouragement to continue from fellow gamblers takes the irrational form of blaming "cold dice" or a "poorly dealt hand." The gambler presents an image of a good sport who accepts the losses. Almost always, compulsive gamblers have a "big win," an amount often equal to their yearly salary. However, they cannot quit when ahead. This windfall seems to be a significant force in locking the gambler into the addiction process. Larger and more frequent bets are needed to achieve the desired excitement. The expression commonly heard from gamblers is "I feel alive when I'm in action."

In the second or losing phase, gambling has become the dominant force in the gambler's life. Martinez (1983) highlights how the compulsive gambler's search for an identity has become organized around his career as a gambler. Increased risk taking and increased betting occurs, and losses begin to accumulate. The need to "be in action" is paramount and must be accomplished at all costs. This magnificent obsession is expressed in the figurative badge compulsive gamblers wear: "The next best thing to gambling and winning is gambling and losing." Lesieur (1984) describes how gamblers in this phase become obsessed with winning in order to recoup losses as they become involved in the chasing phenomenon. They cannot tolerate or accept their losses because they experience losses as a statement about their self-worth. Betting becomes reckless and desperate.

To conceal the extent of losses and to deny the uncontrollable need to gamble, gamblers often succeed in convincing family, relatives, and friends that they need money to pay off debts. Threats from loan sharks or banks usually succeed in the gambler's being bailed out. Of course, the promise to stop gambling is immediately broken as the bailout money is used to gamble again. The bailout is comparable to detoxification for substance abusers. Sobering up substance abusers will not stop the course of the disease, and lack of indebtedness will not stop the gambling illness. In addition, the bailout interferes with the gambler owning responsibility for his actions and making financial restitution.

Finally, in the third or desperate phase, a gambler has most often hit rock bottom (Martinez, 1983). The gambler has continued to bet with utter disregard for consequences. A cycle of lying has been created with relatives, friends, employers. Marriage and other relationships have become dysfunctional. When the compulsive gambler can no longer obtain money to gamble by legitimate means, illegal means will be resorted to (Lesieur 1984). Forgery, theft, and embezzlement are the most frequent crimes committed, although most compulsive gamblers reframe their behavior as borrowing until they win the money to pay back the amount taken. Thoughts of suicide, threats of divorce, the risk of incarceration, or firings from a job simply point up the dismal present and future. The individual's self-worth has been devalued, gambling has lost its excitement, and depression has taken over. This is a dangerous and critical time; one out of every five compulsive gamblers attempts suicide at this point (Custer & Milt, 1985).

Sociocultural Factors and Compulsive Gambling

Sociocultural factors may have important bearings on who gambles socially and who becomes addicted. Lesieur (1984) found Italians, Jews, and the Irish overrepresented among members of GA. The fact that GA chapters exist in many Asian, European, and South American countries leads to the conclusion that compulsive gambling does not stop at ethnic or national boundaries. Again, further research is needed.

Custer and Milt (1985) estimate that there is one female to every ten male compulsive gamblers. In our culture, males tend to have more experience with gambling activities than do females. Wolfgang's study (1988) suggests, however, that personality factors, such as sensation seeking, may be more significant than an individual's gender in influencing an attraction to gambling. Nevertheless, due to stereotypes about male gamblers and the disproportionate number of males versus female gamblers, the latter may go undetected more often even when referred for treatment of other problems or addictions.

In American society, the attitude toward social gambling does not support a cautioning against harmful results, whereas popular beliefs about alcohol and illicit drugs warn users of possible dangerous consequences. Most people begin to gamble with family or friends, and there is ordinarily little objection to engaging in first-time gambling. However, six percent of the callers to the hot line of the Council on Compulsive Gambling of New Jersey (1988) were under 21 years of age—a warning of the growing numbers of youthful addicts.

Cross-Addictions and Gambling

As discussed earlier, pathological gambling has a good deal in common with alcohol and drug addictions. In addition, ingestion of alcohol and/or drugs may lead the compulsive gambler to relapse to gambling. Casinos, tracks, and ball parks all serve alcohol (often free at casinos). Although Ciarrochi's (1987) review of reports on compulsive gamblers who abuse alcohol and/or other drugs indicates a substantial number have severe problems with these other addictions (as many as 45 percent of those seeking inpatient treatment), he cautions that more systematic research is needed. Recovering gamblers who are grieving for their gambling high may change to a different form of mood-altering substance: alcohol and/or other drugs. Conversely, when the alcohol or drug addict is abstinent and begins to gamble, the self-devaluation experienced from gambling losses increases the chances that they will lose their sobriety. Addiction specialists, and the Self-help Anonymous groups, have long held to the belief that abstinence from all mood-altering substances and experiences is indicated in order to maintain recovery.

TREATMENT ISSUES

Treatment programs for compulsive gamblers and family members are a relatively new phenomenon, and there are but a few centers across the country dedicated to treating this client group. In addition, there are very few published reports on the treatment of the disorder. Taber, McCormick, Russo, Adkins, and Ramirez (1987) conclude from their study that compulsive gambling is a treatable disorder in terms of abstinence and general behavioral improvement. When formulating treatment plans with compulsive gamblers, it is crucial to obtain a gambling history. There are different treatment considerations depending on whether gambling is an active problem or whether the recovery process has been maintained for a period of time.

Resistance and Control Issues

Actively gambling clients will need firm interventions to confront and break down the barriers of denial and resistance to treatment. The initial task is to achieve abstinence, to interrupt the gambling. The social worker needs to convey that hope for recovery is possible and to assist in attending to any legal and financial problems. A current medical, alcohol, and drug assessment is necessary. Gamblers may still believe they can exercise control; education is a needed early component. In conjunction with treatment, clients should be enrolled in GA, where group support, confrontation, and continuous sponsorship is available. Since compulsive gamblers can have more than one diagnosis, assessment of severe psychiatric disorders or suicidal possibilities needs to be performed, and where indicated, hospitalization may be required.

The addicted gambler who has achieved a newly gained sobriety, will need a good deal of support and further education. Since compulsive gambling is a lifelong disorder, most recovering gamblers will maintain a long-term affiliation with GA. GA mem-

bers regard their group as lifesaving. As one member put it, "It did not open the door to heaven, but it opened the door to get out of hell." Because debts are always an issue for compulsive gamblers, GA provides a "pressure group" where trusted servants, those members of GA who have achieved sobriety over a significant period of time, help the new member budget and devise schedules of payment to creditors. The client's ego is most often hurt when the transfer of money is made to the spouse or another person, particularly when the client is a male. However, this plan by GA underscores the fact that compulsive gamblers do not value money, nor are they capable yet of handling it. A goal in GA and in treatment is full restitution of money owed (Gamblers Anonymous, 1989). Social workers need to see GA mutual help groups as complementing treatment and to form an alliance on behalf of the compulsive gambler.

Recovering gamblers with a long period of abstinence will seek help from agencies when problems underlying the gambling disorder surface. Marital problems, vocational concerns, child guidance issues, and learning disabilities are commonly presented. Social workers treating these clients and their family members must understand the underlying psychology of the compulsive gambler and the effects of the disorder on the family.

Compulsive gamblers tenaciously hold on to the misconception that lack of money is the cause of their problem. This myth needs continuous confrontation. It is a frequent occurrence for a compulsive gambler to believe that GA gives money! Since compulsive gambling is a disorder of impulse control, gamblers exhibit low frustration tolerance levels and expect immediate gratification. Treatment, therefore, often needs to focus on the connection between the inability to tolerate tension and the accustomed pattern of discharging tension by gambling. In addition, teaching relaxation techniques is useful. For a long period of time the recovering gambler is faced with the serious consequences of the addiction and low self-esteem is a frequent result. Treatment needs to provide encouragement, increase self-esteem, and build confidence. Lessons from the past can strengthen compulsive gamblers in the present, and help them to cope with what is, not what was. The value system of the compulsive gambler in which money and possessions were disproportionately designated as indicators of self-worth must also be examined.

Relapse Prevention

Relapse prevention is an essential part of treatment. As with other addictions, relapse needs to be understood as the last and sometimes repeated event in a dysfunctional process. The assumption that a relapse means a return to chronic gambling is as damaging as it is incorrect. The high percent of relapses in all addictions is well known; and if seen as an opportunity to learn about the cause of the event and how to correct future occurrences, then the recovering person has gained strength (Marlatt & Gordon, 1985). Treatment should focus on cues that have led to the relapse. It is very difficult for recovering gamblers to accept the fact that they can never gamble again. Individuals may succumb to media pressure and purchase a seemingly harmless $1 lottery ticket to test their control. They feel confident they can visit their favorite track and not gamble. Others may recall the high they experienced when gambling and feel the craving. These and other possibilities need to be examined in treatment where support, education, and insight can be provided.

Enhancing Strengths and the Natural Support Network

Compulsive gambling needs to be seen as a family illness, and provisions must be made for treating the family members. Gaudia (1987) and Heinman (1987) have discussed treatment issues in working with the spouses of recovering gamblers. The spouse needs to be seen in relation to her role as an enabler. This partner also will need attention to personal issues. Depression, anxiety, loss of sexual interest, and years of stored-up anger are common issues in treatment. Education about the nature of the gambling disease is indicated and can relieve most spouses or significant others of self-blame and guilt. The gambler is particularly adept at conning others into blaming themselves for the addiction. Facing the huge gambling debts, handling the harassing calls from creditors, and taking charge of the family finances are areas that need immediate attention and are also assisted through Gam-Anon, the self-help group for spouses and others involved with gamblers. Having stayed with their partners during

chaotic and devastating times, many marriages have a strong foundation and strengths that can be called upon in rebuilding the relationship. Of course, as in other addictions, the incidence of divorce is high among compulsive gambling families, particularly those built on the excitement of the gambling scenario.

With those who seek help but whose addicted spouses refuse to participate, the social worker can help by educating spouses about the disease, helping them firmly confront the addicted individual about the present illness, stop providing money to be used for gambling, and use the support of Gam-Anon. Anger and frustration resulting from the severe consequences of the disease are often displaced onto the children. Attention needs to be paid to the guilt felt by spouses for not protecting their children. Although Gam-a-Teen exists for children of compulsive gamblers, hardly any have met nationwide. The reason is not known and there are virtually no studies available on the effect of the disorder on children, an area that sorely needs to be studied.

A MODEL TREATMENT PROGRAM

An example of a social work agency that treats compulsive gamblers and their families is Westchester Jewish Community Services (WJCS), a nonsectarian, New York State licensed family mental health clinic. When utilization review of cases indicated a growing number of clients with gambling problems, a grant was secured from the UJA/Federation of Jewish Philanthropies to begin a Compulsive Gambling Treatment Program. Staff with a background in alcohol and drug addictions obtained specific training in compulsive gambling treatment. The program has three thrusts. First, public education is provided about the nature of the gambling disorder. Media sources have been contacted to get the message across. Second, training to staff in mental health, alcohol, drug, social agencies, and employee assistance programs is being offered. The goal has been to educate and teach the signs of the disease, and to assist referrals to GA and to the agency's program.

Third, an attempt has been made to "mend fences" with GA groups, many of whom had resentment toward mental health workers who were still unaware that the disorder was treatable. A half-day conference on compulsive gambling resulted in recovering gamblers leading workshops along with clinicians. The result of these three efforts increased the number of gamblers who entered the program. The program staff continues to act as consultants to other treatment resources providing services to compulsive gamblers. One staff member leads a group for recovering gamblers, and another has recently begun a group for adult children of compulsive gamblers. The program has received more requests for services than can be handled. As a result, program staff have trained other clinicians in the clinic, acted as consultants, and focused their attention on recently recovering gamblers. The orientation is to attempt to involve the entire family as the individual's natural support network.

The following case example is illustrative of the treatment of a compulsive gambler in the WJCS program:

Nick A. was referred by his lawyer after he had embezzled over $50,000 from a credit union where he had access to customers' accounts. He was facing a possible jail sentence and was ambivalent about going to prison. On the one hand, he felt his family would be better off with him out of the way. Also he thought he could pick up a new vocation in jail as he would have plenty of time to study. On the other hand, he worried how his children would take having a prisoner for a father and if he could tolerate being locked up. His guilt was apparent and, as he faced the consequences of his gambling, he became increasingly depressed. He considered how to cover his contemplated suicide in order to provide insurance money to his family. However, the judge's review of the probationary and treatment reports resulted in a period of probation, mandated therapy, and attendance at GA.

When treatment began, Nick was 41 years old, of white Italian parents, Catholic, married for 16 years, with one 12-year-old daughter and one nine-year-old son. He had a college degree. He had had numerous jobs in business, accounting, and sales. When he did not get sufficient recognition or did not advance quickly enough, he frequently left jobs. Psychological testing to evaluate the extent of his depression confirmed the clinical judgment of a man with superior intelligence, impulsive, narcissistic characteristics, and serious depression.

A gambling history was taken, including the onset of gambling, preparation for the types of gambling preferred, the largest amounts won and lost, illegal activities associated with the gambling, and the effects of gambling on the family and vocational pursuits. The history revealed that Nick gambled as a child and remembered the excitement when winning. In late adolescence he visited the track frequently, bet on sports events, and enjoyed the camaraderie of other gamblers. After his first child was born, he became a more serious gambler, and had a "big win." He had always followed sports events and figured he could win by playing point spreads correctly. He became reckless in his betting, as he could not tolerate the losses. He knew something was wrong and went to a GA meeting at the suggestion of his cousin; however, he did not return as he thought "they were all sick." His problem was bad luck. Relatives bailed him out but the money was used for more gambling. He borrowed from loan sharks and banks, and then embezzled from his employer to obtain gambling money.

Nick is the youngest of five children and the second male child. His father, a heavy drinker and gambler, died when Nick was 16 years old. His mother made few demands of him, and made excuses for his behavorial problems such as early alcohol and drug use. His intelligence got him through school though he often cut classes. He had little contact with his siblings.

The first goal in treatment was to stop the gambling. Nick was still tempted to make a final bet to clear up his problem. GA meetings began to chip away at this fantasy, and education in treatment about the gambling disease reinforced his acceptance of not having control over gambling. Initial individual sessions with his wife, Mary, also provided education about the disease and led to her referral to Gam-Anon. Restitution seemed desirable to Nick since, in his eyes, he had only "borrowed" the embezzled money and the pressure group at GA helped him make a realistic plan of payment. Here, too, GA and treatment complemented each other by blocking his unrealistic impulse to borrow or his fantasy to get some high-paying job to pay off large sums to "those I hurt." His acceptance of Mary's being in charge of money was the first recognition that he was out of control. However, he felt he "would be 101" years old when the debts were paid off, and therefore he attempted to drown his hopeless feelings in alcohol and drugs. Hearing the experiences of other gamblers at GA, he began to think it was possible to get back on his feet.

In addition to individual treatment, he entered a therapy group of compulsive gamblers, which increased his hope as he saw how others had coped with a similar problem. His treatment now focused on his inability to tolerate tension and his subsequent impulsive behavior. Relaxation techniques and methods for thinking out problems were introduced. He was concerned about not having a job. Even though Nick was looking for work, he still had a lot of time on his hands, which only heightened his depression. When he spoke about the poor condition of his house, he was encouraged to paint and fix the roof. He was active in sports and exercised, and working on the house was also physical and at least productive until work could be secured. At first, Nick could not accept revealing his crime on job applications and elected to work in lesser skilled jobs. It was important for him to learn the discipline of work even when the job was not to his liking. Through GA and treatment, his acceptance of his gambling as a disease removed his shame and self-devaluation as "a bum." He secured a job at a computer company after he finally took the risk of revealing his gambling problem to his employer. His self-esteem was heightened, and he began to go to school at night to advance himself.

Marital issues began to surface at this point, and Nick and Mary were seen in treatment jointly. Nick's identification with his father, who was rarely home and showed little emotional involvement with his family, was revealed in the joint sessions. As a reaction, Nick was overinvolved with his children remembering how he missed that contact with his father. He had not yet accepted the need to provide emotional support to his wife, however, and kept her in the passive, non-demanding role his mother took. In Gam-Anon and in therapy, support of Mary's right to have her needs met forced him to examine his self-absorption. Since this was a common theme also in Nick's treatment group, he gained a good deal of awareness about this aspect of the problem.

Prior to joint sessions, Mary's individual treatment focused on her inability to comprehend the damage Nick's gambling had done to family relationships. He had lied and hidden the extent of his losses. Mary came from a middle-class Irish, Catholic family and she was one of five sisters. There was no history of any substance abuse in her family. Since she was a heavy smoker, her nicotine addiction was used to help her accept gambling as an addiction. Gam-Anon also enabled her to understand Nick's gambling disorder and to begin to assert her own needs. In treatment she was able to express her stored-up anger toward Nick.

By the end of the second year of contact, Nick had decreased his debts considerably and had started to pay off the credit union. He had occasional "flashbacks" causing acute sorrow for his past behavior and sessions focused on his need to integrate his past, accept it, and move on. Again, GA members, in recounting their "war stories" of past antisocial behavior during their addiction, helped to lessen a guilt that had no therapeutic value. In addition, since manipulation is a significant characteristic of a compulsive gambler, sessions were used to focus on how to identify his needs, how to express his wants openly and directly, and how to accept that there is no guarantee he will always get what he wants. The treatment group of gamblers is an ideal place to recognize the need for give-and-take rather than the familiar patterns of manipulation. It is an ideal place also to enhance the productive support of a peer network.

As Nick and Mary's relationship strengthened, they presented concern about their daughter's nail-biting and overeating. The assessment of their daughter indicated a child with considerable unexpressed anger, dependency problems, low self-esteem, and confusion about her father's gambling. Since her school sponsored a "rap group," she was encouraged to attend; and individual sessions were also arranged at the clinic with a female social worker. She also attended Weight Watchers, and the parents were offered sessions to enhance their parenting skills.

Both Nick and Mary continue to attend GA and Gam-Anon. Nick terminated his attendance at the treatment group for gamblers but has continued individual sessions on a monthly basis. He has now been abstinent for four years.

IMPLICATIONS FOR SOCIAL WORKERS

Compulsive gambling has been described as an "invisible illness," hidden from professionals as well as from the gambler. Social workers should increase their knowledge about the disorder, and agency administrators can provide in-service training to assist staff in identifying, assessing, and treating the compulsive gambling family. Many agencies include an alcohol and drug history as part of a psychosocial assessment; a gambling history must also be considered. Especially when clients present financial problems, money management problems, and chronic marital disputes about money issues, a gambling assessment is indicated. Families still may cover up extensive gambling problems because of shame or lack of understanding about the disorder. Social workers familiar with the addiction model of alcohol and drug dependence can easily shift to the compulsive gambling paradigm. In so doing, social workers can elicit material about gambling problems and provide help. Social workers who work with drug or alcohol dependency clients also should include a gambling assessment in their work. This is particularly important because of the high percentage of polyabusing gamblers.

The self-help movement continues to grow and many social workers are working collaboratively with self-helpers. We are, all of us, youngsters in the field of compulsive gambling. Natural helpers and professionals have a long way to go. We have a lot in common, and yet there are areas where we need to let each other do what each does best. For example, a compulsive gambler, who has experienced being stigmatized, isolated, and misunderstood, will frequently feel accepted and hopeful about recovery at a GA meeting. Self-help groups are frequently seen as lifesaving. Abstinence most often begins in self-help groups. Support is available continuously; members can contact their sponsors and other members of the group at any time. Professionals, and those with training in addictionology, have special knowledge in helping recovering addicts. Problems that were hidden under their addictive behavior surface, once abstinence is achieved. Marital problems, parent-child difficulties, and vocational issues can be resolved with professional assistance. Alternative ways to cope with problems that were formerly dealt with by addictive behaviors, can be learned through professional treatment. Serious depression can be helped best by professional intervention. GA and social work intervention can dovetail in confronting the denial and resistance to help.

The early phases of a gambler's abstinence are most often based on compliance, a significant other's threat of divorce, or a court mandate to seek help. The gambler has not really "surrendered." Individuals may have made a conscious decision to stop, but they may try to test control or continue to make mind bets. Recovery really begins when the gambler emotionally recognizes that there is a disease to be coped with.

Minuscule amounts of money are available for education and prevention of gambling problems while huge sums of money are spent by governments and the gaming industry to attract people to gambling. The National Council on Compulsive Gambling (1989) has developed television commercials, radio announcements, and brochures to bring attention to the risks associated with compulsive gambling. A speakers' bureau provides educational programs to the community. The National Council does not favor or oppose legalized gambling; it takes the position that states promoting legalized gambling have a responsibility to fund treatment programs. Presently, only the states of New York, New Jersey, Connecticut, Massachusetts, Maryland, Minnesota, and Iowa provide support for gambling treatment programs.

Public schools need to educate students to the problems associated with gambling in the same manner they utilize alcohol and drug prevention curriculum. Berman (1988), at the Compulsive Gambling Treatment Program of Westchester Jewish Community Services, with the assistance of recovering gamblers and wives, has developed a syllabus on gambling problems that can be used in high schools. During workshops given to students, the presenter attempts to be alert to the children who may recognize from the discussion that they have a severe or compulsive gambling parent.

Further deterioration of the compulsive gambling family can be prevented by professionals who are able to identify the signs of compulsive gambling and provide a direct service or facilitate a referral. There is a need to develop educational training programs for school teachers and student assistance staff, for employee assistance personnel, for police, and for personnel in the court system. Special outreach is needed to identify and serve women, African Americans, Hispanics, Asians and other minority groups who traditionally have had less access to the GA or mental health systems. Because compulsive gambling is an "invisible illness," the question is not how many compulsive gamblers have been seen, but how many have been seen and were not known to be compulsive gamblers.

CONCLUSION

The explosion of legalized gambling in the United States during the past two decades has resulted in increased availability of gambling opportunities. Americans have always had a fascination with gambling, and the current trends in the gaming industry indicate that legalized gambling will continue to increase. Many Americans are social gamblers who do not experience problems in gambling, but for many individuals, gambling becomes an addiction. Compulsive gambling is a chronic and progressive disorder in which the individual is unable to resist impulses to gamble. There are devastating consequences resulting from the gambling addiction that are damaging to individuals, families, employers, and society. Compulsive gambling, although affecting millions of people, is a very understudied and neglected mental health concern.

A body of knowledge about compulsive gambling is slowly beginning to emerge. Since the American Psychiatric Association's inclusion of pathological gambling as a mental disorder in 1980, there has been an increase in professional awareness of the problem. Clinicians and researchers have added to existing knowledge about signs, symptoms, and the course of the disease. Postulates concerning the dynamics and etiology of the addiction have provided hope and knowledge for combating the disease. Although there are only a handful of treatment programs in this country treating compulsive gamblers, reports of successful interventions have increased awareness of the skills useful in reaching gamblers. Research is needed in areas such as the effect of compulsive gambling on children, on the role of social, cultural and religious factors, on female compulsive gamblers, and on the growing number of young compulsive gamblers. Community-wide education and prevention programs are very much needed.

Compulsive gambling shares many common factors with alcohol and other substance abuse addictions. A high number of addicted gamblers also abuse alcohol and/or other drugs. The success of AA and other self-help groups in supporting individuals to achieve abstinence has been demonstrated. Social workers treating compulsive gambling families must join forces with Gamblers Anonymous and Gam-Anon; such a partnership increases the rate of recovery. Knowledge that social workers have gained in their work with chemically dependent clients can be called upon in the treatment of compulsive gamblers. Particularly important is utilizing the concepts from the addiction model along with a strengths perspective.

Social workers in agency settings have considerable experience in dealing with families in crises.

Assessments at intake should include gambling histories, particularly with families that present with financial problems. Compulsive gambling is a family disorder, and social work has developed a body of knowledge from family therapy and a person-in-environment perspective which can assist in helping the compulsive gambling family. This is a challenge we cannot ignore.

REFERENCES

American Psychiatric Association. (1980). *Diagnostic and statistical manual of mental disorders* (3rd ed.). Washington, DC: Author.

American Psychiatric Association. (1987). *Diagnostic and statistical manual of mental disorders* (3rd ed. rev.). Washington, DC: Author.

Berman, L. (1988). *The compulsive gambling high school awareness curriculum*. Unpublished manuscript.

Betti, U. (1966). The gambler. In G. Rizzo (Ed.), *Ugo Betti: Three plays* (pp. 135–202). New York: Hill and Wang.

Blackman, S., Simone, R., & Thomas, D. (1986). (Letter to the editor). *Hospital and Community Psychiatry, 37,* 404.

Blume, S. (1988). Compulsive gambling and the medical model. *Journal of Gambling Behavior, 3,* 237–247.

Ciarrochi, J. (1987). Severity of impairment in dually addicted gamblers. *Journal of Gambling Behavior, 3,* 16–26.

Commission on the Review of the National Policy toward Gambling. (1976). *Gambling in America,* Washington, DC: U. S. Government Printing Office.

Council on Compulsive Gambling of New Jersey (1988, Winter). *The Council Connection.* Trenton, NJ: Author.

Custer, R., & Milt, H. (1985). *When luck runs out.* New York: Facts on File Publications.

Gamblers Anonymous. (1989). *Life line bulletin.* National Service Office. Los Angeles: Gamblers Anonymous.

Gaudia, R. (1987, May/June). *Effects of compulsive gambling on the family.* Social Work, 32, 254–256.

Heineman, M. (1987, Spring). A comparison: The treatment of wives of alcoholics with treatment of wives of pathological gamblers. *Journal of Gambling Behavior, 3,* 27–40.

Kaplan, H. R. (1984). The social and economic impact of state lotteries. *Annals of the American Academy of Political and Social Science, 474,* 91–106.

Lesieur, H. (1984) *The chase.* Cambridge, MA: Shenkman.

Lesieur, H. & Custer, R. (1984). Pathological gambling:

Roots, phases, and treatment. *Annals of the American Academy of Political and Social Science, 474,* 146–156.

Marlatt, G. A., & Gordon, J. R. (1985) *Relapse prevention.* New York: Guilford Press.

Martinez, T. (1983) *The gambling scene.* Springfield, IL: Thomas.

Nadler, L. (1985). The epidemiology of pathological gambling: Critique of existing research and alternative strategies. *Journal of Gambling Behavior, 1,* 35–50.

National Council on Compulsive Gambling. (1987, Spring). *Quarterly News.*

National Council on Compulsive Gambling. (1989). John Jay College of Criminal Justice, 444 West 56th St., New York, NY 10019.

Strange, S. (1986). *Casino capitalism.* Oxford, UK: Blackwell.

Taber, J. I., McCormick, R. A., Russo, A. M., Adkins, B. J., & Ramirez, L. F. (1987) Follow up of pathological gamblers after treatment. *American Journal of Psychiatry, 144,* 757–761.

Wolfgang, A. K. (1988, Summer). Gambling as a function of gender and sensation seeking. *Journal of Gambling Behavior, 4,* 71–77.

SUPPLEMENTAL READING LIST

Abt, V., Smith, J. F., & Christiansen, E. M. (1985). *The business of risk.* Lawrence, KS: University Press of Kansas.
A thorough study of legalized gambling since the acceptance of casinos in Atlantic City and the growth of state lotteries. The evolution from gambling in the colonies to the large gaming industry today is also traced. Note is made that "commercial" gambling operators have a guaranteed advantage.

Bergler, E. (1958). *The psychology of gambling.* New York: International University Press.
An early psychodynamic attempt to systematize the gambling disorder. The concept of "psychic masochism," the gambler's unconscious craving for defeat, humiliation, and pain, is posited. Case histories are presented.

Eliot, L. H. (1982). *Pathological gambling.* New York: New York State Office of Mental Health.

A summation of the first statewide training institute. Chapters cover diagnosis, treatment, outreach, public education, legal issues, and self-help groups.

Findlay, J. M. (1986). *People of chance.* New York: Oxford University Press.
The American fascination with games of chance is examined while covering the development of the unique American style of gambling. Historical material is presented. The connection between frontier values, such as risk taking, movement, and gambling values, is made.

Levy, S., & Blume, S. (1986). *Addictions in the Jewish community.* New York: Commission on Synagogue Relations, Federation of Jewish Philanthropies.
Various authors present articles on alcohol, drug, and gambling abuse. Religious and cultural issues are emphasized in the understanding and treatment of the three addictions.

McQuade, C. (1981). *Gamblers digest.* Northfield, IL: DBI Books.
One of many "how to" books inviting people to gamble. The various types of betting and gambling activities are described and strategies to win are provided. The message, "if you lose, you can still win," subtly encourages involvement in gambling.

Report on recommendations of the Governor's advisory commission on gambling. (1988). Trenton, NJ: Author.
The report covers the work of the commission's investigation of casino, track, and lottery gambling in New Jersey. Policies to monitor gambling are proposed. Concerns in relation to the social and economic impact of gambling and of crime are reviewed. Chapters on pathological gambling include recommendations for education, training, and funding.

Sharing recovery through Gamblers Anonymous. (1984). Los Angeles: Gamblers Anonymous.
This "blue book" is used by GA members as an aid toward recovery. Chapters include a history of Gamblers Anonymous, personal accounts of pathological gamblers, the role of Gam-anon and Gam-A-Teen, commentary on the 12-step program, and summaries of professional treatment and research on pathological gambling.

Sternlieb, G., & Hughes, J. W. (1983). *The Atlantic City gamble.* Cambridge, MA: Harvard University Press.
The effects of legalized casino gambling in Atlantic City are covered, and a sobering look at the complexities of legalized gamble is presented. It is shown how the growing industry with tremendous cash flow could be vulnerable to corruption.

Epilogue: Where Do We Go from Here?

Edith M. Freeman
University of Kansas

WHERE ARE WE NOW?

It seems essential to consider, at this point, what conclusions can be drawn about the addictions field from reading this book. To begin with, data show that the picture related to some addictions is changing: for instance, casual use of drugs such as cocaine has decreased while the number of heavy users and the related consequences have increased. Many service providers have worked without adequate data on the assumption that some addictions are similar and, therefore, have ineffectively applied treatments that have proven to be useful with heroin addicts to cocaine addicts. In other instances, researchers and providers may have overlooked some common aspects of addiction that might have been informative; examples include study populations and clients in treatment who have had cross addictions such as eating disorders and alcoholism.

Risk factors have been identified and discussed in the various chapters that predict the potential for use and abuse in certain vulnerable populations and communities. For example, casual drug use has been identified as a risk factor for certain populations that later move on to heavy use. Failure in school, poor family relationships, sexual abuse, and low self-esteem have been identified as risk factors for drug use in some adolescents. Childhood obesity and a pattern of using food to self-medicate hurt feelings at a young age have been associated with the development of an eating disorder in young

adulthood. Inadequate bonding and other factors early in life make it more likely that some individuals will develop sex or love addictions.

Despite the emergence of proprietary treatment programs for addictions and an increase in not-for-profit agencies that serve this population, the numbers of clients who successfully complete such programs and maintain sobriety for one year following treatment has not changed: estimates range from 25 to 33 percent. Recognition of the need for prevention has increased also, although federal cutbacks in funding have seriously decreased the resources available for prevention programs. It has become clear that prevention efforts must be addiction-specific for adolescent and adult populations, while the more generic programs may be effective with younger children. Evaluations of treatment and prevention programs indicate that the field is developing a growing body of data that clarify what interventions work with what addictions and populations under what special circumstances. The field is currently attempting to apply and integrate some of those findings into the design of programs. The movement in that direction is slow, but is gaining impetus.

It is apparent from the topics covered in this book that there are a greater number of complex variables that influence the development, treatment, and prevention of addictions. Increased child sexual abuse, high unemployment, multimember family addictions, larger numbers of homeless families and runaway and homeless youth, clients with a dual diagnosis that includes substance abuse and AIDS or mental illness, the rise of state lotteries and social gambling, and more aggressive advertising by the tobacco industry are but a few of those variables. As these areas have been discussed, the inadequacy of having only one major descriptive model (the disease concept) has become more apparent. Important also is the lack of an integrative theory on etiology that helps practitioners consider all of the bio-psychosocial factors in a client's situation and to intervene based on those guidelines.

WHAT FUTURE STEPS SHOULD BE TAKEN?

Having examined ''where the field is'' throughout the pages of this book, it seems appropriate to also consider in what direction the addictions field should be headed in the future. It will be useful if the field can move beyond its traditional dichotomies in order to address more substantive issues. The old dichotomies include: (1) whether all addictions are the same or different, (2) which of two dual diagnosis conditions is primary or secondary and therefore which can go untreated (based on the chicken-egg dichotomy), (3) whether the priority in effort and funds should be in treatment or prevention, and (4) whether funding priorities should be on the demand or supply side of the drug war (prevention and treatment versus interdiction). The answer for each of these dilemmas is at times neither, and at other times both. The answer is seldom the way those dilemmas are posed for consideration: as either-or propositions.

Moving beyond these dichotomies will permit an opportunity to consider the underlying issues that have become buried under the political implications involved. The following are examples of some of these priority issues that are apparent from reviewing this book:

1. Theory and model building are needed across the addictions that have similar aspects in their development to determine if similar treatment and prevention approaches may be possible for some of them.
2. Development of programs that reach people earlier and more aggressively is necessary; this includes the general public for primary prevention, high-risk populations for early treatment, and treatment on demand for chronic abusers and addicts who walk in by making beds available for that purpose. This may require that a new role, such as a case manager skilled in community work and transition work, be developed for certain practitioners in those programs (providing ''pretreatment'' services so that potential clients will not be lost between referral and intake).
3. A wider variety of treatments should be designed to meet the varied needs of addicted clients: those with cross addictions; those for whom existing treatments are particularly ineffective such as cocaine addicts; those with massive environmental deficits such as housing, employment, and child care; those in need of culture-specific treatment that focuses on the role of racial and gender stress in addiction development and recovery; and those in need of innovative family treatment including in home or residential treatment for multiple-member family addictions.
4. More aggressive, intensive, and longer term aftercare services that last for one to two years for some clients are critical (data indicate the greatest risk of relapse after treatment is during the initial aftercare period); these services should integrate formal aftercare and 12-step group meetings.
5. The development of a continuum of integrated, rather than separated, services for addictions: from prevention, crisis work for moving people into treatment, treatment, aftercare, workshops for maintaining ongoing recovery following aftercare, to crisis and respite services for those who relapse.
6. Systematic and organized advocacy must be initiated to develop greater resources for the addiction field with policymakers (an alliance among treatment, prevention, research, and law enforcement professionals) to reduce competition, increase resources, and provide a more clear and forceful message about the importance of resolving this problem.
7. A model of formalized supports should be developed for practitioners in this high-stress field of practice. This could include guide-

lines for mutual help groups to prevent burn-out, for referring practitioners who desire mental health services for a variety of needs, for reporting and supporting practitioners who are addicted, and for sponsoring addicted practitioners who return to work after recovery.

An important umbrella for the above recommendations is the need to put the concept of ''social welfare'' back into social policies related to alcohol and drug abuse and other addictions. This step could help to improve the quality of life within the environments in which people live out their daily existences. The pernicious effects of poverty in many of those environments have helped to diminish some individuals' hope for an improved quality of life in the future. This loss of hope, along with the negative effects of ''Reagnomics'' on the resources available to the present social welfare system, has greatly impacted the demand side of this country's addiction problems.

The goal must be to develop a set of social policies that improve employment, health, housing, mental health, and the political, educational, and recreational resources available to communities. Simply providing technically effective prevention and treatment services for addictions will not address the underlying environmental conditions that increase the demand for self-medicating substances and other addictive practices. Such policies can help in the development of a more caring and humane society that recognizes the risks of addiction for *all* of its members at this point in time, as well as the costs involved for all.

CONCLUSION

Many of the recommendations summarized in this epilogue, along with the major issues addressed throughout the book, are critical for shaping a future that is more positive than the present conditions. Although the discussions have been far-ranging, the related recommendations are only a tip of the iceberg in terms of the severity and depth of this society's current addiction problems. It is clear that society has the capability to address these problems more productively, but many barriers exist. A number of these barriers have been discussed and analyzed in this book; the proposed recommendations grew out of those discussions. The recommendations represent, therefore, a next step that builds on existing knowledge, skills, effective services, and other strengths within the field of addictions. We need only take that next step.

Glossary

Abstinence Violation Effect. The reactions of an abstaining client following a return to drug use; it often includes self-blame, pessimism about recovery, and premature termination from treatment.

Action. Gambling in general, risk taking by betting to achieve the "gambling high."

Adaptive Model. This model assumes various substitute adaptations, including addictions, are drawn upon by individuals in an effort to cope with a failure to grow up and maintain adult integration. These adaptations are viewed as positive efforts to cope with the individual and environmental factors that contribute to the substitute adaptation. Finding new substitute adaptations that are not harmful is part of the treatment for addictions based on this model.

Addiction. A behavior pattern of compulsive substance abuse, relationships, or other nonconsummatory and consummatory behaviors characterized by overinvolvement with the relationship or abuse as well as a tendency to relapse after completion of withdrawal. Addictions can include the abuse of alcohol and other drugs, eating disorders, sex and relationships, gambling, and tobacco.

Aftercare. A prescribed period of treatment for an addiction that follows inpatient or some other form of intensive treatment; generally the service is designed to monitor treatment maintenance and prevent relapse as well as address other problems which may not have been as high a priority as the addiction during previous phases of treatment.

AIDS. Acquired immunodeficiency syndrome is an infectious disease transmitted through sexual contact and in utero in pediatric populations. A secondary method of transmission is from needle sharing among IV drug users. The syndrome leads to a loss of the body's natural immune system, whereby the body deteriorates and becomes vulnerable to a number of "opportunistic" diseases and serious illnesses that result in death.

Alcohol Abuse or Alcoholism. Heavy alcohol consumption that is characterized by physical and psychological dependence, increased tolerance, withdrawal symptoms during nonuse, and a tendency to relapse after completion of withdrawal. The difficulty in abstaining occurs even when serious physical, social, psychological, and legal consequences occur. Abstinence is usually recommended for some recovering persons, while controlled use may be possible for a smaller number of abusers. See Addiction.

Alternative Family Structures. For pushouts, throwaways, and homeless and runaway youth who cannot return home, an alternative family structure is necessary for facilitating abstinence, unresolved family conflicts, and independent adult functioning. Nonrelated individuals or extended family members provide the lost opportunity for developing trusting and caring relationships with youth.

Anchor. A treatment strategy that helps an addicted client associate recovery with a significant and positive event, site, or person; thus, recovery is enhanced and negative associations that reinforce addictive behaviors are disrupted.

Anorexia Nervosa. Weight loss leading to a body weight of 85 percent or less than is normal for the individual, an intense fear of gaining weight or becoming fat, body image distortion in which the individual perceives herself as fat even when obviously underweight, and in females the absence of at least three consecutive menstrual cycles.

ARC. AIDS-related complex is a condition caused by

the same virus that causes AIDS but it is of a less serious nature; some individuals with ARC go on to develop AIDS, but it is not known at this time how many do or do not later develop AIDS.

Autistic State.   This is a state of absolute primary narcissism where the infant is totally preoccupied with its own well-being.

Bailout.   Money given to gamblers by well-intentioned relatives or friends to pay off gambling debts, but which is generally used by the gambler to continue gambling.

Baseline.   The planned and systematic collection of data on the problem before the intervention or plan is begun, in order to be able to evaluate change. With addictions, the goal is to collect accurate data from a wider variety of subjective and objective sources given the phenomenon of denial.

Big Win.   A series of wins or one "big score" yielding a large sum of money that gives the gambler false optimism.

Binge.   A pattern of cocaine use characterized by continual consumption over an extended length of time. The concept is also applicable to other addictions such as bulimia and alcohol abuse.

Biopsychosocial Factors.   The range of factors in an individual's life situation that influence the development and maintenance of an addiction; they include biological or genetic, psychological, and social factors to be addressed in the assessment and treatment of the addiction leading to a more wholistic view of the client-in-situation.

Biopsychosocial Model.   A systems framework for establishing alcoholism treatment. It depends heavily on assessment at entry and rests on behavioral and cognitive therapy methods. The model assumes the causes of addictions are complex, multifactoral, and include genetic, familial, psychological, and sociocultural influences.

Boarder Hospitals.   Hospitals with obstetrical departments in which addicted women deliver infants who are abandoned or taken from the mothers due to the medical consequences of addiction on the newborns. Infants may stay in such hospitals up to several years for medical reasons and due to a lack of specialized child welfare placements.

Bradycardia.   Abnormal slowness of the heartbeat often occurring in males and females with eating disorders or in substance abusers.

Bulimia Nervosa.   Recurrent episodes of binge-eating; a feeling of a lack of control over eating behaviors during binges; the use of self-induced vomiting, laxatives, diuretics, strict dieting, fasting, or vigorous exercise in order to prevent weight gain; and a persistent overconcern with body shape and weight.

Cerebrospinal Fluid.   Fluid found in the brain and spinal cord.

Chase.   Reckless and desperate betting that is characteristic of compulsive gambling in an attempt to recoup losses.

Co-dependent.   An adult who assists in maintaining the social and economic equilibrium of an alcoholic person to the exclusion of meeting personal needs and in the interest of maintaining the family system's balance and survival. The co-dependent or co-alcoholic can be a spouse, lover, friend, parent, sibling, or other relative who assumes the role responsibilities that have been abandoned by the alcoholic.

Colleague.   A member of the same profession having similar education and credentials or a member of another helping profession who is also engaged in addictions counseling or research.

Combat.   Active engagement of an armed opposing force generally in a situation of war and under great emotional and physical stress that may encourage some form of self-medication.

Community-based Program.   A drug or alcohol abuse treatment program generally located physically within a community from which the client population is drawn and which makes use of the human and other resources from the community as part of its treatment. Inpatient treatment is de-emphasized except when necessary for medical detoxification or other special circumstances, and treatment includes a focus on the special needs of the population served.

Compensatory Model.   A position which argues that addicts should be held accountable for their own recovery, even though they are not entirely responsible for their condition.

Continuum of Care.   Situations in which an entire range of services are offered to meet the differential needs of individual clients, such as assessment, detoxification, residential treatment and out-patient services, alcohol and drug education, 12-step programs, halfway houses, job training, permanent housing, and aftercare.

Controlled Drinking.   Drinking by alcohol abusers after treatment that is not excessive and is said to resemble the drinking style of a nonalcoholic.

Course of the Disease.   Identifiable and predictable stages (winning, losing, and desperation) found in the compulsive gambling, and to an extent, in other addictions.

Crack.   The highly addictive, prepackaged, and smokable form of cocaine.

Crash.   The physical and emotional exhaustion occurring when the euphoric effects of cocaine subside.

Cross Addictions.   The existence of two or more addictions in an individual simultaneously with one substance, behavior, or activity generally compensating for the undesirable effects of the others; also called Polysubstance Abuse or Polyaddictions.

Cultural Ecomap. An adaptation of the ecomap procedure (illustration of the addicted client's current interpersonal and systems connections) which addresses cultural factors in a minority client's life situation that affect the addiction.

Decision Destroyer Technique. A treatment technique that encourages addicted clients to review factors in the past life situation that led to what may have been an adaptive response to stressful factors (the addiction), but which should be reevaluated and redecided in light of the current situation and consequences. The process makes it possible for the addicted individual to modify what has become a maladaptive response.

Dependence. This condition occurs in an individual whose addictive behavior involves both psychological consequences (the person cannot face and handle the life situation without abusing the substance, for example) and physical consequences (when not abusing, the person experiences physical manifestations such as nausea, sweating, and shakiness).

Descriptive Models. Models which describe what happens in the development of addictions without addressing the etiology of the addictions—for example, the disease concept or model.

Diagnostic Criteria. Minimal definitional standards, composed of observable and/or reportable clinical characteristics, that are used to identify ("rule in") or reject ("rule out") the presence of a mental disorder; these are most relevant when a client meets criteria for more than one disorder, as in a dual diagnosis situation.

Differential Diagnosis. The process of identifying the specific and unique set of factors that must be considered during assessment of a client's addiction in order to help determine the most appropriate treatment and the likely response of the client to that treatment.

Disease Concept or Model. A dominant descriptive model of addiction that has been generalized to other forms of addition. Based on the medical model that had been used first to explain organic diseases, this concept assumes that particular individuals have a genetic or psychological predisposition that causes them to become addicted. They are expected to progress through predictable stages of the disease involving the development of tolerance and physical/psychological dependence.

Distressed Professional. A concept closely allied to impairment resulting from an addiction, but somewhat broader. It includes more concern about stress, burnout, and interpersonal relationships.

Double Bind Message. A disordered communication style characterized by conflicting levels of message: a primary negative injunction that includes a secondary injunction that conflicts with the first, with both implying a punishment that appears outside of the receiver's control. This type of communication is often described in dysfunctional and substance-abusing families and families of schizophrenics.

Drinking or Drugging Cultures. Social networks or sites where heavy drinking or drug abuse are encouraged through social relationships and that present barriers to an individual's recovery; examples include the family or peer group as well as the work site.

Drug Abuse. Consumption of illicit or licit drugs to the extent of physical and/or psychological dependency, increased tolerance, withdrawal symptoms during nonuse, and a tendency to relapse after withdrawal is completed. The pharmacological properties and consequences of abusing different drugs varies, as well as the rapidity and intensity of addiction. Abstinence is the recommended course after withdrawal, along with multifaceted drug treatment, and 12-step programs. See Addiction.

Dry Drunk Syndrome. A phenomenon in which a client becomes sober by discontinuing use of an addictive substance, behavior, or relationship but does not give up related interpersonal, emotional, and behavioral patterns that led to or resulted from the addiction.

DSM-III-R. Revision of the third edition of the *Diagnostic and Statistical Manual of Mental Disorders*, published by the American Psychiatric Association and generally accepted as containing the "official" definitions of mental disorder in the United States.

Dual Diagnosis. The presence of two or more recognizable mental disorders. In the substance abuse field, the term usually refers to the co-occurrence of a substance use disorder with another mental disorder, for example, alcoholism and schizophrenia. It can also refer to the presence of two or more different substance use disorders such as alcoholism and heroin abuse. Sometimes used to refer to two or more nonsubstance use disorders such as depression and panic attacks, it is rarely used to refer to the co-occurrence of a mental disorder and physical disorder such as depression and cancer of the lung.

Dysparneuia. Painful genital penetration for a female including painful intercourse.

Eating Disorders. A category of addictions characterized by limiting and excess behaviors related to food. Food consumption is used to provide emotional release and coping in the face of life-threatening physical and psychological consequences. Eating disorders include obesity and overeating, bulimia, and anorexia. See those specific disorders and Addiction.

Ecological Perspective. A view of practice in general including practice with addicted clients that encourages focus on the person within the context of the entire environment rather than in isolation. Resources and barriers to treatment are more readily identifiable as a result of using the perspective.

Empowerment. A treatment technique involving the teaching of key skills (such as assertiveness or problem solving) to a client, which helps to resolve stress and dysfunctional responses such as an addiction, and which enhances coping. The process produces a sense of efficacy and competence in the client and increases motivation to maintain recovery or other productive changes.

Enabling. The behavior of members of alcoholic families that allows the chemically dependent person to continue drinking and increases members' dependence on one another. Enabling behaviors are protective of the family secret of alcoholism through denial of the problem and its effects, and through role assumptions by other members to balance the family system.

Enmeshment. Little or no subsystem differentiation within a family in which the members' interactions are characterized by extreme overinvolvement, poor boundaries, and difficulties with separation that lead to poor interpersonal differentiation.

Euphoric Recall. An addict's tendency to selectively recall only the positive experiences associated with cocaine use; the process can encourage relapse.

Gender-fair Diagnosis and Treatment. Acknowledging that there is no such thing as value-free diagnosis or treatment of addictions, the goal is a position of neutrality in which the practitioner is open to accepting any experience, behavior, and attitude in men and women clients. Another objective is to treat clients as individuals who are influenced by a multiplicity of variables and life experiences, and who have a broad range of skills, problems, options, and possibilities.

Gender-sensitive Diagnosis and Treatment. This concept emphasizes the need for a practitioner to be aware of and incorporate the fact that the realities for women and men in all cultures differ and that this information is useful in the assessment and treatment process.

HIV. The virus that causes AIDS and ARC that is transmitted through sexual contact and contact with contaminated blood products (blood transfusions, IV drug use involving needle sharing, and in utero for the fetuses of infected mothers). See AIDS and ARC.

Homeostatic Family Responses. In families in which two or more members are addicted, when alcohol or other substances are removed from the system, family dynamics are directed toward reintroducing the use of substances in an effort to restore the unit's balance and patterns of interacting.

Hypervigilance. A reaction to stress characterized by heightened awareness and guardedness; also termed "perimeter guarding."

Hypotension. Lowered blood pressure, characteristic of

particular parts of the cycle in clients with eating disorders.

Hypothermia. Low body temperature characteristic of particular parts of the cycle in clients with eating disorders.

Idealizing Needs. An emphasis on needs related to feeling part of an admired other with whose strength, power, and calmness one can merge. This process typically occurs with bulimics.

Identity Confusion: A state in which an individual's identity is in a developmental transition or is arrested in a chronic manner over time; stagnation can occur due to the development of an addiction, or it can lead to an addiction.

Impaired Professional. A member of one of the professional groups whose abilities to practice are diminished by the condition of impairment; also a professional who has overcome this disability. Impairment is often specified as substance abuse.

Impairment. A behavioral, psychological, or physical condition characterized by a diminished ability to function at work.

Information and Education Prevention Programs. These programs provide students with information concerning the health hazards and consequences of taking drugs. The rationale is that once provided with information, adolescents will make healthier choices.

Interoceptive Awareness. The ability to identify internal hunger sensations and feelings, and to be able to differentiate visceral hunger sensations from feelings. This ability is diminished or does not exist in individuals with eating disorders.

Interpersonal Addiction. See Love Addiction.

Interlocking Addiction Process. The existence of two or more addictions that are associated with a particular life-style that can make recovery more difficult. The life-style itself is said to have addictive qualities.

IV Drug Abuser. An individual who injects a non-prescribed drug intravenously.

Lanugo. A fine downy hair often found on the bodies of fetuses and newborns. Also sometimes found on individuals suffering from malnutrition, as when an eating disorder develops.

Least Restrictive Treatment. Selection of appropriate treatment for a client's addiction that yields a minimum loss of freedom and disruption of the life situation, but provides the maximum effectiveness in effecting recovery.

Life Skills Model of Prevention. A cognitive-behavioral intervention approach aimed at developing, enhancing, and maintaining basic intrapersonal and interpersonal skills including problem solving, communication, assertion/refusal, and relaxation that lead to prevention of substance abuse, particularly with children and adolescents.

Love Addiction. A progressive illness that cannot be cured, but can be arrested. It may be expressed in extreme dependency on one person or on many with a chronic preoccupation with romance, intrigue, or fantasy. An obsessive emotional pattern exists in which relationships have become increasingly destructive to career, family, and sense of self-respect.

Maintenance and Generalization. Possibly the most important treatment component to emphasize in addictions counseling. At all times the practitioner must include strategies in the treatment designed to enhance the maintenance of treatment effects over time and the generalization to the natural environment.

Medical Model. The approach to addictions counseling and other forms of treatment that emphasizes a disease perspective, pathology, and a cause-effect relationship in psychological and social areas that is analogous to physiological diseases. The professional as the expert applies treatment to the client. See Disease Concept or Model.

Mental Disorder. According to the DMS-III-R, a mental disorder is a clinically significant behavioral or psychological syndrome or pattern that is associated with distress or disability, but it is not simply a normal reaction to a distressful event (e.g., the loss of a loved one). Regardless of cause, the mental disorder must be a manifestation of a behavioral, psychological, or biological dysfunction in the person. Deviancy (i.e., conflict with society) in and of itself is not a mental disorder unless it is a symptom of a dysfunction in the person. The mental disorder is not a classification of a person but of a dysfunction that a person experiences. While the symptoms of a mental disorder are alike, the individual persons with a mental disorder will differ according to their own personalities and experiences.

Methadone Maintenance Programs. Drug treatment programs in which an addiction to an illicit more harmful drug is replaced with an approved controllable drug (methadone) with less harmful effects and improved consequences for managing the individual's life situation. Such programs also generally include counseling and job training, in addition to the role of methadone in blocking the craving for illicit drugs (heroin, for example).

Minnesota Model. The treatment model developed first in Minnesota that used recovering alcoholics as nonprofessional counselors and integrated professional treatment with the principles of Alcoholics Anonymous.

Mirroring Needs. Those needs related to feeling confirmed, accepted, and appreciated in all one's goodness and wholeness by a significant other. In the lives of bulimics and other forms of addiction, this opportunity may be blocked.

Multiple-Member Addicted Family. Families in which there are two or more addicted members, often involving more than one generation and more than one type of substance or activity; recovery and treatment may be jeopardized if all addicted members do not become abstinent and if nonaddicted members are not involved in treatment and/or 12-step self-help groups.

Multiple Treatment Effects. Situations in which two or more treatments are provided simultaneously in a program for recovery in which the effects of various treatments are interrelated and cannot be isolated to determine their differential effects. While these effects may be positive, it is impossible to generalize the outcomes to other situations or clients.

Mutual-aid Groups. Groups composed of fellow sufferers, with no professional leadership or presence, that charge no dues or fees, where help is received through giving.

Natural Healing. A phenomenon in which individuals recover spontaneously from alcohol addiction without formal treatment or involvement in 12-step programs (it may also occur in other addictions). The phenomenon may occur in 2 to 3 percent of alcoholics, with family members being viewed as a means of social control once changes in use have occurred. See Spontaneous Remission.

Natural Helpers. Those resources in the form of persons, groups, or institutions that are part of one's everyday life but are not specifically constructed to offer service for a designated problem, such as alcoholism.

Needle Sharing. The use of a hyperdemic needle or syringe by more than one person to inject an illicit drug, usually in a drugging culture.

Neonatal Narcotic Abstinence Syndrome. The phenomenon experienced by drug-exposed neonates at the point of delivery in which separation from the mother and an illicit or licit drug leads to physical withdrawal and serious medical complications.

Nicotine Addiction. Nicotine is the drug in tobacco that causes addiction. Specifically, nicotine is psychoactive ("mood altering") and can provide pleasurable effects. Nicotine can serve as a reinforcer to motivate tobacco-seeking and tobacco-using behavior. Tolerance develops to nicotine such that repeated use results in diminished effects and can be accompanied by increased intake. Nicotine also causes physical dependence characterized by a withdrawal syndrome that usually accompanies nicotine abstinence.

Obesity. Abnormally high levels of body fat that produce a weight greater than 20 percent above what is normal for a person's height and age. This does not include situations in which the greater than normal weight is due to an abnormal amount of lean body mass such as might be the case for certain athletes.

Overburdened Self. An individual deficient in self-soothing capacities because of a lack of opportunity to merge with the calmness of an omnipotent self object; food or other substances may be used to self-medicate and make up for this deficiency.

Over-the-counter Drugs. Licit substances that are taken in a manner other than what is recommended in terms of the reason or amount. Such a pattern can lead to compulsive use and negative consequences that affect the person's ability to function adequately.

Para-alcoholic. The children in alcoholic families who learn dysfunctional ways of thinking, feeling, and behaving from both the alcoholic and nonalcoholic parent. These children have neither the choice nor the mobility to enter or exit their relationships with parents; thus, they are different in this respect from adult co-dependents or co-alcoholics in such families.

Passive Smoke. Tobacco smoke entering the environment by two means—exhalation by the smoker (mainstream smoke) and smoke emanating directly from a burning cigarette (sidestream smoke).

Polyaddiction. See Cross Addictions.

Polydrug Abuse. See Cross Addictions.

Primary Prevention. Prevention designed to reduce the incidence of a particular problem or disorder; prevention designed to avoid the onset of the problem.

Psychic Numbing. The voluntary or involuntary blocking of selected affect associated with a trauma. The numbing may be facilitated by a self-medicating substance or activity.

Psychoactive Drugs. Drugs which are mood altering and which produce tolerance and dependence from prolonged heavy use over time. Examples include heroin, ice and other methamphetamines, PCP, marijuana, cocaine including crack, and alcohol.

PTSD (Post-Traumatic Stress Disorder). A cluster of symptoms, cognitions, and behaviors that follows the experiencing of a traumatic event. (See DSM-III-R: previously known as Post-Vietnam Syndrome, Battle Fatigue, Shell Shock, and War Neurosis.)

Rapprochement Phase. This phase of attachment and development denotes the child's ability to tolerate more time away from the primary caretaker; it is important for the development of individuation and trust in the child.

Rapid Assessment Instruments (RAIs). Standardized measures of assessment that are efficient, simple, and effective; when used with other measures and observations they can be particularly useful in assessing addictions, and they are compatible with single system and more rigorous group research designs.

Recovery. A term used in the substance abuse field to indicate that the person is involved in a process of treatment for addiction, is abstinent from substance abuse, and is following one of the 12-step programs based on the Alcoholics Anonymous model. Recovery also includes a salutary change in thinking and interpersonal behavior.

Relapse. Return to symptomatic drinking or ways of thinking and acting that resemble those of the drugging abuse period.

Relapse Prevention. Process of helping clients develop their internal controls to maintain abstinence and the gradual reduction of external controls. Preparation includes teaching clients that a "slip" or relapse is not a discrete, spontaneous event but a return to cognitive and behavioral patterns that are predictable once the "trigger" is identified and addressed.

Residential Drug Treatment Programs. Programs designed to treat alcohol and drug abuse, generally lasting for 28 to 90 days to permit detoxification, restructuring of the individual's way of functioning, and prevention of the escalation of an acute related condition (depression or suicide, for example).

Secondary Mental Disorder. As in a "depression secondary to cocaine dependence," a secondary mental disorder indicates the temporal relationship between the onsets of two mental disorders, with the earliest developing disorder called the "primary" disorder and the later developing disorder called the "secondary" disorder. This does not imply causal relationships.

Secondary Prevention. The early identification and treatment of a disorder that should then curtail the duration of the disorder. Secondary prevention should prevent the aggravation of a problem such as an addiction.

Self-efficacy. An individual's estimate of the ability to successfully perform a behavior or series of behaviors in the future. The level of self-efficacy of an individual is important in the prevention or recovery from an addiction (to cope with stress without self-medication).

Self-in-the-world. One's experience of oneself in consonance with, and in relation to, one's environment; an expectation of the recovery process.

Self-monitoring. Keeping track of one's own behavior, possibly through use of a diary or graph. The process is highly associated with behavior change and recovery.

Self-object. The subjective aspect of a self-sustaining function performed by a relationship of self to objects who evoke and maintain the self.

Self-regulation. The ability to correctly identify, tolerate, and take care of one's needs; to be able to effectively manage drives and impulses; and to soothe and tolerate intense mood states such as depression, anxiety, and anger.

Separation-Individuation Stage. This is the stage in which the child develops a clear sense of self.

Sequential Assessment Model. A behavioral assessment model that emphasizes increasingly refined levels of focus as well as the need to continue monitoring and assessment throughout the addiction treatment process.

Set Point Theory. The concept that humans and animals have a biogenetic predisposition to maintain certain levels of body fat, and that attempts to deviate from one's appropriate level induces metabolic changes designed to restore the preferred level.

Sex Addiction. A progressive illness which cannot be cured but can be arrested. It may be expressed in terms of compulsive need for sex or particular sexual activities that have become destructive to career, family, and a sense of respect.

Sexual Abuse. Any sexual activity without one's consent, ranging form touching to penetration and rape, usually committed by someone who is an authority figure to the victim and who uses emotional and physical coercion in the process.

Sexual Compulsion. See Sex Addiction.

Sexual Dysfunction. The experience of one or more of the following: lack of sexual interest, sexual arousal, lubrication, or orgasm; dysparneuia, vaginismus, lack of erection, premature ejaculation, retarded ejaculation, lack of desire, or lack of pleasure.

Sexual Satisfaction. The degree to which sexual desires are satisfied, and the extent of sexual contentment.

Single-Subject Design. A design that consists of a variety of methods of problem identification and problem solving; data collection and intervention with the design allow the practitioner to evaluate the effectiveness of the treatment intervention with a client or client system of one.

Skill-based Prevention Programs. These programs provide training that will enhance the social and coping skills of youth to offset various influences in the environment and peer group to use drugs. They include assertiveness training, cognitive modeling techniques, and techniques to promote self-control and relieve tension.

Specialized Foster Care. Foster care services designed to meet the special needs of a population of high-risk children (such as those with AIDS or infants born addicted) or adolescents in transition (those needing emancipation services and independent living skills).

Specialized Treatment Programs. Addiction programs designed for the unique needs of special populations including the elderly, women, racial minorities, and the sexually different; programs can include those for prevention and treatment.

Spontaneous Remission. Recovering from or discontinuing abuse of alcohol without formal treatment or help from a source that exists for the purpose of helping the drinker with the problem. See Natural Healing.

Strengths Perspective. A vital part of addictions treatment focused on helping clients to identify strengths and other resources that support recovery and other important changes.

Stress the Family System. A part of the initial treatment process involving families with an alcoholic member in which the homeostatic balance of the system is intentionally disrupted to render the system open to change; a technique which disrupts the general interaction pattern of the unit that may be helping to maintain the family addiction process. An example is eliminating the enabling behavior of a family member to decrease denial and increase awareness of the problem.

Substance Abuse. See Alcohol Abuse or Alcoholism, and Drug Abuse.

Superobesity. Individuals meeting the obesity criteria who are above the 95th percentile for their height and age.

Supply-side/Demand-Side Prevention. The tension or balance deemed necessary between resources available for treatment/prevention and those for interdiction or disruption of drug dealing at local, national, or international levels (blocking access to drugs).

Symbiotic State. The state in which parent and child feel mutual physical and psychological interdependence without experiencing the sense of being separate autonomous beings.

Tertiary Prevention. Intervening with the client after the problem has become severe in order to prevent further problems from occurring or the escalation of an existing alcohol problem. The focus is more on rehabilitation in contrast to primary or secondary prevention.

Theories on Etiology. Theories which explain how and why a particular individual develops a specific addiction, leading to a set of implications for how treatment should be structured. A theory may focus on one type of causality (biological) or a combined set of causal factors (biopsychosocial).

Therapeutic Communities. A type of treatment program associated with a charismatic movement whose goals include global life-style changes as well as drug abstinence and prosocial attitudes and values.

Throwaways. Youth who may be pushouts or runaways whose parents do not encourage them to return home; they are vulnerable to drug abuse, prostitution, and other crimes through exploitation by adults.

Tolerance. A condition that occurs when a given substance or behavior produces decreased effect on an individual after repeated administration; the condition is indicative of abuse or addiction but does not generally occur with "ordinary" usage.

Trauma. An injurious experience, either physical or emotional, that creates a lasting effect.

Twelve-Step Programs. Any program modeled on the Alcoholics Recovery Model such as Al-Anon, NA, or OA. These self-help programs emphasize abstinence, belief in a higher power, and the disease concept of progressive illness.

Vaginismus. Muscle spasms of the vaginal opening that preclude penetration.

Vet Center. The popular name of the community-based Readjustment Counseling Service of the Department of Veterans Affairs. Over 195 of these Centers provide services to Vietnam era veterans, their families, and/or significant others, including addictions counseling and treatment for PTSD.

Ways of Life Model. A model that assumes substance abuse and other addictions may be one of many ways of life or roles which individuals become involved in and which can achieve a position of dominance, leading to an inability to maintain balance and integrity between the different ways of life. Treatment is focused on this predicament and on the process of reinstituting balance by finding other compatible ways of life including abstinence.

Withdrawal. Physical and psychological reactions that occur when an individual discontinues use of an addictive substance, behavior, or relationship; for some drugs such as cocaine, few prolonged, life-threatening withdrawal symptoms usually occur.

Supplemental Resources or Glossaries on Addictions in General

Abel, E. L. (1985). *Dictionary of alcohol use and abuse: Slang, terms, and terminology*. Westport, CT: Greenwood Press.

Abel, E. L. (1984). *A dictionary of drug abuse terms and terminology*. Westport, CT: Greenwood Press.

Abel, E. L. (1982). *A marijuana dictionary: Words, terms, events, and persons relating to cannabis*. Westport, CT: Greenwood Press.

Nelson, J. E., Wallenstein-Pearson, H., Sayers, M., & Glynn, T. J. (Eds.) (1982). *Guide to drug abuse research terminology*. Rockville, MD: National Institute on Drug Abuse.

Author Index

Subject Index

Abstinence. *See* Addiction
Abstinence Violation Effect (AVE), 142–143
Action, high associated with gambling, 239
Addicted infants and children, 110–120
Addicted mothers, 110–120
Addiction, 1, 110–112, 153–157
  child sexual abuse, a factor in, 68–69
  common symptoms, 4
  continuum of involvement, 2
  cross addictions, 4, 84
  definition of, 2
Adult Children of Alcoholics (ACOAs), 43
  assessment strategies, 47–48
  characteristics of, 44–46
  incidence of, 44
  treatment process with, 48–51
Aftercare, 22–23, 52
  continuum of care, related to, 16
  life-style consolidation, associated with, 142–143
AIDS (Acquired immunodeficiency syndrome), 109, 113, 115, 119
  boarder hospitals, as a consequence of, 113
  epidemic, escalation of, 123–124
  high-risk groups, 124
  intervention, community-based, 126–129
    individually focused, 129–130
  intravenous drug use, a factor in, 124–126
    risk factors associated with, 124–126
  research priorities, relevant to, 130–132

syndrome, definition of, 252
Al-Anon Family Groups (AFG). *See* Mutual aid groups
Alateen. *See* Mutual aid groups
Alcohol abuse. *See* Addiction
Alcoholics Anonymous (AA). *See* Mutual aid groups
American Psychiatric Association (APA), 1, 246
Anchor. *See* Relapse
Anorexia nervosa. *See* Eating disorders
ARC (AIDS related complex), 109, 113. *See also* AIDS
Assessment, 29–31
  adult children of alcoholics, related to, 40–47
  child sexual abuse, situations involving, 70–71
  culture-specific tools, useful for, 32–35
  drinking history, in conjunction with, 28–29
  drug history, in conjunction with, 46
  eating disorders, procedures for, 166–170
  gambling history, in conjunction with, 244–245
  multiple member addicted families, barriers to, 54–55
    elements of, 56
  sex and love addiction, process of, 211–216
  social or psychosocial history, content of, 28
  tobacco addiction, process of, 228–229

Bailout. *See* Gambling, addiction process

Baseline. *See* Treatment effectiveness research, methodological problems
Binge drinking. *See* Episodic drinking
Binge eating. *See* Eating disorders
Biopsychosocial model. *See* Theories of addiction, explanatory
Bulimia nervosa. *See* Eating disorders

Casual drug use, 97–107
Child sexual abuse, in alcoholic families, 65–66
  assessment of, 70–71
  consequences, related to, 67–69
  high-risk individuals and families, 69–70
  incidence of, 66–67
  treatment of, 71–75
Children of Alcoholics (COAs), 43–44
  consequences in functioning, 65–66
Cocaine abuse, 136
  absence of withdrawal symptoms, factor in treatment of, 84, 140–141
  addiction development, 109–110, 136–137, 138–139
    demographics associated with, 138
  consequences of, 111–113, 139–140
  crack, a derivative of, 137
  crime, a result of, 140
  cross addictions, characteristic of, 84, 110
  cycles, typical of, 110–111, 138–139
  pregnant women, most common drug of choice of, 110–111
  prevalence of, 110–111, 137–138
  treatment effectiveness, associated with, 84

consequences of, 52
cross-gender addiction, 46
multiple member addicted families,
    dynamics of, 56–57
Intravenous drug abuser, 255. *See also*
    Drug abuse

Least restrictive treatment, 27–31
Life skills model of prevention. *See*
    Prevention, program models

Medical model. *See* Models of
    addiction, descriptive
Methadone maintenance programs,
    256. *See also* Treatment
    effectiveness research
Minnesota model. *See* Models of
    treatment
Models of addiction, descriptive, 1–2
    adaptive model, 5
    disease or medical model, 4
    ways of life model, 5
Models of treatment, 15
    behavioral approaches, 17, 85
    biopsychosocial model, 17
    community-based models, 84–86
    controlled drinking, 17
    developmental model, 16–17
    family systems models, 85–86
    medical detox model, 16
    Minnesota or Hazelden model, 16
    therapeutic community approaches,
        83–84
    traditional psychiatric approaches,
        16, 85
    vocational rehabilitation and job
        training model, 86
Multiple member addicted family, 54
    children, effects of modeling, 55–56
    consequences, internal and external,
        55
    threats to recovery, 57
    treatment with, 56–62
Multiple treatment effect. *See*
    Treatment effectiveness
    research, methodological
    problems
Mutual aid groups, 19–22, 143
    Adult Children of Alcoholics,
        45–46, 51
    Al-Anon Family Groups, 77
    Alateen, 73, 77
    Alcoholics Anonymous, 16, 74, 201
    Gamblers Anonymous, 241–245
    Narcotics Anonymous, 143–144,
        201
    Overeaters Anonymous, 176, 201
    Sex and Love Addicts Anonymous,
        207

Narcotics Anonymous (NA). *See*
    Mutual aid groups
National Association for Children of
    Alcoholics, 43
National Cocaine Hotline (1-800-
    COCAINE), 110, 138
National Council of Alcoholism
    (NCA), 44
National Council on Compulsive
    Gambling, 245
National Drug Control Strategy,
    100–101, 139–140
Natural healing, alcoholism, 13–15
Natural helping, 15
Needle sharing. *See* AIDS, high-risk
    groups; Drug abuse
Neonatal narcotic abstinence syndrome.
    See Addicted infants and
    children; Drug Abuse
Nicotine addiction, *See* Tobacco
    addiction

Obesity. *See* Eating disorders
Outpatient treatment, 82–83
    cocaine abusers, limitations for, 84
    components, essential to, 171–176
    criteria for, 29–31, 105, 171, 184
    group work, as a component of,
        48–51
Overeaters Anonymous. *See* Mutual
    aid groups

Passive smoke. *See* Tobacco addiction,
    consequences
Polyaddiction. *See* Cross addictions
Polydrug abuse. *See* Cross addictions
Poverty, effects on addiction
    development, 6, 118–119, 140
Practice roles, 7–8
    advocate, 7, 62, 117–118, 127, 189,
        199
    alcoholism assessment expert, 76
    broker, associated with collective
        community solutions, 127
    case manager, 6–7, 130
    catalyst, 178
    detached expert, community-based,
        127
    drug assessment expert, prevention
        aspects of, 104–105
    educator, public awareness programs,
        245
    enabler, associated with community
        self-help, 127
    resource mobilizer, 76, 178, 189
    social network intervener, 76,
        113–115, 120
    team collaborator, multidisciplinary
        aspects of, 7, 75–76, 120,
        157–158, 176, 189, 200–201

Prevention
    AIDS and intravenous drug use,
        community-based, 127–129
    alcoholism and child sexual abuse,
        75
        interdisciplinary team practice
            75–76
        public schools, role in, 75
    drugs, demand side, treatment
        aspects of, 101–102
        high-risk groups, 97
        primary, definition of, 96
        skills required, 105–106
        strategies for, 102–104
        supply side or interdiction model,
            100–101
    eating disorders, strategies for, 176
    gambling, public school-based
        programs for, 245
    program models, appropriate for,
        community-based, 103–104
        information and education, 102
        skill-based, 102–103, 232–233
    sex and love addiction, opportunities
        for, 219–220
Primary diagnosis of alcoholism. *See*
    Dual diagnosis
Psychoactive drugs. *See* Drug abuse
Psychosocial assessment. *See*
    Assessment

Recovery. *See* Relapse, prevention of
Recreational drug use. *See* Casual drug
    use
Relapse, 17
    child sexual abuse, perpetrators of,
        73–74, 76
    multiple-member-family addicted
        families, threats to, 57–58,
        60–61
    prevention, process of, 200, 242
        anchor, technique to prevent, 59,
            252
        transition to aftercare, related to
            22–23
Residential drug treatment programs.
    See Models of treatment

Sequential assessment model. *See*
    Assessment; Tobacco addiction
Sex and love addiction, 207–208
    assessment process, relevant to,
        211–216
    consequences of, 208–209
    definition of, 208
    etiology, theories about, 209–211
    prevention, opportunities for,
        219–220
    treatment, strategies for, 217–219